SPARTA'S GERMAN CHILDREN

Frontispiece: The front cover of *Spartanerjungen* by Paul von Szczepański (A. Anton Verlag, Leipzig, n.d.), illustrated by Fritz Buchholz. This work was originally published in 1901 under the title *Spartanerjünglinge*, by which it is better known.

SPARTA'S GERMAN CHILDREN

The ideal of ancient Sparta in the Royal Prussian Cadet Corps, 1818–1920,

and in

National Socialist elite schools (the Napolas), 1933–1945

Helen Roche

To Margaret
with much love
from Helen
4th March 2013

The Classical Press of Wales

First published in 2013 by
The Classical Press of Wales
15 Rosehill Terrace, Swansea SA1 6JN
Tel: +44 (0)1792 458397
www.classicalpressofwales.co.uk

Distributor
Oxbow Books,
10 Hythe Bridge Street,
Oxford OX1 2EW
Tel: +44 (0)1865 241249
Fax: +44 (0)1865 794449

Distributor in the United States of America
The David Brown Book Co.
PO Box 511, Oakville, CT 06779
Tel: +1 (860) 945–9329
Fax: +1 (860) 945–9468

ISBN 978-1-905125-55-5

A catalogue record for this book is available from the British Library.

Typeset, printed and bound in the UK by Gomer Press, Llandysul, Ceredigion, Wales

---

The Classical Press of Wales, an independent venture, was founded in 1993, initially to support the work of classicists and ancient historians in Wales and their collaborators from further afield. More recently it has published work initiated by scholars internationally. While retaining a special loyalty to Wales and the Celtic countries, the Press welcomes scholarly contributions from all parts of the world.

The symbol of the Press is the Red Kite. This bird, once widespread in Britain, was reduced by 1905 to some five individuals confined to a small area known as 'The Desert of Wales' – the upper Tywi valley. Geneticists report that the stock was saved from terminal inbreeding by the arrival of one stray female bird from Germany. After much careful protection, the Red Kite now thrives – in Wales and beyond.

Dedicated to the memory of my father,
Jerome Roche (1942–1994)

CONTENTS

ACKNOWLEDGEMENTS

I am deeply indebted to my supervisors, Paul Cartledge and Robin Osborne, and to my advisors, Anton Powell and Brendan Simms, for their invaluable support and advice. I am also most grateful to my PhD examiners, Stephen Hodkinson and Paul Millett, for their helpful comments and criticisms, which have assuredly improved the finished product to an extensive degree; the remaining flaws in the work are entirely my own responsibility.

Georg Gerleigner deserves especial praise and gratitude for his tireless and wonderfully generous help with German correspondence, without which my attempts to get in touch with the *Zeitzeugen* in the first place might well have foundered. Many thanks are also due to Benjamin Keim and Damian Valdez for their comments and encouragement. I would also like to express my gratitude to all the *Zeitzeugen* who contributed to the project, without whose help and generosity this book could not have existed in its present form.

Research scholarships from the *Deutscher Akademischer Austauschdienst* (DAAD) and the *Geheimes Staatsarchiv Preußischer Kulturbesitz* (*Stiftung Preußischer Kulturbesitz*), as well as funding from the AHRC, the Faculty of Classics, and Gonville and Caius College all made it possible for me to do the requisite amount of research in archives and libraries in Germany; I am therefore grateful to these institutions for their financial support.

During my research-trips to Germany, the support of various individuals was invaluable. Sven Devantier helped me immeasurably – both in terms of negotiating the bureaucracy at the *Bundesarchiv*, and with regard to numerous other matters, practical or otherwise. I am also very grateful to Dr. Andreas Kunz of the *Bundesarchiv-Militärarchiv*, Dr. Reinhart Strecke of the *Geheimes Staatsarchiv Preußischer Kulturbesitz*, Andrea Ribbschläger of the *Bibliothek für Bildungsgeschichtlicher Forschung*, and Petra Dorfmüller, the archivist at Schulpforta, for their help and advice. During my stay in Freiburg im Breisgau, Prof. Dr. Sitta von Reden, Dr. Astrid Möller, and Benjamin Grünert of the *Seminar für alte Geschichte* at the *Albert-Ludwigs-Universität* also made me wonderfully welcome.

Additionally, I would like to thank Pierre Dechant for help with deciphering some of my correspondents' more esoteric handwriting; Raffaella Smith and Christine Enßle for sending on parcels of German books, and Professor Mary Fulbrook, Dr. Arnulf Moser and Dr. Matthias Paustian, among others, for supplying me with useful information.

Last – but never least! – all my love and thanks must go to my mother and Oliver, without whose loving support, intellectual stimulation, and copy-editing this monograph could never have come into being. The work is dedicated, however, to the memory of my late father Jerome Roche, in the hope that – despite its topic being un-musicological – he would have heartily approved of its substance.

LIST OF ILLUSTRATIONS

Note on the illustrations: I am deeply indebted to Amalthea Verlag, Vienna, for giving permission for the reproduction of four plates by Oskar Larsen from Kurt von Borcke's novel *Das sind wir* (1940), and to Reinhard Quenstedt of the *Historischer Bilderdienst* for giving permission to use Figure 1. All other illustrations are either part of the author's own collection, part of the Wikimedia Commons scheme, or have been confirmed as out of copyright.

LIST OF TABLES AND CHARTS

1

GENERAL INTRODUCTION

These days, it is very easy to dismiss the adjective 'Spartan'. It can be used to describe almost anything – from hardy perennial chrysanthemums to terrorists' abandoned flats in London. However, this work aims to portray a place and an era where this epithet was, in its truest and most original sense, crucial to questions of self-definition for hundreds if not thousands of boys, who, as men, would later shape their country's future as high-ranking military leaders. This country, in various forms – Prussia, then Germany, and later, for a short time, 'Greater Germany' – embarked upon what one might almost call a love affair with the Spartan ideal, which, under the influence of National Socialist racial ideology, metamorphosed into a passionate desire on the part of some contemporary Germans to claim the ancient Spartans as their true ancestors. This idealisation and its various metamorphoses in one particular sphere – that of elite education – will be explored and analysed using two case-studies: namely, the Royal Prussian Cadet Schools (*Königlich Preußische Kadettenanstalten*) and the National Political Education Institutes (*Nationalpolitische Erziehungsanstalten*) or Napolas, a type of elite boarding school established in order to educate the future leaders of the Third Reich.[1]

This monograph will investigate both the significant roles which the Spartan paradigm played in the personal lives of cadets and Napola pupils, and the ways in which perceptions of Sparta were integrated into contemporary political attitudes and debates concerning both types of institution.

At the cadet schools, self-identification with young Spartans became instrumental in helping boys to accept the hardships of military socialisation in a 'total institution';[2] this identification was encouraged both by older cadets and by the school authorities. In political debates concerning the cadet corps, ideas of Sparta then became conceptual weapons in the battle between the forces of monarchist conservatism and the adherents of Social Democracy and liberalism.

At the Napolas, National Socialist racial ideology was used to portray Sparta as an ancient precursor of the Third Reich, and boys were particularly encouraged to embrace Spartan models of courage and self-sacrifice, such as Leonidas and the 300 Spartans who fought at Thermopylae. Through correspondence and conversation with around sixty octogenarian ex-pupils of these schools, and by using contemporary documentary sources, I have endeavoured to reconstruct a composite picture of the impact which such Spartan ideology had on Napola pupils on a personal level. At the wider, political level, I have also investigated the ways in which the politicians who founded the Napolas conceived of Sparta as a model for the schools, as well as examining the ideologically-influenced portrayals of Sparta used to foster the National Socialist worldview in lessons at the schools.

History has largely turned a blind eye to these institutions; the cadet schools are seldom mentioned now, and are written about in detail more rarely still.[3] The number of extant monographs on the cadet corps (in any language) can still be counted on the fingers of one hand. One might conjecture that this is not an institution of which Germany is any longer particularly proud, now that both the military mind-set which the cadet schools encouraged, and the 'type' of the Prussian Officer which they produced, have with hindsight been condemned as harbingers of that virulent militarism which embroiled the European nations in two world wars.[4]

The history of the Napolas, meanwhile, has been subject to the turmoil caused by German post-war *Vergangenheitsbewältigung* (seeking to master the past). Many former Napola pupils have kept the truth about their *almae matres* hidden, since discovery that they had been educated at a Nazi elite school could have endangered their careers, their friendships, and even their lives.[5] When books or films on the Napolas are produced, they tend to succumb to one of two flaws: if written by contemporary commentators, they moralise, sensationalise, or even demonise the schools, for their perceived role in the Nazi regime.[6] If written as memoirs by alumni themselves, they may seek to absolve and rehabilitate. Many young Germans today do not want to hear about these schools; they would like to forget the Third Reich altogether; they see it as history, done and dusted, merely the preserve of hysterical schoolbooks which constantly warn against the dangers of forgetting, yet in so doing, engender the act itself.[7]

Sources and methodology

The rest of this introduction will review the relevant secondary literature and source material, before discussing the wider methodological concerns with which the work has had to engage, including the use of eyewitness testimony. In conclusion, the appropriations of Sparta found at the Prussian Cadet Corps and the Napolas will be placed within a broader historical context of German philhellenism and laconophilia.

We shall begin with a brief survey of the existing scholarship which treats these institutions in detail. There are currently four published monographs on the cadet corps; however, one of these, Karl Herrmann von Brand's *Kadetten* (1981), does not fully meet the criteria of a work of scholarship; it was commissioned by the cadet schools' old boys' network in order to provide a rose-tinted celebration of the antiquity and traditions of the cadet corps for those who cared about it most. The work seems in some ways to have been written in a historical vacuum – generally, it does not engage with wider academic debates or theoretical concerns. Nevertheless, it is an invaluable historical resource, particularly since it contains reproductions of a substantial number of original documents.

The first fully academic monograph on the subject was Jürgen-K. Zabel's *Das preußische Kadettenkorps. Militärische Jugenderziehung als Herrschaftsmittel im preußischen Militärsystem* (1978). As has been noted, this work's fundamental flaw lies in its one-sided and excessively critical portrayal of the corps,[8] which is seen as a mere instrument in the bid of the undemocratic Prussian 'military system' to gain ruthless and barbaric control over its citizens. The bibliography is far from exhaustive, and the execution heavy-handed – though this can in part be ascribed to the political context in which the work was written, during which any 'undemocratic' system of rule, particularly one which was seen as the precursor of the Nazi regime, was liable to stringent criticism in the Federal Republic of Germany.

Similar accusations of bias can be levelled at Heiger Ostertag's *Bildung, Ausbildung und Erziehung des Offizierkorps im deutschen Kaiserreich 1871 bis 1918. Eliteideal, Anspruch und Wirklichkeit* (1990) and Steven Clemente's *For King and Kaiser! The Making of the Prussian Army Officer, 1860–1914* (1992), both of which contain sections on the cadet corps as part of a wider discussion of Prusso-German military education.[9] Clemente, in particular, dismisses the cadet corps as a reactionary and academically negligible hotbed of brutality with next to no redeeming features, in thrall to a corrupt regime obsessed with the exclusion of the bourgeoisie from military power.[10]

The second scholarly monograph on the cadet schools, John Moncure's *Forging the King's Sword. Military Education between Tradition and Modernisation – The Case of the Royal Prussian Cadet Corps, 1871–1918* (1993), is the most successful. Moncure gives a well structured and highly readable overview of the cadet corps from 1871 onwards, focusing on boys' experiences and their social background. He aims to rebut the biased views of commentators such as Clemente and Zabel, showing that the corps gradually became more accessible to aspirants of non-noble birth. The most startling omission in Moncure's work, however, is his lack of engagement with the political debates surrounding the cadet corps, along with his apparent ignorance of the government documents on the schools held at the *Geheimes Staatsarchiv Preußischer Kulturbesitz* (Secret State Archives of the Prussian Cultural Heritage Foundation) in Berlin. His depiction focuses primarily on evidence taken from autobiographical accounts and the few official documents held at the *Bundesarchiv-Militärarchiv* (Federal Military Archives) in Freiburg, and he is therefore unable to ground the schools fully in their socio-political context.[11]

The most recent monograph on the corps, which treats the cadet schools alongside the Napolas, is Klaus Schmitz's *Militärische Jugenderziehung. Preußische Kadettenhäuser und Nationalpolitische Erziehungsanstalten zwischen 1807 und 1936* (1997). Schmitz's grasp of both institutions' political background, and of the sources held at the *Geheimes Staatsarchiv*, is admirably thorough. However, he barely describes life at the schools themselves. Thus, the ideal history of the Prussian Cadet Corps would combine the approaches of Schmitz and Moncure, whilst avoiding their omissions.

This, in some measure, has been this work's aim, in that it treats political aspects of the corps' history, as well as considering individuals' experiences of corps life. Moreover, the new contributions which the work will make to existing scholarship can be listed as follows:

Firstly, none of the preexisting treatments have discussed the Spartan *topos*, and most give no indication of its very existence.[12] The following analysis of the socialising function of the Spartan trope, therefore, along with its political uses and their consequences, is completely original.

Secondly, this study covers a wider time-frame in detail than any of the existing histories, since it not only takes 1818 as its starting point (rather than 1860 or 1871), but also considers the afterlife of the cadet-school old boys' associations right up to the early 1990s.[13]

Finally, this analysis draws upon more material than any of the aforementioned scholarly treatments, in terms of both published works and archival documents. In particular, much of the documentation collected by the *Traditionsverbände* (old boys' networks), which includes a large proportion of the current holdings pertaining to the cadet schools at the *Geheimes Staatsarchiv* and the *Bundesarchiv-Militärarchiv*, was uncatalogued or still in the possession of former cadets when Moncure and Schmitz were conducting their research.[14] It is hoped, therefore, that the present study will be extensive in a way that theirs could not have been.

As far as existing histories of the Napolas are concerned, the only serious scholarly works which treat the schools as a whole are the following four: Horst Ueberhorst's *Elite für die Diktatur* (1969), which is essentially a source-book; Erhard Naake's unpublished dissertation, *Zur Theorie und Praxis der Erziehung in den Nationalpolitischen Erziehungsanstalten und ähnlichen faschistischen "Eliteschulen"* (Jena 1971), which, as one might expect for a work produced in the German Democratic Republic during this period, is suffused with Socialist propaganda; Harald Scholtz's *Nationalsozialistische Ausleseschulen* (1973), whose treatment is outdated and fairly cursory (much of the currently available archival material on the schools was still inaccessible or still on the other side of the Iron Curtain at this point), and Schmitz's brief treatment in *Militärische Jugenderziehung* (pp. 245–304), as mentioned above, which only covers the period between 1933 and 1936. Meanwhile, Stefanie Jodda-Flintropp's recent survey *"Wir sollten intelligente Mütter werden". Nationalpolitische Erziehungsanstalten für Mädchen* (2010) focuses upon the four Napolas for girls, which will not be discussed here.[15]

Other recent treatments include Christian Schneider *et al.*, *Das Erbe der Napola. Versuch einer Generationengeschichte des Nationalsozialismus* (1996), the brainchild of a group of psychologists who aimed to prove, without providing a full context for their claims, that the family of any former Napola pupil would be stricken with psychological trauma unto the third generation,[16] and Herma Bouvier's and Claude Géraud's *NAPOLA. Les écoles d'élites du troisième Reich* (2000), a French work which contains many factual inaccuracies. I have not treated the latter as a work of scholarship, though it can provide some useful information, inasmuch as the authors have drawn on evidence supplied by former pupils of Napola Köslin. Alexander-Martin Sardina's *Die Nationalpolitischen Erziehungsanstalten (NAPOLAs) als Beleg für widersprüchliche NS-Erziehungskonzeptionen im Dritten Reich* (2010) is a self-published work, unfortunately riddled with errors; a significant proportion of Sardina's account (including the sole interview with an ex-pupil) relates to a school which was never a Napola at all, and the section which he does devote to the Napolas in general (pp. 44–66) is completely reliant upon secondary sources.[17]

The only other extant literature consists of a number of dissertations, articles and pamphlets, mostly treating individual schools, such as Matthias Paustian's *Die Nationalpolitische Erziehungsanstalt Plön 1933–1945* (1995), an *Abitur* (school leaving exam) project; Arnulf Moser's pamphlet *Die Napola Reichenau* (1997); and Andreas Förschler's MA-thesis *Die Nationalpolitische Erziehungsanstalt Backnang* (Stuttgart 2002).[18]

Once again, none of these works have engaged with, or even noted the existence of, a Spartan ethos at the *Nationalpolitische Erziehungsanstalten*. Additionally, this monograph has been able to draw on a far wider range of sources than had been available to earlier authors, especially those writing before German Reunification. Moreover, many of the relevant autobiographies have been published only recently, or are self-published and unavailable to the general public. The project has also benefited from having had the opportunity to gather a larger corpus of eyewitness testimony than it would previously have been practicable to assemble. As a result, it can fairly be stated that, concerning both types of institution under consideration, this study breaks a substantial amount of new ground.

We shall now look in more detail at the types of sources used, and the caveats intrinsic to each.

Most of the official archival material on the Prussian Cadet Corps was completely destroyed by an air raid on 14 April 1945, which inflicted a direct hit on the *Heeresarchiv* (German Army Archives) in Potsdam.[19] The surviving official documentation on the cadet corps, now held at the *Geheimes Staatsarchiv Preußischer Kulturbesitz* and the *Bundesarchiv-Militärarchiv*, consists of the relatively small number of documents which survived the air raid, and those which were held elsewhere because they pertained to the Ministries of Justice and Education, rather than to the army administration. For this reason, although some information about political debates surrounding the cadet corps can be found in the stenographic reports of the Prussian and German parliaments, it is well-nigh impossible to reconstruct the extent to which Spartan influence played a role in the official running of the Prussian Cadet Corps, since so few of the schools' administrative documents have survived.

The most widely available published sources, therefore, and those which offer some hope of reconstructing a broad-brush portrait of daily life at the cadet schools, are the extant memoir literature, cadet-school stories, and the two official nineteenth-century histories of the schools: Adolf Crousaz's *Geschichte des Königlich Preußischen Kadetten-Corps, nach seiner Entstehung, seinem Entwicklungsgange und seinen Resultaten* (1857),[20] and Louis von Scharfenort's continuation of this work, *Das Königlich Preußische Kadettenkorps 1859–1892 unter den Kaisern und Königen Wilhelm I., Friedrich III., Wilhelm II.* (1892), along with his unofficial volume of cadet-school vignettes, *Bilder aus der Geschichte des Kadetten-Korps für Alt und Jung* (1889).[21] Valuable evidence can also be found in the collections of the cadet-school old boys' networks (held at the *Geheimes Staatsarchiv* and *Bundesarchiv-Militärarchiv*), which consist largely of newsletters containing reminiscences and reports on reunions, former cadets' correspondence, and some unpublished autobiographical accounts and memoirs.

As previous scholars have done, I have worked on the assumption that the depictions of corps life in autobiographical writings and cadet-school stories by former cadets bear a close relationship to the realities of life experienced at the schools.[22] This approach can be justified in a number of ways.[23] Firstly, there is the self-reinforcing nature of the evidence. The portrayals of corps life which we find in the extant histories, in reminiscences found in the writings and newsletters of the old boys' associations, and in the memoirs and cadet-school stories, all present a very similar view of the sorts of practices which occurred at the schools[24] – even if the authors portray these in widely differing moral lights.

Secondly, it seems that, as far as the reception of many of the cadet-school stories is concerned, these really were seen by readers or former cadets who were commenting on them as straightforward statements of 'what actually happened'. Thus, Paul von Szczepański's popular work *Spartanerjünglinge* ('Spartan youths'), which was probably first published in instalments in the weekly periodical *Die Woche*, was sometimes seen not only as an epistolary novel based on the author's own time at a cadet school, but as a series of 'real' letters from a cadet to his mother.[25] Often, contemporary readers seem not to have made clear-cut distinctions between what 'really happened' at the cadet schools, and what they read in volumes such as *Spartanerjünglinge*, Louis von Scharfenort's *Bilder*, or Johannes van Dewall's *Kadettengeschichten* ('Cadet Stories').[26] In general, it seems that public perceptions of life at the schools were based as much on reading these volumes as on individual knowledge. The stories were assumed to present a 'true' representation of corps life, and were quarrelled with only if adherents of the cadet corps thought that the picture they painted was too harsh and negatively nuanced. Even then, the quarrel would often be not so much with the 'facts' represented (for instance, claims that bullying of a certain type was rife) but with the portrayal of this as evil, rather than as a necessary form of toughening up.

Finally, the works of cadet-school fiction which were most popular with the general public, such as those by Szczepański and Dewall, evidently reflected a wide range of expectations among their intended audiences about the nature of life in the cadet corps. It seems unlikely that these works would have been either so widely-read or so beloved by former cadets if they had consistently violated their expectations, or conflicted with their prior knowledge. This assumption may be borne out by the fact that reactions to many of these works of literature explicitly stress the close relationship which their depictions bear to the commentators' own experiences. Thus, the anonymous author of the polemical tract *Unsere Kadettenkorps* (1894) confirmed, with reference to his own cadet-school diary, that almost everything described in Dewall's cadet-school stories was based on reality; however, his fundamental criticism of Dewall's work was that the *Kadettengeschichten* made everything that went on at the corps seem like japes and good fun, rather than harmful bullying.[27] Another example can be found in the correspondence of former cadet Friedrich Carl von Lengerke, concerning Kurt von Borcke's autobiographical novel

Das sind wir, which his friend Werner Hosse had lent him.[28] In a letter dated 13 April 1971, Lengerke comments explicitly on how faithfully Borcke's portrayal matches his own memories of the corps – indeed, posting it back to his friend will be a hard separation, he writes, for it will feel as if he is saying goodbye to his youth for a second time.[29]

The archival sources relating to the Napolas suffered no less drastically during the final years of World War II. A very large proportion of the original documentation on these institutions was destroyed, either in wartime air raids which demolished the relevant administration centres in Berlin and elsewhere, or by teachers at individual schools who were desperate to prevent documents falling into the hands of approaching Allied or Russian troops.[30] The central documentation held by the *Inspektion der NPEA* (Napola Inspectorate) and the '*Dienststelle SS-Obergruppenführer Heißmeyer*' (an administrative office run by the schools' Inspector) was all lost at the end of the war, and, since the Inspectorate had not been required to report to the Reich Education Ministry, very few documents on the schools were duplicated in the Ministry's traditional holdings. Of these, even fewer survived, since the Ministry buildings were also destroyed during bombing in November 1943.[31] Other documents pertaining to the schools were destroyed by the Allies during post-war denazification processes.

Additionally, war losses had decimated the holdings of most German libraries, so that evidence from sources such as official government publications, newspapers and pedagogical journals is also relatively sparse.[32] The contemporary material which I was able to consult during my research therefore consisted of the few surviving government documents held at the *Bundesarchiv* (German Federal Archives) in Lichterfelde (including four files of press-cuttings); textbooks and articles in educational periodicals held at the *Bibliothek für Bildungsgeschichtliche Forschung* (Library for Research in Education History) in Berlin, and copies of various Napola newsletters (either held in libraries and school archives, or made available to me by former pupils). Even if the evidence in some of these sources was designed to portray the Napolas in a particularly positive light, there seems no reason to doubt their veracity as far as references to a Spartan ethos are concerned.

My remaining sources consisted of memoirs written by ex-pupils (both published and unpublished), and personal correspondence with eyewitnesses who attended the schools. These men were, on average, fifteen or sixteen when the Second World War ended in 1945, and it therefore seemed opportune to try to collect some of their recollections before time ran out and no witnesses from the schools were left at all. However, I was aware that the use of such eyewitness testimony raised significant methodological issues, and, in order to establish a secure foundation for this aspect of my research, I have endeavoured to provide here an answer to the inevitable question: 'can utilisation of the type of evidence which I have gained from my correspondence with these eyewitnesses be justified on historical grounds?'

Although (for obvious practical reasons) my researches for the most part took the form of written correspondence, rather than the more common 'live oral history interview', oral history methodologies seemed to match my methods closely enough to provide a useful model and control.

In general, oral history methodologies stress the longstanding and distinguished pedigree which the method has enjoyed since the time of Herodotus and Thucydides through to Michelet and beyond;[33] only the Rankean influences prevalent during the nineteenth-century professionalisation of historiography led to an apotheosis of archival and literary documents at the expense of eyewitness testimonies.[34] Therefore, while scholars of the older generation have traditionally viewed oral history methods with suspicion, today's historians and sociologists generally include oral history interviews in the canon of acceptable sources, whilst taking their particular strengths and weaknesses into account.[35] Although oral histories will always be imbued with an intrinsic subjectivity, they are also extremely transparent regarding their social purpose and authenticity. Thus, while the general rules for examining evidence must hold sway: 'to look for internal consistency, to seek confirmation in other sources, and to be aware of potential bias', these checks and balances also force us to reconsider readily held assumptions regarding the intrinsic primacy of traditional types of documentary evidence.[36] Even supposedly neutral documents such as marriage registers, censuses, or seemingly uncontroversial government memoranda are often subject to falsification, whether due to social pressures (e.g. young newly-weds giving false birth dates in the register to avoid public censure) or desire to please a boss (as one of President Lyndon Johnson's aides did in 1966, writing a false – and subsequently much cited – memorandum to indicate that the TV critic Jack Gould had praised Johnson's graciousness and affability in private; the falsification was only discovered by chance by Gould's son, a professional historian, in the mid-1980s).[37] Yet these types of evidence often go unquestioned, purely by virtue of their documentary nature.

The key to using eyewitness testimony successfully, therefore, is to scrutinise it for bias and potential inaccuracy as rigorously as any other source, and to compare and cross-check it with as much other contemporary evidence as possible. To be sure, 'anyone who relies purely on recounted memories to elucidate social realities is skating historiographically on extremely thin ice';[38] oral history techniques should be considered complementary to other research methods, rather than as providing all the answers.[39] Nevertheless, to ignore such data altogether would significantly impair our knowledge; as Elizabeth Tonkin has put it, 'whether or not a historian specialises in using oral evidence, the importance of eyewitnesses is indisputable.'[40]

Moreover, since I myself was not engaged in the actual processes involved in 'oral history' research *tout court*, some of the methodological weaknesses and 'muzziness' of the interviewing process and its aftermath were circumvented in this research,[41] while many of the advantages were still retained. For instance, my correspondents' social interactions and responses could not be steered in the same way by written correspondence as they could have been by an interviewer, while the problematic nature of interview transcriptions, which are never 100% effective because they simply cannot convey the myriad subtleties and nuances of expression, body language, and tone of voice, do not apply in the same way to the letters and emails which I have received from my correspondents, which are all in the eyewitnesses' own words.

The second, related dimension which I had to consider was the reliability of my correspondents' memories. Given that the time in their life which I was asking them to recall was not only potentially traumatic, but also lay 65 years or more in the past, would the passage of years have led to such a decline in accurate recall that my correspondents' recollections could not be taken seriously?

Psychological studies seem to support the view that the use of evidence from elderly eyewitnesses need not pose a significant problem.[42] Research by two sociologists, Irene and Howard Hoffmann, for instance, has shown that one can generally rely on the consistency of factual content in long-term memories, implying that 'there is a form of long-term memory that seems best described as archival... These are memories that are readily recalled, change little, if at all, with the passage of time, and are resistant to enhancement by the presentation of recognition cues.'[43] In relation to further studies, Paul Thompson has also noted that:

> For the average group tested[,] a decline of memory sets in by the age of thirty and continues very slowly, but is never drastic before either terminal illness or senility is reached. Thus the problem of memory power is not much more serious...with old people in normal health than it is with younger adults... The final stage in the development of memory commonly follows retirement, or some other traumatic process... This is the phenomenon recognised by psychologists as 'life review': a sudden emergence of memories and of desire to remember, and a special candour which goes

> with a feeling that active life is over, achievement is completed. Thus in this final stage there is a major compensation for the longer interval and the selectivity of the memory process, in an increased willingness to remember, and commonly, too, a diminished concern with fitting the story to the social norms of the audience. Thus bias from repressions and distortion becomes a less inhibiting difficulty, for both teller and historian.[44]

In this scenario, then, my correspondents, who had attended the Napolas at precisely the age of the 'reminiscence bump' (when memories are retained most vividly and are most easily recalled during the 'life review' memory process),[45] were more likely to talk truthfully and unhindered about their past lives than they would have been ten or fifteen years earlier, when they were still constrained by fear for their professional reputations and careers.[46] In short, the fact that my eyewitnesses were 'of a certain age' raised no particular methodological issues over and above those which applied to the use of eyewitness testimony in general.[47]

At the same time, however, the very nature of the stage of life which my correspondents were recalling – that is, their schooldays in the service of the 'brown elite' – could lead to involuntary selection and historical revisionism in their recollections, in order to protect themselves from adverse contemporary criticism.[48] As Gabriele Rosenthal has shown in her extensive research on the 'depoliticisation' of memories from the Third Reich,[49] witnesses tend to omit incidents which they find incriminating or embarrassing, and will often endeavour to sever their involvement with the Nazi state from its political context.[50] Examples of this kind of 'depoliticisation' could indeed be found in my own correspondents' evidence; for example, the commonplace that it was only the SS who were truly Nazis, or that education at the Napolas was not really 'political'.[51] One correspondent, Paul F., implicitly wished to prove this point by recounting a couple of stories which showed that respect for the *Führer* was not always paramount at his school, the first of which runs as follows:

> At a rehearsal for an event, we were standing on a dais near a column with a bronze-coloured plaster bust of Hitler. By mistake, someone shoved into it, and the bust fell down into the hall. We gathered up the big shards and wrote 'Adolf Hitler, born on the 20th of August 18..., put out of action on [the Xth of X] 1939 by Class VIb of Napola Rottweil.' We didn't get into any trouble![52]

Nevertheless, this issue does not apply so specifically to the evidence which I have been given regarding Spartan influences in my correspondents' education. Since Sparta was necessarily treated in extremely ideological terms during this period – as a forerunner of the Nazi racial state; a glowing paragon of war readiness and self-sacrifice which the Third Reich could only hope to emulate[53] – it was likely that any ex-pupils who were most concerned to depoliticise their schooldays for my benefit would claim that Sparta had had no part to play in their education at all. Where Spartan ideological influence was adduced by the eyewitnesses, therefore, it seemed probable that their evidence was less likely to have been manipulated (whether consciously or unconsciously) to present a sanitised version of events.

Additionally, it was also possible to check statements from ex-pupils who were in the same class at a particular school to see whether their evidence 'matched'. So, for instance, Kurt K., formerly of Napola Köslin, claimed that:

> When I recall the history teaching, I am in absolutely no doubt that in the Quinta/Quarta (age 12–13) Spartan history was emphasised. The history teacher in any case was in his physical build, his behaviour and his appearance a Spartian [*sic*]. Over 1.80m tall, spoke loud and clear, had fenced as a student and for that reason had a deeply scarred face, clipped manner of giving orders, didn't take any nonsense. His favourite subject in both these years was Sparta. Naturally there was something about it in the history textbook, but he loved to talk in great detail about the hard, plucky life of the Spartan boys, and always made personal, affirmative comments.[54]

That Kurt K.'s portrayal of a Spartan emphasis in history lessons was at least partially accurate could be corroborated by evidence from his former classmate, Joachim D., who had previously written as follows:

> I would like to say that, by some teachers, the 'Spartan' was constantly held up as an example. Particularly in history lessons about the ancient world, the superior qualities of the Spartans – in comparison with the Athenians – were pointed out to us time and again.[55]

Furthermore, one ex-pupil of Napola Naumburg, Karl L., was able to recall – almost verbatim – a text on Sparta which his entire class had been made to learn by heart during the winter holiday of 1943–1944 (see further Chapter 9 below); the first section of this was a nineteenth-century translation of a poem by Tyrtaios (Fr.11 West), while the second section also corresponded in style with other Nazi school propaganda works on Sparta.[56] When questioned, Dr. L. could not remember ever having heard the name 'Tyrtaios'.[57] Therefore it seemed beyond all bounds of probability that he could have deliberately falsified the evidence, constructing a 'forged' document in such impeccably executed style. Rather, his testimony as a whole seemed to support the notion of Spartan influence, at least among certain teachers at Napola Naumburg, which was also borne out by contemporary documentary evidence such as the school newsletter.

In conclusion, then, it seems that, although some of these eyewitness testimonies might be problematic, if taken in isolation or without critical reflection, it is possible to minimise any inaccuracies and distortions by evaluating multiple kinds of sources and divergent perspectives, and by being ever-sensitive to contradictions between and within the sources.[58] Above all, we should try to avoid the flawed view that history is a phenomenon different from and superior to memory; rather, without memory, there could be no history in the first place.[59]

I will conclude my discussion of the sources by making two important observations which relate to the deployment of the source-material within the work as a whole. As mentioned above, previous scholarly work on both the Prussian Cadet Schools and the Napolas is sparse, and none of the works in question have ever engaged with the Spartan *topos per se*. Given the paucity of existing secondary literature, and the absence of many of the primary sources from the public domain (even a significant number of the books in question are unavailable in German state libraries), I have quoted original sources (including eyewitness testimonies) far more extensively than might normally be the case in a monograph of this type. By so doing, I have hoped to ensure that the sources speak sufficiently for themselves, thus forestalling the criticism that my analysis of the Spartan trope is too dependent upon a personal, quasi-unverifiable interpretation. Ultimately, this work endeavours to bring a substantial corpus of primary material to light for the first time, as well as to analyse that corpus in a completely original way.

Meanwhile, the distribution of material within the book (with approximately two-thirds relating to the cadet schools, and one-third to the Napolas) has been essentially dictated by the duration of the institutions' existence, and hence by the amount of available information relevant to each. While the Royal Prussian Cadet Corps (as such) endured from 1819 to 1920, with copious sources by members of the old boys' networks being created until the 1990s, and subsequently archived, the Napolas existed for only twelve years (1933–1945), synchronous with the regime that created them. Additionally, given the schools' taboo status in Germany today, far fewer ex-pupils have been able or willing to publish autobiographical accounts of their time there; nor has most of the material from the Napola old boys' networks yet been archived (if indeed it ever will be). Thus, the book's division into three more-or-less equal parts – the first on personal appropriations of Sparta at the cadet schools (Chapters 2–5); the second on political appropriations at the cadet schools (Chapters 6–7), and the third on personal *and* political appropriations at the Napolas (Chapters 8–9) – ultimately reflects the nature and quantity of the available evidence.

The first part of the work therefore presents the various ways in which the Prussian Cadet Corps appropriated Sparta as a model between 1818 and 1920, and demonstrates how these appropriations of Sparta were also used – both by adherents of the schools and by their critics – as a weapon in political debate, even during the last decades of the twentieth century.[60]

Chapters 1–5, which deal with personal appropriations of Sparta, begin with a general introduction to the aims and ethos of the Prussian Cadet Corps (Chapter 2), before going on to discuss the various ways in which cadets sought – and were indeed encouraged – both to identify themselves with Spartan boys, and to see their tough training in the cadet corps as a modern-day reflection of ancient Spartan educational methods (Chapter 3). The possible origins of this Spartan self-identification are then investigated, exploring both the extent to which cadets' depiction of themselves and their education as 'Spartan' reflects the evidence given by the ancient sources on Sparta, and the degree to which the history textbooks used at the cadet schools would have aided identification with a Spartan model based on those ancient sources (Chapter 4). Finally, it is suggested, using the sociological framework defined by Erving Goffman in his seminal paper 'On the characteristics of Total Institutions' (1961), that the cadets identified with Spartans in this fashion because it helped them to bear the hardships and humiliations of socialisation in the 'total institution' of the cadet corps (Chapter 5).

Chapters 6 and 7 then go on to consider political appropriations of the Spartan trope. Chapter 6 outlines the various educational and political debates in which the cadet corps became embroiled during the nineteenth and early twentieth centuries, and the role which the Spartan *topos* played in these. The fact that the cadet schools had become generally identified with Sparta contributed to the criticisms levelled at the corps, in particular by liberals, anti-militarist thinkers and Social Democrats, who saw the schools as a blight upon the nation, and wanted them abolished.

After Germany's catastrophic defeat in World War I, no holds were barred in these critics' accusations of brutality, which they saw on occasion as having been caused by the schools' flawed appropriation of 'Spartan' values. Thus one author with Social Democratic sympathies, Hans-Joachim Freiherr von Reitzenstein, wrote a short story in 1919 entitled simply 'Sparta', in which the hideous consequences of a ten-year-old cadet's bullying by his seniors nearly led to his losing a hand. Similarly, the new Social Democratic teachers at the schools – which the Ebert government tried to demilitarise following the demands of the Treaty of Versailles – supposedly attempted to demonise the way in which the cadets had always been taught Spartan history (focusing on the glories of Spartan warrior life and the spirit of Thermopylae). The new teachers insisted instead upon the selfishness and bloodthirstiness of the Classical Spartan kings, and on the primacy of the 'socialist' innovations of the Hellenistic reformer kings Agis IV and Cleomenes III (these sources, and others of a similar bent, are discussed in Chapters 6 and 7).

In disgust, the ex-cadets and their reactionary supporters fought back by emphasising what they saw as the truly Spartan virtues of the cadet corps, identifying themselves ever more strongly as '*Spartanerjünglinge*' in the teeth of Social Democratic and anti-militarist opposition. The Spartan *topos* had thus become politically contested, and was taken up by the last generation of cadets as a particular justification against anti-militarist critics, not only in the 1920s and early 1930s, but also in later reactions to detractors of the cadet corps after 1945, who blamed the 'Prussian' spirit of militarism for the rise of Nazism and the evils of the Second World War (all of these sources are discussed in Chapter 7).[61] The section therefore concludes with a discussion of the *topos* in the publications and communications of the old boys' associations (*Traditionsgemeinschaft ehemaliger Kadetten*) in the decades after the Second World War.

Chapters 8 and 9 introduce the discussion of personal and political appropriations of Sparta at the Napolas. Chapter 8 gives a brief overview of these institutions' aims and ethos, before investigating the ways in which the founders of the schools conceived of Sparta as a political model. Chapter 9 begins by examining the politicised portrayals of Sparta which were used at the Napolas in order to foster the National Socialist worldview. Evidence from contemporary documentary material, memoirs, and eyewitness testimony is then used to reconstruct a composite picture of the impact which such Spartan ideology had on Napola pupils on a personal level.

Ultimately, however, it should be understood that this work is not intended to provide an exhaustive analysis of the topic in question. Leaving aside the irredeemable loss of a great proportion of the archival material – which in itself precludes any claim to complete comprehensiveness – it would not have been feasible to unearth every relevant reference to the Spartan *topos*, let alone analyse the potential significance of each one. Indeed, my researches produced many more instances of the *topos* (listed in the Appendix) which it has ultimately been impracticable to discuss in the main body of the text. Rather, the aim of this book is to provide a wide-ranging overview of the use of the *topos* which, it is hoped, will stimulate further research and provoke discussion of those areas to which it has not been possible to give more detailed attention within the scope of a single monograph.

The philhellenist background

Now that the relevant methodological questions have been considered, this introductory section will conclude by situating the particular manifestations of the *mirage spartiate* found at the Prussian Cadet Corps and the Napolas within a wider cultural context of German philhellenism and laconophilia.[62]

As Suzanne Marchand has remarked in her magisterial survey of German philhellenism and archaeology, *Down from Olympus* (1996):

> The obsession of the Schillerian literary and scholarly elite with the ancient Greeks has become an accepted – if severely underanalysed – cliché. Few would [dispute] that the ancient Greeks did indeed entrance the educated elite, particularly in Protestant Prussia, and continued to do so long after the *Goethezeit*...and Greek Wars of Independence. The elective affinity Germans of the late eighteenth century discovered between themselves and the...Greeks became a constantly running motif that resounded through the pages of German prose, poetry and scholarly literature, down (at least) to 1945.[63]

However, the philhellenism which stemmed from the age of Winckelmann is most often seen as privileging the cultural, artistic and intellectual innovations of Periclean Athens (when it did not simply draw upon an all-embracing conception of 'the Greek').[64] As Elizabeth Rawson has shown, although some key figures in the Greek revival, including Winckelmann himself, occasionally had recourse to Spartan ideals, Athens remained their touch-stone, while others, such as Schiller in his *Die Gesetzgebung des Lykurgus und Solon* (1790), saw Sparta in a predominantly negative light.[65] In scholarship, too, the first ever history of Sparta (1800–1805), by J. F. K. Manso, was highly critical of the Spartans' neglect of finer feelings and the arts and sciences – they thus provided a warning example of the limitations of heroic virtue.[66] To some extent, therefore, the idea of democratic Athens as a liberal counterpole to Sparta is the recurring 'theme which goes unseen' throughout this work.[67] It was only in the 1820s, with the publication of Karl Otfried Müller's *Die Dorier*, that a more positive (and later highly influential) image of Sparta began to gain currency; one which represented Sparta as 'the pattern state of all Greece', due to the rigorous and beauty-loving nature of her most purely Dorian inhabitants.[68]

Nevertheless, in less rarefied and intellectual circles, it is possible to discern a rather different Spartan tradition, which seems to have permeated the thought of the Prussian military since at least the late eighteenth century – the catalyst for this may well have been the threats and humiliations to Prussian autonomy brought about by the Napoleonic Wars.[69]

In this variant model, some examples of which will be discussed below, Sparta appears to have been considered the ultimate paradigm of military virtue and patriotic self-sacrifice, and military policies which followed Spartan practices were advocated in Officers' Clubs, or even in Parliament. For Prussian military men, philhellenism and laconophilia often seem to have been synonymous, and emulation of Sparta was commonly seen as a means of improving Prussian patriotism and martial conduct, which could help the national cause far more than the aesthetic Athenophile *Schwärmerei* of the salons or universities. This Spartanism of the military Establishment can therefore be seen in some measure as embracing a more practical application of philhellenism, which was considered capable of solving contemporary problems of the barracks and battlefield.

The first text of this type to be discussed – an article from the *Jahrbücher der preußischen Monarchie* – appeared as early as 1798. This article, entitled '*Wäre es möglich, den patriotischen Heldengeist der preußischen Nation noch mehr zu erheben?*' ('Could it be possible to arouse the patriotic heroic spirit of the Prussian nation yet further?'), begins with the question:

> If that Spartan soldier – the only one left alive out of the three-hundred heroes who died for the Fatherland at Thermopylae – chose death rather than the shame that awaited him, and if this heroic spirit was so broadly prevalent among the Greek peoples, one may fairly ask why our own army, which is by no means inferior to those Greek peoples in the art of war, is not animated by an identical spirit?[70]

The article goes on to discuss the necessity of emulating such a model by creating an *Ersatzreligion* (pseudo-religion), or, failing that, a system of praise, blame, and conscription, which could revitalise the Prussian army's failing patriotic spirit. Following the imperative of the Greek city-state, the author reiterates that anyone who is not prepared to defend the Fatherland betrays the first duty that he owes to the state; he is therefore no true citizen.[71] The implication is that Prussia must equal Sparta in instilling her citizens with self-sacrificial love of the Fatherland, since mercenaries can never form a suitable substitute for heroic citizens.

This passage clearly demonstrates the readiness with which Sparta could be represented as *the* paradigm of Greek military patriotism. Yet, at the same time, we also find Prussia being compared explicitly with Greece, in a way which suggests that such comparison should have meaningful implications for the present. As far as the author is concerned, Greece is not merely a long-dead ancient civilisation; rather, she provides a standard of military excellence which Prussia must match in order to survive the onslaught of Napoleon's armies – just as, in the spheres of art, architecture and literary culture, emulation of Greek style was seen as one of the highest ideals, to be aspired to at all costs. We can therefore see this article not only as an impassioned attempt to bolster Prussian morale in the aftermath of the War of the First Coalition (1792–97), during which Napoleonic forces had already encroached upon German territories in the Rhineland, but also as a military application of that philhellenism which had already become so prevalent in Prusso-German culture since the age of Winckelmann.

That such ideas of Spartan emulation came to the fore not only in merely theoretical patriotic musings in Establishment periodicals, but even on the battlefield itself, can be demonstrated by the conduct of the Prussian General Field-Marshal Gebhard von Blücher (1742–1819) during his campaign against Napoleon in Spring 1813. Karl Freiherr von Müffling (1775–1851), an officer who had been assigned to Blücher's general staff, recorded in his memoirs an account of a Prussian encounter with an overwhelming French force on the Kreckwitz Heights near Bautzen in Saxony on 13 May 1813. Here, he notes that:

> General Gneisenau, on finding [the army's new position] strong, nay impregnable, was somewhat elated; and Blücher, in his harangues to the battalions, designated the Kreckwitz heights as the Prussian Thermopylae... The sounds of the huzzas caught my ear on the way...[72]

Müffling then mentions Blücher's Thermopylaean harangues again on p. 42, describing them as 'an unwarranted misuse of power', in that they caused Blücher and Gneisenau only unwillingly to concede that they must retreat, in order to avoid encirclement and certain death at the hands of Napoleonic troops.

If Spartan warriorhood and the heroic death of Leonidas at Thermopylae were considered appropriate models to spur on the Prussian army during Prussia's desperate struggle to recapture her sovereignty in the Napoleonic Wars, it would seem that the Spartan paradigm had lost none of its power during the process of reform and recovery which followed the Wars of Liberation (1813–14).

In 1821, the *Militair-Wochenblatt*, the official military periodical published by the Prussian Ministry of War, printed an unprecedentedly long-running series of ancient-historical articles entitled '*Alt-Griechische Tapferkeit, oder die denkwürdigen Tage von Marathon, Thermopylä, Salamis und Platäa, hinsichtlich der Kriegeszucht und Stellordnung der alten Griechen*' ('Ancient Greek Bravery, or the memorable days of Marathon, Thermopylae, Salamis and Plataea, with reference to the training for war and rank-organisation of the ancient Greeks').[73]

In an account of Greek *mores* and the art of war which contains a curious yet vivid mixture of fact and fantasy,[74] the anonymous author consistently presents Leonidas' and the Spartans' defence of Thermopylae as the most glowing paradigm of sacrificial heroism, and Sparta as the ultimate purveyor of strict soldierliness.[75] Thus, in his discussion of the ancient Greeks' 'masculine discipline' (*Manneszucht*), he states that:

> The Laws of Lycurgus were intended especially to make fearless soldiers of [the Spartans], and, of all the Greeks, they observed the strictest and most correct military discipline. The power of this little State, in which one could number scarcely 9000 citizens, was founded purely on their gigantic physical strength (*die Riesensstärke ihres Körpers*). As long as they preserved this, they not only shared power over Greece with Athens, but, for a time, they were the sole masters, and increased their power over foreign peoples.[76]

The author implies that, if such a small *polis* as Sparta could manage not only to preserve her autonomy, but also to gain mastery over foreign states, by instilling her citizens with military discipline, then their way of life must certainly be one which Prussia should aim to emulate in the present.

Attention is also frequently drawn to the contemporary relevance of Greek experiences of suppression and slavery under the Persian yoke during the invasions of Darius and Xerxes (499–480 BC). For Prussian readers, who had suffered similarly under French occupation, little imagination was needed to recast the overweening Persian despots as avatars of Napoleon.[77] However, since the brave Greeks had been able to see off the Oriental hordes, just as French troops had finally been driven from Prussian soil, the author comments that 'it should not be untimely to remember these [memorable victories], in order to compile a living proof that true courage and love of the Fatherland are irresistible...'[78]

It should be noted, however, that although the author is impressed with the 'ancient Greek bravery' displayed at the other 'memorable' battles listed in the article's title, none of these are so lauded and lionised as the Battle of Thermopylae. The contemporary relevance of the Thermopylaean example is explicitly highlighted above all in the author's concluding remarks on the battle, and on the other Greeks' desire to emulate the Spartans' heroism:

> *The [Three-hundred] fell so that, even thousands of years later, they could arouse astonished or aspiring admiration in the hearts of all who love their Fatherland, and live once more within them!...* The self-sacrifice of Leonidas and his companions was more effective than the most magnificent victory: he taught the Greeks to know the secret of their strength, and the Persians to know the secret of their weakness...
>
> *One must hold fast to this moment, if ever noble peoples and those oppressed by barbarians wish to rid themselves of their fetters, or if anyone wishes to clap them in chains.*[79]

Emulation of Sparta is depicted here as both prevention and cure for putative future humiliations and incursions by hostile armies – ultimately, the author is convinced that, to achieve liberty in such a situation, or to preserve it indefinitely, one need only follow the ancient Greeks' example. Thus, once again, we find Greek history being portrayed as of direct relevance for alleviating contemporary anxieties precipitated by recent events – particularly Prussia's total and ignominious defeat at Jena (1806), which would remain a running sore in the Prussian national consciousness until her victory over the French at the Battle of Sedan (1871).[80] Here, the warrior-discipline of the Greeks (and the Spartans in particular) is portrayed as providing a useful paradigm which, if adhered to, can save the Prussian people from further ignominy in the future.

If we skip forward a few decades, two instances from the 1860s offer a glimpse of the easy currency which the Spartan example still enjoyed in public debate regarding the Prussian military forty years later, after further internal upheavals (in particular the revolutions of 1848) had weakened the position of the Officer Corps.

At a speech on the 'military spirit' given at an officers' club in Berlin in 1860, and subsequently published by the Prussian Army, the anonymous speaker engages directly with episodes from Xenophon's *Anabasis*. His thesis aims to prove not only that discipline through fear is the best way to command an army, but also that such a Spartan method, advocated in the *Anabasis* by the Lacedaemonian general Clearchus, is in fact the 'original type of old Prussian discipline' (*der Urtypus altpreußischer Zucht*), as instigated by Friedrich Wilhelm I.[81] Although the speaker admits that the Athenian Xenophon's own attempts to lead his men by commanding their willing obedience were initially successful, once the march of the Ten Thousand and its attendant dangers were over, Xenophon was unable to keep them under his control. The moral drawn is that rank-and-file soldiers are simply not always capable of raising themselves to this higher level of obedience unless motivated by fear – they succumb to bad influences too easily. The speaker concludes that, though the rule of fear should, when possible, be tempered by appealing to subordinates' own will to obey, 'the true principle clearly emerges that as far as we are concerned, first and foremost, the Spartan's rigorous discipline must rule'.[82] Spartan techniques of command are thus advocated as useful even for modern armies, since the speaker believes that human nature still responds in much the same way to authority today as it did in Classical Greece.[83]

Meanwhile, during a debate in the Prussian House of Representatives (*Abgeordnetenhaus*) in September 1862, one Freiherr von Vincke attempted to bring his fellow representatives round to his way of thinking regarding the importance of a standing army and a reform of the *Landwehr* (militia) system, by appealing first of all to a Spartan precedent.[84] He begins:

> Gentlemen, the proof is already present in Greek history. Sparta had – that you will acknowledge – the best standing army that a state has ever possessed. The entire ruling class was trained in warfare from infancy, and had no other purpose than to fight for their Fatherland, since all remaining civilian affairs were dealt with by the helots. That was a standing army which can be established as a paradigm and an ideal. In the Peloponnesian War, Sparta was superior to all other states, until these began to train standing armies for themselves.[85]

Vincke proceeds to back up his argument with concrete Thucydidean and Xenophontic examples – claiming, for instance, that the Spartans were only defeated at Leuctra because the Thebans under Epaminondas had finally succeeded in raising a standing army to match their own – before going on to treat an example in Roman history.

However, as soon as he stops talking about Sparta, his listeners become more and more restive – the stenographic reports note that isolated unrest (*Unruhe*) quickly spreads throughout the assembly (*Unruhe in der Versammlung*). It is perhaps noteworthy, given the unruly mood of Vincke's audience at this point, that neither his claims regarding Sparta's absolute priority as the military state *par excellence*, nor his appeal to her paradigmatic worth, appear to have been contested.

By the end of the nineteenth century, once the rise in popularity of the Prussian military following the victories of the Franco-Prussian War (19 July 1870–10 May 1871) had waned somewhat, the Officer Corps began to elicit strong criticism for its descent into luxury and excess.[86] Officers were condemned by contemporary commentators and novelists for 'dancing round the golden calf', in the sense of living far beyond their means, drinking and gambling to disgraceful excess, and constantly seeking 'bad' marriages to wealthy heiresses, known colloquially as *Goldfische* (goldfish), in order to secure undeservedly exalted social status.[87]

In this connection, a two-part *Militair-Wochenblatt* article by the Berlin Military Association, published in 1899 and entitled '*Das Offizierkorps und die Geselligkeit*' ('The Officer Corps and Conviviality'), sought to recall its officer readership to the chaste frugality which had reigned over the Officer Corps seventy years earlier. As one of the crucial conditions for achieving this state, the author invokes that '*Spartanerthum*' (Spartanness) of flesh and blood which once made Prussia great, whose disappearance can only be remedied by a return to the ancient sources of its power, and whose strengthening must be considered a 'categorical imperative'.[88]

These examples of the high value placed on the Spartan paradigm in military circles and contexts can, of course, only touch upon a theme which could no doubt be found in many other similar sources from this period. However, in general terms, we can see that, during the nineteenth century, the Spartan paradigm – often portrayed as representative of ancient Greece as a whole – was repeatedly adduced as a useful model for emulation by the Prussian military, in many different contexts.

I would therefore suggest, in general terms, that the appropriations of Sparta found in the cadet corps follow this tradition of Prussian 'Spartan self-help', rather than being fundamentally rooted in contemporary academic discourse on Sparta. Whilst ideas from works such as Müller's *Die Dorier* almost certainly found their way into some of the relevant school textbooks by the latter half of the nineteenth century,[89] it is unlikely that many military teachers or pupils at the cadet schools would have engaged with such scholarship directly. Certainly, it does not seem that the cadets themselves engaged with the racial ideas stemming from Müller's conception – their appropriations focused primarily on those traits of Spartan education which could be found in the ancient sources (see Chapter 4 below), as well as in more modern pedagogical accounts. Indeed, it is this marked *lack* of engagement with such concepts of race which separates the Spartan tradition at the cadet schools most radically from that found at the Napolas, which seems to have been rooted in a somewhat different conception of Sparta.

*

As we shall see (particularly in Chapter 9 below), the fundamental value of Sparta to the Nazi regime, and hence to the Napolas, was her status as a paradigm of the desired *racial* virtues – in Hitler's view, she was not only the 'purest racial state' in ancient Greece, but throughout recorded history.[90] As the war-years continued, Hitler placed ever cruder stress on the naked power of the Spartan 'master race', and the idea that the Slavic peoples of the East could be termed '*Helotenvölkern*' (helot-peoples) slipped into popular parlance – after all, they would soon be conquered in similar fashion by the neo-Spartan warriors of the Third Reich.[91]

Other Spartan traits which could be characterised as 'proto-National Socialist', such as Sparta's supposedly eugenic social policies, her martial prowess in the 'struggle for life' (*Lebenskampf*), and her emphasis on the community at the expense of the individual, were all attributed to her 'Nordic' or Aryan racial makeup. The Spartans' heroic, immortal achievements as a Nordic warrior race could therefore be claimed as

German (if so desired), and it could even be alleged that German history replicated events in Spartan history. Thus, the disastrous defeat of the Sixth Army at Stalingrad in January 1943 could supposedly be sweetened in propaganda terms merely by recasting it as a second Battle of Thermopylae. Schiller's famous translation of the epigram by Simonides – which Herodotus tells us was placed on the ancient monument to the Spartans who died at Thermopylae – became the keystone of the ensuing propaganda campaign: '*Wanderer, kommst Du nach Sparta, verkündige dorten, Du hast uns liegen gesehen, wie das Gesetz es befahl*' ('Go tell the Spartans, stranger passing by, that here, obedient to their laws, we lie').[92]

Even before the Sixth Army had officially surrendered, on 30 January 1943, Goering delivered a major speech, officially publicised as the *Appell an die Wehrmacht* (Appeal to the *Wehrmacht*), which made the Spartan historical parallel blindingly obvious. The peroration of the speech ran as follows:

> My soldiers! Most of you will have heard of a similar example from the great and formidable history of Europe. Even though at that time the numbers involved were small, ultimately there is no difference in the deed as such. Two-and-a-half thousand years ago, an infinitely brave and daring man stood in a narrow pass in Greece with 300 of his men; Leonidas stood with his 300 Spartiates – men from a race famed for its courageousness and daring. An overwhelming majority, ever-renewed, constantly engaged this small troop. The heavens darkened from the number of arrows which were shot. Then, too, it was an onslaught of hordes which crushed the Aryan men here. A formidable number of warriors were at Xerxes' disposal, but the 300 men did not yield or tremble; they fought and fought a futile battle – yet one far from futile in its significance. Finally, the last man fell. In this narrow pass there stands now an epigraph: 'Stranger, when you reach Sparta, tell them that you have seen us lying here, as the law commanded!' ('*Wanderer, kommst du nach Sparta, so berichte, du habest uns hier liegen gesehen, wie das Gesetz es befahl!*')
>
> They were 300 men, my comrades. Millennia have passed, and today that battle and that sacrifice there still hold good as heroic, as the example of the highest warriorhood. And once again in the history of our own days will it be said: When you reach Germany, tell them that you have seen us fighting at Stalingrad, as the law, the law of the safety of our people, commanded us. (*Kommst du nach Deutschland, so berichte, du habest uns in Stalingrad kämpfen gesehen, wie das Gesetz, das Gesetz für die Sicherheit unseres Volkes, es befohlen hat.*)[93]

Just as the Spartans had bravely sacrificed the flower of their youth, and one of their kings, to keep the overwhelming might of King Xerxes' Persian hordes at bay, so now another barbarian, Oriental horde (this time, the Bolsheviks) had been bravely resisted to the last by the Spartans' twentieth-century heirs.[94]

Yet it was not only the most notorious officials of the Nazi regime who subscribed to what we might term an elective affinity with the Spartans, particularly those who had fought and died at Thermopylae. An example of members of the *Waffen*-SS invoking Spartan heroism for their own propaganda purposes – even before the battle of Stalingrad – can be found in the report of one Paul Falke of Kompagnie Westland (a motorised infantry detachment of the Wiking division, whose makeup included a large number of Scandinavian volunteers). In attempting to reconstruct the events of an engagement which took place at some point during July-August 1941 at Husiatyn on the Eastern Front, during which every member of the SS-troop in question was killed, Falke writes:

> Anyone who saw these men lying there – *Oberjunker* Vogel in front, only a few metres away from his objective, his hand grenade still in his left hand, his machinegun slipping from his right, and behind him the other members of the raiding-party, every last man torn down by enemy bullets as they leapt forward – he must recall the ancient memorial at the Thermopylae-pass, which reads: 'Oh stranger, when you return to Sparta, tell them that you saw us lying there, as the law commanded' ('*Oh, Wanderer, kehrst Du nach Sparta zurück, so kündige dorten, Du habest uns liegen gesehen, wie das Gesetz befahl*') – These men, three Germans, two Dutchmen and a Dane, they lay there, as the law commanded, and that law was: Our lives for Europe's future. The raiding-party did not reach the commanding position, yet the Russians withdrew. They withdrew in the face of the heroic bravery of *Oberjunker* Vogel and his men.[95]

On a less life-threatening level, contemporary scholarly and pedagogical publications also demonstrated a general tendency to equate the Spartan past with the National Socialist present, even during the regime's initial years. For instance, the philologist Hans Bogner (1895–1948), speaking at the first conference of the *NS-Lehrerbund* (Nazi Teachers' Association) in Bremen in autumn 1935, declared that:

> In speech, and in current conceptions both of everyday and of public life in present-day Germany, a new revitalisation of the ancient world, and particularly of Greek antiquity, is revealed... One speaks of Germany as of a new Sparta, and finds here the same spirit of national discipline, self-sacrifice and masculine education in camps, which once made that ancient settlement great in terms of global history.[96]

More forcibly, Helmut Berve (1896–1979), one of Germany's leading ancient historians since the mid-1920s, and one of the quickest to place his scholarly views at the service of the Nazi regime,[97] lost no opportunity in claiming Sparta as 'the most suitable historical model for the "national revolution"'.[98]

In the foreword to his popular book entitled *Sparta*, which was first published in 1937 and intended for a wide lay readership, Berve emphasised that Sparta's education of youth, spirit of community, military way of life, subordination, and heroic desire of the individual to prove himself, were all responsibilities and values that had 'newly arisen' in the contemporary society of the Third Reich.[99] Later on in the work, he stated categorically that the spirit of the Spartans 'shows itself to be related in countless ways to our Germanic way of being'.[100]

In this fashion, ideas of racial – and hence spiritual – kinship with Sparta gradually became incorporated into German national identity during the Third Reich, and leading National Socialists declared that there could be no 'shame' in treating the Spartans as a prime example for emulation, since their blood was in fact *identical* with German blood.[101] Ultimately, this 'Aryanisation' of the Spartans can be traced back, through the theories of post-World War I racial ideologues such as H. F. K. Günther (who considered the Dorians to be the purest examples of the Aryan race in ancient Greece), to the characterisation of the Doric race found in Karl Otfried Müller.[102] In a sense, then, the National Socialist *Spartabild* (image of Sparta) seems to have had a closer connection with previous scholarship (particularly that of the German Social-Darwinist tradition), than had been the case with the nineteenth-century Prussian military *Spartabild*. Certainly, it is through this racial lens that much of the appropriation of Sparta at the Napolas can best be understood, although, as World War II progressed and the German position became increasingly desperate, the Spartans' patriotic heroism against all odds seems to have become an educational aim in itself.[103]

However, what both the identification with Sparta found at the Prussian Cadet Corps, and the racially and ideologically motivated ideas about Sparta which were propagated at the Napolas, had in common, was that they used the Spartan paradigm to illuminate all aspects of school life. Whatever hardships a cadet or Napola pupil had to endure, the idea that he was echoing the fortitude of ancient Spartan youths could serve as a comfort or spur – as will be shown in the following chapters.

Notes

[1] Since this volume is not intended solely for a Classical readership, I have deferred further discussion of its place in the historiography of the 'Spartan tradition' to the Conclusion (ch. 10 below). It is worth noting here, however, that the Spartan idealisation which can be found at these institutions has previously received no detailed attention in Classical scholarship. For more general discussion of the Spartan tradition in Germany, works by Rawson (1969), Christ (1996), Rebenich (2002) and Losemann (2012) can provide a valuable overview. On German philhellenism more generally, see n. 64 below.

[2] See p. 14, and chapter 5 below.

[3] For a castigation of the many biographers who ignore German generals' cadet-school careers when giving accounts of their education, see Moncure 1993, 8–9. It should also be noted that most general histories of the Prussian army, such as Demeter (1965) and Simpson (1985), barely mention the cadet corps.

[4] See, for example, the Treaty of Versailles, Article 176; for more recent condemnations of the cadet schools' spirit of militarism, see Chapter 7 below; also Johann 2003, 222 n. 75.

[5] Leeb 2005, 14; see also my own private correspondence with former Napola pupils (2009–2012).

[6] Schneider *et al.* 1996 and Dennis Gansel's film *Napola* (2004) provide excellent examples of this tendency.

[7] cf. Schlink 2010; also Fulbrook 1999, 235.

[8] Moncure 1993, 10; Schmitz 1997, 3 (for an assessment of these authors' own work, see below).

[9] Schmitz 1997, 3.

[10] The treatment of the corps in Driftmann (1980) is cursory in the extreme, while Markmann (1984) is merely a pamphlet containing a collection of source-quotations strung together by occasional lines of critical commentary.

[11] The same criticism could be made of the brief treatment of the corps in Jörg Muth's *Command Culture* (2011), which is entitled '"To Learn How To Die": Kadetten in Germany' (pp. 85–112). However, Muth's account of the corps is much more seriously flawed – not only is it based on four primary sources alone (and very little secondary literature), but, throughout the chapter in question, Muth puts forward claims about the Prussian Cadet Schools which simply have no basis in fact. In particular, these focus upon the idea that hazing was not a regular feature of life at the cadet corps (pp. 92, 107), and that it 'had no chance of surviving' (p. 110). In general terms, the evidence is also consistently presented in a way which supports Muth's self-evident bias towards portraying Prusso-German officer training institutions as incontrovertibly superior to analogous institutions in the United States (such as West Point). For a full critique of Muth's portrayal of the corps, and an analysis of its lack of scholarly rigour, see Roche 2012f.

[12] See Johann 2003, 248–9, for an interesting (though brief) exception – in the penultimate sentence of the penultimate paragraph of his overview of German-language cadet-school literature (ibid., 217–49; cf. p. 64), Johann remarks: 'It is no coincidence that most of the texts (not only in the title, as in the case of von Szczepański) hark back to Spartan-ness (*das Spartanische*)'. Although Johann does

comment on the general importance of ideas of Sparta for German education in part 6 (pp. 64–6) of his introductory section on *Begrifflichkeiten* (concepts), which is entitled '*Sparta als Bezugspunkt*' (Sparta as reference point), he does not go on systematically to connect his observations with the content of the Prussian cadet-school literature. His work would, however, form a very useful starting point for further research on the influence of Sparta on other forms of German elite education.

[13] 1818 was the year in which the corps was generally restructured. Many of the schools which had formed the nucleus of the corps during the eighteenth century (such as Stolp and Kalisch) were closed down completely, and the new organisation and ethos which arose after the Wars of Liberation (1813–15) formed a significant caesura in the corps' history. See further Chapter 2 below.

[14] In particular the following collections (*Bestände*): GStAPK IV.HA Rep.13 (according to their order-sheets, many of these files had never previously been consulted); BA-MA MSG2 and MSG3.

[15] See further p. 198 n. 4 below.

[16] Frustratingly, the authors did interview a number of ex-pupils, but the testimony quoted is almost exclusively concerned with identifying the supposed after-effects of 'trauma' in the interviewees, rather than with illuminating their school life.

[17] Baumeister (1997) and Gelhaus (2003) also contain sections on the Napolas; however, both are completely dependent on the secondary literature, and add little (if anything) to the wider picture.

[18] Many of these have engaged with a small number of eyewitnesses – normally between three and ten. Brief accounts of various schools' time as Napolas may also be found in historical volumes prepared by the schools themselves, such as Weihe's contribution in Heumann (1994) and Heggen (1993).

[19] For a full account of this disaster, and the extent of the destruction, see Devantier 2008.

[20] The work's official nature is indicated by the following declaration on the title page: 'With the Highest Authority and on behalf of the Cadet Corps' (*Mit Allerhöchster Genehmigung und im Auftrage des Kadetten-Corps*).

[21] There are also a few extant histories of individual schools, such as Gertner (1862) and Masberg (n.d.).

[22] cf. Moncure 1993, 17–18. Unlike British public school stories, many of which were written by authors such as Charles Hamilton or Talbot Baines Reed who had never attended a public school (these included *Greyfriars*, and other famous series which featured in boys' magazines such as the *Boys' Own Paper*, and which thus contributed greatly to popular perceptions of the schools among the general public), almost all the extant cadet-school stories were written by former cadets. In the few cases where an author's provenance is not fully known (as with Paul von Szczepański and Hans Herbert Ulrich), their depictions tally so closely with accounts which we know to have been written by former cadets that it seems highly probable that they, too, attended the cadet schools. In Szczepański's case, this probability is further heightened by what we know of his family connections with the cadet corps (see further p. 55 below).

[23] See also a relevant comment by Peter Parker in his analysis of 'the Great War and the public school ethos' (2007, 69–70): 'By way of illustration I will be referring to fiction in much the same way as factual evidence. In doing so, I am aware that many of the novels bathe the schools in a warm glow of reminiscence rather than in the more direct light of critical enquiry. However, most of the writers attempted to create an authentic atmosphere and to ensure that details were correct... If they do not reflect some of the less attractive characteristics of schoolboys, they at least reflect the codes by which it was intended that the pupils should abide... It will be clear where evidence adduced from fiction appears to be flagrantly at odds with verifiable fact.'

[24] For observations upon these lines by a contemporary commentator, relating to the similarities in portrayals of corps life by Hans-Joachim Freiherr von Reitzenstein and Leopold von Wiese, see Tucholsky 1924 (also p. 154 n. 91 below).

[25] e.g. *Mitteilungsblatt* 24, August 1970, 16–17 [BA-MA MSG3/1186].

[26] For confirmation of this, see ∴ 1894, 12: '*Denn, wie...Dewall den Kadetten schildert, so lebt er noch heute in der Ansicht von Laien.*' ('Dewall's portrayal of the cadet is that which, even today, lives on in the minds of laymen.') For more on Dewall, see p. 75 n. 9 below.

[27] ∴ 1894, 11–12.

[28] GStAPK IV.HA Rep.13 Nr.194, Bl.6–7.

[29] GStAPK IV.HA Rep.13 Nr.194, Bl.4.

[30] e.g. Heggen 1993, 24.

[31] Förschler 2002, 10–11.

[32] cf. ibid., 12.

[33] cf. e.g. Thompson 2000, 31ff.; Ritchie 2003, 20.

[34] cf. Thompson 2000, 25–57.

[35] Thompson 2000, 80–1; see also more generally Grele 1998; Ritchie 2003; Rubin 1995; Yow 2005.

[36] Thompson 2000, 118–20; also 153.

[37] On the often spurious authenticity of marriage registers and other official statistical data, see Yow 2005, 5; on Johnson and Gould, see Ritchie 2003, 117.

[38] Jureit 1999, 10.

[39] ibid., 389.

[40] Tonkin 1992, 40.

[41] cf. Grele 1998.

[42] See further Yow 2005, 41; Ritchie 2003, 31.

[43] Hoffmann 2006, 281, and *passim.*

[44] Thompson 2000, 136–7.

[45] cf. Williams 2009, 46–7.

[46] cf. Leeb 2005, 14.

[47] Thompson 2000, 137.

[48] See further Lambert 2009, Blatz 2009.

[49] cf. Rosenthal 1990, 237–40.

[50] Rosenthal 1986, 24; Rosenthal 1991, 40.

[51] e.g. interview with Ekkehard P., 03/01/2010.

[52] Paul F., private correspondence, 09/04/2010. N.B. All translations of German texts are my own, unless otherwise stated.

[53] See further Roche 2012a and Roche 2012b.

[54] Kurt K., private correspondence, 05/04/2010.

[55] Joachim D., private correspondence, 31/01/2010.

[56] Karl L., private correspondence, 13/01/2010.

[57] Karl L., private correspondence, 01/02/2010.

[58] Here I paraphrase Bergerson 2004, 274.

[59] cf. Tonkin 1992, 118–19: 'Memory is even sometimes treated as if it is pre-historical, a distinction which sits all too neatly with traditional versus modern, primitive versus civilised and oral versus literate – all dichotomies which, in practice, are balanced unequally in favour of "us", not "them".'

[60] In fact, Sparta was even mentioned approvingly as a model by Frederick the Great in his *Dialogue de Morale à l'Usage de la Jeune Noblesse* (1770), which was intended for the cadets of his own day.

[61] From this perspective, the discussion could also illuminate contemporary debates concerning the 'contested' (*umstritten*) history of Prussia, Prussian exceptionalism, and the various ways in which the *Sonderweg* ('unique path') theory of Prusso-German history was received by the German public. For more on this in general, see Clark 2006.

[62] For a full discussion of this work's place in the tradition of scholarship on Spartan reception, and on the idea of the *mirage spartiate* as coined by François Ollier, see pp. 239–41 below.

[63] Marchand 1996, xviii.

[64] See more generally Butler 1935, Marchand 1996, Rehm 1936, Sünderhauf 2004.

[65] Rawson 1969, 308–14. Rawson's conclusions are borne out to a certain extent by analysis of other eighteenth-century and early nineteenth-century publications on Sparta, some of which (e.g. Abbt 1765a, Abbt's judgment on Wegelin 1763 [Abbt 1765b], and Schmidthammer 1809) also tend to portray Sparta as a barbarous and inhumane state.

[66] ibid., 316; Christ 1996, 16–18.

[67] cf. e.g. pp. 77 n. 27; 170, 215, 227 below. It is even possible to conjecture (as Anton Powell has suggested) that Athens may have been considered so prominent in German thought by the end of the eighteenth century that 'Spartanising' reactions were needed to answer criticisms of the military Establishment for not being Hellenic enough (private correspondence, 14/01/2012). However, I have not yet found any evidence either to support or to disprove this view.

[68] Rawson 1969, 323; Christ 1996, 18–20; Losemann 2012, 254–5.

[69] For a full treatment of this phenomenon, including discussion of anti-Spartan criticism of the Officer Corps in the form of Arthur Zapp's *Antimilitärischetendenznovellen* (anti-military novels), see Roche 2012d.

[70] Anon. 1798, 245. I am indebted to Katherine Hambridge for this reference.

[71] ibid., 247–8, 253–4.

[72] Müffling 1853, 39. For more on the history of this campaign in general, see Lieven 2009 (I am indebted to Hanna Weibye for this reference).

[73] *Militair-Wochenblatt* 1821.

[74] For instance, Leonidas' 300 Spartans are referred to as the 'Sacred Band' (2029, 2036); this was actually the title of the troop of 300 homosexually-paired Theban warriors which was instrumental in defeating the Spartans at the Battle of Leuktra (371 BC).

[75] See e.g. *Militair-Wochenblatt* 1821, 2029–30, 2035–6.

[76] ibid., 2004–5.

[77] Examples can be found at ibid., 1994–5, 2021, 2036. Additionally, the 'millions of barbarians who overflooded Greece' are described as 'almost identical to the present-day Turks' (ibid., 1995).

[78] ibid., 1995.

[79] ibid., 2036; emphasis original.

[80] For more on this, see Fesser 1998.

[81] *Militärische Gesellschaft zu Berlin* 1860, 29.

[82] ibid., 30.

[83] ibid., 28.

[84] *Stenographische Berichte des Abgeordnetenhauses* 1862, 45. Sitzung (11/09/1862), 1587.

[85] ibid.

[86] For more on this see also Faller 1901, Stargardt 1994.

[87] *Militärische Gesellschaft zu Berlin* 1899, 2527.

[88] ibid. For another example of 'old Prussian simplicity' (*altpreußische Einfachheit*) being linked to a Spartan paradigm, see Lenski 1922, 34.

[89] e.g. Weber 1847, 38: 'Even Dorian art is characterised...by a prodigious power (*ungeheuere Kraft*), not, as with the Ionic form, by elegance and grace.'

[90] Lankheit 1994, 348. For a full treatment of the attitudes of Hitler and other leading National Socialists towards Sparta, see Roche 2012b.

[91] Keim 1997, 121. Spartan policies were even invoked in the *Generalplan Ost*, Hitler's master plan for the colonisation of Eastern Europe (Kiernan 2009, 22–3).

[92] Schiller, *Der Spaziergang* (1795), ll.97–8, translating Herodotus, *Histories*, 7.228. See further Watt 1985.

[93] Vacano 1943, 120. For more on the national reception of the speech, see Boberach 1984, 4732–5. It is interesting (yet perhaps unsurprising) to note that Goering completely ignores the presence of the 700 Thespians (and other assorted Greeks) who fought alongside Leonidas and his Spartans.

[94] For more on the reception of Thermopylae in German history and historiography in general, see Rebenich 2002 and Albertz 2006.

[95] BA-MA N756/518. I am indebted to Benjamin Haas for this reference.

[96] Bogner 1935, 13.

[97] Berve was later nominated as the official '*Kriegsbeauftragter der deutschen Altertumswissenschaft*' (War-representative of German Classical Studies) by the Reich Education Ministry, and as such was one of the leading lights of *Aktion* Ritterbusch (1940–1945), part of the '*Kriegseinsatz der Geisteswissenschaften*' (War effort of the humanities). For more on both the *Kriegseinsatz* and Berve's involvement with it, see Hausmann 2007.

[98] Rebenich 2001, 472.

[99] Berve 1937, 7.

[100] ibid., 16.

[101] Roche 2012b esp. pp. 99–104.
[102] Rawson 1969, 335–7; Christ 1996, 28, 42; Losemann 2012, 259–60.
[103] See Chapter 9 below.

Fig. 1. The frontispiece from Adolf von Crousaz's history of the Royal Prussian Cadet Corps (1857). An idealised cadet takes centre stage, along with the Prussian eagle and flag. Scenes from corps life, along with miniatures depicting the five cadet schools then in existence (from left to right: Potsdam, Culm, Berlin, Bensberg and Wahlstatt) form a decorative border.

2

PERSONAL AND POLITICAL APPROPRIATIONS OF SPARTA AT THE PRUSSIAN CADET CORPS: HISTORICAL CONTEXT

'The Spartans of Lichterfelde'

Berlin, 5th May 1917: In the *Reichstag*, the German parliament, Representative Mertin is making an impassioned speech on the necessity of the German people's having absolute belief in the Ministry of War and the army high command; in particular, they must have complete confidence in the Chiefs of the General Staff, Paul von Hindenburg and Erich Ludendorff. Without such leaders as these, Mertin argues, it would have been impossible for the army's withdrawal to the Siegfried Line earlier that year to have been received with such gladness and equanimity, both in the field and on the home front.[1] The Independent Social Democratic Party's motion to set up an inspection committee to scrutinise the army high command is therefore ridiculous. Further details are superfluous, he continues. Suffice it to say that Hindenburg and Ludendorff were both educated in the Royal Prussian Cadet Corps; they were '*Spartanerjünglinge*', 'Spartan youths':[2]

> Even in peacetime, the cadets were reared in such a spirit of comradeship, courage, self-denial and self-discipline, all of which we so desperately need in this war. That same spirit guarantees that such men will be at hand... whenever our fatherland is in peril.[3]

His speech is greeted with cries of 'Hear! Hear!' from the Right, duly noted by the stenographer.

Three months later: The future of the German war effort is increasingly uncertain. Russia's Provisional Government is refusing to abandon the struggle on the Eastern Front; the alliance with Austria-Hungary is becoming a dangerous liability, and sailors' peace demonstrations at Wilhelmshaven have only narrowly been prevented from turning into a full-scale mutiny.[4] On July 19th, a majority of representatives in the *Reichstag* had voted for 'a peace by agreement and a permanent reconciliation', and were foiled only by the newly-elected Chancellor Michaelis, who claimed that the *Reichstag* was not a fit body to decide upon such matters of war and peace in the present circumstances.[5]

Shortly afterwards, the *Tägliche Rundschau*, a nationalist daily paper based in Berlin, publishes a morale-boosting article depicting the achievements and way of life of the Royal Prussian Cadets at the central cadet school (*Hauptkadettenanstalt*) in southwest Berlin.[6] It is entitled 'The Spartans of Lichterfelde' (*Die Spartaner von Lichterfelde*).[7]

In an account which is often startlingly reminiscent of Xenophon's portrayal of Spartan education in the *Lakedaimoniōn Politeia* (c.390–378 BC),[8] the author describes the cadets' physical prowess, their strict military subordination, and their readiness to die for their country without a moment's thought. He culminates by emphasising the boys' eagerness to join up and fight for the fatherland, and the final sacrifice which many of them have already made:

> They have done their duty diligently, and sealed their loyalty with death. The blood sacrifices (*Blutopfer*) which their ranks made for their King were great; even in the first months [of the war], many of them had given up their lives – though the first down had yet to appear on their cheeks.

Throughout the article, the author goes out of his way to remind his readers of the 'truly Spartan' nature of life behind the cadet-school walls. The implication seems to be (as with Mertin's speech in the *Reichstag* a few months earlier) that the cadet corps' own reincarnation of 'Spartan' discipline will supply Germany with a steady stream of inspired and utterly patriotic officers, who will save their country from the perils of war through their steadfast loyalty and leadership. The author cannot know that, less than three years later, all the cadet schools will have ceased to exist, having been closed down for good in March 1920 by the dictates of the Treaty of Versailles. The remaining 'Spartans of Lichterfelde' will have lost any chance of pursuing the profession for which they have been trained since the age of ten, and the schools will be criticised from all quarters as 'hotbeds of militarism' (*Brutstätten des Militarismus*). Yet the ex-cadets cannot forget what they should have been; they use their 'Spartan-ness' both as a justification for their education, and as a weapon against their critics.[9]

In 1930, ten years after the closure of the cadet schools and their subsequent transformation into non-military State Educational Institutes (*Staatliche Bildungsanstalten*), Lieutenant-Colonel G. von Unruh reprinted a plagiarised and unattributed version of the article from the *Tägliche Rundschau* on the front page of the *Reichskadettenblatt*, the magazine of the League of Former Cadets (*Reichsbund ehemaliger Kadetten*).[10] He had made one major addition to the text of '*Die Spartaner von Lichterfelde*' – a final paragraph which reads as follows:

> No [German] mother felt it necessary to issue her [latter-day] Spartan youths (*Spartanerjünglinge*) with the warning 'Return home either with your shield or on it'. They all kept their shields of courage and sacrificial bravery intact and immaculate until the last second. That shield forms their gravestone, whether their place of burial be known or unknown.
>
> And when Death comes through sacred strife
> A German foreign field enfolds that life.[11]

This postscript makes even more fully explicit the connection with ancient Sparta which lies at the original article's heart – yet it also implies that the modern '*Spartanerjünglinge*' have outdone their ancient counterparts – for their own mothers did not even need to tell them that they had to do or die.

The reception of the *Tägliche Rundschau* article did not end with Unruh's plagiarism, however. For, on 8 October 1978, a report in the *Berliner Morgenpost* informs us that, in order to revive their failing memories, the elderly ex-cadets attending the *Bundeskadettentag* (a reunion of former cadets from all over Germany) had brought with them 'a yellowed newspaper cutting...from 1917 about the "Spartans" of Lichterfelde'.[12]

'That was exactly how it was', one of the cadets, Joachim Hans Gransow, told the reporter Rudolf Noth, fully endorsing the description which the *Tägliche Rundschau* reporter gave of the cadet corps. From a morale-boosting affirmation of the army's young blood in time of war, the article had become a talisman, a symbol of the ex-cadets' long-lost youth. Even now, as old men, they still clung to their self-definition as *quondam* 'Spartan youths', happily revisiting memories of their 'Spartan' education at the cadet schools.[13] Finally, preserved and mounted with great care, the article was donated to the *Geheimes Staatsarchiv Preußischer Kulturbesitz* (Secret State Archives of the Prussian Cultural Heritage Foundation) in Berlin, along with a collection of other material from the cadet-school old boys' network. It had stayed with the former cadets right until the end.

The reception of this one short article reveals very clearly that the cadet schools' identification with a Spartan model was publicly recognised even during their lifetime. However, it also indicates the important role which this identification played in ex-cadets' own self-definition after the cadet corps had been abolished, even once the gentlemen in question were well advanced in years.

As this case-study and the following chapters will demonstrate, the Prussian Cadet Corps' interpretation of a 'Spartan' model shaped the education and the mindset of Prussian and German military commanders for nearly two centuries. A complete chronological list of references to the Spartan *topos*, along with statistical analyses, can be found in the Appendix below. In general terms, however, it appears that pupils who attended a number of the schools, beginning with Potsdam in the 1820s and Bensberg in the 1840s, recalled emulation of and self-identification with Spartan youth as being a part of cadet-corps life almost immediately after their respective schools had opened.[14] The number of cadets attending the corps who would later go on to praise or draw attention to the schools' 'Spartan education' was to rise steadily until the cadet corps as an institution was disbanded in 1920.

As John Moncure has noted, the impact of the cadet schools on German history was disproportionate to the number of officers which they produced: although only approximately one third of Prussian lieutenants attended the schools, eight of Germany's thirteen Ministers of War before 1914 were former cadets, along with half of the military members of the Kaiser's entourage.[15] By the end of World War II, almost every living graduate of the final class at the *Hauptkadettenanstalt* had become a general,[16] and ten out of the twenty-one General-Fieldmarshals who served during the Second World War were former cadets.[17]

If it is true that 'one approach to understanding the German officer is to investigate his origins', then this work could also claim to be of fundamental importance for understanding the origins of 'the men who directed the most feared war machine of the industrial age'.[18] As William Helmreich points out, those who enter a military educational institution such as the Prussian Cadet Corps are changed, or at the very least affected by their experiences in that institution, once they re-enter wider society.[19] Since military commanders can end up making hugely important life-or-death decisions concerning their own countries (and sometimes concerning those of others), proper comprehension of their educational experiences is paramount.[20]

Therefore, if we wish to understand the officers who commanded the German army during the First and Second World Wars, we also need to understand the education to which those officers were subjected, as well as the aims and ethos of the schools which provided that education. As the following chapters will show, generations of Prusso-German military commanders were not only familiar with a wealth of ancient anecdotes about the ways in which Sparta trained her young men, but were also trained to see 'Spartan' educational methods both as one of the most effective ways of socialising future officers, and as a crucial ingredient of the Prussian military ethos which the cadet schools fostered.

Historical background: the aims and ethos of the Prussian Cadet Corps[21]

The Royal Noble Prussian Cadet Corps was originally founded in 1717 by King Friedrich Wilhelm I of Prussia (father of Frederick the Great), to provide a 'nursery for the Prussian Officer Corps', and to educate the sons of his impoverished officers.[22] During the course of the eighteenth century, the schools remained relatively few in number, and were less than well reputed as academic institutions, despite the best efforts of Friedrich Wilhelm II (1744–1797) and his adjutant, Generalmajor Johann von Buddenbrock (1707–1781), to increase numbers and to improve the education which the schools offered.[23]

However, the Napoleonic Wars heralded a series of attempts to reform the cadet-school system completely. The preeminent figures of the *Reformzeit* (the transitional period of political reform which took place between 1807 and 1815), in particular Gerhard von Scharnhorst (1756–1813), saw the cadet corps as anachronistically aristocratic, and in need of root-and-branch reorganisation, if not outright abolition. 'One could use the money better for something else', Scharnhorst is said to have remarked acidly, after resistance both from King Friedrich Wilhelm III and from traditionalist quarters had forced him to abandon the latter course.[24] Even far less radical plans to reduce the importance of noble lineage as a qualification for admission foundered upon the intransigence of the reformers' conservative adversaries.[25] Finally, in 1818–1819, in the teeth of much opposition, Hermann von Boyen (1771–1848, then War Minister) was able to push through a thoroughgoing reform of the entire system, culminating in the word 'Noble' being removed from the corps' title on 19 March 1819.[26] However, despite this apparent concession to non-noble aspirants, the cadets were still drawn largely from aristocratic (though not necessarily wealthy) families.[27] Over the following decades, the makeup of the cadet corps gradually became more *bürgerlich* (middle-class), although non-noble cadets were still expected to identify with the aristocratic values which the corps had always propagated. Thus, by the end of the nineteenth century, the corps consisted in part of an *Adel der Gesinnung* (those possessed of 'spiritual nobility'), as well as an *Adel der Geburt* (nobility of birth).[28]

In general terms, the continuities in corps life and traditions between the beginning and end of the nineteenth century are striking; contemporary political developments seem to have been largely ignored in the day-to-day running of the institutions, unless revolutionaries actually came knocking on – or breaking down – the schools' doors (as happened in 1848).[29] Aside from the corps' continued expansion, and the authorities' engagement with debates over curricular reform, relatively little change seems to have taken place; indeed, cadets were often deliberately insulated from outside influence, in order to ensure their absolute adherence to the prevailing monarchist value system.[30]

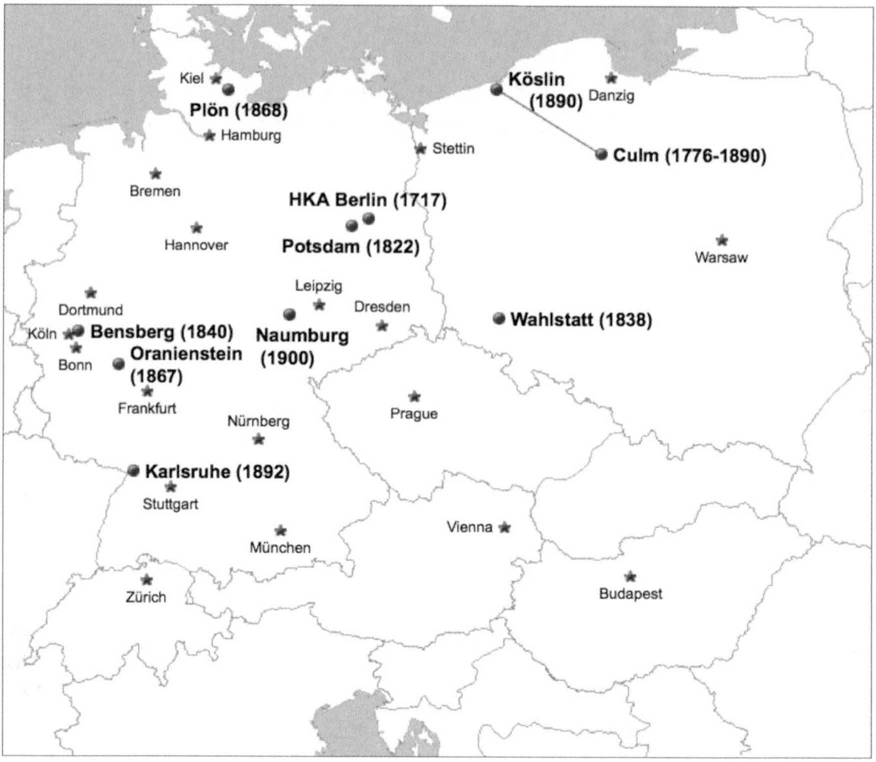

Fig. 2. Locations of the cadet schools and their dates of foundation (superimposed upon modern European state boundaries). The school at Culm (now Chełmno, Poland) was moved to Köslin (now Koszalin, Poland) in 1890. Wahlstatt (now Legnickie Pole) is also now in Polish territory.

By 1900, there existed eight preparatory cadet schools (*Voranstalten*) for boys aged between ten and fifteen, each housing between 150 and 240 cadets. As Figure 2 shows, the school at Culm an der Weichsel in West Prussia, which had been originally founded in 1776, was retained in the new system, with a second *Voranstalt* being re-established at Potsdam in 1822. *Voranstalten* at Wahlstatt in Silesia and Bensberg (near Cologne) followed in 1838 and 1840 respectively, while two others were strategically placed at Plön in Schleswig-Holstein and Oranienstein in Hesse-Nassau in the late 1860s, following Prussia's annexation of these two territories in 1866.[31] In the 1890s, after German unification, *Voranstalt* Culm was transferred to Köslin in Pomerania, and a school was founded at Karlsruhe in Baden in order to exert further influence over non-Prussian territories. Finally, *Voranstalt* Naumburg, the last cadet school to be established, was founded in 1900. These *Voranstalten* all fed into the central cadet school in Berlin, the *Hauptkadettenanstalt* or HKA.[32] By 1914, the total number of cadets had reached 2,650, of whom 1,020 were pupils at the HKA.[33]

All the schools were under the control of the *Generalinspektion des Militair-Erziehungs- und Bildungswesens* (General Inspectorate of Military Training and Education) and the Ministry of War, and regular inspections and running reports from individual school commanders meant that education at all the *Voranstalten* could be broadly unified. Although the preparatory schools were in some ways isolated from one another, each observing a somewhat different code of rules and regulations,[34] they all conformed to the same curriculum and had as their end an identical military training; accounts from all the *Voranstalten* generally portray a very similar ethos and way of life, leavened by slight regional differences. This was an important element in the stability of the system, both because it might be necessary for cadets to move from one *Voranstalt* to another depending upon where their officer-fathers were posted, and because all the cadets were being prepared to feed into the same class at the HKA; radically differing standards of deportment in pupils from the various *Voranstalten* would have been highly undesirable once they reached Berlin.[35]

Since 1877, the schools' academic curriculum had matched that of the contemporary *Realschule* – a type of school similar to the Classical *Gymnasium*, but which placed more emphasis on science subjects and modern languages than on the Classics; Latin was taught, but no Greek. Until the cadets reached Berlin, they underwent little specific training for warfare, although far greater emphasis was placed on gymnastics and other forms of physical education than would have been the case in any civilian school. Specifically military subjects such as tactics and military history were entirely left to the higher education provided at the war academies (*Kriegsschulen*). Although HKA graduates were not obliged to attend the war academy or become army officers, the majority of cadets did embark upon a military career.

Boys were sent to the cadet schools for a number of reasons.[36] Some had always known that they wanted to be soldiers, whether or not they were dutifully following in their fathers' footsteps; others were attracted by a sense of adventure.[37] Many went because the fees at a civilian school were beyond their parents' means (especially if their fathers were prematurely retired officers in reduced circumstances), while yet others were 'problem children', sent to the schools as a last resort to see if the corps' harsh military discipline could curb their bad behaviour where all other methods had failed.[38] If an applicant's father had fallen in battle, or been a meritorious officer – or, indeed, if he had been a civil servant who had performed 'heroic deeds' in the service of the state (though this was less

Fig. 3. Cadets on parade at the *Hauptkadettenanstalt* in Berlin-Lichterfelde (now the site of the German Federal Archives), c.1910.

common) – then the school had the authority to charge substantially reduced fees, or even to offer a full scholarship.[39] The application forms both for admission and for bursaries placed heavy emphasis on genealogy, and the better a boy's noble pedigree and the closer his family's links with the military, the more likely he was to be provisionally accepted. However, his place would be confirmed only once he had passed the school's academic and physical examinations.[40]

In practice, then, the majority of boys who joined the cadet schools were the sons of nobles or officers (fallen or otherwise). That the lives of boys could be made a misery if they were not highly born enough, or if their fathers engaged in the shameful activity of trade, is chillingly suggested in Hans-Joachim von Reitzenstein's cautionary tale '*Der kleine Selcke*'. In this story, a new young cadet, Fritz Selcke, is systematically bullied and ostracised by his noble room-mates because on his first day at the school he let slip that his father, a Lieutenant who lost his arm in battle, now has to make his living as a travelling salesman for a wine company. The other boys force him to eat pieces of half-eaten fruit off the floor as fitting punishment for the 'shame' which his poverty and plebeian origins have brought upon them; they also refuse to share any of the food in the birthday hamper which he has had sent specially to regain their favour. Ultimately, Selcke is unable to bear their cruelty any longer, and drowns himself in the nearby lake.[41]

Certain special privileges were also open only to those of noble birth – in particular, selection for the 'Corps of Pages' at the HKA, whose members were detailed to perform general duties at court (*Hofpagen*), or to attend a member of the Prussian Royal Family (*Leibpagen*).[42] Those disqualified by

Fig. 4. Cadets performing their duties as pages at the Prussian Court, as depicted by 'Othello' (1878).

lack of an aristocratic 'von' to their name often decried the inequity of the custom, though to no avail.[43]

As far as organisation went, the hierarchy in the schools was almost exclusively military. The cadet corps as a whole was commanded by a general, the HKA by a colonel, and each *Voranstalt* by a lieutenant-colonel or a major. Each school was divided into two companies, which were then subdivided into brigades comprising two to three rooms, each containing about ten cadets. Each room (*Stube*) was led by a room-captain (*Stubenältester*), and supervised by an *Erzieher* – a Lieutenant in his early to mid-twenties, who was detailed to watch every cadet carefully and make continual reports on his behaviour and the state of his character, which could later have an important impact on his military career. The cadets' chain of command was parallel to that of the officers; positions such as *Stubenältester*, *Brigadenältester* (brigade captain), *Klassenältester* (form captain) or *Kompagnieführer* (company leader) allowed those considered capable of assuming responsibility to learn essential lessons about how to command their juniors.

This military-style hierarchy reinforced the larger-scale hierarchical relations already prevalent in nineteenth-century Prussia's conservative ruling trinity of Crown, Army and Church.[44] The task of producing officers who were loyal above all to the monarchy and all that it stood for, completely opposed to the anarchist perils of Social Democracy, was taken most seriously by the authorities; no opportunity was lost to remind the cadets that they were royal protégés, or to emphasise their special relationship with the monarch. If the Kaiser met cadets in the street, he would greet them by saying 'Good day, Gentlemen!', not in jest (even though they were still children), but as 'a greeting to his fallen officers, whose sons he saw before him.'[45]

Furthermore, as Moncure puts it, 'the cadet corps calendar was riddled with festivals celebrating the bonds of the cadet corps to the crown and the martial grandeur of the Prussian monarchy'.[46] For instance, the Emperor's birthday was glorified as the 'festival of all festivals', with excitement brought to fever pitch by weeks of preparation and expectation – the cadets were even allowed to sleep late in the morning, and, after a patriotic afternoon spent parading for the Kaiser, to attend a military ball and fireworks in the evening.[47] Meanwhile, the cadets' more humdrum day-to-day existence was watched over by the likenesses of the Kaiser which plentifully adorned the walls of the common rooms and corridors of the HKA.[48]

For individual cadets, however, perhaps the most important ceremony of all, which many remembered with great pride and awe, was that of their graduation. Each cadet would present himself to the monarch, announcing his name, father's occupation, and the regiment which he hoped shortly to join; His Majesty would then, where appropriate, recall the honourable service of the cadet's ancestors. At the end, he would make a short speech declaring how glad he was to have met the cadets, albeit briefly, and telling them to do their duty, be grateful for their education at the state's expense, and evermore hold high the army's honour.[49]

By comparison, the role of the Church was relegated rather to the background; although Protestant chapels were a salient architectural feature at the schools, and church services,[50] graces and prayers were regular features of the cadets' lives, it appears that these were regarded as a mere mechanical duty, 'an unimportant but mandatory hurdle to becoming an officer, a matter of form more akin to table manners or dance etiquette than "moral philosophy".'[51] A quotation from G. R. Halkett's memoir seems to bear this out:

> Service and prayers were hardly to be distinguished from any other military duty in the manner of their execution. Before every meal and before we went to bed, an officer gave the command: 'Let us – pray!' And the cadet Officer of the Day shouted his prayer like so many commands. It was the object of many bets to substitute similar sounding words meaningless or with ridiculous meaning for the prayers, a bet which was always won as nobody ever paid attention to the shouting.[52]

Meanwhile, some former pupils even went so far as to declare that 'prayers stemming from true piety were dead'.[53] Certainly, it was a matter of honour for cadets to try to substitute the usual grace with doggerel such as '*Dem Herrn sei Preis für Igel und Reis*' ('The Lord be prized for hedgehog and rice'),[54] or '*Wir haben gespeist und sind nicht satt,/ und hätten gerne noch mehr gehabt*' ('We have eaten and are not satisfied, and would gladly have had still more'), even though such disrespect often led to severe penalties, or even to expulsion.[55] The boys would also habitually read adventure stories to divert themselves during chapel services, and would mock the chaplain by calling him derogatory names such as '*Himmelsfähnrich*' (Heaven's ensign), or '*Kommißchristus*' (army-Christ).[56]

Ultimately, however, the Church's power over the cadets – and even to some extent that of the State – could never match that of the Army. As the writer and ex-cadet Friedrich Franz von Unruh (1893–1986), who graduated from the HKA in 1911, put it, 'the all-powerful longing for the military, which filled almost everything, tore [the cadets] with it...'[57] This was perhaps only to be expected, given the avowedly military orientation of the schools. Although formal military instruction did not form part of the corps curriculum (except in the Selekta, a special stream for the most gifted at the HKA), and the education received at the schools could hypothetically prepare cadets for careers in many other walks of life,[58] the boys' world was fundamentally a military one, in which they learned to think like military men and devise military solutions to problems. As Louis von Scharfenort, a Captain and librarian at the HKA, explained in his later-nineteenth-century history of the cadet corps, even though the younger boys did not take part in any exercises with weapons, their drill, with its training in obedience, self-discipline and alertness to their superiors, was far more about preparing them for their later calling than it was about simple physical fitness.[59]

Likewise, athletics and team-games were seen by the authorities as a vehicle for character-building, and for the development of the coordination, strength and teamwork which were vital to military efficiency.[60] Gymnastics was also considered important for its ability to develop boys' courage, determination, self-confidence, alertness, endurance, strength and agility, all of which they would need in their later careers as officers.[61] Certainly, success on the parade-ground and the sportsfield or in the gymnasium was prized far above success in the classroom,[62] and there existed an elaborate system of rewards for those who performed well: gaining the coveted black-and-white ribbon of the *Voltigeur-Abzeichen* (for gymnastic prowess) or the deathshead badge of the *Totenschwimmer* (meaning you could swim for an hour without stopping) were seen as crowning moments in a cadet-school career.[63] Those who demonstrated physical prowess were also far more likely to be selected for the highly competitive HKA elite class, the Selekta, which enabled a cadet to gain his full commission without having to attend the war academy (*Kriegsschule*). Not for nothing was it often noted by cadets that, although the motto over the front of the HKA read '*Martis et Minervae alumnis*', the cause of Mars was exalted above all else.[64]

From the very beginning of their school careers, the importance of the boys' future profession was impressed upon them; Ernst von Salomon's introduction to drill by a military teacher on his first day at *Voranstalt* Karlsruhe in 1913 ran as follows:

> '"Gentlemen!" You have chosen the most splendid profession on earth. The highest goal on earth looms before you. Here we will teach you to reach that goal. You are here to learn the meaning of your life. You are here to learn how to die... Everything you have experienced, seen and understood you must forget. Everything you now experience, see and understand, you will embrace as a goal. From now on you have no free will; you will learn obedience in order later to command.'[65]

The cadets were also surrounded by reminders of the glory of their forebears in the form of statues of kings and famous fieldmarshals, paintings of former corps commanders in the hall, and even trophies of famous battles such as the Lion of Idstedt.[66] Small wonder, perhaps, that they too might long for the chance to fight and win laurels of their own, as Paul von Hindenburg (who graduated from the Selekta in 1866) did at the outbreak of the Danish War in 1864:

> Unfortunately for me I was too young to be in the number of that highly-envied band [of cadets who set off for the war]... We followed the course of military events with the greatest eagerness, and, quivering with excitement, were joyful spectators when the captured guns were paraded round and the troops made their triumphal entry... Was it to be wondered at that henceforth we were all impatience for the day on which we ourselves would enter the army?[67]

Meanwhile, on the 7th May 1866, a group of young Primaner at the HKA wrote a letter to King Wilhelm I begging him to let them join the army straightaway, and give their young blood and lives for His Majesty and their dear fatherland; their sole wish was to take part in the war, and show the enemy that the cadets of 1868 were worthy to take their place alongside those of 1813, who had fought in the Wars of Liberation.[68]

Daily life at the schools also had its official rituals designed to promote patriotic self-sacrifice. On the 25th anniversary of Sedan-day (1 September 1895), a sermon celebrating the occasion was given in the park of *Voranstalt* Oranienstein by the school chaplain, *Kadettenpfarrer* Gelpke, the peroration of which ran as follows:

> On one of the battlefields lay a fatally wounded soldier. 'Are we victorious?' he asked one of his comrades, and when he heard the words 'Yes, we are', he raised himself for one final time with the last of his strength, and cried: 'Long live Germany.' Then he died. God fulfilled my brother's greatest wish...: he died for King and Fatherland. And our wives and fathers and children, they have not only sung 'Dear Fatherland, be at peace!'; they have given their loved ones, have let them go into battle, yes, with pain and tears, but also gladly; they have sacrificed them for the Fatherland... A widow, who had lost two sons at Metz, sent a wreath for their grave on the 18th of August. She had written 'for their day of death' (*Sterbetag*), but then she had crossed out the word '*Sterbetag*' and substituted it with 'day of honour' (*Ehrentag*). Still more could be told of the joy in sacrifice (*Opferfreudigkeit*), which at that time showed itself in the home as well as on the field; and you...can certainly provide still more examples of such heroic bravery and sacrificial spirit.[69]

Paul von Lettow-Vorbeck (who graduated from the HKA in 1888) also recalled that cadets whose fathers had fallen in battle were made to present themselves in great rows and announce where their parents had died – resulting in a recitation of famous battles such as Beaumont or Sedan. He describes the experience as 'thrilling' (*ergreifend*).[70]

Given this unrelenting emphasis upon the military and the patriotic, it is perhaps unsurprising that the highly ideological, monarchist and militaristic training provided by the cadet schools did not find a great deal of favour in non-conservative circles, and the corps had to sidestep a sizeable amount of criticism, particularly from politicians of a liberal bent.[71] Twice, the schools narrowly escaped complete abolition (first in 1848, after the March revolution, and then again in the early 1860s). Commentators claimed, in particular, that boys were being placed in a 'professional school' before their talents or inclinations had had any chance to develop, and that they were being 'programmed' to become soldiers by an education that was one-sided and far too harsh.

In his autobiographical work *Aus einem Soldatenleben*, Erich von Manstein (1887–1973), one of Germany's most prominent generals during World War II, admits that the cadet schools' preparation of their pupils for the soldier's life may have been harsh and concentrated, but that this was a great advantage, in that it 'accustomed the boys to fit into a larger community. Comradeship stood above the wishes of the individual.'[72]

But what precise forms – other than a great emphasis on drill exercises and physical education – did this harsh and concentrated preparation take? Often, the instruments of toughening were not so much the school staff as cadets further up the hierarchy, who, frequently with the tacit connivance of the *Erzieher*, would impose their will on their younger charges, claiming '*Tertianerrechte*' (third-formers' rights of overlordship) over them. The sociologist and ex-cadet Leopold von Wiese describes some typical occurrences dating from his time at *Voranstalt* Wahlstatt in the late 1880s:

> The invention exercised [by the boys] was astonishing – even the influence of changing fashions presented itself. In the study hour at that time the '*Gardereiter*' were *de rigueur*. Needles or pen nibs were hidden in a tough india-rubber, on which one was forced to sit by an energetic shove on the shoulders. Nastier yet was the fitting of *Gradehalter* with *Gardereiter*. In every room there were two or three of these official instruments of torture, which could be fastened to the tabletop. The chin had to rest on a little wooden saucer, which was brought to such a distance from the table that one was forced to sit with a straight-stretched back. The affair became painful via the introduction of inky, rusty *Gardereiter* onto the wooden plate. Above all it proved that pen and ink were not only – as in civilian life – weapons for a malicious intellectual quarrel, but were also adaptable to many forms of physical torture. The deputy *Stubenältester*...took great pleasure in the fact that he had made the bonces of both the Sextaners at his table the target for his darts. First he dipped the pens which stuck out of the holder in ink and then threw them at our heads. It was because of this that the missiles stuck in our scalps.[73]

Friedrich Franz von Unruh, who was a pupil at *Voranstalt* Plön at the turn of the twentieth century, was also present during some fearsome torments – on his very first evening in the corps, he had to witness his younger brother being hung out of a fourth-storey window.[74] Later, he discovered that such 'japes' as dropping hot sealing wax onto another boy's chest, or getting under someone's bed and rocking the iron frame so that it hit him on the head as he fell (*Kippen* or *Stülpen*), were all *de rigueur*.[75] Various forms of beating might be supplemented by even crueller tortures, such as making the younger boys grow their fingernails long and then nailing them to the desk so that they would be late for roll-call, or sewing buttons into their flesh.[76]

The prevailing view of such ill-treatment was of the 'what doesn't kill you will make you stronger' variety. Rudolf Görnandt, who attended *Voranstalt* Bensberg during the same period, admits that although such bullying was officially deprecated in public, it was not only tacitly tolerated by the authorities, but even seen as a good thing. Those who had endured such hardships themselves saw their prerogative of inflicting them on the new cadets as a divine right: 'We had to go through it...and it didn't kill us!'[77] It was all just part of the cadet corps 'tradition', necessary to make the new boys into 'useful members of the human race'.[78] One could not even always expect sympathy from one's parents; Kurt von Borcke (who attended *Voranstalt* Karlsruhe during the 1890s) tells us that his father's opinion was 'if boys beat each other up, it's their own affair...'[79] However, one happy ending caused by a father's intervention can be found in Paul von Schoenaich's autobiography, describing an incident at *Voranstalt* Culm which took place in the 1870s:

> The [improvement of the situation with regard to bullying] came about because of a small cadet, von C., whose father was General of a garrison close to Culm. This von C. had poured out his heart to his father during the holidays. Each morning, the boys in von C.'s *Stube* themselves had to put the canes, with which they were later to be beaten indiscriminately in the evening, in water, so that they would 'sink in' better. The scene for this thrashing was set each evening at 8.45pm on the dot. General von C., who knew this precisely from his son, paid a surprise visit to Culm, and at forty-five minutes past eight entered the company building in uniform. He ordered the old porter to lead him to *Stube* number four, his son's room. Upon the General's entrance the small boys were standing in rank and file, torsos naked, in front of the cane-wielding third-years. The General shouted at the astounded gang 'Everyone stay exactly where you are'. Then he let the porter go in order to fetch the commander, the company captain and the room's commanding officer. A denial was impossible. The officers, mortally ashamed, could do no other than promise a severe punishment.[80]

As this account, in which the authorities take measures against ill-treatment only when it is forcibly brought under their noses by a senior officer, suggests, help in such circumstances could not necessarily be expected from the *Erzieher.* In fact, some handbooks suggest that hazing (abusive or demeaning treatment of pupils, often in an initiatory context) had potential benefits, and was less dangerous to the boys than would have been the harmful destruction of the atmosphere of comradeship (so important to a military organisation) which would have resulted from the boys 'informing' on each other. For instance, at *Voranstalt* Karlsruhe, the house rules stated explicitly that:

> Every cadet considers it a matter of course that he should protect himself and his comrades from misconduct and punishment. Talebearing, known colloquially as *petzen*, is abhorrent, and is objectionable to no one more than it is to the superior involved.[81]

When Kurt von Borcke explains to his *Erzieher*, Lieutenant Knobelsdorff, that his best friend Udo von Gaisberg's death was ultimately the result of

Fig. 5. Lieutenant Knobelsdorff visits Udo von Gaisberg's deathbed (painting by Oskar Larsen).

persecution in their first few years by a bullying Count called Reising, Knobelsdorff replies that the fault was really Gaisberg's mother's for insisting on sending him to *Voranstalt* Karlsruhe when he was completely unsuited to the corps lifestyle. Although assuring Borcke that Reising wouldn't have got away with it on his watch, Knobelsdorff continues:

> 'We can't be everywhere – we're officers, not nannies... We want to train up boys who've got guts, not wet dishcloths. We have to bring out their characters; that's how our education differs from other boarding schools', where all the value is placed on dry-as-dust knowledge... We did everything humanly possible for Gaisberg...but the weak must go under; only the strong remain. That's how things are, both in nature and in human society.'[82]

Notes

[1] The withdrawal to the Siegfried Line (also known as the Hindenburg Line) was ordered by the Kaiser on 3 February 1917; however, the Line was pierced by the Allies during the Battle of Arras (April 1917).

[2] *Stenographische Berichte des Reichstages* 1917, 101. Sitzung (05/05/1917), 3089.

[3] ibid.

[4] Gilbert 1994, 355.

[5] ibid., 347.

[6] Boys educated at the *Hauptkadettenanstalt* would have been aged between fifteen and nineteen. See further n. 32 below.

[7] Sch. 1917 [GStAPK IV.HA Rep.13 Nr.70, Bl.16].

[8] Parallels include the author's depiction of the cadets' modest public demeanour (cf. *L.P.* 3.4): 'They appear grave, silent, and controlled far beyond their years, in full consciousness of their soldierly dignity' (*Sie scheinen über ihr Alter hinaus Ernst, schweigsam, gemessen, im Vollgefühl der soldatischen Würde*), and his emphasis on older boys commanding their juniors in the corps (cf. *L.P.* 2.11): 'From a very young age they are trained to have a sense of responsibility. A Tertianer is already in charge of how-ever-many comrades, whom he must not only command, but also supervise. Nowhere else is self-discipline so pronounced; wrested away from the framework of the family, the older boy trains the younger; the sense of honour already forms characters from their tenderest youth.' (*...sehr früh werden sie zum Gefühl der Verantwortung erzogen[;] ein Tertianer ist schon der Vorgesetzte von soundsovielen Kameraden, die er nicht nur kommandieren, sondern auch betreuen muss. Nirgends ist die Selbsterziehung so ausgeprägt; losgerissen aus dem Rahmen der Familie; erzieht der Ältere den Jüngeren, das Ehrgefühl bildet schon in frühester Jugend Charaktere.*)

[9] See further Chapter 7 below.

[10] G. von Unruh 1930. The smaller changes which Unruh made to the article's original text normally follow one of three patterns: firstly, all present-tense verbs are changed to the past tense; secondly, the original author's turn of phrase is often replaced by a different expression with exactly the same meaning; thirdly, information is added or corrected in places where Unruh, as a former cadet, knows more about the corps than the original author did – e.g. ibid., 298, where he states that the word '*Schule*' (school) was frowned upon, and replaces it with '*Klasse*' (class).

[11] *Reichskadettenblatt* 20, October 1930, 299. Interestingly, one of the epigraphs to the article, a quotation from Ernst Wildenbruch's *Der deutsche König* (Act V Scene 3), also implicitly refers to another Spartan apophthegm: 'Our bodies are our city-walls'.

[12] Noth 1978.

[13] For many more examples of this tendency, see Chapter 7 below.

[14] See further the accounts by Corvin and Dewall, discussed on pp. 59–64 below.

[15] Moncure 1993, 5–6.

[16] *Berlin Observer*, 5 September 1985, 4.

[17] Lübcke n.d., 17. See also Scharenberg 1979 for a full list of ex-cadet generals up to 1919.

[18] Moncure 1993, 5, 1; cf. Trotha 1912, 3.

[19] For examples of former cadets thanking the cadet corps for teaching them 'everything that they are, that they know and are capable of' (to paraphrase War Minister Albrecht von Roon, quoted in Ostertag 1990, 129), see *Reichskadettenblatt* 11, October 1927, 145 (Paul von Hindenburg); GStAPK IV.HA Rep.13 Nr.101, Bl.56 (Maximilian Perkun).

[20] Goffman 2007, xii–xiii.

[21] It should be noted that this account cannot be comprehensive; for a more extensive portrayal, see Moncure 1993.

[22] Military Education Commission 1870, 202.

[23] For a brief account of the early years of the cadet corps, see Moncure 1993, 30–5. See also Crousaz 1857, 14–286.

[24] Poten 1896, 309.

[25] In fact, such strife between the adherents of '*altpreußisch*' (old Prussian) conservatism and '*bürgerlich*' (middle class) liberalism was to dog the cadet corps until its final abolition in 1920 under the terms of the Treaty of Versailles (Article 176). See further Chapter 6 below.

[26] Moncure 1993, 43; cf. Crousaz 1857, 287–95.

[27] Crousaz (1876, 58–9) suggests that this was in part because the nobles continued to take up their accustomed *Schwertberuf* (military career), while the middle classes needed time to accustom themselves to the idea of pursuing a career in a sphere previously so alien to them. Other more hostile commentators saw the lack of *bürgerlich* cadets as part of an aristocratic conspiracy to keep the middle classes out of the officer corps (e.g. *Anlagen zu den Verhandlungen des Hauses der Abgeordneten* 1862, *Dritter Theil,* Aktenstück No.126: *Bericht der Kommission zur Prüfung des Staatshaushalts-Etats über den Etat der Militair-Verwaltung pro 1862*, 1202–3: *Militair-Erziehungs- und Prüfungs-Anstalten*).

[28] cf. Moncure 1993, 66, quoting Kaiser Wilhelm's Highest Cabinet Order (*Allerhöchste Kabinettsordre*), 29 March 1890.

[29] cf. Moncure 1993, 42; see further Chapter 6 below.

[30] cf. Moncure 1993, 100–1.

[31] cf. Moncure 1993, 53.

[32] The central cadet school will henceforth be referred to simply as the HKA. Until 1878, the HKA occupied premises in the Neue Friedrichstraße in Berlin, but for reasons of space and hygiene, a new site was developed in Groß-Lichterfelde during the 1870s, which became the home of the HKA from 1878–1920 (for more on these developments, see Lichtenstein 1890). It should be noted that the *Voranstalten* covered

the years from Sexta (age 10–11) to Obertertia (14–15); the years at the HKA ran from the Untersekunda (15–16) to the Oberprima (18–19).

[33] Schmitz 1997, 127.

[34] This can be attested by the regulation books belonging to each school, which differ from each other in various ways – e.g. Oranienstein 1908, Plön 1911, Karlsruhe n.d. (c.1914).

[35] On arriving at the HKA, cadets might try to cling to the specific slang of their own *Voranstalt*, or call cadets from other schools by disparaging names – the Culm cadets were often known as 'bears' because they had arrived from the uncultivated wilderness of West Prussia (cf. Moncure 1993, 60). Yet these differences seem for the most part to have been subsumed into the general *esprit de corps* as the cadets became more accustomed to life in Berlin. It appears that, in general terms, a greater difference was perceived to lie between the *Voranstalten* and the HKA than between individual *Voranstalten* (for an example of this attitude, see Dewall 1878, 4–6).

[36] For a full discussion of these, see Moncure 1993, 79–98.

[37] Some boys might even be packed off to the corps without any say in the matter, if their father or guardian were a high-ranking military man who deemed the life of an officer the only possible career for his youthful charge. Thus, for instance, Cordt von Brandis ended up at *Voranstalt* Köslin through the good offices of his Uncle Ernst, 'the *Jupiter tonans*' of the family. Once 'Uncle Jupiter' had sent his 'thunderbolt'-decree that '[the boy] must be enrolled in the cadet school at Köslin in Pommern at once!', there was no gainsaying him, for he was a General (Brandis 1966, 11–12, 19). For a somewhat similar view taken by Fritz and Friedrich Franz von Unruh's father, also a General, see Friedrich Franz von Unruh 1967, 59.

[38] Moncure 1993, 83, 86, 98.

[39] This latter was the case with Udo von Gaisberg in Kurt von Borcke's autobiographical cadet-school novel *Das sind wir* (1940).

[40] Moncure 1993, 90–1, 98.

[41] Reitzenstein 1920, 17–27. On the autobiographical nature of Reitzenstein's work, see Chapter 6 below. A similar case is also described in Borcke's *Das sind wir* (1940) regarding one cadet Kiekebusch, the son of an émigré German businessman who runs a Brazilian coffee company; however, his brush with bullying did not end so tragically.

[42] For more on this, see Glinicke's memoir *Aus den Memoiren eines Leibpagen* (1957), which contains numerous colourful anecdotes about cadets' time at court.

[43] Take, for example, the bitter recollection of Erich Ludendorff (1865–1937): 'Jealously I viewed cadets who were permitted to serve at the galas held for the royal family. Because I was "bourgeois" I was not permitted such a position of trust.' (Ludendorff 1933, 7).

[44] Moncure 1993, 100.

[45] Lettow-Vorbeck 1957, 29. The Kaiser's personal enthusiasm for the cadet corps was also evidenced both by his support for new building programmes (Lorentzen 1977, 3), and by his frequent visits to the schools, such as one paid to *Voranstalt* Bensberg on 18 August 1906 (Feiber 1939, 60).

[46] Moncure 1993, 122.

[47] ibid., 125.

[48] Ilgner 1932, 60.

[49] Hindenburg 1920, 16. The wonder and joy which cadets felt at having the Kaiser officiate at their graduation, which led their hearts to beat faster, their knees to tremble, and caused them to vow then and there to die for him if need be, is expressed powerfully by von Altrock (1925, 52). For an example of one of the Kaiser's graduation speeches, see the article '1914: "738 Kadetten zum Eintritt in die Armee!"' in *Reichskadettenblatt* 9, May 1927.

[50] Five of the *Voranstalten* also had smaller Catholic chapels, and the HKA Protestant chapel had a Catholic 'annex'. For more on religion at the schools, see Moncure 1993, 126–36.

[51] Moncure 1993, 127–8.

[52] Halkett 1939, 58.

[53] Schoenaich 1926, 23.

[54] Instead of '*Dem Herrn sei Dank, für Speis' und Trank*' (The Lord be thanked for food and drink). *Igel* ('hedgehog') was cadet slang for meatballs.

[55] Schoenaich 1926, 24.

[56] Fritz von Unruh 1963, 221. For an instance of cadets mocking a parson's religion class, see ibid., 262. See also various episodes in Borcke 1940 (including that described on pp. 101–2 below).

[57] Friedrich Franz von Unruh 1967, 60.

[58] Indeed, a good proportion of our sources were produced by cadets turned writers, dramatists, film producers, or sociologists.

[59] Scharfenort 1892, 66. On the introduction of instruction in rifle marksmanship and field craft, see Moncure 1993, 219–20.

[60] A passage from the *Hausordnung des Kadettenhauses Karlsruhe* (c.1914, 20) similarly emphasises that whenever the cadets are not carrying out academic or other duties, they must engage in as much healthful outdoors activity as possible: '[The cadet] must tumble around outside as much as he can; he must show that he is no lazybones or mummy's boy, but a real man, who stands his ground in every game and every physical activity... The cadet must also learn through [outdoor] games to humble himself and subordinate himself to the collective; he must feel himself to be part of the whole, cultivate consideration, and therefore, by good comradeship, help younger and weaker cadets to come into their own...'

[61] Moncure 1993, 222, 227.

[62] Wiese 1924, 46.

[63] Brandis 1966, 34–5; Isenburg 1958, 63.

[64] e.g. Salomon 1933, 17.

[65] ibid., 29.

[66] The Lion of Idstedt (also known as the *Flensburger Löwe*) was a monument created by the Danish sculptor Hermann Wilhelm Bissen in 1862, recalling the victory of Danish troops over those from Schleswig-Holstein on 25 July 1850, which had enabled the city of Flensburg to remain in Danish hands. In 1864, however, Prussian troops returned in greater force, defeating Denmark and capturing Schleswig-Holstein and Northern Schleswig. The great bronze lion, which was treated as a symbolic spoil of war, was displayed first in the Berlin *Zeughaus* (arsenal) and then transferred in April 1878 to the courtyard of the new HKA in Groß-Lichterfelde. The cadets became very fond of the lion, and treated it as a kind of mascot, often playing pranks such as

dressing it up, or filling it with snow or water so that it would look as if it were relieving itself.

[67] Hindenburg 1920, 15.

[68] Scharfenort 1892, 94.

[69] *Zur Erinnerung an die 25. Wiederkehr des Sedantages und seine Feier im Kadettenhaus Oranienstein* (Diez an der Lahn, 1895), 7. The subject of the sermon was in fact 'Psalm 126, verse 3'.

[70] Lettow-Vorbeck 1957, 24. For a depiction of a similar occasion at *Voranstalt* Culm, see Szczepański 1910, 36–7.

[71] For a more thorough discussion of critics' attitudes to the cadet corps and their political implications, see Chapter 6 below.

[72] Manstein 1958, 22.

[73] Wiese 1924, 12–13.

[74] Friedrich Franz von Unruh 1967, 62–3.

[75] ibid., 87–8.

[76] Schoenaich 1926, 19.

[77] Görnandt 1966, 27.

[78] Borcke 1940, 243.

[79] ibid., 145; cf. Fritz von Unruh 1983, 134.

[80] Schoenaich 1926, 19–20.

[81] Karlsruhe, n.d., 16. Interestingly enough, the author of the *Vorschriften für die Erzieher des Kadettenhauses in Bensberg* (n.d., c.1906) takes a much stronger line (9–11); all abuses of younger cadets by their older comrades are potentially harmful to the corps spirit. However, cadets are forbidden on pain of punishment to mention maltreatment to anyone *except* the *Erzieher*, so that anyone who tells tales to their parents at home will be considered culpable (33–4).

[82] Borcke 1940, 380–1. Sometimes, of course, it was the *Erzieher* who posed the problem, as Paul von Schoenaich (who attended *Voranstalt* Culm during the late 1870s) was to find to his cost (1926, 22): Lieutenant T. von B. he describes as 'chronically sadistic... His victim was a cadet T. who was in his *Stube*, whom he hazed in an absolutely refined way. His room-mates were forbidden on pain of the strongest punishment possible to speak a word to this completely harmless, but less gifted, youth. He had to eat his breakfast in a corner with his face turned towards the wall. Into the bargain, the boy received such beating from this beast in human form, that he could barely take any more. I never did find out the reason for this ill-treatment.' Another *Erzieher*, B., would always complain that Schoenaich's *Stube* was too hot or cold; he would either open the window and leave the cadets to freeze, or make them stoke up the stove when the temperature was already boiling. When the cadets were late for lessons, he would force them to 'present arms' for minutes at a time.

3

SPARTANERJÜNGLINGE, OR THE IMPORTANCE OF BEING SPARTAN

How to become a Spartan Youth

The cadet-corps authorities' *laissez-faire* attitude to bullying, along with the widespread abomination of talebearing at the schools, were both combined in the idea that a boy's strength of character and 'guts' could best be demonstrated by his ability to suffer in silence. Both these phenomena were important elements in the nexus of ideas which led cadets to identify themselves with 'Spartan youth' on a personal level, and which also led authors writing about the schools to portray them as such.

Perhaps the finest – and most publicly explicit – example of this aspect of the Spartan *topos* can be found in one of the most famous of all pieces of cadet-school literature – an epistolary novel by Paul von Szczepański (1855–1924) set in the preparatory cadet school at Culm-on-Vistula, entitled *Spartanerjünglinge* ('Spartan youths'). Szczepański himself appears to have been a precocious author as well as an established member of the Prussian Officer Corps, publishing his first novel at the age of 24, and quickly establishing himself as the editor of numerous newspapers and periodicals, including the *Deutsches Tageblatt*, *Daheim*, and the *Berliner Lokal-Anzeiger*. It seems likely that *Spartanerjünglinge* is based on Szczepański's own personal experience as a cadet, or on that of other family members who joined the cadet corps (at least six had done so, four of whom, including his elder brother Gerhardt, definitely attended *Voranstalt* Culm).[1] The novel, which was first published at the turn of the nineteenth century,[2] went into as many as twenty editions over the following decades (including an illustrated version with the variant title *Spartanerjungen*),[3] and was translated for publication and use in schools even in non-German-speaking countries.[4] It was widely considered as a paradigmatic example of the cadet-novel genre, which any mother anguishing over her son's possible fate at a cadet school would make a point of reading,[5] and at one point – towards the end of the First World War – it was even referred to in the *Reichstag* as a 'famous novella' (*bekannte Novelle*).[6]

This titular identification of Prussian cadets with young Spartans raises a number of interesting questions. For instance, why had Szczepański chosen this particular title for a novel which, in W. D. Lowe's English translation (1910), is merely rendered 'Letters from a Cadet to his Mother'? Could we deduce that the equation of cadets with young Spartans had become a *topos* in the cadet corps and the public imagination at this time, or did it merely suit Szczepański to identify the cadets in this manner because of his own private conceptions of Sparta and of cadet-school life?

The key to these questions seems, in part at least, to lie with the overt references to Sparta in the novel itself.[7] For instance, at p. 19ff., cadet von Gottwein (the narrator) and a group of his company embark upon a night raid to steal pears from the garden of Mr Winter, the school chaplain. Those left behind in the dormitory are menaced with dire threats – every bone in their bodies will be broken if they tell – while the brave band of thieves stealthily clambers out of the dormitory window and down the side of the school building with the aid of a conveniently placed trellis. All goes well until one of the younger boys, von Sendrecki Minimus, cuts his hand on the trelliswork and lets out an involuntary cry. Castigated by his peers because he might have brought about their discovery, Sendrecki Minimus bravely smashes his hand into a mirror the next morning so that the school doctor will not guess the true reason for his injury. Gottwein's mother, disapproving, rebukes him in her next letter for taking part in the escapade – to which Gottwein earnestly replies (p.26):

> If you had learnt history you would certainly understand: we learn history and all about a Spartan boy who was a hero because he had stolen a fox and hid it in his clothes, and the fox bit the boy in the chest till he died, but he never made a sound so that people should not notice it. And the Spartans set up a monument to him, and we are taught about him in our history lessons. Now just think...if the trellis-work of the vine had broken, we should have broken our necks and been killed too; it is just the same...

On two other occasions (pp. 53, 65), Sendrecki Minor calls Sendrecki Minimus, his younger brother, 'my young Spartan' – both times in the context of opening his mouth or keeping quiet when he would have been better advised to do exactly the opposite. For example, the first time this appellation is used occurs when Sendrecki Minimus is too dumbfounded at being accused of stealing another boy's possessions to deny the charge, and is almost throttled by his oldest brother, Sendrecki Major, on account of his untimely silence (Gottwein saves him from asphyxiation in the nick of time by revealing the truth).

These incidents, and the particular (one might go so far as to say peculiar) emphasis supposedly placed on a version of Plutarch's 'fox-tale' (*Lyc.* 18.1)[8] in actual academic lessons, suggest both that boys were encouraged to identify themselves to some degree with young Spartans

Fig. 6. The pear-stealing expedition, as imagined by Fritz Buchholz.

(a matter to which we will return below), and that the most telling way in which life at the cadet school is supposed to be 'Spartan' is that one learns to bear the worst of hardships with never a complaint. In the boys' parlance, this is translated into an utter abhorrence of 'sneaking'; one learns never to tell tales or reveal bullying to the authorities, even if one's life were, literally, to depend upon it.

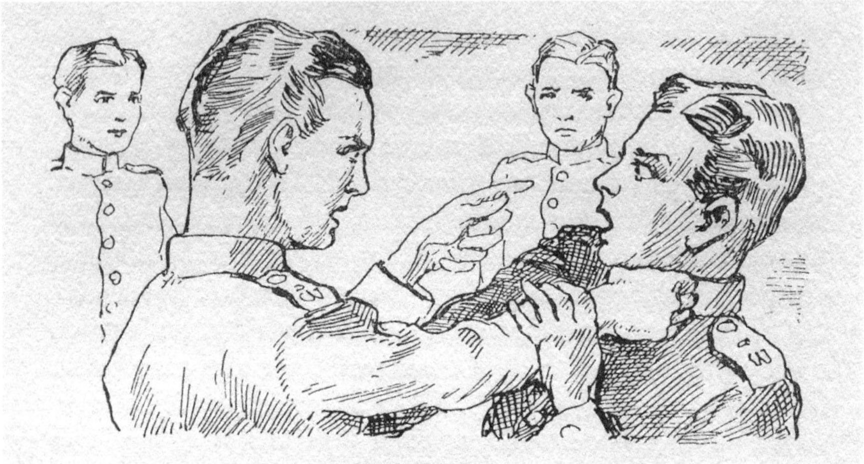

Fig. 7. Sendrecki Major throttling his brother Sendrecki Minimus, on the assumption that he is a thief.

Fig. 8. The bully Bendling forces Gottwein to undergo the trial of 'bacon-swallowing' (*Speckschlucken*).

The importance of keeping one's mouth shut even in the face of the most vicious bullying or most sorrowful situations is a recurring theme in the novel, and is repeatedly portrayed as eminently praiseworthy behaviour. In his first letter home, Gottwein tells his mother that although many of the new boys are homesick and have been subjected to maltreatment by the archbully Bendling, 'we mustn't cry under any circumstances; cadets never cry' (p. 4). Shortly afterwards, when being subjected by Bendling to the disgusting torture of being made to swallow a piece of dried-up bacon on a thread, which is then pulled out of one's gullet and forced down the next boy's throat, Gottwein writes of the dreadful persecution inflicted on sneaks (pp. 7–8); they get a 'licking' from the entire form, and are called 'cads', which is the worst ever insult: 'a cadet must never sneak...it hardens you to be bullied.' At the novel's end, Gottwein himself is killed by a bout of pneumonia induced by the bully Bendling's cruellest prank – leaving him locked up all night in midwinter in a freezing ground-floor locker room – yet Gottwein is saluted above all by the school's Commandant (and, we might surmise, by the author himself) for never revealing the true reason behind his incarceration, and claiming instead that he got himself shut in by accident (p. 73ff). The truth is only revealed when the commander reads Gottwein's last unfinished letter to his mother.

The theme of boys being considered 'Spartan' through their silent and stoical bearing of hardship is not unique to Szczepański's novel, however. Johannes van Dewall (1889–1823) also expounds this idea in an autobiographical book of cadet-school stories (*Aus meinen Kadettenjahren*), inspired by his time at *Voranstalt* Bensberg in the early 1840s, and first published in 1877.[9] On pages 7–8, Dewall describes his heart-rending parting from his loving family as he climbs into the coach bound for Bensberg, leaving behind his home in Minden and all that he knows:

> With all my will I choked back my weeping, even though my heart was hurting so and I was frightened, now that I was separated from my family home – but two real cadets were standing nearby, so I was ashamed of my tears, and, like a young Spartan, forced them heroically back.

Here, the idea of being like a 'young Spartan' (*junger Spartaner*) is equated with holding one's tongue; not losing face through showing pain or emotion.

Later on in the book, we also find the idea (touched upon in *Spartanerjünglinge*) that 'sneaking' (*petzen*) was something to be avoided – or punished – at all costs, *because* of its thoroughly un-Spartan nature.[10] In the absence of their *Erzieher*, *Gouverneur* Justus, the boys in Dewall's *Stube* are whiling away the private study period with forbidden pleasures such as reading Red Indian novels by James Fenimore Cooper, writing home – or, in the case of one boy, Thilo – simply having a snooze. Thilo's room-mates, annoyed by his loud snoring, decide to see what it will take to wake him. First, they put a lighted spill under his nose, so that he breathes the smoke – but he doesn't awaken. Then Risius, another of the boys, crawls

Fig. 9. Johannes van Dewall bids a tearful farewell to his family before getting on the coach bound for Bensberg. The sight of the two cadets in the background forces him to hold back his tears 'like a young Spartan'.

underneath the table and sticks a piece of gum to Thilo's boot, which he sets alight with the aforementioned spill. It burns right through the leather and causes a huge blister on Thilo's foot, as well as awakening him most rudely. All laugh at his howling and antics, but...

Fig. 10. The baiting of Thilo. Risius burns a lighted spill into a piece of gum stuck to his boot.

> Thilo was not enough of a Spartan...to bear the pain of his wound stoically; the next morning he went with the duty NCO to the sickbay, where he took the doctor into his confidence and revealed that someone had stuck the gum to his boot.[11]

To punish Thilo for his lack of *Spartanertum* (Spartan-ness), the boys lie in wait for him on his return and subject him to the torture of the 'Spanish rack' (in which the victim's hands are tied with a leather strap or handkerchief and pushed over his knees, while a bat or broom is stuck

Fig. 11. Thilo is punished with the torture of the 'Spanish Rack'.

obliquely under them) so that he is helpless to prevent the beating which follows (accompanied by a stern lecture on the evils of talebearing), or to extricate himself from the large metal washing-bowl into which they decant him until it is time for class.

Elsewhere, we find another aspect – though one quite closely related – of the boys' continual anxiety to be 'Spartan' enough; one which even caused them to coin a new verb, '*spartanern*' (to be like a Spartan).[12] This word was used not so much in connection with putting up with others' bullying as with the endurance of *self-inflicted* torments, as Dewall describes on page 49:

> Twenty-five strokes of the cane on the muscles before breakfast; why, that's nothing, no one turns a hair at that anymore, even when it hurts so much and one's arms are streaming with blood – fifty with the whip, that's laughed to scorn; someone took this so far, that he let a piece of sponge burn into his hand, just because he had read somewhere-or-other that someone else had done it. So, ultimately, everyone vies with everyone else in '*spartanern*', attempting the most incredible and reckless deeds... The Schnappsacks [new cadets] hear and look on, astounded, and naturally they try to follow in the footsteps of their older models until they surpass them.

Dewall goes on to present this competitive masochism as all part of the schools' way of putting 'steel' into the boys' backbones:

> With good nature, thick skin and some cunning, we found the heavy yoke becoming lighter with each day that passed, and with each day we felt more plainly that we had taken the *steel* within us... [By the end of the year,] no one can deny that *the little man has truly turned into steel*... His muscles are firm, his body is toughened, he has a lively sense of honour and he is ready to die for his comrades. Thus there lies already in each Schnappsack all the traits that make a future general-fieldmarshal![13]

A more detailed account of this interpretation of the Spartan ideal, in which 'being like a Spartan' is taken to mean bearing dreadful discomfort or distressing ordeals without flinching, laughing in the face of pain, and always wishing to go one better in acts of reckless daring than cadets who have gone before, can be found in Otto von Corvin's autobiography *Aus dem Leben eines Volkskämpfers* (1861), which details his experiences at *Voranstalt* Potsdam during the 1820s:

> [One of the other boys] threw me down in wrestling, and my left arm was very badly dislocated. I delayed going to the doctor; but I was in the most awful pain all night, and my arm was double its size next morning. Dr Baumann handled it somewhat roughly, and when I could not suppress a little cry of pain, he said, in a sneering manner, 'Pshaw! a soldier should be able to dance on needles!' which mortified me much, and hurt me more than my arm, which I had to wear in a sling for nearly two months...

> The example of the Spartan youths appealed to us greatly as a model – we used to drill ourselves in enduring all possible tortures,[14] and it was for this reason that the Doctor's scorn wounded me so deeply. Bearing blows, sticking needles into our flesh or making deep cuts were the usual; however, some of these exercises were even more refined, such as the burning of elastic bands into our hands, melting a snowball over the palm of the hand, or letting a cockchafer crawl over your face without turning a hair. This last is not as easy as it might sound, especially when the cockchafer tickles your mouth or nostrils with its prickly feet... For a time running was the fashion, and you might see long files of cadets, their arms akimbo, and handkerchiefs in their mouths, trotting for hours in the yard, until they almost dropped from fatigue...[15]

A further example can be found in Kurt von Borcke's autobiographical recollections from *Voranstalt* Karlsruhe during the 1890s:

> The cadets in my *Stube* were all very smart at bearing pains, and Gersing [the *Stubenältester*] was very firm on the point that we were being brought up after the Spartan fashion. Interesting bets were made on [for example...] who could stand for longest with a compass between his legs doing kneebends, or with a washboard with glasses on it balanced on his outstretched arms.[16]

Louis von Scharfenort, Captain and librarian at the HKA, also mentions the custom in his *Bilder aus der Geschichte des Kadetten-Korps für Alt und Jung* (1889) – a little book which aimed to present any interested parties (though particularly cadets past, present and future) with 'cultural-historical portraits, which stand out from the broad background of the history of our great fatherland', weaving together selected vignettes from throughout the cadet corps' existence in order to help illuminate Germany's history.[17] In a section aimed at warning prospective cadets what they might be let in for if they joined the corps, he writes:

> The dream is shattered; harsh reality rules. Now one must get dressed in a few minutes so as not to be last in the washroom, at the entrance of which an officer stands guard, watch in hand, in order to spot the slowcoaches. There the new boy begins to discover what it means to be a Schnappsack, but his fate will seem bitterer by far when the '*Bolle*', the harsh cadet corporal, scrapes the butter from his morning roll and, at midday, when there is mashed potato and meatballs, makes the little Schnappsack's portion disappear without the slightest qualm.
>
> Woe betide you, poor boy, if you don't learn to bear your sufferings with dignity and humility. Those who now torment you will someday also introduce you to 'stargazing' and the 'Spanish rack'.
>
> Pay close attention: if someone holds a tunic in front of your face for 'stargazing' and you have to look up at the heavens through the stiffly-stretched sleeve, someone will pour a glassful of water down it from above. Certainly the 'Spanish rack' is no laughing matter, particularly not when it

> is arranged with a long broomstick stuck through under the knees, and you have the opportunity, sitting in a washtub, to consider the lovely moon there outside.
>
> Just don't 'sneak' and 'toady'. These torments against each person, which you think are devised at your expense alone, are simply what you have to do in order to become an 'old hand'. Alongside this, like the 'Spartan youth' (*der 'spartanischen Jugend' gleich*), you must inure yourself against all forms of physical pain. Learn to 'endure blows, stick needles in your flesh, or even – however, only the bravest do this – burn india-rubber into your hand or let a cockchafer crawl over your face, without turning a hair.'
>
> Insults, my young friend, can only be atoned for with a weapon in your hand. Where to get a weapon from? If you don't have a little wooden children's sword, then take a switch, perhaps with thorns – then, mark well, blood must flow – afterwards one embraces one's friend, and the matter of honour is concluded.[18]

The fact that the example of the '*spartanische Jugend*' is considered directly relevant, even highlighted, as part of this 'fatherly advice' which all prospective cadets are hypothetically intended to read, not only corroborates still further the idea that Spartan self-identification was considered important by cadets, but also implies that such identification was actively encouraged by the cadet-school authorities (further evidence of which will be discussed below).[19] Significant, too, is the point that this depiction is not an isolated memory from one school alone. Rather, it is included as part of a supposedly comprehensive picture of any *Voranstalt*, which anyone who had once been a member of the corps could presumably be expected to recognise, and which is intended by Scharfenort to be handed down to posterity. Thus, competing for the title of being a 'Spartan youth' through toughness and resilience to pain and discomfort becomes something to which the author expects cadets to aspire even at considerable personal cost, since '*spartanern*' is depicted as being as much part of the tribulations of corps life as the trials such as 'stargazing' (*Sternegucken*), which new boys were made to undergo each year.

Scharfenort's description also raises another interesting point – that being Spartan was not seen solely as an aid to the endurance of self-inflicted pains, but could also help inure cadets to the ill-treatment which they would have to undergo to become 'old hands'.[20] That former cadets also linked such toughening through bullying with the idea of 'being educated after the Spartan fashion' is demonstrated by a passage from the autobiography of officer-turned-pacifist Paul von Schoenaich (1866–1954), who attended *Voranstalt* Culm during the late 1870s:

> Mistreatment of the little ones by the big boys was...always on the agenda... So, for example, even today I still have a scar on my hand, where my table-

> officer, cadet von F., burned me. He used to put the scissors under the lamp until they became red hot, and then I had to show him how long I could stand it when he held them against my hand. At bottom, von F. was a very good-natured person – just rough like a boisterous dog. Mostly, I suffered from his insatiable appetite. In the long break-time we got buttered rolls, called *Bobel*. For von F., one of these was like a drop of water on hot stone. When he had gobbled his *Bobel* in one minute, he would come up to me and insist that I should, just this once, let him have a bite of mine. Resistance was futile. Then he would open his mouth...impossibly wide, and bite my finger so hard that I would instantly let go, and watch my *Bobel* vanish, never to be seen again. More disturbing were the so-called 'stomach-promenades' (*Bauchpromenaden*), which one had to undergo if convicted of some small misdemeanour by the *Stubenältester*. This involved the culprit being laid on a table, in the middle of which was a raised inkwell. A large youth sat on the convict's back; four others grabbed him by the arms and legs, and then they spun him like a merry-go-round, giving him hell. I think that one little Sextaner got a serious internal injury from this and had to go to the sickbay. Naturally he had to tell the doctor that he had hurt himself by falling from the high bar. I admit now that at the time I did not consider these things tragic... Yes, perhaps it is even a good thing that the boys were brought up to a certain Spartan toughening...
>
> I also wish to count the boys' punch-ups under the chapter-heading 'Spartan-ness', since they went far further than those which are otherwise usual amongst boys. Namely, these consisted of an official battle – that is, one ordered by the *Stubenältester* – which was only considered at an end when blood flowed. So one had to punch one's opponent in the face. These duels were tacitly tolerated by the officers, since one had to ask for permission afterwards to put the bloody jackets in the wash.[21]

Interpreted another way, this sort of 'Spartan toughening' was seen by some who underwent it as all being part and parcel of Spartan-influenced methods of teaching the young to obey, in order that they might later be good commanders.[22] Thus, Peter von Heydebreck (1889–1934) writes of his time at *Voranstalt* Köslin at the turn of the twentieth century:

> Even by contemporary standards our life was Spartanly hard; by the opinions of our time, unquantifiably so. In particular, the [Schnappsacks] had nothing to laugh about. They had to do menial cleaning tasks for the older cadets, collecting up tennis-balls in their free time or, on winter days, pulling [them] round the courtyard on sledges for hours at a time. A small example to illustrate my point:
>
> My deputy *Stubenältester* was a lanky fifteen-year-old, nicknamed Uhle. He only ever addressed me as 'swine' or 'stupid old hen'. Besides that, three times a day, he administered the 'muscle-strapping' (*Muskelsträmmer*) to me. These are blows to the muscles of one's slightly bent-back upper arm. Whether the 'muscle-strapping' was lighter or harder, and given with his

> fist or with his bootjack, depended on his mood, and on how capable I had shown myself in the performance of my *Sack*-duties. Mostly they were of the lighter sort, since Uhle only did it because he wanted to do his best for me. At least, he himself assured me of this each time with the words: 'You'll be grateful to me for this later on, swine, when I've made a strapping young man of you.'[23] I must admit that his teaching did me no harm. Generally, in his own way he was good to me, and protected me from others' harassment. There was only one thing I hated him for, and that was his lizards, which he reared in a preserving jar. I had to supply those beasts with food. One day he found a dead fly in the receptacle, and, inflamed with rage, took me to task: 'Stupid old hen, do you think that my upstanding lizards will eat your filthy flies!' For the next two weeks I went fly-hunting in all places, accessible and inaccessible, since, as a punishment for my incompetence, each day I had to produce thirty live flies, and, as atonement for the offence caused to his lizards, an extra thirty dead flies, well packed in matchboxes...
>
> The transfer to the HKA at Groß-Lichterfelde was linked with the promotion to the Untersekunda. One became a *Sack* again and had to do menial cleaning tasks for the NCOs. And that was good. After the last year in the preparatory corps with the authority of senior cadets...it meant that now we had to obey again, in order later to be able to command properly. For that was the point of this Spartan educational system: the Prussian Cadet Corps was a school for leaders, which could not have been better devised. Whoever grows up surrounded by military constraints throughout his long years of youth has the opportunity to consider his superiors critically, and will later avoid falling into those mistakes which once had caused him to suffer. What a subaltern (*Fahnenjunker*) who comes out of the school first has to learn, the cadet brings into the army with him. He has understanding for the joy and suffering of his subordinates and can sympathise with them. One of the most important attributes of a leader, since it secures him the trust of the men who follow him.[24]

However, Sparta could also be invoked as a more general paradigm for the harshness of life in the cadet corps, often in comparison with the comforts of home life; take for instance the reflections of theatre- and film-director Herbert Maisch (1890–1974), who attended Oranienstein and Karlsruhe between 1900 and 1906. He writes:

> When I have often looked back in later life and wondered whether it was necessary to tear me away so young from the tender care of my Swabian parental home and give me over to the Spartan world of Prussian discipline, simply because, with regard to my future, the question of schooling seemed a difficult one, nowadays I no longer have any quarrel with my dead father's [decision]. His initiative turned out well for me. Not only because this Prussian discipline awakened my character, strengthened my inner rebellious streak, and in many ways made me into a useful person, no – odd as it must sound – it was via this path that I discovered my artistic temperament.[25]

By this definition, it seems that some cadets considered that *Spartanertum* and 'Prussian discipline' (*preußische Zucht*) were well-nigh interchangeable,[26] an attitude which is also reflected in Friedrich-Wilhelm Isenburg's recollections of his time at *Voranstalt* Plön just before the turn of the twentieth century:

> 'Sparta embraced us with arms of steel', one reads in [Dr. Klüver's little book of cadet memoirs]. That hits the nail on the head... [T]he future officers (*Offiziernachwuchs*) were trained in seclusion by tough discipline (*strenger Zucht*)...[27]

Isenburg does, however, also touch upon another aspect of the Spartan trope – that is, that the cadet-corps training was 'Spartan' because it facilitated endurance of material discomfort such as extremes of heat and cold. On the experience which led to his gaining *Totenschwimmer* status (see above, p. 44) he writes:

> After half an hour I was already badly frozen, and I knew how bitterly hard it would be for me to stick it out until the fifty minutes were up; as I was swimming near the escort boat I counted the seconds and time seemed to stand still. But this was the most admirable part of the cadet-corps education, that one learned to grit one's teeth and was ashamed to be feeble. In this regard, a passage...from Field-Marshal von Manstein's autobiography should be mentioned; he too was a cadet at Plön in 1900. He writes:
>
> 'Even in that freezing winter, when the Rhine was already covered with ice, Colonel-General von Rundstedt still wore only a thin raincoat. When I protested that he would catch his death of cold, he merely retorted that he had never possessed a greatcoat in his life, and was certainly not going to buy one at his age! And neither did he, for even after all these years the old gentleman still bore the imprint of his Spartan training in the cadet corps.'[28]

We might perhaps compare these with Graf von Holleben's account of his 'Spartan' education at *Voranstalt* Potsdam in the 1840s:

> In the [attic] dormitories...the temperature in summer would rise to an unbearable heat, and in winter it sank so low that the water in the basins was crusted with ice. Our beds were extremely simple; an iron bed-frame, mattress, a hard bolster; in summer one, in winter two woollen blankets, a rough sheet... In winter one used the second blanket to swaddle oneself like a mummy, without anyone considering what diseases might have been caught from it... When we romped about in the thick snow in the courtyard, we sat down to the private study period in the same socks and shoes... [Washing was considered unimportant...] Cadets who felt unwell had to trudge over to the sickbay through the snow... But despite all this we grew up into a sturdy generation. Our whole education was a military one; perhaps too Spartan for boys, but it certainly trained future soldiers.[29]

Franz von Papen's less lengthy description of life at *Voranstalt* Bensberg during the 1890s also forms a variation on this theme:

> I had little idea what a Spartan profession I had chosen. We slept on camp beds, the great, vaulted rooms of the old castle of Bensberg were unheated even in the depths of winter, and the food consisted mostly of soup and bread. It was a harsh introduction to life for a boy of eleven, but it seemed to do me little harm. I grew up healthy and happy, and learned habits of hard work and personal discipline which I have kept all my life.[30]

Von Papen's mention of food, however, also brings us to another (quasi-constant) form of material discomfort which the cadets thought of as quintessentially Spartan – that is, hunger. In this connection, let us take Ernst von Salomon's description of his first meal in the Karlsruhe corps (c.1913):

> For breakfast there was flour soup (*Mehlsuppe*), a roll and a little bit of butter. I had once heard in passing about a Spartan meal, and this tied in exactly with my vision of the famed black soup, so I was pretty disappointed to find floury goo in it, neither black nor made of blood. Anyhow, by itself it was scarcely edible; at home I had always made the glue for my kites out of a mixture of flour and water, but had never thought that such a paste could be considered fit for human consumption.[31]

The authorities, however, took such Spartan comparisons rather as a compliment, if we are to believe Kurt von Borcke's account of a tongue-lashing which the (unfortunately rather corpulent) Commandant of *Voranstalt* Karlsruhe gave the cadets there for complaining about their meals:

> 'Cadets!' bellowed his fearsome voice, 'It has come to my knowledge that complaints have been raised about the food here. I have personally made on-the-spot investigations *re* your diet and have found that it is simple and tasty. I love the simplicity of the Spartans, just like His Majesty, our supreme commander, who has recommended it for the education of the replacement officers in the army, that the army may follow his good example in every regard.' – Pause – Does the Kaiser really eat meatballs with sweet rice, or 'Kilometre-sausage' with dried-up vegetables, I wondered? 'A cadet must eat what has been put in front of him. I do not want to hear any more complaints about this matter.'[32]

In fact, Louis von Scharfenort tells us that, at one of the extremely grand meals after the annual cadet-corps sports-festival, 'Spartan soup' (*spartanische Suppe*) was actually on the menu.[33] Is it too far-fetched to wonder whether, since the boys had just proved themselves as Spartan-like young athletes at the aforementioned sporting celebration, the authorities might have considered it particularly appropriate to serve a Spartan dish in their honour?

The endorsement of *Spartanertum* by cadet-corps authority figures

As noted briefly above, the idea that teachers and *Erzieher* at the cadet schools might have seen identification with a Spartan model as something which they wished to encourage is suggested both by the emphasis supposedly placed on Spartan history in lessons, and by the treatment of *spartanern* as a perfectly normal part of cadet-school life in Scharfenort's semi-official *Bilder aus der Geschichte des Kadetten-Korps für Alt und Jung* (1889). However, more explicit examples of military superiors holding up a Spartan example to cadets as worthy of emulation can be found in several sources of widely differing types, three of which will be discussed here.[34]

The first work is one of a series of children's career guides, entitled *Der Offizier. Das Buch der Berufe: Ein Führer und Berater bei der Berufswahl* (1901), by Major Ernst Faller. If a boy wants to become an officer, the Major informs his youthful readers, one of the best ways to achieve his goal is to join the cadet corps. But (here Faller takes an admonitory tone reminiscent of Scharfenort's *Bilder*) he must know what he is letting himself in for: education in a Spartan and frugal sense.[35] Faller proceeds to list a number of other characteristics which we have already seen linked with cadet-school *Spartanertum*: habitual subordination of individual wishes to those of the collective; punctuality; order; vigour and endurance. The cadet must not be sluggish or cowardly; above all he must not 'sneak' if ill-treated, or he will be a lost soul, thrashed by his comrades (whose task it is to train him out of weakmindedness, snivelling, and mummy's-boyishness).[36] Faller praises particularly the equality of all cadets, which ensures that the noblest Count and the lowliest *bürgerlich* cadet must endure the same uncomfortable bedding, the same frugal food, and the same strict discipline and beatings.[37] Only once the cadet has undergone such a training can he take up an officer's career, fully possessed of the necessary 'Spartan-soldierly traits' (*spartanisch-soldatischen Eigenschaften*) and warrior virtues – which he must be careful not to lose through succumbing to the dangers of luxurious living.[38]

The second example is taken from the recollections of Henning von Koss, formerly of *Voranstalt* Köslin, which were published in the Köslin former cadets' newsletter in 1973.[39] The following incident, von Koss recalls, took place in 1903, when he was in the Untertertia.[40] One evening, the cadets' beloved duty-officer, Lieutenant Freiherr von Houwald, entered their *Stube* and, having received the obligatory report from the *Stubenältester*, showed the cadets his lighted cigar and asked them if they were '*Spartanerjünglinge*'. They replied with a unanimous '*Jawohl, Herr Leutnant!*' Houwald replied:

'Great, let's see if it's true. Now, I'll hold my burning cigar to the tip of each of your noses for exactly a second, and anyone who doesn't bat an eyelid will win a beer-with-a-shot (*Weiße mit Schuss*)...'

No sooner had he spoken than he had pressed the cigar to the nosetip of the righthand-most cadet. Water streamed from his eyes, but he didn't blink. The other nine did the same.

'You *are Spartanerjünglinge*,' said Houwald approvingly, and left the room.

The boys think that this is hilarious, until they realise that each has an utterly unconcealable blister on the end of his nose. How can they possibly explain this? To betray Houwald would be unthinkable, so von Koss suggests the implausible story that each boy in turn had tried to get the *Stube*'s stove to draw by blowing on it, leaning over too far and burning his nose on its iron door in the process. Despite hour-long interrogations by the authorities, the cadets stick to their story, and within a few days, the matter is closed. However, an epilogue was to occur the following Sunday, when an orderly from the officers' mess appeared and served them up ten beers and thirty pancakes ('no comment necessary', von Koss remarks).

This tale is significant not only because it illustrates how keen the cadets were to be considered *Spartanerjünglinge*, but that the identification was imposed upon them by an *Erzieher*, who was both a responsible adult and a member of staff. Even if Lieutenant von Houwald did behave in some ways like one of the nastier *Stubenältesten* mentioned above, his standing, and the boys' 'love' for him, gave his behaviour a very different gloss. They longed for nothing more than to prove to him that they were *Spartanerjünglinge*, rather than having this designation inflicted upon them unwillingly.

What is more, the anecdote has implications for the way in which the Spartan trope in the cadet schools may have been diffused. As Moncure has noted, many ex-cadets returned voluntarily – or were even requested – to serve in the corps as *Erzieher* in the early stages of their careers.[41] This could mean that officers who, as boys, had had the idea of *Spartanertum* instilled by their elders, might have created a self-perpetuating cycle of Spartan identification, had they then imposed this model upon their charges once they became members of staff.[42]

In the final source under discussion, Fritz von Unruh's autobiographical novel *Im Haus der Prinzen* (1967), based on his time at *Voranstalt* Plön at the turn of the twentieth century, we find an authority figure holding up ancient Spartan youths as a fine example not just for any cadets, but for two of the Kaiser's sons, the royal Princes August-Wilhelm and Oskar (whose education, along with that of a small group of selected fellow-pupils, including Unruh himself, took place at the so-called *Prinzenschule* [princes' school], a residence in the grounds of *Voranstalt* Plön).[43] However, when the novel's protagonist, von Unruh's autobiographical alter ego Kaspar-Friedrich Uhle (otherwise known as 'U2', Unruh's own cadet-school nickname), actually tries to copy the Spartan behaviour which has been expounded to him as desirable, he almost gets expelled.[44]

It all begins when U2 is invited to dinner with Princes Auwi and Oskar, along with their tutor, Major Gordat. Firstly, Gordat rebukes Prince Auwi for not eating up his soup:

> 'Yes, by golly! Prince Auwi, to wit, in Sparta, there they would certainly have had the famous national dish, the "black soup". A sort of porridge, cooked with blood and mixed with vinegar. So why are you leaving half your bowlful? Are you being fussy again?'[45]

The conversation then moves on to swimming lessons (the Princes' mother is worried that these will cause them to catch cold), and it transpires that U2's father (a General) taught him to swim the hard way – by having a corporal push him off a high tower into the river Leine, and forbidding any of the other soldiers to rescue him, so that U2 had to paddle like a dog to keep afloat. Gordat uses this story as the entrée for a lecture on the merits of Spartan education:

> 'By golly, Prince Oskar, you can thank your stars that his Excellency didn't get his hands on you! But that's exactly what I call Spartan education! Your Majesty is far too timid! In Sparta, there the lads were the property of the State. Immediately after their birth, they were correctly and competently inspected. Those too weak to live (*die Lebensuntüchtigen*) were simply abandoned in the canyons of Mount Taygetos for the wild beasts. That's right, Prince Auwi! They were exposed, without a doubt! Stop eating so much of the red fruit jelly! You'll get too fat! You've remained far too long in the custody of your royal mother. In Sparta, there they simply took the lads away from their parents when they were just seven. Frugality was the motto. And so little to eat, that the boys often had to steal things secretly. – By golly! That's right! That was truly Spartan! And that's Prussian too! Anyone who got hungry, he had to steal something for himself! – eh?... No!' he fended off the footmen, who wanted to put the fruit on the table, 'There'll be no feasting here; take the sweet things away too!' The footmen disappeared.
>
> 'By golly, even in the harshest winters, the lads in Sparta had to go around barefoot, with only a shirt to wear. They had to sleep on hay or straw, not on such soft mattresses as you've got upstairs, my honoured pair of Princes! That cadet there has harder bedding, thank the Lord. Prince Auwi, pay attention when I'm speaking! Here you're not under the wings of your royal mother in Potsdam any more.' He rang the bell. A footman appeared.
>
> 'Yes, by golly, where's the wine then? I've only just noticed that you haven't poured out any wine!'
>
> 'Herr Major', whispered the footman, 'I understood that things were to

> be conducted Spartanly!' Gordat looked up at him, nonplussed. Then he ordered:
>
> 'Would you kindly pour out the wine directly!'[46]

Once Gordat has his wine, he proposes a toast:

> 'Yes!... Let's drain this glass to Sparta! Every year at the festival of Artemis, there the Spartan youths (*spartanischen Jünglinge*) were beaten bloody! By golly! That's right, Prince Auwi, beaten bloody! And many a one sank down dead during the scourging, without having blurted out a single cry of pain.'...
>
> 'Herr Major', Prince Auwi dared to ask, 'Will we have to be scourged to death too?' Gordat regarded him first coldly, then angrily. The two Princes winked at each other.[47]

Inspired by this impromptu hymn of praise to the ways of the ancient Spartans, a few days later U2 is overcome by hunger, and steals some cake and chocolate from his room-mate's cupboard. When found out, he eventually admits the theft, and the reason for it – he expects that his hunger will exonerate him; he was just following the Spartan example and stealing to supplement his meagre diet. However, Gordat is furious; he bawls U2 out in front of the Princes and all their fellow pupils (the *Prinzenmitschüler*), demanding to know the meaning of his treachery and dishonourable behaviour:

> 'You stole a piece of cake from your room-mate Rappert's parcel? Why, may I ask?' The cadet blanched.
>
> 'Because I was hungry, Herr Major.'
>
> 'And you stole for that reason?' U2 stared at the Major and answered:
>
> 'Yes, Sir! I stole for that reason, just like the Spartan youth (*spartanischer Jüngling*), when he was hungry.'
>
> At that, Gordat's black pupils became keen with hate. But the cadet held his gaze.
>
> 'So?' Gordat's eyes twitched ironically, 'Like a Spartan youth? You don't say!' Suddenly he yelled: 'Turn round and look in the mirror!' U2 obeyed. 'Who do you see there?'
>
> 'Myself, Herr Major.'
>
> 'No! There you see a dishonourable cadet, but no Spartan youth. He stole, because he was hungry? – Prince Auwi, what does a human being deserve, if he behaves dishonourably? Eh, by golly! What does he deserve, I'd like to know!'[48]

U2 narrowly escapes an on-the-spot thrashing – in front of the Princes and everyone else – only because he had proved himself a first-class marksman the day before.

This, then, is an intriguing example of what can happen when Spartan self-identification goes too far. Unlike the Princes, U2 took the *Spartanerjünglinge* too seriously as a model, and is then caught out –

completely uncomprehending – when the conventions of contemporary Prussia do not measure up to his Spartan expectations. The correlation between the German state and the Greek city-state which Gordat implied in their after-dinner conversation has been revealed to be worthless, and the only response he can muster to Gordat's vitriolic denunciation is an inarticulate cry – his assumption of identity between Sparta and Prussia has been revealed as both false and treacherous, and he is inconsolable.[49]

The second issue which the passage raises superlatively well is that of engagement with the ancient sources. As we shall see in the following chapter, all of Gordat's claims about Spartan education can easily be identified in Classical authors' accounts; they also highlight many of those aspects of cadet-corps life which we have previously seen termed as 'Spartan' by the boys themselves.

It should be noted here that both of Fritz von Unruh's autobiographical novels which depict his time at Plön – *Der Sohn des Generals* (1957) and *Im Haus der Prinzen* (1967) – are highly politicised, and portray the cadet corps very negatively (traits which other ex-cadets often decried); Unruh had been a staunch pacifist since the 1920s, and had even, in a speech given in 1948, characterised the cadet schools as the 'original model' for later concentration camps.[50] A parallel reading of these passages might suggest that Unruh has a consciously ironic deconstruction of the *Spartanerjünglinge* trope in mind. Nevertheless, for such satire to be effective, the discourse being satirised must be widespread enough to be recognisable as a part of real-life experience, and von Unruh's depiction of U2's bitterness at the injustice of the whole affair also smacks of autobiographical recollection.

Therefore, whether we read Unruh's account as a satirical exposure of the hypocrisy and vapidity of the royal *Erzieher* in particular and the officer class in general, or as straightforward autobiography, these passages have great significance – both for our understanding of the boundaries and preconceptions which governed the use of Sparta as a paradigm for the Prussian Cadet Corps, and for our conclusions regarding how much cadet-corps educators may really have known about education in ancient Sparta.

Notes

[1] I am deeply indebted both to Peter Hennings, and to Alfons D. Szczepanski, chief archivist of the Szczepanski Family Archives in Delmenhorst, for providing me with information on Paul von Szczepański's life and career, as well as biographical details of other family members. Although there is no record of Szczepański's having joined the corps at Culm, Alfons Szczepanski believes it 'very probable' that he would have attended at least one of the cadet schools (private correspondence, 02/08/2012).

[2] According to the Szczepanski Family Archives, the work was first published by Georg Wigand Verlag, Leipzig, in 1901. Luserke (1999, 52) suggests that the work originally appeared in 1898; however, all his subsequent references refer to a later edition. Jany-Hamburg (1926, 68) remembers that *Spartanerjünglinge* was published in *Die Woche*, which was founded in 1899; if the novel first went to press here, it would therefore have had an initial publication-date of 1899 or later. These chronological difficulties are compounded by the fact that very few subsequent editions of the novel possess any publication-date at all.

[3] My copy of this version, published by A. Anton Verlag, Leipzig (12th edition, n.d.) and illustrated by Fritz Buchholz, bears the inscription '9.1925[?] To my dear brother for his fourteenth birthday, dedicated by his sister Liesbeth' – which may provide some small insight regarding the novel's (intended or actual) readership.

[4] e.g. Joseph Moncrieff Morrison's 'authorised edition' (Edinburgh 1903), entitled *Spartanerjünglinge, edited with notes, vocabulary, and letters for retranslation*, or W. D. Lowe's *Inner Life of the Prussian Cadet* (London 1910), a volume containing translations of *Spartanerjünglinge* and Ernst von Wildenbruch's best-selling cadet-school novel *Das edle Blut.*

[5] For an example of this, see Maisch 1968, 38.

[6] *Stenographische Berichte des Reichstages* 1917, 101. Sitzung (05/05/1917), 3089. For more on the work's reception after 1945, see p. 172 below.

[7] Page numbers and translations are taken from the English edition by W. D. Lowe (London, 1910).

[8] 'The care which the boys take over their stealing is illustrated by the story of the one who had stolen a fox cub and had it concealed inside his cloak: in order to escape detection he was prepared to have his insides clawed and bitten out by the animal, and even to die.'

[9] The book went into several editions, and was adored by fans of the cadet corps – one admirer in the *Reichstag* described it as the 'best-beloved book about cadet-school life' (*Stenographische Verhandlungen des Reichstages* 1888, 22. Sitzung [26/01/1888], 507). However, the work was vilified by critics of the cadet schools (such as the anonymous author of *Unsere Kadettenkorps* [1894]) for portraying corps life and its hardships as mere harmless fun – though present-day readers would probably baulk at such an assessment. See further p. 7 above. N.B. Dewall's real name was August Kühne. Like Paul von Szczepański, he was also an extremely prolific author, with over forty novels to his name (many of these also gained a wide readership in English and Swedish translations). He probably took up the pseudonym as a means of differentiating himself from the author Gustav Kühne (1806–1888). For further information on Kühne's life and career as an artillery officer, serving

in both the Austro-Prussian and Franco-Prussian wars, see his entry in *Meyers Konversations-Lexikon* (Leipzig, 1888).

[10] Dewall 1884, 50–3.

[11] ibid., 53–4.

[12] This word has not yet been found elsewhere in the corpus; however, it is treated hereafter as a conveniently concise shorthand for traits or actions denoting 'Spartan behaviour', equivalent to similar, wordier, expressions such as '*Spartanerjüngling sein*', '*der spartanische Jugend gleich sein*' (to be, or to equal, Spartan youth), etc.

[13] Dewall 1884, 50, 56 (emphasis original).

[14] Interestingly, Graf von Haslingen (1906, 32–3) quotes a slightly altered version of this passage, which reads 'The example of the Spartan youths, *which we read about in class*, appealed to us greatly as a model – we used to drill ourselves in enduring all possible tortures', using it to exemplify how rare it was for cadets ever to cry (my emphasis). Again, we find the idea that Spartan history was a staple of the cadet-school curriculum; this will be discussed in detail in the next chapter. It should be noted that, occasionally, other figures from ancient history were also included in the cadets' recreations in a similar fashion to the Spartans – most commonly, these involved Mucius Scaevola (to whom I have found four references). Red Indian novels such as James Fenimore Cooper's *Last of the Mohicans* were also popular at the schools, and a handful of references to Indians or Mohicans can also be found. For more on cadets' engagement with history and the Classics generally, see Roche 2012e.

[15] Corvin 1861, 75–6. Corvin (1812–1886) gave up his military career to become an author, and later formed a literary circle dedicated to furthering the cause of democracy against autocracy. He took part in the revolutionary uprisings in Paris and Berlin, and was one of the leaders of the Baden revolt in 1849. This led to his being imprisoned for six years in Bruchsal (where he wrote much of *Aus dem Leben eines Volkskämpfers*); he then went into exile in London, where he lived until the late 1860s. It is interesting to note that in the English version of his autobiography (*A Life of Adventure*, London 1871) the translation of the second part of this passage merely reads: 'The doctor's taunt had hurt me deeply, because we tried to imitate the Spartans, and endure all kinds of pain without wincing' (p. 116). If we glance at Corvin's preface (p. vi), it appears that this omission may in fact have been one of the abridgements made at the publisher's behest, to ensure that the book would be 'fit for every drawing-room table, [or to] be read even in the nursery without injury to the feelings of the most immaculate governess.' The first paragraph and the last sentence of the translation are also taken from this edition (p. 115).

[16] Borcke 1940, 227.

[17] Scharfenort 1889, v.

[18] ibid., 77–8.

[19] Even if some of the material in this passage has been taken from other existing sources, rather than from Scharfenort's own personal experiences of corps life, the fact that he specifically includes instances of '*spartanern*' in his advice to new cadets about what they ought to expect upon their arrival in the corps seems significant.

[20] For the sociological relevance of Scharfenort's depiction of '*spartanern*', in which emulating 'Spartan youths' seems to be part and parcel of boys' general initiation into life in the cadet corps, see Chapter 5 below.

[21] Schoenaich 1926, 20–1. One might perhaps compare Pausanias' descriptions of

Spartan youths' battles at the river Platanistas, which also set great store by the 'blooding' of one's opponents (3.14.8–10) – or simply the fights between Spartan youths described in Xenophon's *Lakedaimoniōn Politeia* (4.6); cf. Ducat 2006, 208–9.

[22] For an emphasis on obedience in the ancient sources on Spartan education, see e.g. Plutarch's *Life of Lycurgus*, 16.5–6.

[23] Balthasar von Aulock-Radau (1955, 7) relates that *Stubenältesten* at *Voranstalt* Wahlstatt (which he attended between 1896 and 1900) used similar reasoning to justify inflicting 'truly Spartan methods' of toughening on their charges. We might compare Kurt von Borcke's advice to a new cadet called Kiekebusch on how to cope with the bullying which he will inevitably encounter (1940, 289–90): 'You must grit your teeth. It's common knowledge that we are brought up in the Spartan fashion... If at any point you get beaten once too often, though, and can't bear it in your company any more, come to me and I'll see what I can do to help you.'

[24] Heydebreck 1931, 9–10. Heydebreck served as an officer in the First World War, and went on to become first a leader of the *Freikorps* (see below pp. 158–9) and then a member of the SA. This move was eventually to cost him his life, since he became one of the victims of the Röhm Putsch (the so-called Night of the Long Knives) on 30 June 1934.

[25] Maisch 1968, 31.

[26] cf. *Der Plöner: Kadetten-Mitteilungen des Vorkorps Plön* 16, Dec. 1975, 6: '...everything was simple and prosaic, in Spartan and Prussian fashion.'

[27] Isenburg 1958, 10. Other descriptions of the cadet-corps education's *Spartanertum*, contrasted with a more cultured, 'Athenian' way of life, can be found in Salomon 1933, 95, where one of the civilian teachers, *Studienrat* Bösser, wishes hopelessly that 'the *Spartanertum* [prevalent in the corps] might unite with the richness and wisdom of Athenian life, which he so prized', and in Manstein 1958, 23: 'the cadet-corps education was modelled in far stronger measure on Sparta than on Athens...' This sentiment is also repeated in Manstein's foreword to Isenburg's work (1958, 3).

[28] Isenburg 1958, 63. The English translation of von Manstein is taken from Anthony G. Powell's translation (*Lost Victories*, London 1958, 69).

[29] Quoted in Brand 1981, 217–18. Holleben went on to become Commander of the Cadet Corps during the 1860s (Moncure 1993, 166), and then Commander of *Voranstalt* Potsdam between 1879 and 1874.

[30] Papen 1952, 5; cf. also Dünheim 1873, 3 (*spartanische Wohnungsausstattung* – Spartan living arrangements); Feiber 1947, 41 (*spartanische Bettdecke* – Spartan coverlet); Werner n.d., 2 (the corps as a *spartanisches Heim* – his Spartan home).

[31] Salomon 1933, 42. Nickol (1935, 99–100), Nimz (1979, 9) and Lorentz (1980, 23) also compare *Mehlsuppe* with Spartan fare. For an ancient reference to Spartan soup, see e.g. Plutarch's *Life of Lycurgus*, 12.6–7.

[32] Borcke 1940, 224.

[33] Scharfenort 1889, 129. For further references to the supposedly 'Spartan' nature of cadet-school cooking see e.g. *Reichskadettenblatt* 16 (1929), 245 (*spartanische Kadettengerichte* – Spartan cadet-meals); Feiber 1947, *97 (*die Verpflegung war spartanisch einfach* – 'the food was Spartanly simple').

[34] See also e.g. Gruhl 1928, Kostorz 1928.

[35] Faller 1901, 30.

[36] ibid., 30–1.

[37] ibid., 31–2. This emphasis on equality might recall to us the vaunted *homoiotēs* (homogeneity) of the original Spartans.

[38] ibid., 72.

[39] Koss 1973, 2–3.

[40] It may well be significant that this incident occurred shortly after the publication of Szczepański's *Spartanerjünglinge* (and that it also took place at Köslin, the school to which all cadets from *Voranstalt* Culm had been moved in 1890).

[41] Moncure 1993, 181–2.

[42] These conclusions must remain hypothetical unless and until corroborating evidence can be found; however, if it could be proved that Lt. von Houwald had been himself a cadet, this would have interesting implications for the propagation of the cadet corps' *Spartabild.*

[43] This work is the second in a projected set of eight autobiographical novels recounting the author's life (*Lebensromane*); however, Unruh only ever completed three of these before his death in 1970, the first being *Der Sohn des Generals* (1957), the second *Im Haus der Prinzen* (1967), and the last *Kaserne und Sphinx* (1969). Karola Schulz describes these novels as Unruh's attempt to make the past his own property and translate his experiences 'into his own language' (Schulz 1995, 234). Unruh was also deeply concerned by the remilitarisation of the German Federal Republic under Chancellor Konrad Adenauer during this period (1949–1963), having recently returned from exile in America. Throughout these autobiographical works, Unruh deliberately problematises the Federal Republic's political attitudes and rearmament policies as potentially leading to a renewal of turn-of-the-century nationalist militarism (cf. ibid., 235), a development to which he was deeply opposed, by placing them within a 'frame' (*Rahmen*) set in the 1950s. For more on Unruh's life and writing generally, see Schulz 1995. The autobiographical works themselves seem to have been relatively neglected in modern scholarship, especially when compared with Unruh's early dramas (which were heralded as works of genius when they were first produced at the beginning of the twentieth century), or the works which he wrote whilst in exile.

[44] On U2 as Fritz von Unruh's '*Roman-Ich*', see Wernfried Schreiber's afterword to Fritz von Unruh 1983, 634. The autobiographical nature of *Der Sohn des Generals* and *Im Haus der Prinzen* is also borne out by the fact that they include real (still living) people who were at Plön at the time, such as Friedrich-Wilhelm Isenburg and Erich von Manstein, as well as Princes August-Wilhelm (with whom von Unruh later developed a strong friendship) and Oskar. For the account quoted here, see Fritz von Unruh 1967, 68–83.

[45] ibid., 69.

[46] ibid., 70–1. For previous laconophilia ascribed to Gordat, see Fritz von Unruh 1983, 76, which describes his letter to U2's father asking the latter to allow his son to be a *Prinzenmitschüler* (fellow-pupil of the Princes): For the sake of the Hohernzollern dynasty (he writes) the Kaiser's sons must be 'worthy heirs of a Spartan ethos' (*würdige Erben einer spartanischen Gesinnung*).

[47] Fritz von Unruh 1967, 70–1. See also p. 74: '"Prince Auwi, by God in heaven, stop standing there so flabbily! Even if we're not in Sparta, *all the same* (*doch immerhin*) we reside in Prussia! Please hammer that fact into that illustrious head of yours!"'

[48] ibid., 81–2.

[49] ibid., 82. For another instance of 'U2' considering Spartanism and Prussianism

to be two sides of the same coin, see ibid. 101–2, where he remembers the bravery of his father, who insouciantly bore the agony of a horse biting through his arm to the bone and then having the gaping wound cleaned out by his mother with aluminium acetate, describing the whole time how his grandfather Eberhardt, having had his leg shattered during the Battle of Leipzig in 1813, wrote a letter home to his mother while the limb was being sawn off in a field hospital, without mentioning the matter. Echoing Gordat's words, U2 comments 'Yes, that was truly Spartan! That was Prussian!' He then recalls that the thought of having such formidably brave relatives helped him to grit his teeth and bear the pain of having a boil lanced by his mother. This passage recalls that element of cadet-school Spartanism which emphasised that one must bear all pain without complaint – perhaps this is the real, common-or-garden *Spartanertum* which U2 now realises that he should cling to, rather than taking Gordat's more precise parallels too literally.

[50] Fritz von Unruh 1957, 147 (*Rede an die Deutschen*). See n. 43 above.

4

CREATING THE CADET-CORPS' *SPARTABILD*: TEACHING, TEXTBOOKS AND THE ANCIENT SOURCES

The characteristics of Spartan education expounded by Major Gordat in Fritz von Unruh's account of his post-prandial lecture to the Princes, quoted extensively at the end of the previous chapter, actually resembles nothing so much as a compressed version of the *Life of Lycurgus* by Plutarch (c.46–120 AD),[1] one of the few surviving ancient accounts of Spartan education and *mores*.

The fact that the *Life of Lycurgus* was written several hundred years after the Classical period which it purports to describe (c.5th–4th centuries BC) is a matter of permanent frustration to scholars of Spartan history, since it means that Plutarch's account is partly based on personal observation of the Sparta of his own day, and can no longer be seriously regarded as a faithful description of Classical Spartan *mores*.[2] However, in this context, the fact that Plutarch can never tell us 'how it really was' in Classical Sparta is irrelevant; what matters is that Plutarch's depictions of Spartan history formed the basis of almost all the portrayals of Spartan education to which boys and teachers at the cadet schools would have had access, at a point in time when the veracity of his descriptions was not regarded with so much scholarly suspicion.

Given the fact, therefore, that the sources discussed in the previous chapter indicate that many cadets and cadet-school staff saw the cadet corps as a form of 'Sparta *rediviva*', it seems appropriate at this point to investigate both how and why this collocation might have come about, enquiring both to what extent the ancient sources on Spartan education justify an identification with the Prussian Cadet Corps, and how well boys and teachers at the cadet schools would have known those sources. This can be done most effectively by analysing, firstly, the relationship of the ancient sources with cadet-corps life, and, secondly, the ways in which history textbooks used at the cadet schools summarised and presented the material from the ancient texts in a way which encouraged pupils to draw explicit parallels between Spartan education and education in contemporary Germany.

We will begin by examining how far the ancient sources on Sparta in general, and on Spartan education in particular, justify the Spartan trope. Was the identification of the cadet corps with Sparta by the authors of the cadet-school stories and autobiographies discussed in Chapter 3 merely based on a series of misapprehensions, or did there genuinely exist any specific similarities between what the authors would have known about the training of young Spartans, and their own training in the corps? And, in the latter case, which were the aspects of ancient Spartan education that actually matched the Spartan image of the cadet corps which these authors had created?

The content of five extant history textbooks known to have been used at the cadet schools strongly suggests that the knowledge of Spartan education imparted there would have been based mainly on a simplistic reading of Plutarch's *Life of Lycurgus* (with occasional additions from his

Fig. 12. A cadet-school classroom, as depicted by Oskar Larsen.

Moralia and his two collections of *Spartan Apophthegms*), as well as extracts from Xenophon's *Lakedaimoniōn Politeia* ('Constitution of the Spartans'), and a smattering of information gleaned from Herodotus, Plato, Aristotle, and possibly Pausanias.[3] Various accounts of contemporary history teaching methods also suggest that teachers at the schools would not have relied upon textbooks alone for teaching material, but might well have read the ancient sources (at least in translation) when they were preparing their lessons, in order to make them as lively as possible.[4] The normal history teaching method in Prussia from the mid nineteenth century onwards consisted of the teacher giving an 'off the cuff lecture', treating the material freely, rather than being dependent upon the material given in the textbook.[5]

The present analysis will therefore concentrate for the most part on the accounts of Sparta presented in Plutarch's *Life of Lycurgus* (henceforward abbreviated as *Lycurgus* or *Lyc.*) and Xenophon's *Lakedaimoniōn Politeia* (abbreviated as *L.P.*), which seem to have provided most of the material for these nineteenth-century Prussian views of Spartan education. These resemblances between what we know of Spartan education and cadet-school education are not being highlighted purely for the sake of comparison – the issue at stake is *why* the Prussians were so convinced of these similarities that the cadet schools' status as '*neu-Sparta*' became such a widespread theme throughout all genres of cadet-corps literature.[6]

The Spartan trope and the ancient sources

The first writer to make mention of an easily attributable Classical anecdote is Paul von Szczepański, in *Spartanerjünglinge.* Here, the connection of an ancient text (*Lyc.* 18.1) to an essential part of corps life – abhorrence of 'sneaking' (*petzen*) – is perhaps less direct than some of the more straightforward similarities which will be discussed below. Nevertheless, cadets would surely have recognised in the refusal of the 'fox-boy' to 'squeal' (either literally or metaphorically) a distorted version of their own honour code, which saw *petzen* as the worst possible sin against the arcane discipline (*Arkandisziplin*) of their world.[7] Boys claimed that they 'would rather go to hell than sneak', and one cadet at Bensberg apparently went so far as to let himself be expelled for stealing apples (even though he was commanded to do so by a third-former) rather than tell tales – perhaps this could almost be considered as a contemporary equivalent of the fox-boy's self-sacrifice.[8] If such sacrifices were not made, painful punishment from one's comrades would certainly ensue, such as the much-feared 'stomach promenades' (described on p. 66).[9] Indeed, if there were even the slightest suspicion that a cadet might tell tales, his life would be made unbearable unless he proved himself worthy of his fellows' trust once again, as a passage from Dewall's *Kadettengeschichten* (cadet stories from his time in Berlin) well illustrates:

> The Schnappsack Max von Eberstein, nicknamed the *Zuckermäulchen* (Sweet Tooth) had been cheeky to one of the 'demigods' (boys in the penultimate year), and had, naturally, to be punished for it in exemplary fashion. They put him in the 'Spanish rack' and gave him a proper licking right where it hurt etc. But little Max was so lean that instead of flesh, each blow struck bone and hurt him so much that, half out of his mind with desperation, he threatened to complain to the Major if they didn't leave him alone. This filled the demigods with a veritable storm of indignation – so to make a fool of him [they put the bat under his knees and tied his arms] and, with general jubilation, dragged him downstairs to the Major and left him outside [his] door...

Fig. 13. The *Zuckermäulchen.*

> so that his knees and forehead were resting on the floor. The Major, hearing the ruckus, opened the door so violently that the poor, tightly-gagged *Zuckermäulchen*...was thrown onto his side... [Yet still he did not tell on his persecutors, but lied and said that he was looking for his key] – he did not want to betray his comrades, so he came up with this emergency white lie.[10]

As noted above, the parallel between the fox-boy's silence and that of the cadets is not a complete one, since the fox-boy is resisting the temptation to reveal his *own* misdemeanour rather than that of his comrades. Nevertheless, it seems likely that the relevant passage from *Spartanerjünglinge* could have been highly influential in causing cadets to equate the fox-boy's silence with that which they felt obliged to keep.

From another perspective, the fox-tale's significance could be linked with the extraordinary emphasis placed by exponents of the Spartan trope on the cadets' ability to endure all kinds of physical maltreatment – whether at their own hands or at the hands of others. The fox-boy is so determined to appear completely impervious to the pain of the fox gnawing at his vitals that he suffers the extreme consequence – death. Plutarch's descriptions of the Spartan boys' endurance of vicious scourging at the Artemisian ritual of the *bōmolochia* in his day could also have been a source of inspiration for the cadets' adulation of Spartan endurance:[11]

> The boys in Sparta were lashed with whips during the entire day at the altar of Artemis Orthia, frequently to the point of death, and they bravely endured this, cheerful and proud, vying with one another for the supremacy as to which one of them could endure being beaten for the longer time and the greater number of blows. And the one who was victorious was held in especial repute. (*Moralia* 239d)

One might also suggest an identification with the terrible tests of endurance (*deinai karterēseis*) which Plato's Spartan interlocutor Megillos mentions in the *Laws* (I.633b–c), such as 'the systematic training in the endurance of pain which is undergone in our own community...both in group fights with bare knuckles and also in the process of certain acts of theft which take place amid a constant hail of blows.' Even if any of the cadets had been aware of the religious context of these tests of endurance, this would probably not have altered their belief that the quintessence of being truly like a Spartan youth lay in bearing extremes of pain and hardship, no matter what the cost.

Other kinds of hardship which the cadets had to undergo could also seem to mirror the endurance of the Spartans. Upon reading *L.P.* 2.4 ('Instead of their clothes serving to make [the Spartan boys] delicate, [Lycurgus] required them to become used to a single cloak all the year round, the idea being that thereby they would be better prepared for both cold and heat'), a cadet might recall bitterly his being forced to wear only his thin *Litewka* (military jacket) rather than a coat when being taken for winter walks, even when the temperature was twenty below zero – this too was construed as a test of healthiness; a '*Gesundheitsprobe*'.[12] Or he might compare the Spartans' lack of underclothing in the form of a tunic (*Lyc.* 16.6) with the cadet schools' prohibition of warm socks or undergarments – what Dewall calls an 'unknown luxury' – even when the unheated rooms were so cold that the water in the washbasins froze.[13] Certainly Friedrich Franz von Unruh's description of his bedding – 'a seagrass mattress and clammy sheets' on an iron bedstead – might have seemed only marginally more comfortable than the reed-bedding by the Eurotas which was the lot of young Spartans in Plutarch's account (*Lyc.* 16.7),[14] while Dewall's catalogue of the hardships which the cadets had to learn to endure uncomplainingly (cold, heat, hunger, thirst) could almost seem to be a paraphrase of *L.P.* 2.3–5.[15]

That such hardships were intended by the authorities to prepare the cadets for the harsh exigencies of the soldier's life may be exemplified by a quotation from an article in the *Militair-Wochenblatt*, describing the appointments of the new HKA-building in Lichterfelde in 1873:

> In general, any luxury in the facilities must be deliberately eliminated, for this would irresolvably contradict the necessity of making sure that the education of future soldiers places habituation to frugality and modesty in the foreground.[16]

As we have seen above (Chapter 3), criticisms of cadet-school food were also often presented as stemming from its overtly 'Spartan' quality. Such complaints about the notable insufficiency of the boys' diet as that of G. R. Halkett: 'It seems to have been part of the educational principles to starve us...' – or that of an Englishman educated at one of the schools, who noted that 'the food was neither of good quality nor sufficient in quantity' – could, in a Classical context, have been echoed by Spartan youths: compare *L.P.* 2.5:[17]

> As for food, [Lycurgus] instructed the eiren to furnish for the common meal just the right amount for [the Spartan boys] never to become sluggish through being too full, while also giving them a taste of what it is not to have enough. His view was that boys under this kind of regimen would be better able, when required, to work hard without eating, as well as to make the same rations last longer, when ordered; they would be satisfied with a plain diet, would adapt better to accepting any type of food, and would be in a healthier condition.[18]

Moreover, as in Sparta, this undernourishment, so often highlighted in cadet memoirs, often led the boys to supplement their official meals by means of thieving expeditions.[19] For instance, in his book of *Kadettengeschichten* (1909), Hans-Herbert Ulrich describes an elaborate plot by cadets at Wahlstatt to raid the extensive larder of the *Oekonom* (quartermaster), while Rudolf Görnandt tells us in his memoir *Rabenschloß und Rote Mauern* (1966) of the many expeditions which he and his companions made into the officers' gardens at Bensberg to plunder ripe chestnuts, and the red-veined pears which were a regional speciality.[20] Even Paul von Hindenburg, then President of the Weimar Republic, who asked (whilst visiting his *alma mater* Wahlstatt) whether stealing apples was still as strongly forbidden then as it had been seventy years before, reminisced happily about his own thieving exploits: 'In my time, I made sure that there weren't too many apples left on the trees for everyone else.'[21]

While officially frowned upon, escapades such as those described here (and in *Spartanerjünglinge*) were also secretly seen by the authorities as marking out those who would display exemplary leadership qualities at a later stage in their military career; these were often left unpunished if no hard evidence could be found to condemn the culprits, even when circumstantial evidence clearly pointed to them.[22] This treatment can perhaps be considered in the same light as that of Spartan boys who were only punished for stealing if they were actually foolish enough to allow themselves to get caught (e.g. *L.P.* 2.6–9).

Another aspect of corps life which bore some similarity to ancient Spartan *mores*, though one more liable to understatement or suppression in the cadet-school sources, was that of the homoerotic relationships between older and younger boys.[23] The descriptions of a completely chaste pederastic relationship, aimed only at bettering and educating the younger boy, which we find in Xenophon (*L.P.* 2.12–14) or Plutarch (*Moralia* 237c), seem comparable to these depictions by Rudolf Görnandt and Gustav Hillard:

> The *Schuß* (younger boyfriend) was protected and given gifts by his older friend – generally without any hint of immoral behaviour... These harmless friendships were a sort of substitute for family life in the parental home.[24]
>
> *Kadetteneros*...[manifested itself as] the older boy wanting above all to care for the younger, taking care that he behaved in an upstanding manner both in his *Stube* and in the Company... Whether [the authorities] recognised the pedagogical value of this Eros and attempted to direct it remains to be seen.[25]

A more impassioned description can be found in an autobiographical account from 1901 by the liberal novelist Werner von der Schulenburg (a harsh critic of the cadet corps, which he had left only two years earlier),[26] describing his 'first love' at the HKA:

> My first love...was possibly the most passionate of my whole life, and I was only able to endure the grim time at Lichterfelde because of it. I loved a cadet, Rolf Freiherr von Bergstetten. He wasn't a particularly handsome boy, but he was absolutely as attractive as a woman... My passion for Bergstetten was pathological. I would remain constantly melancholy if I were unable to see him. A quarter of an hour spent arm-in-arm with him sufficed to comfort me despite everything that afflicted me... Every cadet had his '*Schuß*'... Often the couples invited each other to meet at night...and boiled hot chocolate over a paraffin lamp and chatted, ensuring the most genteel form of company. Invitations to these parties would read: 'Herr and Frau von ... take the liberty of inviting Herr and Frau von ... to dinner tonight at 3am in *Stube* Nr. 14.' We often sat up until 5am, and this seemingly pointless bodily exhaustion gave my spirit ever more buoyancy. When I thought of the possibility of spending the night together with Bergstetten, the exertions of the day, the dullness of the drill, and the lack of any intellectual stimulus were all forgotten.[27]

Although in Sparta the roles in the pederastic relationship of *erastēs* (lover) and *erōmenos* (beloved) were taken by a young man and a boy, rather than by an older boy and a younger, the gap in age would probably have been similar.[28] The real point, however, is that a Prussian cadet or cadet-school observer, who did not possess the detailed knowledge which ancient historians today have of age-grade systems or comparative pederastic practices in other societies, might quite possibly have seen the incidence of homosexual attachments in the schools as yet another way in which they did recreate a (partially) Spartan ethos.[29]

Perhaps the most significant similarity of all, however, is to be found in the Spartan and Prussian educational hierarchies, and the ways in which boys in both societies were supervised and disciplined. In the cadet schools, there existed a complex chain of leadership responsibilities which were awarded to boys depending on their conduct and the potential for leadership which they demonstrated.

The boys' chief arbiters in this regard were their *Erzieher* (educators). These men (usually in their early to mid-twenties) were young regular army officers who were detailed from their regiments to serve as examples to the cadets, to cultivate in them the desired personality traits, and exact high standards of military discipline. They were supposed to be 'the embodiment of how the little cadet saw himself ten years in the future', playing the roles of 'teacher, father and friend', planting seeds of virtue in the cadets' hearts, and understanding and having sensitivity for their emotional crises.[30] Even more than the cadets' commanding officers, the *Erzieher* were responsible for leadership training, each guiding about twenty cadets through their developing years; they were therefore the principal executors of the training programme, particularly outside the classroom.[31] Only the best officers, therefore, were selected to take on the role of *Erzieher*, and each boy was only given responsibility to the extent that the *Erzieher* felt he could accept it – the aim being deliberately to create an atmosphere in the school which would help to teach 'the desired [character] attributes, and discern who accepted them most readily and most thoroughly'.[32]

The *Erzieher*s' responsibilities were so wide that they could monitor all aspects of the cadets' lives, as well as being entitled to punish them if necessary; however, such chastisement was supposed to go no further than that which a good father might inflict upon his son – 'cane-happiness' was severely frowned upon.[33] In the *Voranstalten*, each *Erzieher* inhabited a small apartment with glass doors which was situated in between two *Stuben*. He was thus able to observe the cadets from his living quarters, and kept a report book (*Zeugnisheft*) on each cadet, commenting on his character, virtues, talents, intellectual ability, enthusiasm for work, love of order, social adaptation, comradeship, and even the purity of his heart.[34] Such observation ensured that the responsibilities given to individual cadets would match their character and ability.

Thus, at the lowest level in the *Voranstalten*, cadets would answer only for themselves and their personal space; later, they might be selected to have responsibility for (but no real authority over) their living quarters and their dining table at meals, and then become section or company leaders. As they grew older, cadets also gained the power to punish their fellows (this could either be a sanctioned part of their duties or take the form of hazing); any official punishments had to be written in the 'Company Punishment Book' (*Kompagnie-Strafbuch*) and submitted to the company commander for review.[35] At the HKA, these same duties entailed some authority over younger cadets. Privileges and rank devolved upon those cadets who had such duties thrust upon them, however, so that they became seen not as onerous chores but as marks of honour, strengthening the connection which the officer corps wished to maintain between responsibility and privilege.[36]

However, the effect of the *Erzieher*s' constant surveillance, well intentioned though it may have been, could at times seem rather too oppressive for comfort. For instance, Paul Deichmann, former pupil of *Voranstalt* Bensberg, remembers of his time there:

> We stood day and night under the gaze of our *Erzieher* or duty officers. Eating in the mess hall, playing in the great courtyard or in the great park belonging to the institution and even during our free time, an officer was always watching.[37]

Looking at this system of discipline and supervision, therefore, can we see any resemblances with the structure of education in Sparta? Self-evidently, both systems of education were in the control of the state, rather than being left to the whim of individual families, and both also involved the removal of boys from their home sphere. However, many more detailed comparisons can be made.

One might, for instance, argue for an equation of the eirens (young Spartan men in their twenties, whose task it was to supervise the youths) with the *Erzieher*; their age-ranges would certainly have been similar. What is more, both played a vital role in supervising the boys when higher authority (in the form either of the commanders of the cadre or of the *paidonomos*) was absent (*L.P.* 2.11); both were regarded as the 'father, tutor and commander' of each boy (*Lyc.* 17.1), and were also charged with keeping the boys up to the mark intellectually (whether by ensuring that they did not fail exams or by making sure that they were able to respond to questions with sufficient concision and critical appraisal [*Lyc.* 18.2]). Boys' punishments – both in the cadet schools and in Sparta – were subjected by superiors to rigorous scrutiny in order to ensure that they were fairly administered, whether through the medium of the Company Punishment Book or through the chastisement having to be administered under the eyes of the elders (*Lyc.* 18.3).

The emphasis found in the cadet schools on constant supervision of the boys to determine which were most worthy of the rewards of leadership can also be discerned in Sparta: '*as they exercised, the boys were constantly watched by their elders*, who were always spurring them on to fight and contend with one another; *in this their chief object was to get to know each by character*, in particular how bold he was, and how far he was likely to stand his ground in combat.'[38] The cadets' exploits certainly mirrored those of their Spartan counterparts as far as their continual fighting was concerned. Otto von Corvin describes one such:

> [...W]e fought very hard cavalry battles. The strongest took on their shoulders others, who held themselves on with their feet... Thus the two parties advanced upon each other, and though only the use of fists was permitted, blood was frequently drawn. A few fractured arms occurring, these cavalry fights had to be discontinued, and to give way to another game. The parties fought on crutch-stilts; and as everyone had tried to outdo the other in the height of these stilts, the game became still more dangerous than the previous one.[39]

Dewall also gives an account of bloody company-versus-company snowball fights at Bensberg, in which *Erzieher* often had to prise boys off each other.[40]

Fig. 14. Snowball fights at Bensberg, as depicted by 'Othello'.

If the cadets had known of the Platanistas battle (described by Pausanias, 3.14.8–10) or Megillos' 'collective bare-hand combats' (*en te tais pros allēlois tais chersi machais* – Plato *Laws* I.633b), might they have inferred that this penchant for massed fighting might have been yet another reason why they, above all, deserved the epithet 'Spartan'? Certainly Gertner's assertion that 'the *Erzieher* [made sure] to lead the boys' games in a direction of military usefulness', spurring them on in their snowball fights and attacking of snow-forts, fits rather nicely with Plutarch's observation on the way that the eirens spurred the boys on to fight and commanded them in battle (*Lyc.* 17.2).[41]

It is also true that the captaincy of both an *agela* and a cadet squad 'was conferred upon the boy who displayed the soundest judgement and best fighting spirit', and that 'the others kept their eyes on him, responded to his instructions, and endured their punishments from him, so that altogether this training served as a practice in learning ready obedience' (*Lyc.* 16.6).[42] One might even mention that, just as Spartan eirens had their small 'fags' to assist them whilst preparing meals, the youngest cadets were also charged with performing whatever menial duties were required for their superiors at table.[43]

To sum up, then, let us consider the following description of the cadets' education:

> [The Prussian cadet] was best known for the 'military' qualities he acquired during the carefully planned and deliberately administered socialisation process... [He] learned, foremost, unquestioning obedience to orders. He was inured to physical hardships intentionally to prepare him for the rigours of the campaign. He played sports, not as recreation, but to harden his body and learn the meaning of teamwork. He was rewarded for demonstrating leadership skills, and he was placed in responsible positions over junior cadets.[44]

If each instance of the word 'cadet' were to be replaced with 'young Spartan', this depiction would bear a striking resemblance to those found in the work of many ancient historians who take Xenophon's *Lacedaimoniōn Politeia* or Plutarch's *Life of Lycurgus* as their starting point for portrayals of Spartan education – one might compare Plutarch's assertion that 'all the [Spartan] boys' education was directed toward prompt obedience to authority, stout endurance of hardship, and victory or death in battle.'[45] Ancient historians such as Jean Ducat have often seen Spartan education in terms of a carefully planned and deliberately administered socialisation process,[46] while a paramount emphasis on obedience is a recurring theme in our sources on Sparta.[47]

Meanwhile, the preoccupation with training boys of the right 'character' which can be found in ancient sources on Spartan education (*L.P.* 4; *Lyc.* 16.5) finds its counterpart in the rhetoric of the cadet schools: 'the profession of each teacher and *Erzieher* demands chiefly the care of the noble buds of the blossoming race; your holy duty is above all to provide a foundation for the excellence of character'.[48] The form which the perfect boy's 'character' took could be summed up in a list of exemplary virtues: honour and chivalry, obedience, the overcoming of fear through pride and a sense of duty, unbreakable comradeship, (self-)discipline, self-denial, dedication and patriotism. These virtues were often seen as embodying 'the spirit of Prussia', yet they were traits which one could argue would also have been prized in Sparta.[49]

The all-encompassing enthusiasm for such virtues in both societies can in general be ascribed to their importance in the formation of military men – if we are to believe Plato and Aristotle (*Laws* I.626c; *Politics* 2.1271b.1–6), Spartan education aimed 'only and above all' at military excellence; such, too, was the aim of the cadet-school training. As General-Major Walther Reinhardt (1872–1930) put it: 'The spirit of the cadet corps was also the spirit of the army. Its goal was the development of a hardy race, sound in body and soul...true to duty, comradely, honourable, and above all enthusiastic.'[50] As mentioned above, it was a common complaint of commentators that cadets in the Prussian Cadet Corps were placed in a 'professional school' before their talents and inclinations had had a chance to develop, that they were 'programmed' to become soldiers at too early an age; the same sentiment (with appropriate reservations) can be attributed to some Classical authors' criticisms of Sparta. The boys' forms of exercise in both societies certainly seem to have been similarly calibrated to equip them physically for future military hardships.[51]

Contemporary criticisms of academic shortcomings in both educational systems, resulting from their self-confessedly military orientation, were also prevalent to a greater or lesser extent in the cases of both Sparta and Prussia. While the Spartans were often castigated by hostile commentators from *poleis* outside Sparta (Isocrates, for instance) as illiterate, and Plutarch's description of Spartan boys' learning as sufficient to enable them 'to read and write no more than was necessary' (*Lyc.* 16.6) has often been interpreted as an indictment of Spartan anti-intellectualism, the cadet schools were also plagued by criticisms of their academic standards throughout their existence.[52] This is borne out in many of the cadet memoirs; Leopold von Wiese comments that the schools did not really care about intellectual development and that physical education was considered far more important than any academic subject,[53] while the author of *The German Army from Within* provides a telling example of the lack of intellectual rigour at the school which he attended (p. 32):

> Many of my fellow cadets were extremely weak in English or French, and when papers were given in these subjects, they invariably came to me. By this 'ghosting' I was able to make quite a good thing in the shape of hard-boiled eggs or meat rissoles. My corporal's English exercises I was privileged to write for no reward whatever, except an occasional hammering.

Furthermore, General von Hake, Prussian Minister of War from 1819–1833, is in fact on record as stating that it was sufficient for an officer to know only how to read, write and do basic arithmetic;[54] older officers were often decried as being unable to write grammatically, and the general consensus among the military Establishment seems to have been that a good all-round education was unnecessary if cadets displayed the right 'spirit' and zeal for their military vocation.[55]

Bearing all these points in mind, therefore, it might not seem too farfetched to conjecture that, when a cadet – who had (to paraphrase *Lyc.* 16.6) been placed from earliest youth in a squad of his peers, with whom he was accustomed to live, learn and play in order that he might later fulfil his military duty to his state – came across descriptions of Spartan education in his primer or history book, he might have been moved to cry: "Why, *this* is Sparta!"

Cadet-school textbooks as potential sources for the Spartan trope

That the cadets would indeed have had such primers at their disposal will be illustrated in the following section, which will examine the content of five history textbooks used in the cadet corps, and their relationship with the ancient sources on Spartan education.

At the cadet schools, ancient history – including Greek history – took up far more time in history lessons than might have been expected at a school which did not teach Greek, and which was certainly not focused on 'the Classics' in the same way as the contemporary *Gymnasium*. Some commentators went so far as to suggest that in this regard the cadet corps actually went one better than the *Gymnasien*, in that cadet-school history teaching was not completely subordinated to the study of ancient languages.[56] Greece and Rome actually had a higher profile than Germany and Prussia in the list of historical subjects about which cadets were supposed to have special knowledge, both in the cadet schools' ordinance sheet from 3 February 1844,[57] and in the syllabus for the HKA Lieutenants' exam, the *Portepée-Fähnrichsexamen*.[58] Sample papers show that a large proportion of the historical questions on this examination concerned the ancient world – including 'The Lycurgan Constitution'.[59]

Extant syllabuses from the 1840s onwards show that the amount of time spent on ancient history increased rather than decreased over the years. In the 1840s and 1850s, the Sexta (10–11-year-olds) covered an overview of history in its entirety (including ancient history) 'linked with the biographies of famous men'.[60] In the following year, the Quinta, ancient history was the only topic on the history syllabus, and in the Sekunda, ancient history was also revised (along with medieval history).[61]

By the 1880s, the biographical history being taught in the Sexta (now only one lesson a week) was purely ancient-historical in its choice of subjects.[62] In the Quarta or the Untertertia, Greek and Roman history was still the sole subject;[63] in the Obertertia and/or the Untersekunda, ancient history would be revised; in the Obersekunda (four lessons a week), all history would be revised in its entirety, and in the Unterprima, both History (three lessons a week) and Geography covered the Graeco-Roman world,

Fig. 15. Cadets in a Geography lesson at the HKA, c.1910.

'in particular with respect to the Greeks' and Romans' lives *re* their respective constitutions, art and literature.'[64] One undated syllabus from this period even states that tales from Classical times were taught in German lessons in the Quinta and Untertertia.[65]

Small wonder, therefore, that in his Highest Cabinet Order (*Allerhöchste Kabinettsordre*) of 13 February 1890, Kaiser Wilhelm was concerned to stress the importance of more modern German history, and to insist that more emphasis should be placed on the history of the Fatherland in cadet-school curricula.[66]

However, this appeal was not greeted with the widespread approval – or the alacrity in instigating suitable change – which the Kaiser might have wished. It seems that the (rather reactionary) cadet-corps authorities often preferred to emphasise that part of the Highest Cabinet Order which described ancient and medieval history as highly useful – inasmuch as these epochs could provide important models of heroism and historical greatness.[67] One *Studienrat* Bösser, describing the cadet-school curriculum in the late 1890s, states that, although more emphasis was now placed on the history of the Fatherland in the Sexta, some people did not always agree with this 'going crabwise into history'.[68] Material from Classical history was still being taught in German lessons in the Quinta, the Untertertia and the Oberprima.[69] In the Untertertia, history and geography still focused on ancient history, and in the Oberprima, the two tasks of the boys' four history lessons a week were not only to bring them up to scratch on present-day history, but also once again to revise all history, 'in particular that of Greece and Rome'.[70]

That this debate was still raging even at the beginning of the new century may be nicely illustrated by a letter concerning changes to examination syllabuses, which states that it would be no good at all if the lieutenants' exam were no longer to contain any Greek or Roman history, as suggested in the first appendix to the *Offizier-Ergänzungs-Vorschrift* (18/03/1905, Abschnitt VIII), because this was what the boys had spent so much of their time on. The history of the Fatherland may be important too, but if there are no questions on ancient history, then the cadets will simply be unable to use any of the knowledge which they have acquired.[71]

In general, Kaiser Wilhelm's edict seems to have been seen by the schools as a challenge to make ancient history as useful as possible for contemporary military ends.[72] As Major Fleck, one of the cadet corps' representatives at the 1890 school conference, had put it, the highest aim of education was to instil future soldiers with readiness to die 'for Kaiser and Reich, for King and Fatherland'.[73] The best way to ensure this was to teach history in a way that satisfied boys' imaginations and stirred their emotions, as well as giving them appropriate heroic models. In his history of the cadet corps, Louis von Scharfenort expands upon this point:

> For this reason, the Sexta and Quinta should only deal with biographical portraits, but in a way that presents not people as the main point, but deeds, which are either linked to those people, or which took place in their era. Tales from myth are not permitted too much space, since the characters of Greek, Roman, and German men, and men and rulers of the fatherland, provide richer and more lively material for the intellectual development of a young schoolboy...[74]

It was in this context, and particularly in the teaching of the Sexta, that contemporary reworkings of Plutarch's *Lycurgus* could really come into their own. Plutarch's text itself fits Scharfenort's recommendation perfectly, in that it brings the deeds of 'Lycurgus' far more to the fore than his enigmatic, and ultimately imaginary, personality.

It should therefore come as no surprise that several of the textbooks used to teach the Sexta – in particular Dr. Ludwig Stacke's *Griechische Geschichten: Erzählungen aus der griechischen Geschichte in biographischer Form* – present a more-or-less abridged translation of Plutarch's *Lycurgus*.[75]

In his foreword to the first edition, Stacke states that he aimed to write a textbook for the lower classes of the *Gymnasium* which would take account of the fact that, nowadays, history for younger children was supposed to be taught in a 'biographical' fashion. He wished to follow a middle way between the comprehensiveness of 'greater works' and the compendious qualities of a historical handbook (*Leitfaden*), so that his book would be suitable both for pupils' preparation and for further reading. At the same time, the work should not render the teachers' lectures superfluous; rather, it should help to secure the memory of these in the pupils' minds.[76]

Stacke states that he has striven, wherever possible (and particularly when quoting Herodotus and Pausanias) to use translations of the ancient authors' own words[77] – this is certainly borne out by his adaptation of Plutarch's *Lycurgus* in the book's seventh chapter. As Table 1 (an analysis of the relationship which portrayals of Spartan education in the textbooks bear to the descriptions given in the ancient sources) demonstrates,[78] almost all the passages from the *Life of Lycurgus* mentioned earlier in this chapter – including the fox-tale and an account of the whippings at the temple of Artemis Orthia – are quoted by Stacke verbatim in the passage which he devotes to Spartan education (pp. 96–7).

The same can be said of Johan Matthias Schrökh's *Algemeine Weltgeschichte für Kinder* (1788), which was used in the cadet schools during the earlier part of the nineteenth century.[79] Schrökh's aim was to portray for his youthful audience 'revered men and deeds worthy of admiration and emulation', as well as the laws, *mores*, art and invention of the various peoples which he described.[80] Although Schrökh does seem to have gleaned some of his facts from sources other than Plutarch (for instance, it seems probable that his depiction of Spartan boys climbing precipitous peaks barefoot is based on Xenophon *L.P.* 2.3),[81] the bulk of his account does appear to be based on Plutarch's *Lycurgus* and *Moralia*. In this regard, he also mentions most of the passages from *Lycurgus* cited above (see Table 1). However, his criticism of the Spartans' focus on warlike pursuits at the expense of intellectual and spiritual delights (pp. 290–1) also suggests some further engagement with the Platonic and Aristotelian passages mentioned above.

Nevertheless, Schrökh also goes out of his way to assure his young readers of the highly respect-worthy (*hochachtungswerth*) nature of a military career even in his own day, giving the following reasons:

> [The soldier] must have so much love and loyalty to his Fatherland and his sovereign, must apply himself so keenly to the strictest order, discipline and compliancy, be so fearless, vigilant and courageous both in attack and defence; he must also be able to bear countless troubles so lightly, that even the common soldier who achieves these things cannot be underestimated, not to mention a commander of soldiers, in whom a variety of knowledge,

> wisdom and other profound traits must be sought. Therefore Lycurgus did very well in teaching all Spartans to be cunning, and spurring them on from earliest youth to defend their Fatherland.[82]

This passage, which is explicitly addressed to the youthful readers of the work, would surely have encouraged cadets to link such fulsome praise of their own future careers as 'commanders' with that soldierly career which, Schrökh tells us, was the most highly prized of all in Sparta.[83] What is more, the Prussian cadets might have felt that they could embrace the idea of being new, contemporary Spartans, without the danger of that 'wild', 'raw' anti-intellectualism which Schrökh decries in the Spartans of old – after all, the cadets did have to undergo some form of academic education.[84]

The third textbook, Schillmann's *Vorschule der Geschichte* (1881), which was also used to teach the Sexta, is the most novel in style and conception, since it contains sections not only on Greek and Roman history, but also on Greek and German myths and legends. The work was conceived by Richard Schillmann, a Berlin school inspector, after the success of his *Leitfaden für den Unterricht in der deutschen Geschichte*, which led to numerous requests for him to put together a collection of stories from German and Classical myth and history which ten- to eleven-year-olds would find particularly appealing.[85] The collection comprises the sum of those stories which, throughout Schillmann's many years of personal experience, pupils in the second year at various *Gymnasien* had found most engaging, and is designed in such a way that individual tales can be left out without spoiling the effect of the whole, and so that teachers can easily supply any material which they feel to be lacking.[86] The historical sections, though covering much the same ground as more conventionally organised textbooks, are clearly oriented around certain key personalities – such as Leonidas in the tale of Thermopylae, or, later, Themistocles and Alcibiades.

However, in some ways the most interesting aspect of the work, regarding the light which it can throw on Prussian cadets' perceptions of Spartan education, is Schillmann's description of the Spartan way of life (pp. 118–9). 'The Spartans...', he writes:

> ...wanted nothing more than to be warriors; therefore their entire occupation consisted of exercises, which made their bodies strong, nimble and tough in bearing hunger, thirst, heat, cold and all the hardships of war, and their souls courageous in all perils... The healthy boys remained with their mothers only until the age of seven, then they were taken to collective educational institutes (*gemeinsame Erziehungsanstalten*), where they spent the whole day being educated for their military careers. They had to practise gymnastics diligently, bathe in the Eurotas' cold stream, and toughen themselves by only wearing light clothing, which remained the same both in summer and

> winter. They only received such food as was sufficient to satisfy them, for they were not allowed to accustom themselves to pleasures which would cause them to become pampered. For the same reason, they slept on a pallet of reeds, which they themselves had to cut from the banks of the Eurotas. If they grew up to become youths, then they were further prepared for war by military exercises. They did not receive academic education; they were only instructed in music, and they also learnt certain poems by heart, which instilled them with courage and love for the fatherland... [Even as men over the age of thirty,] they did not live with their families, but, as the soldiers do here (*bei uns*), lived together in close quarters. Here they also ate together, but they had the same meal almost every day, namely a *Schweineschwarzsauer*, called black blood soup.

Here we find echoes of a number of elements of the Spartan trope found in the cadet-school literature (as described above): toughness and endurance of all physical hardship; lack of luxury; and, of course, the notorious black soup. Although Schillmann's account of Spartan education obviously draws heavily on that of Plutarch (and perhaps also on Xenophon, Plato and Aristotle – see Table 1), it is far from being a mere translation or paraphrase. In particular, we can discern certain elements of his portrayal which would surely have had a strong resonance with any cadets who read the work, or who had it read to them. For instance, the idea that Spartan boys were sent to '*gemeinsame Erziehungsanstalten*' (communal education institutes), combined with Schillmann's initial emphasis on the Spartans' self-proclaimed military vocation, would in all likelihood have evoked an image of the cadets' own educational institutions, given their administrative designation as *militärische Erziehungsanstalten* (military education institutes). Meanwhile, the idea that Spartan education *in toto* was designed purely to serve military aims, focusing on physical education at the expense of the academic, and culminating in full military drill and exercises, would not only have seemed to reflect the cadet schools' own hierarchy of educational values, but also to mirror the complaints which contemporary critics of the schools often made about their shocking lack of academic rigour. The notion that what non-physical education the Spartan boys did receive aimed to instil them with *Vaterlandsliebe* (patriotism) could also have reminded a contemporary reader of the constant emphasis on serving – and, ultimately, dying for – the fatherland, which could be found throughout the cadet corps.[87]

What is more, Schillmann's depiction of Spartan boys' education is somewhat abridged and sanitised, in that it leaves out those elements which might hamper readers' identification of the system with that of contemporary society. We would not expect pederasty to be mentioned, perhaps, or the boys' lack of baths (indeed, this is gainsaid by Schillmann, in his description of the boys' bathing in the Eurotas) but we also find no mention of their going barefoot, their unusual punishments, or of their being encouraged to steal – curiosities in which it might be expected that the author's intended audience might take a keen interest. That Schillmann might wish his readers to draw explicit parallels between Sparta and the Germany of his day can in fact be adduced from his remark that adult Spartans' barrack life is identical with the way in which soldiers live '*bei uns*'.

The *Vorschule der Geschichte*, however, is not the only one of the textbooks to portray Spartan *mores* and education in a way which the cadets might have found illuminating (it is worth noting here that, barring Schrökh, none of the textbooks mention Athenian education, or forms of education in other Greek *poleis*). The other textbooks also emphasise those points which might most have appealed to a reader searching for similarities between Spartan education and military education in contemporary Germany.

For instance, Weber's *Lehrbuch der Weltgeschichte* (1847) highlights the public role of the State in taking boys away from their parental home, and the central part which exercises in the *Turnanstalten* (gymnastic institutes) played in their education, as well as the paramount importance of subordination and obedience towards one's superiors throughout the educational system as a whole.[88] More interestingly still from the point of view of the cadet-school sources, the description of Spartan education by Holtze and Berduschek in their *Übersicht der Weltgeschichte* – although only a couple of sentences long – particularly mentions Spartan boys' ability to bear pain and hardship, in language which seems to echo some cadet-corps descriptions of *spartanern*:

> Civil life was ordered by the state, with preparation for war as its particular aim. The young Spartiates were educated with great strictness in state-established units, led by state officials, [and trained] in cunning, strength and the suffering of pain (*Erduldung des Schmerzes*), and in modest and concise (laconic) speech.[89]

The authors then go on to link this education with Sparta's success as a '*Militärstaat*' (military state) and the constant readiness for war of all her adult citizens – a theme which recurs in several of the other works.[90] In particular, some of the textbooks' descriptions of the Battle of Thermopylae seem specially calculated to arouse the interest of adolescent boys, and to appeal to them as the paramount example of heroism and self-sacrificial love of the Fatherland – traits which, as we have seen, were frequently emphasised at the cadet schools.

While Stacke (as his foreword promised) mainly adheres to the Herodotean account – which is exciting enough – the accounts of both

Weber and Schillmann place even greater emphasis on Leonidas' and the Spartans' honouring of patriotism above all else, their immense bravery, and the incredible gruesomeness of the battle. For Weber, even the Spartans' swords are *tapfer* (valiant), and they themselves are possessed with *Löwenmuth* (the courage of lions).[91] Meanwhile, Schillmann uses the word '*Blut*' (blood) and its cognates at least five times in his description: the Spartans create a 'great bloodbath' (*großes Blutbad*) when they first attack the Medes with their long lances; the Persians suffer a 'bloody defeat' (*blutige Niederlage*) when they are fooled by the Spartans' deceptive retreat; the following night they are also driven back 'bloodily' (*wieder blutig abgewiesen*); finally, during the Spartans' last stand, Leonidas and his men once more bring about a 'terrible bloodbath' (*furchtbares Blutbad*).[92] Once their power is exhausted, the Spartans die happily because they are serving their fatherland.[93]

That the Thermopylaean example was actually absorbed by boys at the cadet schools, and adopted into their system of values (even if in a distorted fashion) alongside examples of daring and self-sacrifice from more recent history, can be nicely illustrated by an extract from Kurt von Borcke's autobiography.[94] The cadets in Borcke's class make a plan to get revenge on the chaplain (*Kommißchristus*) because he had placed Cadet Wilamowski under arrest merely for asking sincere questions about the feeding of the five thousand.[95] The deputy *Stubenältester* Heinz von Bonin, one of the most intellectually gifted cadets, hatches a plot which he wishes to be remembered with amazement by their 'children and children's children', and by posterity.

> 'We must undertake something, like Leonidas, who defended a Thermopylae pass against two divisions of Persians with heavy artillery alone for two months, day and night – without sleeping – until he could do so no longer. We must imitate Pionier Klinke of the Danish Wars, who sprang into the air with a sack of gunpowder!'
>
> 'But what are we going to do to carry out our plans?' asked Obertertianer von Kleeman, 'We have neither a pass nor a sack of gunpowder, only our Schnappsacks, and they explode mostly from behind...'[96]

Using the protesting Schnappsacks' uniforms, the boys create a fake cadet out of pillows and a pumpkin, calling it 'Cadet Keller', the name of a cadet from another *Stube* who is currently in the sickbay, and throw it out of the window so that it will look as if a cadet has tried to commit suicide in the chaplain's garden. When the Lieutenant on duty does discover the prank, he assumes that it has been carried out by Cadet Keller's own room-mates, and Bonin and his accomplices go unpunished.

That the treatment of Sparta in history lessons had an effect on cadets more generally is also borne out by Johannes van Dewall, who states,

Fig. 16. Karlsruhe's Chaplain (*Kommißchristus*), giving a blessing to one of his youthful charges before his confirmation (painting by Oskar Larsen).

immediately after a declaration that every new cadet 'must become a proper Spartan!', that 'the cadets' minds were haunted wonderfully by hearing all the Greek and Roman history.'[97]

Perhaps, then, in these textbooks – which we know to have been included on nineteenth-century cadet-school history syllabuses – we can find a partial answer to the question of where the persistent *topos* of Spartan self-identification in the Prussian Cadet Corps originated. Although we can never know the extent to which teachers would have supplemented the facts which these textbooks provide, we can still gain some idea of the general background in Greek and Spartan history which the cadets would have been given, and which they would have needed to revise more or less diligently in order to pass their final exams.

Fig. 17. Cadets revising for their final exams.

Table 1

Analysis of the relationship of portrayals of Spartan education in textbooks with the descriptions in the ancient sources

Aspect of Spartan Education (ancient ref.)	Schrökh 1788	Weber 1847	Schillmann 1881	Stacke 1894	Holtze 1899
Inspection of Infants/Apothetae (*Lyc.* 16.2)		§51	p. 118	p. 96	
Taught to be unafraid of the dark/being alone (*Lyc.* 16.3)	p. 286				
State education for all from age 7 (*Lyc.* 16.4)	p. 286	§51	p. 118	p. 96	p. 11
Boys leading other boys, who obey them (*Lyc.* 16.5)				pp. 96–7	
Surveillance by elders (*Lyc.* 16.5, 17.1; *L.P.* 2.10, 6.1)	p. 288			p. 97	
Little academic education (*Lyc.* 16.6) But importance of music/poetry (*Lyc.* 21.1)	pp. 284–5 p. 285	§51	p. 118 p. 118	p. 97	
Educational aims (*Lyc.* 16.6): *Physical training* (cf. *L.P.* 2); *obedience to commands*; *military excellence*; *endurance of hardships – including hunger, thirst, cold, heat* (*L.P.* 2.4–5)	p. 286	§51	p. 118	p. 97	p. 11
Barefootedness/nakedness (*Lyc.* 16.6/*L.P.* 2.3)	p. 286			p. 97	
Inadequate clothing (*Lyc.* 16.6; *L.P.* 2.4)			p. 118		
Self-made reed bedding (*Lyc.* 16.7)			p. 118	p. 97	
Paidonomos (*Lyc.* 17.2; *L.P.* 2.2)				p. 97	p. 11
Eirens (*Lyc.* 17.2; *L.P.* 2.11)				p. 97	p. 11
Insufficient food (*L.P.* 2.5)			p. 118	p. 97	

Aspect of Spartan Education (ancient ref.)	Schrökh 1788	Weber 1847	Schillmann 1881	Stacke 1894	Holtze 1899
Stealing (*Lyc.* 17.3; *L.P.* 2.6) *Cunning/ Military ends* (*Lyc.* 17.4; *L.P.* 2.7)	p. 288	§51		p. 97	p. 11
Fox-tale (*Lyc.* 18.1)				p. 97	
Artemisian whipping-contests (*Moralia* 239d, *Lyc.* 18.1; cf. *L.P.* 2.9, *Laws* I.633b)	pp. 286–7			p. 97	
Questioning by eirens (*Lyc.* 18.2)	p. 287				
Punishment before elders (*Lyc.* 18.3)				p. 97	
Laconizein (*Lyc.* 19.1)	pp. 284–5	§51	p. 118	p. 97	p. 11
Pederasty (*Lyc.* 17.1, 18.3; *L.P.* 2.12–14)	–	–	Not mentioned	–	–
Fights (*Laws* I.633b; Pausanias 3.14.8–10)	p. 286				
Respect for elders (*Lyc.* 15.1, 20.5; *L.P.* 2.10, 10.1)	pp. 287–8	§51	p. 118	p. 97	
Only oriented to war (*Laws* I.626c; *Politics* 2.1271b.1–6)	pp. 290–1	§51	pp. 118–9	pp. 97–8	
Black soup (*Lyc.* 12.6)		§51	p. 119	p. 96	

The publication dates given above denote the editions used here. Schrökh, Weber and Schillmann are all first editions; however, it has been impossible to trace the original publication date of the works by Stacke and Holtze. Research using the *Karlsruher Virtueller Katalog* suggests that Stacke's volume was first published in 1852; the original volume by Holtze and Berduschek seems to have been published in 1859, but the new, revised version, intended for the cadet corps, probably only appeared in the late 1860s or early 1870s. In terms of teaching, Stacke is first recommended for the Sexta in the corps syllabuses in 1880/1 and 1883/4; Schillmann is recommended likewise in 1881 and 1887 – individual schools may have decided which work was to be used. Holtze was recommended for the Quarta and Obertertia in 1880/1 and 1883/4, and for the Untertertia in 1887. On Schrökh and Weber, see n. 79 and n. 88.

Notes

[1] Spartan characteristics in the order that Gordat mentions them: black soup: *Lyc.* 12.6; exposure of weak infants: *Lyc.* 16.1–2; state education for all from the age of seven: *Lyc.* 16.4; stealing food to obviate hunger: *Lyc.* 17.3–4; simple clothing and going barefoot: *Lyc.* 16.6; bedding made of reeds: *Lyc.* 16.7; Artemisian whipping contests: *Lyc.* 18.1.

[2] On these problems see in particular Kennell 1995, Ducat 2006.

[3] See Table 1 and discussion on pp. 104–5.

[4] See in particular *Stenographische Berichte des Abgeordnetenhauses* 1890, 33. Sitzung (20/03/1890), 852–3.

[5] Albertz 2006, 228.

[6] While it may be true that retrospective representations of the cadet corps and its life-style as resembling Spartan *mores* could have been subject to some form of cross-contamination by the 'Spartan' reputation already attributed to the cadet corps, and that ancient accounts of Spartan education may not merely have drawn attention to cadet-corps parallels, but have actively influenced and shaped the perceptions and practices of staff and pupils, there is no way in which such effects can realistically be measured or assessed. In general terms, it could be argued that the nature of the Spartan trope was always to some extent self-reinforcing; once it had been taken up enthusiastically by one generation of cadets, it was likely to be imposed upon younger year-groups as part of the trials and tribulations which they would have to endure as a matter of course, and then might even be adopted by officers serving in the corps as *Erzieher*, such as Lt. von Houwald. It is also possible that works such as Dewall's *Aus meinen Kadettenjahren* (1877), Scharfenort's *Bilder* (1889) and Szczepański's *Spartanerjünglinge* (1901), which may have been widely read by prospective cadets and their families (cf. Scharfenort 1889, vi; Maisch 1968, 38), could, as time went on, have influenced subsequent behaviour in the corps. One might even suggest (cf. p. 78, n. 40 above) that there is some significance in the fact that the '*Spartanerjünglinge*' incident with Lt. von Houwald took place only two years after Szczepański's novel was first published. However, unless a piece of evidence were found which definitively stated that cadets had engaged in Spartan behaviour because they had taken such works as a model, these ideas must remain in the realm of pure conjecture. In similar fashion, given the current state of the evidence, it would be impossible to prove definitively that practices at the cadet corps actually became more 'Spartan' due to the influence of ancient accounts of Sparta on the cadets and their educators.

[7] Hillard 1954, 47.

[8] C. von der Goltz 1932, 24–5; Görnandt 1966, 25.

[9] Feiber 1947, *89; Neumann n.d., 11.

[10] Dewall 1878, 74–5.

[11] Indeed, at *Lyc.* 18.1, Plutarch explicitly links the fox-boy's endurance with that of the boys undergoing the *bōmolochia*; the sentence following the end of the fox-tale states that: '[Even] this story gains credence from what the [Spartan] youths now endure, many of whom I have seen dying under the lash at the altar of Artemis Orthia.'

[12] C. von der Goltz 1932, 27; also Scharfenort 1889, 79, and Steynitz's recollections in Nimz 1976, Anhang, 32.

[13] Dewall 1884, 68; C. von der Goltz 1932, 27.

[14] Friedrich Franz von Unruh 1967, 66. See also Bösser 1897, 7.

[15] Dewall 1884, 40.

[16] *Militair-Wochenblatt* 1873b, 324.

[17] Halkett 1939, 60; *The German Army from Within*, 29. An old street-song on this theme (with many variants) runs as follows: '*Kadett, Kadett, Kaldaunenschlucker/ Hosen ohne Unterfutter – / Rothe Kragen,/ Nichts im Magen,/ Goldne Tressen,/ Nichts zu essen!*' (quoted in Dewall 1884, 22). Halkett provides an incomplete, yet pleasing, translation: 'Cadet, cadet, feeds on tripe: Scarlet collar, golden stripe...' A typical daily menu might run as follows: Breakfast – very weak coffee and a piece of *Schwarzbrot*; Breaktime – a bread roll; Lunch – a small portion of meat and vegetables with a piece of *Schwarzbrot*; Supper – bread, cheese and soup.

[18] The cadets were also strictly forbidden luxury foods such as sweets and chocolate – parents were instructed that in food parcels to their offspring they should include only healthy fare such as fruit. Isenburg (1958, 25) describes a sneaky method of smuggling chocolate into the *Stube*; he instructed his mother to put the prohibited bars right at the bottom of the hamper underneath a cornucopia of apples and pears. The *Erzieher*, who had been a cadet himself, turned a blind eye and did not search the hamper thoroughly. In this regard, General von Neumann's comment (n.d., 5) is illuminating: 'We were brought up very Spartanly [in Köslin], inasmuch as one was only allowed to receive a parcel three times a year – namely on one's own and the Kaiser's birthday, and on Sedan Day.' Sedan Day was a national celebration, held each year on the anniversary of the Prussians' capture of Napoleon III and his troops at the Battle of Sedan (2 September 1870) during the Franco-Prussian War.

[19] cf. Plutarch, *Instituta Laconica* (*Moralia* 237e-f)/*Lyc.* 17.3–4. The real difference here, of course, is that Plutarch presents the Spartan authorities as *intending* the boys to steal as part of their training; any benefit perceived in cadets' stealing by the school authorities was incidental, rather than being officially sanctioned. In any case, stealing from one's comrades (as opposed to 'appropriation' [*organisieren*] of fruit etc.) was considered utterly abhorrent – cf. Gordat's reaction to U2's theft, as described in Chapter 3 above.

[20] Ulrich 1909, 25–35; Görnandt 1966, 28. Descriptions of similar exploits can be found in *Mitteilungsblatt* 5, March 1964, 32 [BA-MA MSG3/1186] (stealing coal to keep warm in the winter of 1919–1920); GStAPK IV.HA Rep.13 Nr.121, Bl.96 (stealing apples from the *Prinzengarten*, the garden of the Princes' royal residence in Plön); *Potsdam Brief* August 1971, 4 [GStAPK IV.HA Rep.13 Nr.123] (an altercation with a gardener over stolen apples).

[21] Quoted in *Reichskadettenblatt* 14, October 1928, 212.

[22] e.g. Szczepański 1910, 23.

[23] For depictions of such relationships, see for example Reitzenstein 1920, 68–71; Salomon 1933.

[24] Görnandt 1966, 16.

[25] Hillard 1954, 55–7.

[26] For more on Schulenburg's background, see http://www.wernervonderschulenburg.com/widerstand.htm; also Johann 2003, 240.

[27] Schulenburg 1919, 81. For an anonymous ex-cadet's analysis of a number of these relationships (including love letters), which also explicitly links such homoerotic relations with the Greek idea of *erōs*, see BA-MA MSG2/17007, 7, 11.

[28] For more on this, see Cartledge 2001a.

[29] Interestingly, some homoerotic relationships are documented between *Erzieher* (i.e. young adults) and boys; however, if these went any further than a generalised *Schwärmerei*, and any overtly sexual element to the relationship were discovered, this was treated as scandalous; in at least one instance the Lieutenant involved committed suicide. See further Hillard 1954, 57; Görnandt 1966, 16, 56. For an example of the role which positive ideas about Sparta and Spartan 'virility' played in contemporary discourse on military homosexuality, see Karl Franz von Leexow's pamphlet *Armee und Homosexualität. Schadet Homosexualität der militärischen Tüchtigkeit einer Rasse?* (Leipzig, 1908); I am indebted to Norman Domeier for this reference.

[30] *Militair-Wochenblatt* 1899, 2273–5. Henning von Koss also remembered his first *Erzieher*, Lt. von Tramnitz, as a 'fabulously able *Kadettenvater*' (GStAPK IV.HA Rep.13 Nr.111, Bl.58).

[31] Moncure 1993, 180–1.

[32] ibid., 209.

[33] cf. disciplinary regulations quoted in Clemente 1992, 246.

[34] Moncure 1993, 192–3. This full report was forwarded on to the cadet's future regiment when he left the school. Such a meticulous record was essential because each *Erzieher*'s duty period only lasted two years, and his successor would need as complete as possible a picture of each cadet's development.

[35] ibid., 199–201.

[36] ibid., 180.

[37] Deichmann 1979, 13–14. Neubourg (1890, 38) confirms this observation: 'During playtime, the cadets in the courtyard are never without supervision; the duty *Erzieher* watches over the whole lively troop with a sharp eye...'

[38] *Lyc.* 16.5 (emphasis mine).

[39] Corvin 1871, 115; cf. e.g. Halkett 1939, 61.

[40] Dewall 1884, 69–70.

[41] Gertner 1862, 104–5. N.B. Once again, the point here is not to emphasise *actual* similarities with Spartan education, but to highlight what the cadets themselves, and those in charge of them, would have *perceived* as similarities with Spartan boys' way of life.

[42] Indeed, groups of boys in the cadet schools were also often called a '*Herde*' (herd) – a meaning analogous with that of the Spartan *boua* (or *agela*, as Plutarch calls it). Examples of this can be found in Dewall 1878, 223; Reitzenstein 1920, 13.

[43] Moncure 1993, 116; *Lyc.* 17.2.

[44] Moncure 1993, 20.

[45] *Moralia* 237a; *Lyc.* 16.6.

[46] e.g. Ducat 1999, 2006.

[47] *Lyc.* 16.5–6, 30.3; *L.P.* 8.

[48] Oberst von Brause, quoted in Meier-Welcker 1964, 71.

[49] Moncure 1993, 187–8.

[50] Quoted in Brand 1981, 341.

[51] cf. Moncure 1993, 222ff.; also *L.P.* 2.6–9; *Lyc.* 16.6.

[52] Moncure 1993, 166. See also Boog 1998, 119ff.

[53] Wiese 1924, 46–7.

[54] Craig 1955, 79.

[55] cf. Clemente 1992, 10, 14; Moncure 1993, 143–5.

[56] *Militair-Wochenblatt* 1873a, 194–5. If Albisetti's portrayal of a general lack of enthusiasm for Classical subjects in the *Gymnasien* during this period is correct (1983, 42–9), then the cadets may well have shown more enthusiasm for ancient history than many of their civilian counterparts.

[57] GStAPK IV.HA Rep.13 Nr.25, Bl.157.

[58] Military Education Commission 1870, 183. For more on the exam in general, see Moncure 1993, 234–8.

[59] Military Education Commission 1870, 184, 531–4. Friedrich-Wilhelm Isenburg actually remembers revising 'Lycurgus' in 1899 – as well as Solon, the Persian and Peloponnesian Wars, and fifth-century Athens – for his final exams (1958, 78). At the Prussian War Academy, officers in training also had two lessons a week purely on the art of war of the ancient Greeks and Romans (Lenski 1922, 127).

[60] *Grundzüge der Organisation des Königl. Cadetten-Corps*, Berlin 1844, 27; Crousaz 1857, Beilage C, 44–9. All forms were allotted two hours' history teaching a week, unless otherwise stated.

[61] *Grundzüge* 1844, 28–31.

[62] The textbooks used were those by Schillmann and Stacke (see further discussion below).

[63] One textbook used was Holtze's and Berduschek's *Leitfaden* (see below).

[64] *Aufnahme-Bestimmungen und Lehrplan des Königlichen Cadettencorps*, Berlin 1887: 19, 25, 31, 34, 37. See also *Wissenschaftliche Anforderungen für die Aufnahme in das Kadettenkorps*, 1880/1 and 1883/4.

[65] *Abgeänderte Lehrpläne des Kadettenkorps* (n.d.), in GStAPK I.HA Rep.76 *Kultusministerium*, IV.Sekt.1.Gen.aa,19 Bd.2.

[66] Quoted in Stübig 1983.

[67] cf. Neuber 1903, 11. Two authors writing in the *Militair-Wochenblatt* in 1891 complain of this tendency: it is argued that history in the cadet-schools has heretofore been too much oriented towards the Greeks and Romans and their respective heroic figures as models, particularly at the beginning of boys' school careers (Kinsky 1891, 2111); even the chronological organisation of the textbooks means that boys know much more about the Greeks and Romans than they do about their own fatherland (*Militair-Wochenblatt* 1891a, 2349).

[68] Bösser 1897, 17.

[69] ibid., 13–14.

[70] ibid., 20–1.

[71] GStAPK I.HA Rep.76 *Kultusministerium*, IV.Sekt.1.Gen.aa,19 Bd.4, Bl.175.

[72] See further *Militair-Wochenblatt* 1890, 586–7.

[73] Cited in Stübig 1988, 518.

[74] Scharfenort 1892, 26.

[75] The text of the 27th edition, which was published in 1894, will be discussed here. The work may have been originally published in 1852.

[76] Stacke 1894, v.

[77] ibid.

[78] Table 1 can be found on pp. 104–5.

[79] Haslingen 1906, 14, quoting *Soldatenfreund* 1861–2, 'v.K. *Aus dem Jugendleben*'. It is not made clear exactly which classes would have used the work, though it seems likely that it would have been used primarily with the Sexta.

[80] Schrökh 1788, unpaginated foreword.

[81] ibid., 286.

[82] ibid., 289–90.

[83] The comment 'In Sparta, the soldier's estate was the most praised above all, and almost the only one to be honoured' (ibid., 285) could have applied equally well to Prussia at various points in her history.

[84] ibid., 290.

[85] Schillmann 1881, unpaginated foreword.

[86] ibid.

[87] e.g. Scharfenort 1892, 5.

[88] Weber 1847, 38–9. This work seems to have been supplied to the cadets for recreational purposes; E. Neubourg, writing in 1890, uses the *Lehrbuch der Weltgeschichte* as an example of the type of book of which plentiful copies would be left in the cadets' *Stuben* (p. 44).

[89] Holtze 1899, 11. This work was recommended for use by the Quarta and Tertia (see p. 105).

[90] ibid. cf. also Schrökh 1788, 285–6; Schillmann 1881, 119.

[91] Weber 1847, 48.

[92] Schillmann 1881, 119–21.

[93] ibid., 120.

[94] Borcke 1940, 203–8.

[95] ibid., 203: 'Had there been more or fewer men there than in a German army-corps, and had a quartermaster supervised the division of leftovers?... "I will report you for punishment to the Captain; then you can consider your spiritual questions in the *Arrestlokal* [detention room]."'

[96] ibid., 203–4.

[97] Dewall 1884, 49.

5

OF SPARTANS AND SOCIALISATION: THE FUNCTION OF '*SPARTANERN*'

Although the possible sources of the Spartan identification found in the cadet schools have been discussed at some length, an equally pressing question still remains unanswered: what was '*spartanern*' *for*? Why would cadets, realistically, have thought it useful or helpful to emulate the scions of an ancient Greek warrior caste which had died out countless centuries before? Furthermore, why did the cadets' conception of Spartan education always cleave most closely to those ancient historical facts which bore most relation to their own training? In this chapter, it will be argued that one of the most important functions of what the cadets termed '*spartanern*' or 'Spartan behaviour' was that it enabled them better to bear the hardships of the 'total institution' in which they found themselves.

The term 'total institution' was first coined by the Canadian-born sociologist Erving Goffman in his seminal paper 'On the characteristics of Total Institutions', which was first presented in 1957, then published in full in 1961. Goffman invented the term in order to describe institutions which exhibited certain characteristics: firstly, they were places both of residence and work, and secondly, they contained a large number of individuals sharing equivalent status. These individuals were to a great extent cut off from normal civilian life; they would stay there for a considerable length of time, and together they would lead an enclosed, formally regulated way of life.[1] The examples used in Goffman's survey range from mental asylums to concentration camps, convents and officer training camps. Goffman's work has already been cited in relation to the Prussian Cadet Corps by Zabel (1978), Driftmann (1984) and, most recently, by Schmitz (1997). Indeed, the extreme emphasis placed on military discipline and the subordination of the individual to the collective at the cadet schools means that they fit the 'total institution' model rather better than do the English public schools, which were analysed from this perspective by John Wakeford in his study *The Cloistered Élite* (1969).

As this chapter will demonstrate, according to Goffman's criteria, the cadet schools were indeed 'total institutions'. In particular, they exemplify that type of total institution which pursues an instrumental, 'worklike task', as opposed to institutions such as prisons and sanatoria, which aim to segregate inmates from the outside world either for others' safety or for their own, in order to cure, to punish or to reform them.[2] As schools, they belong to that category of organisation which aims to 'work on' people in order to change or socialise them: 'People constitute the *raison d'être* of these organisations, and...the desired product is a new or altered person.'[3] Those characteristics of total institutions which bear most resemblance to those of the Prussian Cadet Corps will be examined first; these correlations will then be put into context, the better to demonstrate that the function of the Spartan *topos* can indeed be illuminated by an analysis based on Goffman's theory.[4]

The anatomy of the total institution

Three of the most obvious aspects of total institutions, Goffman tells us, are the topographical and psychological isolation of their inmates from the outside world (they are incompatible with family life);[5] the clear distinction which they make between inmates and supervisory staff,[6] and the fact that they cause inmates to perform regulated activities in large groups or 'blocks'.[7] He expands upon this system of 'regimentation' as follows:

> First, all aspects of life are conducted in the same place under the same single authority. Second, each phase of the member's daily activity is carried on in the immediate company of a large batch of others, all of whom are treated alike and required to do the same thing together. Third, all phases of the day's activities are tightly scheduled, with one activity leading at a prearranged time to the next, the whole sequence of activities being imposed from above by a system of explicit formal rulings and a body of officials. Finally, the various enforced activities are brought together into a single rational plan purportedly designed to fulfil the official aims of the institution.[8]

Surveillance is therefore one of the total institution's distinguishing features, since any lack of compliance with the regimentation, or infraction of the regulations, must be promptly dealt with.[9]

The admission procedure of a total institution often takes the form of a *rite de passage*, an important part of which will include 'a leaving off and a taking on, with the midpoint marked by physical nakedness.'[10] One may lose one's name (or a familiar form of it, at least), be stripped of one's possessions, and given instead standard-issue replacements, 'uniform in character and uniformly distributed'.[11] The admission process in general can be seen as shaping or coding the new inmate as a mere object to be fed into the administrative machinery of the establishment.[12]

Upon entering the total institution, an individual is also stripped of the comforts and assurances of his home life and subjected to a series of 'abasements, degradations, humiliations, and profanations of self', which Goffman collectively terms 'mortification'.[13] This means that new members of the institution will often be required to perform menial tasks, or to behave in demeaning ways which have symbolic connotations that are alien to their status in the outside world.[14] The new inmate is also likely to have to undergo initial tests of obedience or 'will-breaking contests', which ensure that he gives his new superiors due deference (particularly if, in the outside world, no such deference would be forthcoming).[15] As a part of this initiation, the recruit may often be called by derogatory terms which indicate his exceptionally low status.[16]

Neither does the total institution guarantee its new members protection from physical harm. The recruit is often exposed to beatings or other maltreatment, and, if he reacts badly to this, may be subjected to 'looping'. This term indicates a process whereby an inmate's reaction to his own situation is collapsed back into the situation itself, so that, for instance, any reaction to bullying leads only to more bullying, and any attempt to make an expressive response to degradation (such as a grimace or a *sotto voce* profanity) can lead to yet more humiliating demands, as punishment for perceived sullenness or insolence.[17]

The inmate of the total institution will also be subjected to constant physical discomfort and 'exposure'; this may take such forms as unpalatable food, hard bedding, doorless toilets, and large communal sleeping-quarters which allow no privacy.[18] Even the inmate's relationships with significant others may be exposed 'contaminatively' – if personal mail is read or censored, for instance, or private communications are made fun of in front of his face.[19] In general, the inmate must accept loss of autonomy and self-determination,[20] and submit to the 'regimentation' and 'tyrannisation' which may govern every waking moment at the total institution.[21]

In order to survive in a total institution, therefore, the inmate has to learn any and every behaviour that may possibly help him to survive the regimented tyranny of his new environment. He must learn as quickly as he can the appropriate forms and patterns of deference which his superiors will teach him.[22] He must acquire knowledge of the system of rewards and privileges laid down by staff in return for obedient or praiseworthy behaviour, and above all, he must gain acceptance from his fellow inmates.[23] He must learn the institutional lingo which both inmates and staff use to describe events or behaviour which are important in the world of the total institution, and discover the 'secondary adjustments' or 'ways to get by' in that world.[24] And, very importantly, he must not violate the code that forbids an inmate to inform on his fellow inmates to the staff, or he will find himself forever typecast as a dishonourable, untrustworthy 'stoolie' or 'finkrat', never a 'right guy'.[25] Members of the institution generally expect loyalty to their group to be a given, and they will exhibit great hostility to any who break solidarity with them.[26] Ultimately, the inmate must 'rationalise' his mortification and live according to the terms of the total institution, if he is to survive his time there.[27]

If the time spent at the total institution has led to a gain in 'proactive status' upon leaving or graduation, as in the case of elite schools or Officer Training Corps, it is likely that former inmates will institute jubilant official reunions, and proclaim their pride in the institution publicly.[28]

The Prussian Cadet Corps as a total institution

It is clear that very many of these characteristics of the total institution can be found in the life of the Prussian Cadet Corps. As Moncure has shown in his detailed analysis of the cadet schools' physical locations, the cadets (like inmates of other types of total institution) were isolated as far as possible from the world outside – in part to protect them from that civilian society which 'posed a threat to the development of soldiers much as might a disease to the newborn'.[29] During term-time, cadets were completely cut off from family life.[30]

That cadet-corps life exemplified the massed regimentation and constant surveillance so typical of the total institution may be demonstrated by a passage from Friedrich Franz von Unruh's autobiography, which describes the interminable drill that turned each boy into nothing more than 'a standard, a number among numbers':

> One was never alone... The lessons, drill and gymnastics..., the meals in the great hall, were all held communally. We sat down, ate, stood up, and moved on command, and even that most personal thing of all, prayer, happened to order. [More than a hundred boys slept in each dormitory...] and an Officer patrolled and policed the communal going-to-sleep.[31]

Friedrich Franz von Unruh's portrayal of the admission process also possesses that initiatory quality which Goffman describes: the donning of the new (though often rather shabby) cadet-corps uniform was termed a '*Mauserung*' or 'moulting', and served to destroy the new boys' individuality as much as possible; they must forget that they were all individuals with intrinsic capabilities and a particular parental home. Now they were all the same: they had the same uniform, the same kit, and the number assigned to them symbolically replaced their name (use of which was reduced to the absolute minimum) – forenames, as an obvious relic of civilian life, were dropped immediately. As von Unruh puts it: 'It was all aimed to transform [us] from individuals into members of the community (*Gemeinschaftsglieder*).'[32] Zabel, in his analysis of various cadet-school autobiographies, also characterises the diverse elements of admission into the corps – the medical exam, the exchange of civilian clothes for uniform, the speech telling the cadets that their purpose in life was to serve and die for their country – as an initiation rite which facilitated loss of personal identity and ushered in the learning process, which had obedience as its ultimate aim.[33]

Like new inmates of other total institutions, new cadets would be challenged and forced into deference to their elders as soon as they entered the corps, as the first speech given to Cordt von Brandis by his '*Bärenführer*' ('bear-leader'/sheepdog) can illustrate:

> 'You're not in the *Penne* (civilian school) now! You call yourself a Royal Prussian Cadet; you will be fitted out as such directly. But you won't be a cadet for a very long time. First, you're just a miserable Schnappsack. In the next year you're a "bread-sack", and in the third an "old cadet". Only then can you have your say!'[34]

As even this short passage shows, cadets would quickly have to get up to scratch on the 'institutional lingo' of their *Voranstalt*; each school had different names for the various year-groups – for instance, at Köslin, Sextaner were called '*wandelnde Misthaufen*' (mutant dung-heaps), and Quintaner were known as '*Fröscher*' (frogs).[35] However, the cadets also gave special names to all the tortures and initiatory rituals (mortifications) which older cadets inflicted upon their younger charges. One cadet dictionary lists some of these (many of which have already been mentioned by Wiese, Szczepański and Scharfenort) as forming part of an '*Einweihung*' (initiation ritual) which would generally take place about three weeks after the Schnappsacks arrived. The trials involved included: *Sternegucken* (star-gazing); *Klo-papiernummerieren* (looroll-counting); *Speckschlucken* (bacon-swallowing); *Schlüsselbeißen* (key-biting), and *Gardereitern* (sitting on an eraser with a needle stuck into it).[36]

As we have seen in Chapters 2 and 3, such initial, literally ritualised mortifications were then subsumed more generally into the type of 'menial tasks' and demeaning treatment characteristic of a total institution. One might compare the cruelty of the Tertianer (described by Leopold von Wiese or Paul von Schoenaich), who whipped younger boys daily or tortured them with pen-nibs, or Peter von Heydebreck's endless task of finding flies for his *Stubenältester*'s lizards. Anyone who turned to the *Erzieher* for help was a no-good *petzer*, a sneak, who would suffer even more maltreatment from his comrades once they discovered his disloyalty.[37]

Interestingly, the 'tyrannisation' of 'inmates' at the cadet schools was often carried out not by staff, but by older pupils, whose position was intermediate, poised between the new boys and the staff members. However, they could still claim certain 'staff-like' powers and privileges in relation to the lowliest members of the institution.

„An Grabes Rand": Einweihung

Fig. 18. New boys at Karlsruhe being subjected to an 'initiation' ceremony (painting by Oskar Larsen). The caption reads: '"On the edge of the grave": Initiation'.

In general terms, cadets also had to bear the hardships of discomfort and 'exposure', sleeping in huge unheated dormitories, eating poor-quality food, and having no privacy, even in the washrooms and lavatories. However, if cadets ultimately managed to survive all these hardships and mortifications, the general consensus upon graduation seems to have been that these had been exactly what they needed to turn them into first-class military men and commanders. After all, it was just part and parcel of that famous Prussian 'character education' (*Charaktererziehung*) which was seen as the only true way to instil cadets with the traits that they needed to become officers prepared unquestioningly to sacrifice their lives for their Fatherland. Thus one justification for the harsh nature of the cadet-school training (as expressed by Louis von Scharfenort) lay in the inability of family life to prepare the child for life as a useful member of society as a whole. At the cadet school, however:

> The newcomer is integrated into a collectivity, in which he must create a place for himself, but in which he can do so, and where by listening and sharing his character is toughened, his mind is satisfied; he must acquire friends through his dealings with his comrades, and seek within himself the source of his joys. A fickle disposition, an arrogant superciliousness, those products of a pampered home education, find no fertile soil here. The community trains and educates... One of the most salutary claims which the education can make here finds its vindication: Surmounting one's selfishness for the benefit of the rights of the community, which lays down the laws that give the cadet more opportunity to subordinate himself than at a [civilian] school which can only work on him educationally for a few hours each day.[38]

These methods and aims could therefore be used to justify what the anonymous author of *The German Army from Within* terms the 'systematised brutality' of the training which the cadets had to undergo.[39]

The function of '*spartanern*'

Since the cadet schools do fit the model of a total institution in a significant number of ways, it seems highly probable that '*spartanern*', in its various manifestations, became institutionalised because it helped cadets to bear both the hardships of their initiation, and their subsequent life in the total institution of the cadet corps. In the rest of this chapter, I will therefore argue that *spartanern* formed an important – if not crucial – part of the 'rationalisation process' which enabled both cadets and staff to justify the mortifications (or 'systematised brutality') which the boys had to endure. This self-identification with a Spartan model even fits exactly one of the patterns of socialisation which Goffman describes, in which some total institutions 'offer the inmate an opportunity to live up to a model of conduct that is at once ideal and staff-sponsored – a model felt by its advocates to be in the best interests of the very persons to whom it is applied.'[40]

In fact, using this particular sociological model also explains why descriptions of *spartanern* are found much less frequently in stories and memoirs from the HKA, such as Johannes van Dewall's *Kadettengeschichten* (1878) or Gerhard von Heinz's *Kadettenliebe* (1908) – something which puzzled me during my initial research. By the time that cadets reached the HKA, they felt themselves to be 'men'; physical maltreatment was therefore less common, and was considered by many to be simply out of the question.[41] In terms of socialisation, 'the primary goal of forming a cohesive corporate body had been accomplished by the time a boy had been a cadet for five years'.[42] Thus, it should come as no surprise that the 'Spartan' elements of such socialisation were also no longer in evidence – the function which *spartanern* served had already been accomplished.

As we have seen, the idea that boys could be designated '*Spartanerjünglinge*' or '*spartanische Jugend*' often cropped up in cadet-school vocabulary, and boys at Bensberg also seem to have coined the verb '*spartanern*' (to behave like a Spartan). This terminology evidently represented an important concept in the institutional world, since it had worked its way so thoroughly into that 'institutional lingo' which is one of the most common manifestations of the total institution. Furthermore, this concept of 'being like a Spartan' seems to have been used by the authors of our cadet-school sources to 'rationalise' a whole variety of their total institution's features, beginning with the initial *rites de passage* and mortifications, and extending to the day-to-day bearing of hardships and the institutionalised hatred of '*petzen*'.

Johannes van Dewall's account of his first days at *Voranstalt* Bensberg, taken from *Aus meinen Kadettenjahren* (1884), forms a promising starting-point for such an analysis. As we have seen, Dewall uses the idea that crying is un-Spartan to force himself to hide his homesickness; that is, he is using a Spartan model to help him endure that stark isolation from home and family which admission to a total institution always entails.[43] Later, Dewall also links 'becoming a Spartan' with overcoming a whole catalogue of regimentations and mortifications which seem to match Goffman's descriptions uncannily:

> [The new cadet's] things are all State property... At meals he gets the smallest portions; in games he has to be the horse [whom the others ride...] Naturally he gets beaten up all the time. He needs to pull his socks up and become a Spartan (*Er soll ein ordentlicher Spartaner werden*)![44]

This isolation and regimentation of corps life is also mentioned in the recollections of Eugen Jany-Hamburg, published in the *Reichskadettenblatt* in 1926:

> Our life in the institution (*Anstalt*) was very monotonous: practically monastic, so to speak. We really were '*Spartanerjünglinge*', as a novella which was published some years ago in *Die Woche* was called, in which a little cadet poured out his heart to his mother in a childish fashion.[45]

In Kurt von Borcke's autobiography, we also find Spartan emulation linked to a cadet-school *rite de passage* which was inflicted upon Borcke and his friend Udo von Gaisberg by Graf Reising, their *Stubenältester*. As the two new boys in the *Stube*, Borcke and Gaisberg are forced to undergo various initiations which will end in a 'festival of manliness' – the only thing that can ensure their entry into the circle of the initiated. As the centre-piece of his oration, Reising reminds his charges that this is just the sort of thing that happened in Sparta (though his facts seem a little confused): '"The Spartans laid their boys for hours at a time in the freezing water, to produce Spartan simplicity in them..."'[46]

Such ideas come to the fore in Reising's mind once again when he becomes afraid that a medical examination of Gaisberg, who has been taken ill, will lead to discovery of the scars from the beatings which Reising has been giving him.

> That could be very awkward. The senior physician had no sympathy for the cadet education and would report such things to the Captain... People shouldn't send such weakly cadets into the corps. The ancient Spartans threw their useless infants into the water and let them drown if they couldn't swim.[47]

Invoking the Spartan example, particularly with reference to the Spartans' education in obedience, can also be found as a rationalising response to further mortification and 'tyrannisation' during the first few years at the cadet schools, as the recollections of former cadets such as Peter von Heydebreck and Magnus von Eberhardt show. Heydebreck saw enduring constant 'muscle-strapping' from his *Stubenältester* Uhle, or going on fools' fly-catching errands for him, as instilling that crucial subordination in order to command which was 'the point of this Spartan educational system'.[48] Eberhardt expands upon this theme as follows:

> Much has been written and spoken about the tough education and discipline in the cadet corps, and I can only confirm that we lads were called '*Spartanerjünglinge*' not without reason. Despite all prohibitions, we were soundly thrashed by our superiors and older comrades for 'educational reasons'. For particular ill-doers there were massed beatings ['*Rutschen*'], where the whole class, room or company apportioned the punishment... But none of that harmed anybody, and I think that the overwhelming majority of former cadets would share my view, that such training, which often seemed over-harsh, still had its good side. We had to be trained to

> become real men with strong characters, leaders of the people in arms in time of peace and war; there one can't have any infirmities or weaknesses.[49]

The horrible punishments or tests of endurance inflicted by *Stubenältesten*, such as burning hot pen-nibs into younger cadets' hands, are also often rationalised as being all a normal part of 'education in the Spartan fashion'.[50] The implication seems to be that 'if the Spartans could bear it, so can we!' Similarly, the boys' pathological hatred of '*petzen*' (another feature of the total institution) is rationalised by an appeal to Spartan history: a cadet should not act in this way because it is 'un-Spartan'. 'The fox-boy died rather than blurt out a word, and so should you!' could be one reading of *Spartanerjünglinge*, and of certain passages of Dewall's *Aus meinen Kadettenjahren*.

In this light, we might even see the prevalence of Spartan *self*-mortification, in which cadets have to prove themselves masochistically (described above by Corvin, Scharfenort and Dewall), as an attempt on the younger boys' part to recapture their own autonomy from the demeaning forces which have hitherto left them the passive victims of older boys' tortures. At least taking the torture into one's own hands allows for a certain amount of self-determination (the lack of which is one of the characteristics of the total institution), and if the cadet can prove himself a 'true Spartan' in this manner, perhaps he will regain so much respect from his comrades that they will no longer seek to mortify him themselves.

Finally, bearing of general hardship and 'exposure' in the schools is also rationalised with reference to Spartan *mores*. Such features of the total institution as poor food and uncomfortable living and sleeping quarters were often accepted more readily because they were 'Spartan' (cf. Chapter 3); Emil Ilgner's description of hardships at *Voranstalt* Culm nicely illustrates this:

> The cots stood in long rows, and the mattresses and pillows had, in Spartan style (*nach Spartaner Art*), an enviable hardness... It was strictly enforced that each boy should strip his torso and wash with cold water in an orderly manner. With some Mummy's boys who weren't accustomed to such Spartan ablutions, there was blubbering and chattering of teeth. But such an educational method is a real blessing; it's damned bad luck that families put it into practice far too little.[51]

The equation of 'Spartan' training with future effectiveness in one's military career is made strongly by other commentators such as Isenburg (1958, 63) and Gertner (1862, 101); Henning von Koss also provides an example, in his examination of 'How one came to join the cadet corps at the turn of the century, and how things went for a new boy before he had become integrated into the cadet corps':[52]

> There has been a lot of belly-aching about the cadet corps, but I have never been able to find any justice in the grumblers' accusations. Of course things went along in a Spartan fashion at the cadet corps, and of course military perspectives predominated. It was considered a matter of course that a cadet would or should become an officer, and his training was tailored to that end.

Cadets who went on to be successful in their later lives tended to look back with rose-tinted nostalgia at their training into '*Spartanerjünglinge*', which 'made them the men they were'.[53] This characteristic can even be found in the recollections of Paul von Hindenburg, as he remembers his time at *Voranstalt* Wahlstatt fondly:

> The serious matters, the joys and the sorrows of those boyhood years form emotional experiences which pass vividly before my mind's eye. The fear of God; strict Spartan discipline, consciously borne; effective self-discipline taught among ourselves;...healthy and toughening training of body and spirit to aid willpower and determination, and thus the development of character – those were the fundamental building-blocks of our education.[54]

As Schmitz has noted, the cadet schools needed in some way to foster an acceptance of the hardships of the training which they provided, and, in the absence of most official evidence,[55] the memories and memoirs of ex-cadets are some of the best sources which we have for discerning the methods of socialisation at work in the corps.[56] Given the frequency with which the Spartan *topos* appears in this context in the relevant literature, seeing Spartan identification as an unofficial – yet sanctioned – method of helping boys to bear their frugal (and to some extent brutal) existence seems completely logical.

In this way (to paraphrase Goffman), we can see that the cadets did indeed espouse a Spartan model of conduct which was at once ideal and staff-sponsored; they both aligned themselves with this model, and to some extent espoused the torment themselves – often inflicting the burden of 'having to be Spartan' on other new cadets in their turn.[57] Thus their 'Spartan' self-identification fits exactly that model which Goffman's theory might lead us to expect – its function being to provide a context and a deeper meaning for the hardships which the cadets had to suffer every day, particularly during the socialisation process which immediately followed their recruitment into the total institution of the Royal Prussian Cadet Corps.

Notes

[1] Goffman 1961, 17. One might suggest that the textbooks which portrayed Sparta as most similar to contemporary German education (discussed in the previous chapter) actually attempt to force ancient Sparta itself into the mould of a 'total institution'.

[2] ibid., 16,

[3] Street *et al.* 1966, 3, cited in Wakeford 1969, 42.

[4] Not all Goffman's observations on total institutions are relevant to the cadet schools. However, given his preliminary caveat that 'none of the elements I will describe seems peculiar to total institutions, and none seems to be shared by every one of them; what is distinctive about total institutions is that each exhibits to an intense degree many items in this family of attributes' (1961, 17), a focus on those elements of Goffman's analysis which do apply to the cadet schools seems methodologically justifiable.

[5] Goffman 1961, 15–16, 22. Visits from or to people outside the institution may be completely curtailed, at least at first (ibid., 24).

[6] ibid., 18. However, in the cadet schools, the 'social distance' between cadets and staff did not take such a severe form of alienation as that which Goffman goes on to describe. Additionally, older cadets had some 'staff' attributes, in that they took on disciplinary roles. See further below, including n. 15.

[7] ibid., 17–18.

[8] ibid., 17.

[9] ibid., 18.

[10] ibid., 27.

[11] ibid., 27–8.

[12] ibid., 25–6. As examples, Goffman mentions medical examinations, haircuts, the allocation of uniform, etc.

[13] ibid., 24.

[14] Wakeford (1969, 41) links this practice with 'fagging'.

[15] Goffman 1961, 26–7. In Goffman's example, the superiors in question are prison-warders breaking in a new prisoner; in the cadet schools, older cadets could fulfil this function.

[16] ibid., 27. The examples given by Goffman include 'fish' and 'swab'; we might compare cadet-school designations such as '*Schnappsack*' or '*Scheißtaner*' (a vulgarisation of *Sextaner* [sixth year, the lowest year], to 'shit-year').

[17] ibid., 41.

[18] ibid., 32, 47.

[19] ibid., 38. For such censorship at the cadet schools see Salomon 1933, 50. Woe betide the cadet who attempted to pass off a sweetheart as a 'male cousin' to get past the censorship control: he could easily find himself asked in front of the entire company whether said cousin had always exchanged 'intimate kisses' with him.

[20] Goffman 1961, 47.

[21] ibid., 42.

[22] ibid., 107–8.

[23] ibid., 51–3. Sometimes, pairs of inmates become 'buddies' (not necessarily with any sexual element involved) whose mutual pairing is recognised by other inmates and who come to rely on each other for a wide range of assistance and emotional

support (ibid., 60). One might compare such pairings with the cadets' '*Schuß*' relationships described in Chapter 4 above.

[24] ibid., 55. This might even involve learning how to traffic in 'illicit commodities', i.e. how to work the black market. Cadets also found such 'ways to get by': food became 'a medium of exchange or ransom' (Moncure 1993, 116), and help with homework could constitute a fitting trade for some meat or eggs (see above, p. 93).

[25] ibid., 56.

[26] ibid., 61.

[27] ibid., 49.

[28] ibid., 70.

[29] Moncure 1993, 104–5.

[30] Cadets even had to wear their uniform and abide by a set of corps regulations throughout the holidays – in this sense, the total institution had not fully released its grip upon them even when they were at home. For an exhaustive list of these rules, see Schaarschmidt 1911/12, Section 21.

[31] Friedrich Franz von Unruh 1967, 66.

[32] ibid., 65.

[33] Zabel 1978, 194–7.

[34] Brandis 1966, 24.

[35] Nimz 1976, 57, 85. See also Brandis 1966, 25, and the 'cadet dictionaries' compiled by Berkun (n.d. c.1930) and Anon. (1972).

[36] Anon. 1972, 14. In Szczepański's Culm, such initiations took place under the aegis of the 'Fehmic Court' (1910, 27–31) – even including a ritual biting of the initiand's thumb (which might delight seekers after gratuitous Spartan parallels, even if it had no direct Spartan connection – cf. *Lyc.* 18.3).

[37] This matches the description of 'looping' in Goffman's account (see above).

[38] Scharfenort 1892, 74–5.

[39] *The German Army from Within*, 26.

[40] Goffman 1961, 64.

[41] e.g. Schoenaich 1926, 24.

[42] Moncure 1993, 207.

[43] Dewall 1884, 7–8.

[44] ibid., 49.

[45] Jany-Hamburg 1926, 68.

[46] Borcke 1940, 63.

[47] ibid., 86–7.

[48] Heydebreck 1931, 10.

[49] Eberhardt 1929, 236–7.

[50] Borcke 1940, 289–90; Aulock-Radau 1955, 7.

[51] Ilgner 1932, 15–16.

[52] Nimz 1976, 58.

[53] Eberhardt's recollections (see above) also exemplify this tendency. These cadets are therefore equivalent to Goffman's former inmates with 'proactive status'.

[54] Quoted in Brand 1981, 266.

[55] Due to the destruction of the *Heeresarchiv* Potsdam in 1945 (cf. Devantier 2008).

[56] Schmitz 1997, 3–12.

[57] cf. Goffman 1961, 64.

6

THE CADET CORPS AND ITS CRITICS: EDUCATION, POLITICS AND THE PRUSSIAN MILITARY

The cadet corps, politics and *Spartanertum*, 1840–1900

Thus far, life at the Prussian Cadet Schools has been examined from the perspective of staff and pupils; both the nature of the cadet corps' collocation with Sparta, and the probable reasons for its prevalence, have been documented in depth. The descriptions of the Spartan *topos* which have been discussed so far mainly illustrate the ways in which Spartan self-identification impinged upon cadets' lives on a personal level, yet many of these portrayals did not seem to have any overt political significance or intent. However, the present chapter will focus upon the role which the Prussian Cadet Corps played in contemporary Prusso-German politics, and the effect of this political engagement upon the deployment of the Spartan trope. Often, the schools polarised public opinion, provoking violent controversy and vehement parliamentary debate.

Since the cadet corps was considered a bastion of aristocratic, militaristic and ultramonarchist conservatism, it was never without its detractors – particularly among politicians of a more liberal or Social Democratic persuasion. At the same time, among those conservatives whom scholars have dubbed the Prussian '*Militairpartei*' (military party), and particularly among the officer class, such critics' condemnation was vehemently rebuffed.[1] Thus, a pattern of liberal demands for the abolition or financial restriction of the cadet schools, followed by reactionary counterattacks from the schools' supporters (often abetted by the current monarch), can be discerned throughout the nineteenth century.[2]

However, during the last decades of the nineteenth century, the schools began to attract attention from another perspective – in the context of the ongoing debate over German secondary-school reform and the necessity (or otherwise) of Latin and Greek as compulsory qualifications for many forms of higher education. Indeed, it was the Kaiser's decision to make the cadet schools conform to the curriculum of a *Realschule* which provided a significant catalyst for the ground-breaking educational reform conferences (*Schulkonferenzen*) which were convened in 1890 and 1900. Following the curricular reforms of the late 1870s and early 1880s, the cadet schools had become far more subservient to the education ministry, and had to make a firm commitment to follow the same curriculum as non-humanistic civilian schools. Yet the fact that boys who attended the cadet schools would not normally take the *Abitur*, the school leaving examination which qualified one for higher education, led to a declining number of applicants. If boys proved physically unfit for military service, or were wounded and unable to pursue their military careers further, their parents wanted the guarantee of a position in civilian life which only a conventional school leaving certificate could give.[3] Thus the cadet-school commanders' desperation to have cadet-corps education considered an acceptable and equal substitute for education at a civilian *Realgymnasium* or *Gymnasium* led them to encourage the Kaiser in his conviction that a thoroughgoing reform of the German secondary-school system was really necessary.[4]

We will now consider the various educational and political debates with which the cadet corps became embroiled between 1840 and 1900, including the part which the Spartan *topos* had to play in these.[5] This discussion will then be followed by an examination of the role which the Spartan trope played in liberal and left-wing criticism of the corps, as demonstrated by various literary manifestations of anti-militarist attitudes towards the cadet schools which appeared during the first two-and-a-half decades of the twentieth century.

By the early 1840s, the two original *Voranstalten*, Potsdam and Culm, had been supplemented by the foundation of Wahlstatt (1838) and Bensberg (1840). The total number of cadets supported by the state now numbered over 800. However, in many ways, both the Prussian Officer Corps and the cadet corps were still as 'Junker-heavy' during the 1840s as they had been during the Napoleonic Wars.[6] In the *Vormärz* period leading up to the revolutions of 1848, aristocratic military families, obsessed with maintaining the exclusive noble ancestry and *esprit de corps* of the officer class, were intent on preserving the social homogeneity of the cadet schools at all costs.[7] This effective upper-class monopoly on high-flying military careers, along with the considerable and, as many saw it, overweening influence of the officer corps on contemporary politics, contributed to the hatred of the military which was to become so apparent once revolution had broken out.[8] The 'soldierly spirit' of the '*Militairmonarchie*' (military monarchy) was seen as fundamentally opposed to the revolutionary ideologies of liberalism, egalitarianism and democracy;[9] the reactionaries' disdain for such ideas can be well exemplified by the slogan '*Gegen Demokraten helfen nur Soldaten!*' ('Soldiers are the only answer to democrats!').[10]

It may therefore come as no surprise that, during the revolutionary days of March 1848, the cadets themselves became prime targets for radical violence. They were seen as the seeds from which the detested '*vertierte Soldateska*' (brutish soldier-thugs) would arise, in urgent need of extirpation.[11] In Bensberg, citizens of the town instigated demonstrations against the cadet school and attempted to storm it; other *Voranstalten* also saw direct conflict between cadet-school personnel and revolutionary elements.[12] In Culm, local rabble-rousers were even joined by disaffected Polish nationalists seeking to further their aims of 're-Polonisation' (*Polonismus*) in the area.[13] Meanwhile, in Berlin, the authorities feared that the HKA in the Friedrichstraße would be stormed at any moment, so grimly were the cadets hated by the revolutionaries.[14] General von Below gathered together a group of officers to resist hostile incursions; the cadets, however, were bitterly disappointed when a dispatch from the King ordered them to retreat to the safety of Potsdam. One commentator notes that ammunition had to be deliberately withheld from the cadets, who were so keen for battle that it was feared they would force a confrontation by opening fire onto the street below the building.[15]

Later that year, discussion in the newly-convened Frankfurt Parliament focused upon more rational means of eradicating the cadet corps than those deployed by the revolutionary mob. The current liberal Minister-President and War Minister, Ernst von Pfuel (1779–1866), was particularly keen to resolve the problem posed by the cadet schools.[16] The cost of maintaining the schools, the unnatural onesidedness of their education, their promotion of the exclusive spirit of the aristocracy, and the 'danger which they presented to the welfare and safety of society', were all cited as grounds for their abolition.[17] A commission was set up to investigate the possibilities for reform of the 'Cadet Institutes', and their report was presented at the end of September 1848. The commission whole-heartedly decried the anachronistic nature of the cadet corps, claiming that it should never have survived the reforms of 1808 or 1813. The very fact that the schools insisted on training boys as military men from a tender age was seen as contravening all the basic rights of a free people. The commission recommended that the *Voranstalten* should all be transformed into ordinary *Realgymnasien*, whose only link with the army would be the provision of a number of free places and bursaries for the sons of dead or invalid officers.[18]

Further recommendations from 1 October 1848 stated that the *Voranstalten* should be renamed 'Royal Education Institutes' (*Königliche Erziehungsanstalten*); the HKA would be renamed the 'Royal Military School' (*Königliche Militairschule*). The schools would have Directors, Inspectors,

Governors and teachers with the highest academic qualifications, and all military drill would be replaced with gymnastic exercises. Culm would be remodelled as a fully-functioning *Realgymnasium* whose pupils could choose any career at eighteen, and only the HKA would still retain any vestige of military organisation. Two days later, King Friedrich Wilhelm IV agreed to these changes – it seemed as if the revolutionaries had won the day, at least as far as the cadet corps was concerned.[19]

However, the liberals' high expectations of the King's willingness and capacity to introduce a new era of political reform, which would pave the way for a relaxation of class distinctions and a diminution of the nobles' monopoly on political influence, were soon shattered. After the King's refusal to submit to the demands of the army and of his brother, Prince Wilhelm (the future King and Kaiser Wilhelm I), to put down the revolution by force, the Prussian '*Militairpartei*' were even more concerned to preserve their position and ensure that the cadet-school question, the '*Kadettenhausfrage*', would be resolved to their satisfaction.[20] Military journals such as the *Wehrzeitung* mounted campaigns against all the proposed military reforms, including the abolition of the cadet corps,[21] and Prince Wilhelm lent his weight to their protests,[22] proclaiming at one point that, if the King got rid of free places at the cadet schools, he himself would fund them – to the tune of 6000 Thalers a year – out of his own pocket.[23] This obstructive criticism of the reforms was evidently successful in wearing Friedrich Wilhelm down,[24] and by 1850 all the most radical plans for reform had been watered down or abandoned, following the resignation of Ernst von Pfuel.[25] Ultimately, even these were sabotaged by the conservative cadet-corps commanders, so that the only remnant of the revolutionary reforms lay in the euphemistic renaming of each *Voranstalt* Commander as a 'Director', and each officer commanding a company as an *Abteilungsvorsteher* (section headmaster). The original titles were reinstated in 1862.[26]

During the whole of this period, the officer corps and the liberal revolutionaries were conducting a battle of pamphlets concerning the pros and cons of cadet-school education.[27] Foremost among these was an anonymous pamphlet entitled *Das Kadettenkorps sonst und jetzt* (1848), which one reviewer described in the *Militair-Literatur-Zeitung* as concerning nothing less than the struggle of the military value system against the newly-founded liberal party-state.[28] In sum, the pamphlet's author claims that all the reformers' criticisms are based on entirely false premises. The headings of the first section nicely summarise his rebuttal of these: 'The cadet corps is no longer an aristocratic institution' (p. 5); 'The cadet corps is no longer a mere vocational school, but teaches to the standard of a

Realgymnasium' (p. 12); 'Preferential treatment of cadets as opposed to officer-aspirants from the ranks has ceased' (p. 14); 'The cadets can dedicate themselves to any other career than that of the military' (p. 15). In any case, the author argues that the cadet schools are vital to protect Prussia's time-honoured glory in warfare (p. 21).

In general, the adherents of the '*Militairpartei*' were unprepared even to entertain the possibility that the cadet corps might have any flaws – still less to learn any lessons from the upheavals and vilifications of 1848.[29] If the schools had ever conformed to the critics' stereotypes, they would argue, then that had been long ago, and had no bearing on present-day debates.

Interestingly, such refutations of the tribulations of cadet-corps life may also have had an influence upon the deployment of the Spartan *topos* by the schools' first historian, Adolf von Crousaz, sometime Captain and Company Commander of the Tenth Infantry Regiment. Published less than ten years after the revolution, Crousaz's *Geschichte des Königlich Preußischen Kadetten-Corps, nach seiner Entstehung, seinem Entwicklungsgange und seinen Resultaten* was intended as 'a literary monument to the glorious King of Prussia', which would prove the extraordinary contribution of the cadet corps to the Prussian military spirit and the military intellect of the Fatherland, celebrating the achievements of the brilliant men who had been educated there.[30]

In his depiction of the cadet corps under King Friedrich Wilhelm I and his son, Frederick the Great, Crousaz repeatedly comments upon the 'Spartan' qualities of the cadets' way of life in the eighteenth century. He describes the first cadets as being subjected to Spartan strictness (*Spartanischen Strenge*) in order to knock off their rough edges,[31] and in his conclusion to the chapter entitled '*Das Kadetten-Corps unter König Friedrich Wilhelm I*', remarks that:

> The men from the school of the cadet corps in its infancy were without scholarship and refinement, but full of circumspection and intelligence, full of soldierly routine, full of drive and morality. One is aware that these were fruits of the ground in which they were raised; one sees that this sphere of education was strong and simple, without intellectual pleasures, but it certainly developed healthy heads and hearts. A Spartan education was at odds with the interests of gentility, and is also not always possible in all centuries, but it always provides good soldiers, and was at that time the only means to the end.[32]

In the next chapter, comparing this situation with that of cadets under Frederick the Great, he writes:

> At that time the Cadet Corps was a half-monastic, half-Spartan institution, excellent in training and vigour, but without intellectual vitality, without

> outside attractions. All the teaching consisted of mechanical and elementary exercises; the staff were devoid of scholarship and inconsequential, the system of punishment iron-hard; one lived closely packed together, the house was in a shameful condition etc. One trained excellent men, exactly like those which once the Lycurgan Constitution had also trained, but it was still a bleak view, insufficient to the demands of the human spirit.[33]

It seems highly probable that Crousaz has used the Spartan *topos* in this way in order to deflect criticism in the same manner as the author of *Das Kadetten-Corps sonst und jetzt*. When used by the cadet corps' foes, the *topos* could have a potentially damaging propagandistic effect (as will be demonstrated below). Therefore, in the aftermath of the revolution, and given the cadet schools' lack of cooperation with or support for liberal policies, it might have seemed safer – at least in an official publication – to link the cadet schools' Spartanism most explicitly with their earliest days. At the same time, the implicit link of the cadet-corps education with Spartan virtues more generally, and the continuities which Crousaz's history portrays with corps life in his own day, could still have made an impression on those who knew of the schools' contemporary reputation as '*Neu-Sparta*'.[34]

However, in the following decade, the cadet corps was to face renewed challenges and threats to its existence, to which at least one commentator would counterpose a more explicitly political appeal to the value of the Spartan paradigm. It is to this period that we shall now turn.

During the later 1850s and early 1860s, the Ministry of War constantly found itself in such a parlous financial state that the indexes of the parliamentary reports for this period often read 'For "Military Administration" (*Militairverwaltung*) see "Lack of Funds" (*Geldbedarf*)'. This was partly due to a series of prohibitively costly yet ineffective campaigns in the Crimea and in Schleswig-Holstein, and partly due to the army's perpetual plans for expansion. The new War Minister, Albrecht von Roon, himself a former cadet, increasingly perceived the role of the officer-elite as that of the 'Protector and Saviour of Monarchy and Order' from the bourgeois parliamentary powers.[35] In general, the nobility were gaining more influence in the highest echelons of the military than ever before, as those who had been educated as cadets from the time of Scharnhorst's reforms and onwards began to reach the top of the military ladder. These officers, and Roon in particular, felt that they owed their success to the cadet corps; they therefore wished to ensure that former cadets would continue to predominate in the officer corps by augmenting the number of cadet-school places on offer, and by improving the quality of the training. It was hoped that, even in competition with outside applicants, the cadets could then continue to find their way to the peak of the military organisation.[36] Only then would the army fulfil its true vocation as a regulatory force free from all *bürgerlich* inclinations, able both to quell the unruliness of bourgeois society, and to preserve the age-old relationship of mutual loyalty and dependence between the nobility and the crown.[37]

Yet, at the same time, the liberals were gaining so much ground in the House of Representatives (*Abgeordnetenhaus*) that, with the advent of the newly-formed *Deutsche Fortschrittspartei* (German Progress Party) in 1861, they actually held a majority. Matters soon came to a head between the army, the new King Wilhelm I, and the predominantly liberal parliament, in the constitutional crisis over Roon's proposed military reforms (the so-called *Heeres- und Verfassungskonflikt*) which began in that year, and which was only resolved by Bismarck in 1866.[38] In this atmosphere of heightened political antagonism, attitudes to the cadet corps soon became symbolic of deeper ideological stances or rifts. The fact that the liberal majority in the *Abgeordnetenhaus* had the power to veto the phenomenal sums which Roon wished them to grant towards the expansion of the cadet corps was a thorn in the side of both the King and the War Ministry, who believed that it was the Government's absolute duty to support any expenditure which lay in the army's interest.[39] Yet the funds demanded by the military administration for the proposed enlargement of the cadet corps (amounting to tens of thousands of Reichsthalers) were denied them not only in 1860, but also in 1861.[40] The acrimonious parliamentary debates on the subject ranged widely, often touching upon criticisms similar to those which the Frankfurt Parliament's *Fachkommission* (expert commission) had made in 1848: children should not be forced into a military career so young; the academic education provided by the cadet corps was insufficient; furthermore, the schools encouraged a caste mentality and were prejudiced against admitting middle-class pupils.[41]

By 1862, the liberals' hostility to the concept of the cadet corps, and to Roon's cavalier dismissal of their criticisms, could no longer be contained. The 'Commission for the Examination of the National Budget, concerning the Budget of the Military Administration for 1862' voted that the Government should transform all the cadet schools into civilian boarding schools (*Realschulen* and *Gymnasien*) and that they should be placed under the administration of the Minister of Education.[42] They considered the cadet schools to be not only anachronistic, superfluous, and inexpedient, but also positively detrimental to the intellect and characters of the boys whom they educated, as well as contradictory to the prevailing spirit of the country.[43] Once again, the cadet corps was fighting for its life, and the odds in favour of its survival seemed to be poor indeed.

On 20 September 1862, Government Commissioner General Karl Rudolf von Ollech (1811–1884) was requested by Roon to make a speech in parliament which would sweep away all such opposition.[44] It was hoped that Ollech, as a former cadet, former *Erzieher*, and now the current Commander of the Cadet Corps, could convince his hostile audience that it was in the public interest to retain the cadet corps in its current state, rather than to complete the work which the 1848 revolutionaries had left unfinished.

Fighting to be heard amongst constant cat-calls and disruption, Ollech first attempted to appeal to the principles of Frederick the Great, and all the other Prussian kings who had endorsed and supported the work of the cadet corps. Quoting the statutes of King Friedrich Wilhelm III, which stressed the necessity of the schools' military focus, he went on to emphasise the cadets' happy demeanour, and the lessons of fair leadership which their military education instilled in them, without which the officer corps could never have raised Prussia to greatness. Sarcastically, Ollech demanded of his listeners whether they thought that the cadets should be imbued instead with hatred and contempt for the army and their future careers, or whether they should be taught lawlessness and insurgency rather than discipline and order? He stressed that, since the cadet corps' foundation, there had not been a single battle fought by the Prussian army in which former cadets had not battled and bled alongside their troops. Accusations of aristocratic privilege and academic inadequacy in the corps he dismissed as mere poppycock: were his listeners suggesting that nobles should be shut out of the army, or that only the bourgeois should be allowed to be officers? The education provided was certainly academic, and furthermore was 'a true, through-and-through military training, with a fresh, lively spirit, just as King Friedrich Wilhelm III wished.' If the 'young sabres' in the corps were 'forged harshly', this was only so that they could lay down their lives, just as he himself would, to uphold the glory and greatness of the Prussian Fatherland.

Although Ollech's speech gained little or no respect from the majority of its parliamentary audience, its consequences were far-reaching. Roused to still further hatred by the liberals' mockery and ill-treatment of their champion, the '*Militairpartei*' proceeded to strengthen their stand against the powers of the parliamentarians. In the following spring, a 'Highest Cabinet Order' (*Allerhöchste Kabinettsordre*) was passed which effectively vetoed the bill passed by the 1862 commission, confirming that the military character of the cadets' education should in future be intensified.[45] All vacancies previously reserved for civilian teachers were to be given to military staff, and civilian tutors (known as *Gouverneurs*) were to be reduced in numbers and replaced with *Erzieher* from the officer corps.[46]

This controversy was widely commented upon, and soon led to the use of the Spartan *topos* as a vehicle for political justifications of the education provided by the schools, in the guise of former cadet August Gertner's volume commemorating the twenty-fifth anniversary of *Voranstalt* Bensberg in 1860, *Bensberg und sein Kadettenhaus* (published in 1862). Gertner came from a distinguished military family, and the work itself was dedicated to Crown Prince Wilhelm, in thanks for the patriotic spirit with which the cadet schools had imbued the author, and the education which he had received there (p. 8). The work consists of three sections: the first a topographical and historical exploration of the Bensberg region; the second a history of the cadet school; and the third dealing with 'legends and tales from the Bensberg region'.

In the second section, Gertner's discussion of the advantages and character of education in the cadet corps in general (and at *Voranstalt* Bensberg in particular) clearly engages with the criticisms which liberals were levelling at the corps at this time. However, one of the principal means by which Gertner defends the corps from accusations of untimely militarisation and academic insufficiency is to draw a direct parallel between the cadets' education and that employed in ancient Sparta:

> If the cadet corps is to achieve its goal, to be a nursery for the army's officer corps, then the entire physical and mental education of the cadets must be directed towards this goal from the outset. Even if special concern can only be dedicated to the military elements at the HKA in Berlin..., the provincial houses, since they create the basis of the entire cadet education, must make it their central task to give their pupils a practical military training, to have an additional effect on the development of the military spirit and to bring the first buds of soldierhood to unfold, by which the pupils will already at an early age be made accustomed to what must some day be the purpose of their lives... Military nature must merge into the flesh and blood, so that one is 'every inch' a soldier.
>
> So one must not be persuaded that there's always time for that when the pupils enter the Berlin house. When the Spartan youth became state property for their public education, its aim was toughening, efficiency in war, and patriotic feeling, and what other aim does the cadet house have? We recall here the proverb 'he who wants to excel must start early'.
>
> Therefore, in a sense, the cadet school must be considered a Spartan institution. This really does not rule out the fact that, regarding the principle of practical military training, the pupils at the [*Voranstalten*] are capable at a tender age of suffering commensurate restrictions... Although a certain onesidedness is unavoidable, it will be found everywhere...when one...is dealing with a particular vocational training which aims to achieve a specific goal. The cadet corps educates its pupils for military service. Not only will they be trained in the sense that this is their future; on the one point of

> soldierliness they will concentrate in all their deeds and thoughts, and will early be accustomed to self-control, military discipline, obedience and order. As sons of soldiers and militarily schooled, they will one day see the regiment as their cradle and service as their homeland...
>
> [However], regarding the cadet-corps curriculum, [the reproach that the corps destroys individuality and is nothing but a breaking-in] is utterly groundless, since the curriculum is practically identical to that of the *Realgymnasium*. Thus, henceforth, there is absolutely no disadvantage in pupils leaving the cadet corps with the aim of following a career other than the military – if, for a people like the Prussians, who should and must be a 'people in arms', a military education of youth can be called a disadvantage. And when the first memory of a boy is none other than of his father's sword, then the sword will become for him the particular aim of all his striving and his ideas; he will hold true to this aim, even unto the bounds of possibility.[47]

Although Gertner's work might not have enjoyed a particularly wide readership beyond the Cologne region, this passage is certainly of interest, since it represents the first extant instance of the cadet schools' identification with Sparta being used in an explicitly politicised context, as well as presupposing a widespread knowledge of and sympathy for Spartan *mores* among his readership. Gertner is setting out a programme for the schools which is deliberately designed to allay sceptics' fears and to dispel the liberal criticisms which had been levelled at the corps in parliament, and he evidently believes that an appeal to Sparta as paradigm will convince his readers of the value of his argument. Ultimately, the implication is that Prussia needs cadets who have been raised in Spartan fashion if she is to fulfil her military potential.

During the remainder of the decade, the military continued to consolidate their position, and the influence of civilian teachers in the cadet schools steadily decreased. Bismarck's victory over the liberals in the *Verfassungskonflikt* (constitutional crisis), along with the military successes of the Prussian Army in 1864–1866, led to the silencing of the cadet corps' liberal opponents, who were forced to accept the expansion of the corps with two new *Voranstalten*, Oranienstein (1867) and Plön (1868). The military's newly-restored prestige, won by cadet-school alumni in the wars with Denmark and Austria, meant that politicians who opposed these costly building projects could be accused of pacifism, lack of patriotism, or insufficient gratitude to the soldiers who had given their lives for them.[48] German Unification as such made little difference to the running of the cadet schools or to the aims of their commanders – it merely meant that further *Voranstalten* could be established beyond the boundaries of Prussia.

Even though plans for a new, bigger HKA in Berlin-Lichterfelde were initially opposed due to their exorbitant cost (2.46 million Thalers when first proposed), this opposition was overcome once the authorities calculated that the old HKA in the Friedrichstraße could be sold off for 1 million Thalers, reducing the cost of the new building to a mere 1.46 million.[49] Schmitz believes that this lack of opposition can in part be ascribed to the rise of 'social militarisation' in all political parties, even the liberal parties, so that they too accepted that a military educational institution should be granted special status.[50]

By 1900, two further *Voranstalten* had been founded in Karlsruhe and Naumburg an der Saale respectively, and extended facilities had also been built for the schools at Köslin and Potsdam.[51] Although opposition to the cadet schools was to reappear once the newly-decriminalised Social Democratic Party had begun to make headway, the political discussions surrounding the cadet corps in the last decade of the nineteenth century were mainly of a rather different – and generally more positive – nature.[52]

Between 1873 and 1890, German educators had generally divided into two camps, the first claiming that the humanistic education offered by the *Gymnasien* could be the only true guarantee of academic worth, and the second wishing to introduce a common framework for all secondary education which would dethrone the *Gymnasien* from their privileged position as the principal purveyors of the qualifications needed to proceed to higher education.[53] People began to speak of a '*Schulkrieg*' (educational war) or '*Schulkampf*' (educational battle), and it was becoming increasingly obvious that there was a pressing need for more focused debate on these issues than the discussions in the House of Representatives (mainly concerning budgetary matters) could provide.[54] Since the cadet schools had held the status of a *Realschule* since 1877, it was in their interest to ensure that the supporters of the *Gymnasien* should not win this battle hands down. From this perspective, they had one unbeatable ace up their sleeve – the unconditional support of the Kaiser.

Wilhelm II wanted his schools to be filled with fit, well trained, disciplined young men, not bespectacled swots overburdened with Greek grammar. He believed that subjects which contributed to military expertise (such as modern languages, sciences and maths) should be emphasised over the Classics.[55] In speeches, and in his 'Highest Cabinet Order' (*Allerhöchste Kabinettsordre*) concerning the cadet-school curricula (13 February 1889), the Kaiser set out what many saw as a programme for thoroughgoing educational reform.[56] He called for an emphasis on practical subjects, and for the propagation of a cultural outlook which exalted Germany's greatness while emphasising the wickedness, ruinousness and impracticality of Social Democratic politics. The school was to become the 'battlefield' on which all Socialist and Communist views would be combatted.[57]

Conservative voters and members of the press were instantly impressed by the Kaiser's engagement with such pressing contemporary social problems so soon after his accession, and the ramifications of the cabinet order were widely debated.[58] Surely Wilhelm's educational decrees and plans for the cadet corps must apply, *mutatis mutandis*, to the *Gymnasien* as well?[59] Some saw such programmatic and detailed intervention in school curricula as posing a constitutional danger,[60] while others argued that it would be eminently desirable if the Kaiser were to lay out as detailed a plan of reform for the entire secondary-school system as he had for the cadet corps.[61] Still others, in particular supporters of the *Realgymnasien* or the '*lateinlose Einheitsschulen*' (Latin-less comprehensive schools) were filled with optimism by the Kaiser's evident endorsement of an institution which followed the curriculum of a *Realgymnasium* and did not teach Greek.[62] From being a reviled and academically vilified institution, the cadet corps had suddenly become a beacon of hope for those hoping to crush the 'gymnasial monopoly' (*Gymnasialmonopol*). Furthermore, due to the cadet schools' patronage by Germany's first 'educator King', their representatives were now guaranteed a leading role in the proceedings of the educational reform conferences – and hence could exert a significant influence over the future of German education as a whole.

In the very first words which he spoke at the school conference in December 1890, the Kaiser made it clear that, as far as he was concerned, a militarily oriented education was in no way to be considered a disadvantage: 'I seek soldiers... We want to raise an athletic generation who will serve the Fatherland as intellectual leaders and administrators.'[63] Throughout the sessions, the cadet schools were held up as a pattern for the education system of the future. It was argued that the highest, most important and most responsible career to which young Germans could aspire was that for which the cadet schools educated their pupils.[64] As a type of *Realschule* which achieved good results on its own terms, the cadet schools were hailed as a set of '*Musteranstalten*', or prototypes for further reform. Thus, in the first session of the conference, when one Dr. Uhlig was trying to make a case for humanistic education, he did so by explicitly identifying the *Gymnasien* with the cadet schools:

> The cadet schools are rightly famed as institutions from which excellent officers emerge, partly because their pupils are instilled with a military sense from earliest youth. Now, Gentlemen, I believe it would be no false comparison if one were to call the *Gymnasien* the cadet schools of the

universities, and, inasmuch as the ambition of the *Gymnasien* is to prepare for studies at university, if they were to be constrained by other curricula, they would provide a less adequate preparation for academic studies.[65]

At a later sitting, Dr. Paulsen, taking an opposing view, praised the cadet schools as awakening that enthusiasm for Kaiser and Reich, King and Fatherland, which the *Gymnasien* were incapable of developing.[66]

Meanwhile, other supporters of the *Realschulen* saw the cadet schools as a truly 'realistic' type of *Realgymnasium*; since they had developed so well under the Kaiser's guidance, then surely all other *Realgymnasien* could do no better than to follow their lead:

> [Just as the cadet schools do,] we wish to educate pupils who will embrace the exigencies of contemporary life, and if Officers need no Greek, then ultimately our pupils cannot really need it either.[67]

In further discussions concerning the evils of *Überbürdung* (overburdening) in the *Gymnasien*, Gymnasiasts' general unsuitability for military service was compared unfavourably with the cadets' eminent suitability. The cadets' eyesight was better, they were physically fitter and healthier, and they already met the highest criteria of war readiness both in body and soul – the supreme aim of German youth.[68]

However, when it was the turn of the representatives of the military administration to put their views on the subject forward, Major Fleck chose to intersperse his depiction of the spirit of healthful military exercise which the cadet schools imparted with reference to Greek examples:

> The cadets' clothing is calculated to provide protection against the weather whilst simultaneously aiming to impart a reasonable toughening... The food is tasty and sufficient, but very simple. As far as drink is concerned, we pay homage to the principle: *ariston men to hudōr* (water is best)... This simple nourishment is extraordinarily beneficial not just for the body, but also for moral education... The youth learns that one can also be happy without dissipation!... Only when all powers work together for the hygiene of body and soul, only then will we reach that which the Greeks held up as the aim of all education: '*kalokagathia*' (nobility and bravery).[69]

That such a portrayal should bring visions of Spartan education to mind may well have been no accident, for in the fourth session, the Major had concluded a speech on the value of modern languages by stressing that, at least as far as the army was concerned, the roots of German success were not merely Greek, but specifically Spartan:

> We too wish the young man who enters our ranks to be equipped with a harmonious education of his intellect, heart and character, and we too wish him to be conscious of the position of his Fatherland among modern

> cultured peoples, so that he can grasp his own time and its tasks, but also so that he does not forget what the roots of our culture are. In a nutshell, in peacetime we are creators, educators, and teachers; in wartime we are commanders. For this, we need men who are thoroughly imbued with the highest ideals, and who will never forget that the great spirit which swept over the battlefields of Vionville and Gravelotte was the same one which could be sensed around all the crags of Thermopylae: '*O xein', aggellein Lakedaimoniois hoti tēde keimetha tois keinōn rhēmasi peithomenoi.*' ('Go, tell the Spartans, stranger passing by, that here, obedient to their laws, we lie.')[70]

Here, we have an example – in an official and highly politicised context – of a cadet-corps official portraying the Spartan spirit of Thermopylae as something which a cadet must never forget, an inspiration for those victories which had led to '*Preußens Gloria*' and the founding of the Second Reich. At the same time, the cries of 'Bravo!' which greeted Fleck's peroration suggest that a great many of the delegates agreed with his sentiments, and that, when they went on to praise the military, patriotic spirit which the cadet corps instilled, they might have been in some sense endorsing the Spartan elements of that education also.

At the conclusion of his closing speech, the Kaiser himself picked up on Fleck's words, using the historical treatment of Thermopylae as a symbol for the sort of change which he wished to encourage in Germany's schools:

> Previously, if I may put it thus, the way led from Thermopylae via Cannae to Rossbach and Vionville. I will lead the young from Sedan and Gravelotte, via Leuthen and Rossbach, back to Mantinea and Thermopylae. I believe that that is the right way, the way which we and our youth must take.[71]

*

In general terms, Wilhelm's educational reforms soon came to fruition. Curricula were reformed in all schools, from the *Volksschulen* (elementary schools) upwards, to reflect his views on politics, the importance of German culture, and physical fitness. By the time of the second school conference in 1900, the *Gymnasien* were fighting a losing battle, and Wilhelm even intervened in curricular reforms planned by the *Kultusministerium* (Ministry of Culture), in order to allow cadets to take up further study in medicine and law without needing to study Greek or take additional Latin lessons.[72] Thus, royal patronage of the cadet corps had increasingly led to far-reaching changes in the academic and social structure of the German educational system, paving the path to professional careers not only for cadets unsuited to military life, but for middle-class school leavers who would previously have been unable to fulfil the required language qualifications for higher education. Not only had the 'cadet-school question' proved as pressing as the '*Gymnasium* question', but it had eventually become inextricably bound up with it.

Yet the underlying identification of the cadet corps with Sparta would not be eradicated by any of these reforms. During the first decades of the twentieth century, its political significance would continue to increase, whilst also becoming the subject of controversy and contemptuous criticism in left-wing circles.

Anti-militarist attitudes: Sparta as a byword for brutality in liberal and socialist thought

The rise of anti-militarist sentiment towards the turn of the twentieth century meant that, despite the Kaiser's support for the cadet schools, they came increasingly under attack in certain liberal and socialist milieux, where literary weapons such as satire and the 'cautionary tale' could be deployed in order to vilify and destabilise the legitimising power of the Spartan model. This can be seen in part as an attack upon the Establishment endorsement of the Spartan paradigm discernible in the official or semi-official sources discussed in the previous section.

One of the earliest manifestations of this tendency can be found in the well-known Bavarian satirist Ludwig Thoma's second set of *Lausbubengeschichten* (Tales of a Little Rascal), entitled *Tante Frieda*, which was first published in 1906. Starring one of Thoma's most successful comic creations, a Bavarian 'Just William' figure also named Ludwig, the *Lausbubengeschichten* were an instant success, and were widely read throughout the twentieth century.[73] The final tale in *Tante Frieda*, '*Hauptmann* Semmelmaier', features a satirical depiction of Prussian military education which takes particular pleasure in mocking its 'Spartan' pretensions.[74]

In the story, Ludwig's parents have despaired of his bad behaviour, and decide that the only solution is to consign him to the care of Captain Semmelmaier, whose newspaper advertisement claims that his school can reform all unruly boys and instil in them an iron sense of duty (*eisernes Pflichtgefühl*). At an interview with Ludwig and his anxious mother, Semmelmaier lies to her, telling her that his old boys are always coming back to thank him for making them into useful members of society. However, a friend of Ludwig's family called Heiß, when informed about the new plan for Ludwig's future, hopes that Semmelmaier is not in fact the same man as an extraordinarily stupid Lieutenant, Joseph Semmelmaier, with whom he served in the War, who was nicknamed the '*Hornpepi*' because he always hid whenever there was shooting. His mother says that would be impossible, but when Ludwig gets to the boarding school he discovers from his new-found friend Max that the captain's Christian name is Joseph, so he must surely be the same man.

'By the time I had been there a month,' 'Ludwig' writes,

> I had seen enough to know that I didn't like it at Semmelmaier's at all. They gave us terribly little to eat, and when I said that I was hungry, he lectured me on how he didn't know how Germany could continue to exist when its youth were so ungrateful. He had not eaten or drunk for three days, when he was in the war, and on the fourth day that there was no meat, only dust and lead, he had not made anything of it, because he loved the Fatherland. And if the young wanted to eat all the time, things must go badly for Germany. And then he would go to the pub again. He bought lots of beer with the money which he got from our parents...
>
> Every Sunday we only get flour soup (*Brennsuppe*), and Semmelmaier said that he is testing us, to see if we are Spartans.
>
> We are not Spartans, however, and it always made me so hungry that I wrote home about it.

Ludwig's mother writes back saying that she has told Semmelmaier of his complaint; perhaps he didn't realise how big Ludwig's appetite was. Semmelmaier calls him to his office, and gives him a ferocious telling-off for lying about how hungry he is. He points to one of his decorations, and asks Ludwig what he thinks it is. When Ludwig replies simply 'brass', he gets extremely angry:

> He said that it was a decoration from the highest Commander-in-Chief, and if I thought that people won it when they wrote complaints home about flour soup, then I was wrong. Instead, one must be a Spartan and make sacrifices and sweat and freeze and stare death in the face. One gained it because one was a courageous Spartan, and he had to train the boys so that they would some day win this decoration, and we must eat flour soup every Sunday because it was a preparation for war. He said that he wanted to give us kidneys every day, and it would give him pleasure if we ate lots of them, but he could not, because then we would not become Spartans, only self-indulgent boys. And he would have to write to my mother and tell her that he could give no guarantees for me if I wanted to eat lots of kidneys all the time.
>
> [In the next letter from Ludwig's mother, she tells him that] the Captain had explained everything; it is not because of miserliness that we have to eat flour soup, but it is part of the training, and I should not complain, but be glad that I am with a man who will turn me into a Spartan.

Thoma's satire is noteworthy in one sense because it implies that Prussian adulation of Spartan models of discipline and frugality was sufficiently widespread and well known to attract the attention of non-Prussians, and that these Spartan pretensions could be mocked throughout Germany to great humorous effect. However, when viewed from the perspective of

Thoma's pre-war left-liberal political views and his strong Prussophobe sentiments (frequently demonstrated in his contributions to the satirical periodicals *Simplicissimus* and *März*, which he edited), one might suggest that he was also using his knowledge of the cadet schools' self-identification with Sparta to disseminate a specifically anti-militarist, anti-Prussian message. The character of Semmelmaier himself, with his stupidity, ceaseless hypocrisy and obsessive laconophilia, can be read as embodying precisely those elements of Prussia which Thoma hated most: her chauvinism and her '*pickelhaube* militarism'.

Whether or not such sentiments were connected with the Spartan trope in anti-militarist literature more generally, remains to be seen.[75] However, given the popularity of the *Lausbubengeschichten* throughout the rule of the German Empire, it seems likely that Thoma's portrayal of Semmelmaier's academy might well have both reflected and influenced public perceptions of Prussian military education.

In general, Thoma's work fits into a pattern of anti-militarist thought which had first appeared in the 1860s, when the idea of German unification began to gain momentum. All the political groups opposed to a *kleindeutsch* solution of the unification problem (that is, German unification without Austria) had shared a common horror of the Prussian army's 'militarism', even if they could not agree precisely on what this meant.[76] As Nicholas Stargardt has noted, South Germans in particular

> regarded Prussia from the outside[,] and had least trouble linking the garrison state with the ordinary lives of its citizens via the conveyor belts of police-minded rules and regulations, military service and 'blind obedience' to superior officers. Not surprisingly, they were most concerned to forestall their own inclusion in this 'ruthless' system.[77]

However, after Unification, anti-militarist rhetoric became much more the preserve of the Social Democratic Party,[78] who were keen to exploit any military scandals or controversies as grist to their political mill[79] – including those which concerned the cadet corps. Having been subjected to a period of 'draconian' repression during the 1870s and 1880s,[80] in 1912 the Social Democrats went on to become the largest-polling party in Germany, and Prussia became 'the stamping-ground of Europe's largest and best-organised socialist movement'.[81] The socialists were well aware that officers and soldiers alike had long been indoctrinated against the 'poison of Social Democracy',[82] and one contemporary analysis of the cadet corps by the Social Democratic Party declared that the corps 'makes from the children...soldiers of true Prussian worth and character – human machines who endure the highest possible hardships without a murmur [and] blindly obey the commands of their superiors.'[83] In practice, this meant that any hostility towards the cadet corps – as expressed in publications such as the anonymous pamphlet *Unsere Kadettenkorps* (1894), or in anti-military novels of the period – were dismissed by the cadet schools' supporters as libellous socialist filth.[84]

That the political danger of such exposures was felt keenly by the authorities at the schools themselves is implied by a passage from Fritz von Unruh's autobiographical novel *Der Sohn des Generals* (1957), in which one of the cadets at Plön runs away, is caught, put under arrest, and promptly hangs himself.[85] The Corps Captain's first reaction to his initial disappearance is not concern for his fate, but for the reputation of the school:

> 'A scandal!... If only the *Plöner Wochenblatt* won't find out about it! Otherwise the editor will bring it to the attention of the *Reichstag* straight away! And then of course the Berlin press will have it said that our Plön is a "Torture-Institution", where your Captain pricks you with redhot needles every Sunday. Eh? What! These damned Sozis! They're gaining ever more ground...'[86]

When the editor of the local paper does hear of the affair, he reacts with righteous anger to the idea that the Commander wishes to suppress his report – in any case, censorship would be fruitless, since he has already received a good dozen telegrams about the affair from the Plön *Reichstag* representative.[87] After the scandal has died down somewhat, the Captain tries to ensure that the younger cadets are not being bullied by their *Stubenältesten*, not because he really cares for their welfare, however, but merely because he fears further bad publicity: '"The eyes of the *Reichstag* are watching us. The Social Democrats have their spies everywhere."'[88]

The cruelty of the cadet-corps regime therefore became a frequent theme whenever socialists wished to make political headway against the Establishment. However, it was not until after the red revolutionaries' dissolution and overthrow of the Monarchy and the Establishment in November 1918 that it became open season for the cadet schools' detractors. From 1919 onwards, a steady stream of socialistically-minded publications which portrayed the schools in a peculiarly unfavourable light began to appear – at least three of which made explicit mention of the corps' 'spartanism' as a key component in its day-to-day ritualisation of brutality.[89]

*

Fig. 19. The front cover of Hans-Joachim Freiherr von Reitzenstein's *Vergitterte Jugend* (1920).

One of the most harrowing of these publications is a collection of cautionary tales of cadet-school life by writer and sometime cadet Hans-Joachim Freiherr von Reitzenstein (1881–1935), entitled *Vergitterte Jugend* (Youth behind Bars). Though partly written before the war,[90] the collection was completed in 1919 and published the following year. That the stories are indeed autobiographical is confirmed by an interview which Reitzenstein gave to the prominent left-wing journalist, author and satirist, Kurt Tucholsky (1890–1935), shortly after the work's publication. When asked whether the book's novelistic framework had still allowed him to engage with the realities of his erstwhile life at the cadet corps, Reitzenstein told Tucholsky that 'the reality had been a thousand times more gruesome' and that the fictional form had by no means 'severed his connection with the truth'. Rather, the stories simply contained 'the most lamentable and brutish torments which cadets inflicted upon each other, atrocities of an almost chronic degree, completely backed up by military education and the military system.'[91]

In his foreword, Reitzenstein characterises '*Kadettentum*' (cadet-hood) as a sort of serfdom, an unsavoury fossil of times long past, a type of servitude and subordination that may have been necessary in ancient and medieval German times, but which has no place in modern society. Reitzenstein argues instead for a Utopian ideal of socialist peace and brotherhood, in which people will laugh at the very idea that there ever existed a 'youth behind bars'. The 'spirit' of those bars leaves cadets devoid of humanity and the 'spirit of life'; indeed, it symbolises all the cadet corps' faults – its monarchist sycophancy, its lack of proper education, its blind unthinking obedience and arrogant pride – all of which are unnecessary now that Prussia is no longer surrounded by powerful enemies or fighting the Seven Years' War.[92]

Many of the tales in the collection can be interpreted as providing a systematic debunking of all the arguments with which the cadet corps' supporters were accustomed to defend the institution. In the first story, entitled *Kameradschaft* (comradeship), a new boy (nicknamed the '*Gehirnathlet*' [brainbox] because he has recently joined the corps from a *Gymnasium*) is about to take a beating for his lack of '*Kameradschaft*' because he refuses to let all his classmates copy his maths homework. Amazingly, the *Gehirnathlet* manages to persuade his ignorant and venal companions that their entire honour code (in which cheating is *de rigueur*, but asking the teacher for help is a sign of weakness) is dangerous hogwash. However, after the teacher punishes the class because he cannot be bothered to explain the maths problems to them, the class turn on the *Gehirnathlet* and beat him within an inch of his life.[93]

In another story, *Die Ehre der Sexta* (The Honour of the Sexta), the ten-

or eleven-year-old ego-narrator is about to undergo a similar beating because he has besmirched his comrades' honour by bringing his beloved teddy bear to school. An inquisition takes place, at which his classmates ask him the burning question 'But what do you *do* with it!?'. In answer, he makes the bear march around as it might do in the wild, then stands it up like a man and makes it do funny things, losing himself in his make-believe. The others are fascinated and for a brief time they become nothing but 'happy, laughing children'. The final judgement is that the bear is '*ein durchaus schicker Apparat*' (a thoroughly nifty piece of kit), but there is a danger that other classes will 'misunderstand' if it is discovered in their *Stube*. The narrator says that he must send it home, at which all the boys are disappointed, wishing to touch it one last time. They make a bed for the bear in a beautiful box in which it will be packed, giving it various gifts (a scented pillow, a china dog and a tiny infantry sabre) to keep it company, in a moving but unacknowledged ceremony of farewell to childhood.[94] The tale as a whole exemplifies one of the collection's leitmotifs, highlighting the dichotomy between the brutality of an institution which forces the cadets to feign contempt for childish things when they are still of an age to be fascinated by them, and the sadness of that lost innocence of which they have far too soon been robbed.

Other stories in the collection deal with the utter hypocrisy and powerlessness of the cadet-school authorities in the face of cruelty and ill-doing – they know what goes on but close their eyes to it – and its corollary, the poisonous power of superiors who give unfair punishments which lead to a chain reaction or 'avalanche' of unfair treatment, all the way down the hierarchy of command. There are also treatments of the pernicious influences of homoeroticism in the corps, leading in one case to a suicide, and of older cadets' entrapment by prostitutes. In total, the twelve stories in the collection contain two suicides, three instances of cadets being beaten or bullied until they are in a critical condition, and countless instances of cruel and pointless punishments.

In the final story, *Material*, a new teacher called Dr. Michael, fresh from the '*Penne*' (civilian school), and filled with humanity and Social Democratic ideas, manages to win over the cadets' hearts and minds. However, he is instantly dismissed for teaching them that democracy need not be evil, and that there is 'a little bit of Social Democrat in everyone'.[95] The Major who has sacked him tells him that, as far as the cadet schools (and their history textbooks) are concerned, the year 1848 never existed:

> 'Your duty...should have been to educate...officers and nothing but officers, who keep their gaze rigidly fixed on the narrow path of their duty, without looking to left and right...'[96]

Dr. Michael realises that the cadet school is nothing but a factory for fanatical career-officers, and that his mistake lay in believing otherwise, and trying to make the boys think for themselves.[97] Nowhere are Reitzenstein's Social Democratic leanings more apparent than in this story, and in some ways Dr. Michael is the most sympathetically-drawn character in the collection.

However, it is one of the tales at the work's heart which deals explicitly with the evils endured in the name of cadet-school '*Spartanertum*'. One of the longest stories in the collection, it is entitled simply 'Sparta'.[98]

The story begins with Dallwitz, an arrogant *Stubenältester*, boasting to his peers about his power to make the cadets in his charge do anything he tells them. He invites the other *Stubenältesten* to pay him a visit that evening, to witness his methods in practice. He starts off his exhibition of cruelty with a number of typical trials – forcing the younger boys to swallow a dried-up piece of bacon on a string, which is pulled out of each boy's gullet and given to the next one, or making them curl their hands into 'cats' paws', and beating them with a cane. The other *Stubenältesten* aren't yet very impressed – that's all small beer, the kind of thing which they had had inflicted upon them a couple of years before. But then Dallwitz decides to create a tableau...

The two biggest cadets are chosen to be the 'Brandenburg Gate', the rest, from the deputy *Stubenältester* down to the smallest cadet, are the 'Lindens'. The Brandenburg Gate pair have to bend over, curved, so that their fingertips are just touching in the middle. On top, Dallwitz lays a heavy oak board, and puts on top of it inkpots and the most fragile knick-knacks from their cupboards. The 'Lindens' he makes stand on their heads in straight rows leading in two lines towards the 'Brandenburg Gate', decorating the soles of their feet with inkpots, knick-knacks, lightbulbs, glasses and similar ornaments, so that if they even move a muscle, and let the knick-knacks fall, they will be punished by the authorities for making a mess.

Dallwitz regards his handiwork, pleased – his audience can't deny that this is his own individual artistic creation. The tapering arch of the Brandenburg Gate gives the whole a pleasing moral aspect. Holding the tableau positions becomes more and more uncomfortable for the cadets, but none dare move.

> 'Tell me how you came up with that,' asked one of the guests.
> 'You know, I really can't say,' said Dallwitz, 'I find tableaux so dignified...'
> 'How long,' asked another, 'before they keel over?'
> 'That depends,' Dallwitz informed him. 'We've done up to ten minutes in the past.'

'Now that I don't believe!'

'You can wait that long.' Dallwitz knew he could rely on his *Stube*. Admittedly, it had taken enough trouble. Then his gaze fell on the smallest of them all, who had been left over and had remained idle all this time, as if he would rather have stolen away. When his eye was caught, something like terror flitted over his childish face, then he lowered his eyes. Perhaps he would get away with it.

'Schmeling!' The little one cringed. So, he would not. Ah well, it would soon pass. He came and stood in front of Dallwitz.

It seemed to his guests as if Dallwitz had suddenly forgotten something. With a sickly, morose expression he stood next to his desk, and his eyes glittered with an urgent, undetermined desire. There was something predatory in it. Now he grabbed a penholder and held the nib under the glow of the table-lamp. A smell of varnish began to spread, and the metal became red right up to the wood.

'Raise your hand!' commanded Dallwitz, and approached Schmeling.

A remarkable transformation had come over him. Every trace of fear and humanity seemed to have fallen from him. Quickly and mechanically, like an obedient robot, he stretched his right hand in front of him. He stared straight in front of him with a completely uninterested expression, and his eyes gazed unmovingly past the whole thing, somewhere into the distance.

Dallwitz stepped forward, and pressed the pen-nib, sizzling, into the hard little palm of his hand.

'Had enough?' he asked, after the pen had cooled down a little.

'No,' answered Schmeling imperturbably.

'Will you sneak?'

'No,' came the peaceable reply.

Then Dallwitz pulled the pen slowly from his flesh, and, almost as if bored, Schmeling let his hand drop. Then he turned so sharply that his heels clicked, and was dismissed. In the corner by his cupboard he hastily wiped his brow, bothered by a couple of sweat-beads. For him, the matter was over.

Somewhat sheepishly, the three guests stood to one side. One had gone rather pale and walked slowly to the door. The second said, *sotto voce*,

'Good night, then,' and followed him. The third said, somewhat forced:

'Even Old Nick could learn something from you...' Then he disappeared with the others.

Meanwhile, Dallwitz seemed to have found a response. With a nervous agitation he waited until the door had closed. Then he let the deputy *Stubenältester* release the 'Lindens' and the 'Brandenburg Gate', and with an abrupt command transformed the motionless composition back into humans, uniformed children, swaying a little as they took their seats...

'You did fairly well. Your good luck, that none of you made a fool of me,' said Dallwitz, somewhat unsure of himself. 'And that was also my goodbye present to you – so that you don't forget me during the long holiday.' That sounded insulting and sarcastic as ever.[99]

Now the scene changes to the Schmeling family dinner table. Schmeling's mother would much rather have kept him at home, but as a widow with three children (two daughters as well as a son) she had too much to cope with – and everyone knows that a boy needs a strong hand. Yet she is wretched to see how pale and thin he looks – and why is he picking at his food with his fingers like that? She seizes his hand, which appears to be swollen, and finds 'a hideous, suppurating wound, whose edges had turned black.' Schmeling is furious at the fuss, pushing away from her angrily; when questioned, he shouts: 'For goodness' sake, I'm no infant who goes running to someone when he makes a slip and pricks himself with his pen!'[100]

By the end of the holiday, Schmeling's hand is almost healed as good as new – but the deep scar would stay with him forever.

> In fact, the hand ought to have been cut off, but he had fought against that with all his might. To be an invalid of state at only eleven would have been a big mistake. He would rather take the risks. So the wound was burnt out, and the long beautiful days of the holiday were taken up with the treatment. The hand was saved, and he had borne all the miserable pain without turning a hair. One just couldn't talk to him, though, because he had become insolent and petulant once again.[101]

One evening, his mother tries to get to the bottom of his moodiness, trying to get him to tell her his woes. Perhaps it's because he's sad to be away from the corps, she asks?

> No reply. Then she saw that his chin was trembling slightly. She lifted his head – his eyes were dry and stared fixedly past her.
>
> 'Fritzel,' she said, gently, softly. And at her tone of voice, the young Spartan's resolve cracked. His mouth opened and sucked in ever more air. His face became immeasurably crumpled; quickly, he began to weep, just as very small, helpless children do.
>
> His mother held her arms out to him and took her chick onto her lap. And with the tears came all the laments, and with the laments all the terrors and fears of an afflicted child. His mother just sat there holding her child, stock-still with horror. And before the little boy's every sentence she had to swear that she would never tell, and never, ever sneak.
>
> 'But my child, my child...'
>
> 'Leave it, Mummy. He means well. He is only educating us in awe of our masters.'
>
> 'But my child, one word, and that bully will be expelled.'
>
> 'It wouldn't be any use, Mummy. Another one would just come along. And who knows what he would educate us in.'
>
> She fell silent, at a loss. Whatever could she do? She should just be happy that the spell had broken, and that her child was a child again. Fear gripped her. At this time on the day after tomorrow, it would begin again.

> 'Tell me, Fritzel, wouldn't you rather stay here with Mummy, where no one can do anything to you...?'
> 'Oh no, it would happen again.'
> Her fear weighed down on her ever more heavily.
> 'But Fritzel, my child, how can you bear it at all...?'
> 'Oh, Mummy, here we go again,' he said softly, and from his weeping eyes there came a smile so gentle, as if an angel had come to console the despairing mother: 'You know, it will only last another four years, until *I* become a *Stubenältester*, you know, Mummy.' And at these words the angel disappeared from his eyes, and instead there came into them that same glint which had glittered in Dallwitz's eyes, when he took up the red hot pen.[102]

While the reason for the title of the tale is made explicit only at its very end, both the atmosphere of terror created by Dallwitz, and the poignancy and horror of the maimed Schmeling's metamorphosis from victim to potential torturer, can be seen as symbolic of the brutalisation and loss of innocence to which *spartanern* could lead. Instead of emphasising the affirmatory, self-imposed nature of *spartanern*, as described by Dewall and Corvin, Reitzenstein focuses on the scars – both mental and physical – which such tests of endurance must necessarily leave behind. Reitzenstein's 'Sparta' stands for a world in which sadistic superiors can subject their subordinates to any torture in order to ensure their obedience and 'make men of them' – the implications for any officer educated at the schools are horrific. In a sense, both this story, and the collection as a whole, can be read as an exploration of the Social Democratic Party's analysis of the cadet corps as '[making] from the children...soldiers of true Prussian worth and character – human machines who endure the highest possible hardships without a murmur [and] blindly obey the commands of their superiors.'[103]

This characterisation of Sparta as symbolic of cadet-school brutality was also explicitly noted by the Socialist critic Kurt Tucholsky, writing in the weekly magazine *Die Weltbühne* later the same year. In an article which begins by characterising and taking to task what he sees as the essentially vapid genre of 'sea cadets' or ensigns' literature' (*Seekadetten oder auch Fähnrichsliteratur*), Tucholsky goes on to single out Reitzenstein's *Vergitterte Jugend* as a work which seems at first glance to belong wholeheartedly to this genre, but which actually possesses a very different character. Surprisingly, however, he then goes on to accuse Reitzenstein of betraying a certain pride in the Spartan trope:

> Yet, from out of the bitterest criticism, a form of boastfulness regarding this education (or is it just boastfulness and ruefulness regarding the human 'material'?) sometimes seems to speak. Groß-Lichterfelde? It's Sparta, my dears, Sparta (*Sparta, meine Lieben, Sparta*).[104]

Since the setting of Reitzenstein's 'Sparta' is evidently a *Voranstalt* rather than the *Hauptkadettenanstalt* at Groß-Lichterfelde, we might wonder whether Tucholsky's comment here was also partly stimulated by his having seen the *Tägliche Rundschau* article from August 1917 entitled '*Die Spartaner von Lichterfelde*' (as described in Chapter 2 above). Alternatively, we might simply conjecture that the collocation of Spartan brutalities with the cadet corps in general was so widely prevalent at this time, at least in left-wing circles, that Tucholsky saw the concept of 'Sparta' as embracing the whole of Reitzenstein's collection (including those stories set at the HKA), rather than the eponymous tale alone.

In similar vein to his criticism of Reitzenstein's portrayal of *Spartanertum*, Tucholsky ironically accuses even stories such as '*Die Ehre der Sexta*' of peddling an ideal of collective honour which is criminally deceptive, while the book as a whole still seems to him to possess a regrettable focus upon obedience to authority figures. He dismisses the collection in general terms as 'scribbled down – not really literature', although he admits that the stories are not entirely devoid of literary merit. The broader moral which Tucholsky draws from Reitzenstein's work, however, and one with obvious relevance to the fragile political situation in the newly-created Weimar Republic, runs as follows:

> No corporate body has the right to escape the community of all its fellow men and create an evil world of its own (*eine üble Sonderwelt zu bilden*) – just because it is easier to do so. How they close ranks! As they do in the cadet corps. How they lie when prestige is on the line! As they do in the cadet corps. How they dissemble! How they use their offices in order to accomplish their own shabby interests! As they do in the cadet corps. And the consequence? This country has masters and beggars. It has no men.[105]

*

Leopold von Wiese's cadet-school memoir *Kindheit*, published three years later (and also reviewed by Tucholsky), provides a similarly negative characterisation of the cadet corps' collocation with Sparta.[106] Wiese's foreword makes it clear that he is presenting his experiences in an unfavourable light, and also that he wishes his portrayal to have a certain political impact. He notes that:

> Many parents and teachers today long to have the old, more or less military education system back, and labour under the delusion that the training and bonds of the old type of boarding school, in particular the cadet corps, is urgently needed for their children. Everywhere in Germany there are signs of a voluntary 'militarisation' of education, by which I mean not external

> preparation for war, but in particular the inner formation of youth according to the rules and principles of an unfree spirit.[107]

Wiese chronicles the torments which he was forced to endure at *Voranstalt* Wahlstatt in painful detail, beginning with his first introduction to cadet-corps life – a slap in the face from his *Stubenältester* for failing to get changed at the right time, accompanied by the comment '"You seem like a right idiot"'.[108] He remarks on the awful comparison between 'the friendly, free holiday time at home, and the *Spartanertum* of the cadet school',[109] and at a later point characterises the hellish atmosphere as that of a 'Sparta *rediviva*':

> If the two poles of human development are power and love, then one must consequently deduce from the hunger for power – which found so much fuel in the complete mastery of the stronger over the weaker – that the charming god Eros could not have found much to busy himself with on the fields of this *neu-Sparta*.[110]

When the League of Former Cadets published a review of Wiese's book soon after its publication, they took issue not only with its underlying premise, accusing Wiese of peddling falsehoods under a sociologist's disguise and fouling his own nest, but also with his understanding of cadet-corps *Spartanertum*, linking his work explicitly with that of Reitzenstein.[111] The review itself was entitled *Vogel Wiedehopf* (the hoopoe bird), probably a play on the German phrase '*stinken wie ein Wiedehopf*' (to stink like a hoopoe), a reference to the fact that hoopoes' nests are considered peculiarly disgusting and malodorous. The reviewer swore that the League of Former Cadets could vouchsafe that, harsh though it might have been, the cadets' 'truly Spartan education' had been wholly sound in nature. This, he claimed, could be witnessed by anyone, from Reich President von Hindenburg right down to the very smallest cadet who had never even had a chance to join the army. The review therefore provides an excellent example of the way in which, after the end of the First World War, every accusation of Spartan brutality by the cadet corps' opponents would be countered by former cadets with a defiant reiteration of the corps' Spartan virtues.[112] This use of the Spartan *topos* as a means of self-justification by cadet-school alumni following the Treaty of Versailles will form the subject of the next chapter.

Notes

[1] For more on this, see in particular Trox 1990.

[2] For instance, we might compare the criticisms levelled at the cadet corps by Wilhelm von Humboldt in his tract *Über Kadettenhäuser* (1809) with those described below. Humboldt raises many of the conventional objections to cadet-school education, decrying the schools' onesidedness, their caste mentality, the fact that they take boys from their homes too early, and even do violence to human nature. He argued that a non-military school which offered good gymnastic training would prepare future officers just as well as the cadet corps.

[3] Schmitz 1997, 68–70.

[4] ibid., 79.

[5] For an indication of the way in which these instances fit in to the overall pattern of evidence for the Spartan trope, see the Appendix.

[6] Trox 1990, 36.

[7] ibid., 83.

[8] ibid., 18.

[9] ibid., 281–2.

[10] ibid., 114.

[11] Anon. 1898, 34. This was a common designation for the army in political debate at the time.

[12] Neubourg 1890, 64f.; Schmitz 1997, 55.

[13] Crousaz 1857, 387.

[14] ibid., 385.

[15] Anon. 1898, 35. For a vivid eyewitness account of the revolution from a cadet's perspective, see Hohenlohe-Ingelfingen 1897.

[16] Schmitz 1997, 55. Pfuel had himself attended the cadet corps in Berlin in its pre-1819 incarnation.

[17] *Justizministerium* 1848.

[18] ibid.

[19] *Vorschläge zur Umgestaltung des Kadettencorps*, quoted in Schmitz 1997, 55.

[20] Crousaz 1857, 388–90.

[21] Trox 1990, 229–30.

[22] ibid., 248.

[23] Anon. 1898, 34.

[24] Trox 1990, 252.

[25] Schmitz 1997, 56.

[26] *Militair-Wochenblatt* 1896, 1623.

[27] Crousaz 1857, 388–9.

[28] Trox 1990, 250.

[29] Schmitz 1997, 56–7.

[30] Crousaz 1857, x–xi.

[31] ibid., 69.

[32] ibid., 98.

[33] ibid., 145. Spartan references continue on p. 146.

[34] That the Spartan *topos* was present in at least some of the schools from the 1820s onwards, and was becoming more widespread by the 1850s, is strongly suggested by

evidence from Otto von Corvin, Johannes van Dewall, Graf von Haslingen and Eugen Jany-Hamburg (see further the Appendix below).

[35] Schmitz 1997, 57.

[36] ibid., 59.

[37] ibid., 57.

[38] ibid., 59. References to further literature on the *Verfassungskonflikt* ad loc.

[39] e.g. *Anlagen zu den Verhandlungen des Hauses der Abgeordneten* 1860–1861. *Vierter Theil*, Aktenstück Nr.170 (7.Band), *Erster Bericht der Kommission über den Etat der Militair-Verwaltung für 1861*, 1329.

[40] ibid., 1333; see also *Dritter Theil*, Aktenstück Nr.144 (5. Band), *Bericht der Kommission zur Prüfung des Staatshaushalts-Etats für 1860 über den Etat der Militair-Verwaltung, zweiter Theil*, 1017–9; *Stenographische Berichte des Abegordnetenhauses* 1859–1860, 35. Sitzung (18/5/1860), 1167–74; *Stenographische Berichte des Abgeordnetenhauses* 1860–1861, 59. Sitzung (29/5/1861), 1458–71.

[41] See nn. 2, 17 above.

[42] *Anlagen zu den Verhandlungen des Hauses der Abgeordneten* 1862. *Dritter Theil.* Aktenstück Nr.126 (7.Band), *Bericht der Kommission zur Prüfung des Staatshaushalts-Etats über den Etat der Militair-Verwaltung pro 1862*, 1202–3. The motion was passed with 21 votes to 5.

[43] ibid.

[44] *Stenographische Berichte des Abgeordetenhauses* 1862, 51. Sitzung (20/09/1862), 1797–1804.

[45] Quoted in Schmitz 1997, 60.

[46] *Allerhöchste Kabinettsordre*, 29 April 1863.

[47] Gertner 1862, 102–3.

[48] Schmitz 1997, 61.

[49] ibid., 63–4. Representative Eugen Richter, one of the schools' remaining 'stiff-necked' critics, denounced the new HKA as a '*Kadettenschloß*' (cadets' castle), but ultimately his dissent went unheeded.

[50] ibid., 65–6.

[51] The cadet school at Culm was moved to Köslin in its entirety, for reasons of space.

[52] The so-called *Sozialistengesetz* (Socialist Law) was repealed in September 1890.

[53] Führ 1980, 194–5.

[54] ibid., 193.

[55] cf. Schmitz 1997, 96.

[56] For further discussion of the *Allerhöchste Kabinettsordre*, see p. 95 above.

[57] Schleunes 1989, 209–10.

[58] Schmitz 1997, 89–90.

[59] Keller n.d., 8 [GStAPK I.HA Rep.76 *Kultusministerium*, IV.Sekt.1. Gen.Z Nr.115 Bd.1, Bl.107].

[60] Führ 1980, 203–4.

[61] *Stenographische Berichte des Abgeordnetenhauses* 1890, 31. Sitzung (18/03/1890), 780.

[62] ibid., 33. Sitzung (20/03/1890), 846–7.

[63] Quoted in Schubert-Weller 1988, 594.

[64] Heydorn 1973, 17.

[65] *Verhandlungen über Fragen des höheren Unterrichts* (1891), 90.

[66] ibid., 239.

[67] ibid., 365. Indeed, by the end of the conference, such sentiments were so strong that the Kaiser felt the need to take its proponents to task in his closing address (ibid., 771): 'Gentlemen, the cadet corps is completely unique; it has a particular aim, ...stands directly under My command, and really does not concern us in this context.'

[68] ibid., 440–7.

[69] ibid., 534–5. It seems possible that the Major decided to intersperse his speeches with original Greek quotations so that none of the *Gymnasium* teachers could accuse him of being a mere uneducated soldier.

[70] ibid., 229.

[71] ibid., 771. Presumably the Kaiser is referring to the First Battle of Mantinea.

[72] For a detailed account, see Schmitz 1997, 104–114.

[73] They even spawned a well-loved TV series, first aired during the 1960s.

[74] Text can be found at http://gutenberg.spiegel.de/buch/712/12.

[75] For discussion of Sparta as a theme in the anti-militarist novels of Arthur Zapp, see Roche 2012d, 31–3.

[76] Stargardt 1994, 21.

[77] ibid., 22.

[78] ibid., 20.

[79] ibid., 35–6. Stargardt's study of the critics of German militarism does not discuss reactions to the cadet corps at all, which seems a rather startling omission.

[80] See n. 52 above.

[81] Clark 2006, 563.

[82] Trotha 1912, 8.

[83] Quoted in Clemente 1992, 132.

[84] e.g. Wülfingen 1894, 5–6.

[85] For more on the context of the novel, see p. 78 n. 43 above. For a similar depiction of a fictional cadet-school scandal which could supposedly have placed Bismarck's coalition government in jeopardy had it not been suppressed, see Bedford 1954.

[86] Unruh 1983, 101.

[87] ibid., 175.

[88] ibid., 597–8.

[89] One might surmise that it had been relatively difficult to find a publisher for such works *before* the Revolution – as is suggested by the fact that Werner von der Schulenburg's hostile tract on the cadet schools, *Meine Kadettenerinnerungen (1892–1899). Ein Beitrag zur Lösung einer Zeitfrage*, was first written in 1901, but only published in 1919.

[90] Tucholsky 1920, 236.

[91] Tucholsky 1924, 734. Tucholsky goes on to comment upon the remarkable way in which the details of cadet-school life, as depicted by Reitzenstein, are confirmed by Leopold von Wiese's description of his time at *Voranstalt* Wahlstatt (see pp. 150–1).

[92] Reitzenstein 1920, 5–6.

[93] ibid., 7–16.

[94] ibid., 59–64.

[95] ibid., 135.

[96] ibid., 141.

[97] ibid., 142.

[98] ibid., 36–51.

[99] ibid., 44–6. For other depictions of this particular type of maltreatment, see Borcke 1940, 228–9; Fritz von Unruh 1983, 110. cf. p. 134: When U2's mother had complained to his father, the General, that their son was coming home from Plön with suppurating fingertips, he merely remarked 'We all had to go through that. What I won't have is one of my sons becoming a "sneak".'

[100] Reitzenstein 1920, 48.

[101] ibid., 49.

[102] ibid., 50–1.

[103] See above, n. 83.

[104] Tucholsky 1920, 236.

[105] ibid.

[106] Tucholsky 1924.

[107] Wiese 1924, 5.

[108] ibid., 9.

[109] ibid.,79.

[110] ibid., 86.

[111] H.F.H. 1925, 54–5.

[112] Compare the opening statement of an autobiographical account by von Altrock (1925, 38), published in the previous issue of the *Reichskadettenblatt*: 'The time after the revolution brought with it the radical wasps, nibbling away at all the honourable trappings of state. The cadet corps has also fallen prey to this fate. Anyone who knows what a high number of brave men emerged from the cadet-corps education, anyone who has seen that even those of average ability were firmly forged in body and spirit by this training, can only deplore the fact that this outstanding school (*Lehrschule*) has been taken from the German people. The former cadet soars smiling above all attacks, and thinks gladly of the time when he was still a cadet. In the gilded light of memory the old times pass before his mind's eye, even if they were sometimes hard and stormy too, as in the school of the *Spartanerjünglinge*.'

7

RAGING AGAINST THE REPUBLICS: 'SPARTAN' SELF-DEFINITION IN THE CADET-SCHOOL *TRADITIONSGEMEINSCHAFT*, 1920–1995

Spartan Youth versus the Spartacists:[1] The contested nature of cadet-corps *Spartanertum* during the Weimar Republic

As Christopher Clark has noted, the old Prussian elite was one of the social groups most affected in the upheavals unleashed by Germany's defeat in World War I, in particular the socialist revolution of 1918–1919, the forced abdication of the Kaiser, and the dissolution of the monarchist Establishment.[2] 'For the older generation of the Prussian military nobility, defeat and revolution brought a traumatic sense of loss', culminating in a shared awareness that 'the old order had collapsed and no longer had a future.'[3] As for the cadets, their whole world had been turned upside down – literally, in the case of those at *Voranstalten* such as Plön or Bensberg, which had been stormed and looted by adherents of the red revolutionary Workers', Soldiers' and Sailors' Councils.[4]

On 16 December 1918, the Councils passed a resolution demanding that the German military be completely restructured. Hindenburg must be dismissed from his position as Chief of Staff, the cadet schools must be closed down, and all distinctions of rank abolished. In future, officers would be elected by the troops, and a people's militia (*Volkswehr*) would supplement the army.[5] Unsurprisingly, Hindenburg refused even to consider these proposals, and informed the new socialist government (led by Friedrich Ebert) that any attempt to implement them would lead to an instant withdrawal of his support. When the Ebert government announced its intention of obstructing the Councils' demands, however, the Independent Social Democratic Party (USPD) and the Spartacus League (the future Communist Party) were furious, and began to mobilise supporters across Berlin. On the 23rd of December, open conflict broke out, and by 16 March 1919, the death-toll numbered over 1000.[6]

Yet, in the midst of this anarchy, the cadet schools still continued to function more or less normally, even enrolling new pupils for 1919 and 1920. The authorities did not believe that the cadet corps' end could really be nigh; indeed, the new alliance between the Social Democratic government and the army seemed to imply that the schools' future was secure.[7] It was only at the beginning of 1920 that the military became fully aware of the contents of the Treaty of Versailles, including Article 176, which spelled the end of the cadet corps. The military's loathing for the '*Novemberverbrecher*' (November traitors) in government, fuelled by the ever-prevalent 'stab-in-the-back myth' (*Dolchstoßlegende*), rose to fever pitch. Nevertheless, they realised that, if the schools were to survive in any form whatsoever, some concessions to the government would have to be made.[8]

The ultimate decision was that the cadet schools should be transformed into non-military state-run boarding schools called *Staatliche Bildungsanstalten* (or Stabilas for short), which would employ civilian teaching staff and female house-matrons (*Hausdamen*) to look after the boys. Though highly unsatisfactory to the War Ministry, this motion was voted through almost unanimously.[9] With bitter resentment and mournful ceremony, the cadet corps was officially disbanded on 20 March 1920; present and former cadets processed through Berlin to the Brandenburg Gate in full regalia, knowing that this was the last time they would ever be part of the corps as a living institution. A quotation from cadet-school pastor Jäckel's speech sums up the mood of the occasion:

> We are standing at the grave of the Prussian Cadet Corps... Griefstricken, [those attending] look upon their smart uniforms, which they are wearing today for the last time, and this pain convulses them, convulses us all, when we see the proud banners, which afterwards, in the last parade march, will fly one more time, before being rolled up and taken away. – Ach, we do not wish to analyse how this all came about, [we know] that this closure of the military educational institutions due to a shameful and ignominious peace (*Schand- und Schmachfrieden*) was forced by our enemies' fear; for it was here that that spirit could be cultivated which could help our people once again; because the *Schand- und Schmachfrieden* was only made possible by the insanity of our people, to deprive themselves of all weapons and then come to terms with a hate-filled, revengeful enemy...[10]

Among the former cadets, the *Auflösung* (dissolution) of the cadet corps was a running sore, and many who were old enough ran away to join the *Freikorps*, a group of reactionary terrorist bands with an expressly anti-civilian ethos.[11] This trajectory is well exemplified by Ernst von Salomon, who went on to become a celebrated and murderous *Freikorps*-member as well as a successful author.[12] In his autobiographical novel *Die Geächteten* (The Outlaws), Salomon describes the hideousness of the fact that the revolution has robbed all his family's military mementos of their meaning; his mother unsews his precious cadet-school epaulettes from his coat and he immediately, rebelliously, sews them back on.[13] He sees the hopeless ordinary folk in the streets as nothing but rats or rabble, and joins the *Freikorps* along with a group of other ex-cadets who are determined to stick together to 'smoke out the red swine'.[14]

The former cadets who were forced to remain at or return to the former HKA at Lichterfelde to complete their studies were utterly disgusted by its new incarnation as a Stabila. At the opening ceremony on 5 May 1920, it was reported that pupils wearing swastikas in their buttonholes had tried to pull down the red, black and gold flag (symbolising the new Republic) which adorned the building.[15] They also distributed flyers which decried all the new *Erzieher* as filthy Jews who would never be worthy of Germany, and encouraged all pupils to fight back against their new teachers with 'passive aggression'.[16] Many of the ex-cadets had been sent back to the school to gain some qualifications after having spent time in the *Freikorps*, and had thus been instilled with its anti-republican spirit – including a strong element of anti-Semitism. They felt betrayed by the socialist government which would not allow them all to be enrolled in the new (dramatically reduced) German army, the *Reichswehr*, and were determined not to lose the role of 'active fighters' which they had gained in the *Freikorps*, battling against the 'reds' alongside much older military men who had nevertheless respected them as equals. As the oldest pupils at the school (all aged between sixteen and twenty), it was easy for the former cadets to organise resistance to the new Social Democratic school authorities, especially the freshly appointed Jewish Director, Friedrich Karsen.[17]

In 1921, anarchy erupted at Lichterfelde in the form of the 'cadet revolts' (*Kadettenrevolte*), in which one of the new house-matrons was attacked and subjected to extreme verbal abuse because she had denounced another matron for inviting boys to tea on the Kaiser's birthday and allowing them to sing patriotic songs. Needless to say, the 'revolts' were raked over in the press, and discussions raged in parliament regarding suitable punishments for the cadets involved, and the ways in which the Education Ministry should defuse the dangerous influence of the older cadets' anti-republican, monarchist convictions.[18] At one point, the parliamentary debate grew so heated that one representative threatened to box another's ears, while a representative from Neukölln threw a pile of documents at an adversary.[19] The cadets were branded '*Hurrabengel*' (jingoistic whippersnappers) and '*Arbeitertöter*' (worker-killers), while the school at Lichterfelde was presented as a reactionary hotbed, stirring up hatred against civilians. However, one of the few representatives who was prepared to make a case for the cadets, Representative Oelze of the *Deutschnationale Volkspartei* (German National Peoples' Party, a far right nationalist party), tried to use the 'Spartan' nature of the cadets' education as an excuse for their behaviour. Oelze argued that the entire problem lay in the fact that it had been psychologically ludicrous to expect the cadets to accept the female authority of the house-matrons at such an advanced age.

> [At the onset of puberty,] pupils are averse to being made directly subject to female influence. The astute and pedagogically-informed mother holds back in these years and, perhaps precisely through this withdrawal, secures the strongest influence over her growing sons. Whether it was appropriate to give these pupils governesses, if I may use the expression, when they were expressly attuned to a Spartan education... (cries of 'Hear! Hear!' from the Right)... I really do not know. They ought to have confined themselves to employing such female educational assistants with younger pupils, where they are in their element.[20]

One may be able to take the cadet out of Sparta, Oelze implies, but one cannot take Spartan education out of the cadet.[21] He accuses the Education Minister, Dr. Boelitz, of ruining the cadets' lives by expelling them before they can take their exams (*Abitur*), to which the Minister replies that it is such unscrupulous demagogy which has poured so much oil on the flaming waters of the incident.[22]

While it is noteworthy that the cadets' 'Spartan education' could be cited as an extenuating circumstance for their potentially criminal behaviour in no less a forum than the *Landtag*, the Prussian state parliament, this debate is also interesting for the light which it throws on an autobiographical novel which describes precisely this period, Hanns Nickol's *Der letzte Kadett* (1935), which gives an account of the life led by the ex-cadets at Lichterfelde and their struggles against the new regime. To these disillusioned adolescents, even the school's new name, 'Stabila', was an insult: '"It sounds like a type of *Kinderwagen* (pram)..." "Yes...we're just a *Kinderbewahranstalt* (crèche) now."'[23]

The work's protagonist, Wolfgang Hartwig, is an embittered former cadet company commander who is desperate to return the former HKA to its old glory.[24] Hartwig pits himself against various adversaries who do not share his militaristic views, such as his thoughtful, intellectual comrade Krüger, and the 'weak' civilian *Erzieher* who have taken over the school. Hartwig hates the loss of military duties, which erases meaning from his life;[25] he hates the new Director, a Jewish Socialist who stands for the new regime and everything Hartwig despises;[26] most of all, he hates the house-matrons: 'They want to make our steel-hard hearts pliant and docile; they want to make us receptive to their babble about universal brotherhood and humanity and true democracy.'[27]

When Hartwig learns that Krüger has taken the treacherous step of agreeing to take tea with one of the matrons, he determines to make him see the error of his ways and boycott all such invitations. 'It's begun; the red poison has started to work!'[28] When Hartwig reaches Krüger's room, he finds him asleep holding, of all things, Heinrich Mann's anti-nationalist novel *Der Untertan* (better known in English as *Man of Straw*, *The Patrioteer* or *The Loyal Subject*).[29] The contrasts in Hartwig's and Krüger's respective characters ('Hartwig, the soldier and nothing but a soldier; Krüger, the rebel')[30] are highlighted by Nickol's descriptions of their living quarters; much is revealed by the 'un-Spartan' character of Krüger's room, even before the reader has had a chance to meet him in person:

> Anyone who had seen the cadets' *Stuben* and dormitories, these simple, strict and clinical rooms, which lacked any comfort and cosiness, should have been astounded to see [Krüger's] room. Here there was nothing left of the barrack room and the Spartan spirit... Several armchairs, even a sofa... Had it not been for the great gold-framed paintings – of battles, of the Kaiser – which implied the military connection, one could have believed one were in the rooms of a gentleman's club.[31]

Hartwig does his best to persuade Krüger that the house-matrons are mere tools of a system which must be defeated:

> 'Our common enemy...stands without the walls. This Republic! This Government!... We must fight against them. Not with weapons. That is forbidden to us. A battle of attitudes. Of training. Of ethos. They have taken our uniforms away. They cannot take our spirit away...'[32]

To Hartwig's chagrin, Krüger will have none of this, telling him that he sounds 'like a commander without an army, a general attempting to fight a battle without any soldiers.'[33] Later, Krüger confides to the house-matron that he feels Hartwig is so exclusively fixated upon his military obsessions that 'he is not human anymore; he is becoming a "commando-machine".'[34]

As far as lessons are concerned, Hartwig and Krüger are once again divided by their opinions of Dr. Hinrichs, one of the new young Social Democrat teachers. Hinrichs' character and his educational methods are closely modelled on those of a real master at the Stabila called Robert Zwetz, whose teaching Nickol had experienced at first hand.[35] Like Reitzenstein's Dr. Michael in *Vergitterte Jugend*, Hinrichs succeeds in winning the cadets over with his entertaining and unorthodox methods. Yet Hartwig is filled with horror at the ideas which are being put into the cadets' heads by this besandalled, patch-trousered traitor in their midst – such as the notion that history is more than just monarchs and battles, or that wars are not necessarily the peak of historical achievement.[36] However, the lesson which really leads Hartwig to feel that Hinrichs has gone far too far is the one in which he reveals to his astonished listeners the left-wing version of Classical history:

> They knew about Julius Caesar. They knew about Romulus and Remus... But that ancient Rome was already known to have had slums and housing shortages was fantastical, and sounded just as unbelievable as the things which Hinrichs told them about the Spartans, with whom until this point they had always found it so flattering to be compared. Sparta! A people of heroes, who were brought up on blood soup; that very soup which must have tasted similar to the slop made of flour and water which they pumped into their fasting stomachs morning after morning, only it would have had a bit more taste to it... Sparta! Leonidas! The Battle of Thermopylae!
>
> And now this King Leonidas was suddenly supposed to have been a thoroughly disagreeable fellow. Noble, generous, ready to help the poorest; that was what his rival Agis IV was supposed to have been; he had wanted to divide up the land in a new, fairer fashion. However, the hero of Thermopylae, if one followed Dr. Hinrichs correctly, had worked out how to foil the land reform plans of his young rival king; he had come down on the side of the landowners, the rich, the super-rich, who couldn't stand to put their wealth at the service of the general public.
>
> Could be, could be, thought the cadets. They could not check whether the things Hinrichs was telling them had any bearing on reality...
>
> It's gone too far! thought Hartwig apprehensively. Where will it all end?[37]

In this passage, Hinrichs' handling of Spartan history is treated as paradigmatic of the way in which the new Social Democratic authorities attempted to instil the ex-cadets with their own worldview, as opposed to that fostered by the cadet corps in former times. Spartan history is portrayed as a moral and political battlefield, on which the spirit of the Republic battles with that of the reactionary Establishment; the winner will gain the cadets' hearts and minds.

Strikingly, Nickol's portrayal of Hinrichs' teaching also suggests that he had not fully explained that although Leonidas II, rival of the idealistic reformer king Agis IV, bore the same name as the cadets' ultimate Spartan hero, he had actually lived two-and-a-half centuries later. If we assume that this vignette is autobiographical, and that Nickol has not simply forgotten or failed to realise that Hinrichs was talking about Leonidas II and not Leonidas I, this might imply that Hinrichs is deliberately denigrating the cadets' ideas about the 'hero of Thermopylae' in order to expunge the pernicious influence of what they had been taught about Sparta before 1920. Alternatively, this could be a clever piece of characterisation on Nickol's part – suggesting that Hinrichs is falsifying Spartan history deliberately, and thus undermining the reader's estimation of the worth of left-wing teaching. However, the ideas about Agis IV and his reforms expressed by Hinrichs in this passage do have real-life parallels in the work of socialist Classical scholars working on Sparta during this period, such as Ernst Bux.[38] For Hartwig, the reactionary protagonist, this scene merely exemplifies the extreme political manipulation to which the cadets are constantly being subjected by the new regime; the corruption of 'their' idea of Sparta is thus symptomatic of the sickness which lies at the heart of the Stabila.

Finally, in a run-in with his arch-enemy, the civilian *Erzieher* Herr Knust, Hartwig is confronted once again with what he considers to be utterly wrong-headed Social Democratic views on the worth of the cadet corps' 'Spartan' training. Hartwig has been caught forcing the younger boys to undergo a '*Kostümfest*' (a punishment which involved getting changed into and out of many different types of uniform within a couple of minutes) to keep them on their toes.[39] Knust calls him to his study and accuses him of bullying. Hartwig tries to explain why such drills are necessary, but Knust argues that his 'hymn of praise' to military discipline is flawed.[40] He must know that once the cadets become officers, their Spartan way of life (*spartanische Lebensführung*) quickly goes by the board, and they become depraved drunks, gamblers and womanisers.[41] The interview ends in disaster when Knust finishes his lecture by insulting the honour of Krüger, who ran away to fight alongside the *Freikorps* against Spartacist elements and has just been reported killed in battle.[42] Hartwig slaps Knust in the face, and only escapes expulsion because the Director and his lackeys have found the Stabila too hot to handle and have decided to leave at the end of the term.

These references to the Spartan *topos* in Nickol's work all serve to illustrate its extremely contested nature during the political upheavals of this period. Hartwig's cadet-school definition of *Spartanertum* is in constant danger of being undermined by the hated representatives of the Social Democratic regime, or even by renegade ex-cadets such as Krüger who have decided to move on from cadet-corps life in a way that Hartwig finds simply impossible.

Furthermore, the fact that Sparta was considered as one of the key historical subjects concerning which the ex-cadets had to be re-indoctrinated (or even mis-indoctrinated) suggests that the new regime was well aware of Sparta's significance in a cadet-school context. The self-sacrificial heroic patriotism of the 300 is no longer a politically correct model, but must be replaced with tales of tamer 'reformer heroes' recast in a socialist mould. Even if we ignore the incontrovertibly autobiographical elements in *Der letzte Kadett*, the very fact that Nickol has chosen to illustrate his portrayal of the changing nature of teaching material at the Stabila with this Spartan example speaks volumes for Sparta's symbolic political significance at this point. In their bid for power, the 'damned Sozis' had even pinkwashed the Spartan paradigm – what could be more indicative of the old order's demise?

*

The cadets who had left Lichterfelde, however, had no intention of relinquishing their Spartan self-identification merely because the cadet corps had ceased to exist. This reactionary tendency can most readily be observed in the newsletters of the *Reichsbund ehemaliger Kadetten* (League of Former Cadets), first formed in 1920 following the corps' dissolution, which contain a wealth of references to the Spartan *topos.*[43] On the very first page of the first edition of the League's newsletter, published in September 1920 under the title *Deutsche Kadettenzeitung*, the League's 'mission statement' describes the cadet corps through the ages as serving 'Spartan pedagogy, German-style' (*spartanische Pädagogik deutscher Art*), as well as emphasising the hope that its spirit will survive and arise phoenix-like from the ashes of the destruction which lily-livered pacifists have forced Germany to suffer.[44]

The League declared its initial aims as follows:

1. Fostering of Tradition and Comradeship.
2. Fostering of a national, loyally German cadet ethos (*treudeutschen Kadettengesinnung*).
3. Care of...pictures and rolls of honour, and their safekeeping...
4. Setting up a roll of honour for those comrades who died for Germany's honour, and erection of a memorial.
5. Supporting our members to the best of our power if they are in need.
6. Economic control over all these areas...
7. Editing the *Deutsche Kadettenzeitung.*
8. The widest possible circulation of cadet memorabilia and distribution of written recollections (*Erinnerungsschriften*).[45]

This first edition also contained a reprint of commiserations from the *Deutsches Offizier-Blatt* on the dissolution of the cadet corps. This 'obituary' describes the 'Spartan simplicity' (*spartanische Einfachheit*) of cadet-school education as being entirely in accordance with the spirit of the army as a whole, in that it trained men who saw the strictest military fulfilment of duty as their only life's work. The endorsement concludes with the following wish: 'May the spirit of the cadet corps, even after its abolition, be preserved in our future peace-time army.'[46] In both these passages, the Spartan character of cadet-school education is defined as a crucial component of that 'cadet-corps spirit' which the military aimed to preserve at all costs, despite the terms of the Versailles Treaty, the diminution of the army, and the dissolution of the cadet schools themselves.

For other members of the League, such praise of the schools' Spartan spirit was mixed with heavy-hearted nostalgia. A former Potsdam cadet and later Captain on the General Staff ruminated in an article (reprinted from the *Deutsches Adelsblatt*) that seeing Potsdam now awakened in him memories full of sadness and times long past.

> All the many who once wore the military dress with its six buttons and red epaulettes, or who were gladdened...to see the tiny yet important cadets...will recall the old Potsdam cadet school and its *Spartanerjünglinge* fondly.[47]

Similarly, a military chaplain recalled his time at *Voranstalt* Bensberg:

> For decades, the castle was the site of Spartan educational practice (*spartanischer Erzieherarbeit*) and therefore a romping ground for the freshest and gutsiest lads... For lads cut from such cloth, the cadet corps was a school for life, and Bensberg, with its summer joys in water and woods, with its winter joys on the skating rink and toboggan run, was a boys' paradise despite its Spartan, but oh so healthful discipline (*trotz spartanischer, ach so gesunder Zucht*). Whoever went through this school might have a couple of carefree years as a Lieutenant, but ultimately he was an Officer, just as the King needed him to be: steeled to his duty and physically tough, capable of obeying, of commanding, the first to engage with the enemy as a matter of course, and – just ask the old soldiers, who so often in the field say 'if only we had our first Captain still!' – whose first thought was care for the men and only then for himself, wherever he made camp...[48]

It seems that, for those who contributed to and edited the *Reichskadettenblatt*, linking the cadet corps with Sparta, and the cadets themselves with *Spartanerjünglinge*, was considered an essential element in the preservation of the all-important cadet-school tradition. In particular, whenever the League organised some sort of ceremony of remembrance, images of Sparta often came to the forefront of the ex-cadets' minds.

Thus, at a *Heldengedenkfeier* (a celebration of all those cadets who had fallen in battle) which took place on 4 March 1928, a military chaplain gave a speech at the cadets' memorial on the necessity of those who had survived emulating the dead heroes' spirit in order to save their Fatherland:

> We have accepted a sacred legacy from the dead – to finish what they have begun. In battle *behind* the Front, it lies to us to prove what the heroes demonstrated at the Front; through smart self-discipline, through wise economy, through a Spartan way of life... Like a stone-hard command of soldierly duty [their call] resounds...: Make yourselves worthy of us! You, our brothers, must defend the future of your people and your children, you

> must secure that which we conquered for you, hold honour and the true fame of our entire country high.[49]

Meanwhile, at the fiftieth anniversary celebration of the establishment of the HKA at Lichterfelde in October 1928, which doubled as the second official reunion for former cadets from all over Germany, a former cadet chaplain gave a rousing speech on the virtues of the cadets' Spartan education in times past:

> No state has *thought* through its ideas with greater consistency or put them into practice with greater energy than ancient Sparta, and this spirit of total devotion should have become second nature to our young comrades here.[50]

The *Neue Preußische [Kreuz-]Zeitung* reported on his speech as follows:

> Consistory Councillor Gruhl, the old cadet pastor, who had himself confirmed many of those gathered here today, and had also exhorted many of them from the pulpit with manful words before their departure for battle, opened the celebration with an address in which he brought the old cadet existence back to life once more. He recalled that the cadets were frequently called '*Spartanerjünglinge*', often in jest, but often also with meaningful seriousness. Yet this Spartan education became exactly the means by which they found themselves able, often at such a very young age, to prove themselves as men and as Prussian soldiers; not for the first time in the World War, no; the many names hewn in stone on the walls of the school chapel bear witness to the fact that the cadets had always known how to fight and bleed for their country.[51]

That such an emphasis on the Spartan elements of cadet-corps education, and the continued remembrance of the cadets' collocation with *Spartanerjünglinge*, was considered appropriate in a speech which not only opened one of the League's most important festivities, but which took place almost exactly ten years after the end of the First World War, implies strongly that this Spartan identification remained very dear to the ex-cadets' hearts. Here, Gruhl openly claims that it was the cadets' '*spartanische Erziehung*' (Spartan education) which had made them into true men and Prussian soldiers ready to die for their country, whatever the cost – one might even conjecture that he could have urged the cadets to follow the Spartan example when he harangued them from the pulpit with '*mannhafte Worte*' (manful words) in former times. Gruhl also explicitly links the corps' methods of education with those employed in ancient Sparta; another instance of cadet-school authorities imposing Spartan self-identification from above.

In a sense, the fact that the former cadets had all once been considered '*Spartanerjünglinge*', exposed to the same hardships and tribulations of the

'Spartan' cadet-corps education, was felt to be an important tie which could still bind them together. Even if they had long since gone their different ways after leaving the HKA, erstwhile cadet-comrades could still be concerned about each other's fates, asking, as did one Ernst Kiock in a *Reichskadettenblatt* article in 1929: 'What has become of them now, the former *Spartanerjünglinge* of Lichterfelde?'[52]

In conclusion, it appears that many members of the League of Former Cadets still saw *Spartanertum* as a defining feature of their educational experiences, whether these had been entirely framed by the cadet corps, or whether they had had some experience of life at the Stabilas under the new regime. Their self-identification as 'Spartan youths', and their continued and belligerent approbation of the 'Spartan' virtues of their education, can be seen as signifying both a desperate wish to cling on to an idealised vision of their past, and a keen desire to counter the constant criticism of the corps which, as detailed in Chapter 6, portrayed cadet-school Spartanism as horrific and dangerous, and the cadet-corps mentality in general as flawed and treasonable.[53]

Although political attitudes to the cadet corps were to change radically and repeatedly during the next few decades, the cadets' comradeship ultimately survived Nazism and the upheavals of World War II more or less unscathed. In a less centralised form, their *Traditionsgemeinschaft* (old boys' association), reconstituted as the *Bund der ehemaligen königlich preußischen und königlich sächsischen Kadetten* (League of former Royal Prussian and Royal Saxon Cadets), remained active until the early 1990s, surviving communism and Reunification as well.[54]

The afterlife of the *topos*: 'Spartan' self-definition and nostalgia in the cadet-school *Traditionsgemeinschaft* post-1945

Self-definition (*Selbstbestimmung*)
For Tommies it's just natural,
For Frenchies patriotic,
Yet one deems it full of shame,
or even idiotic,
if Germans should venture
to long for the same.

Must it be? (*Muss das sein?*)
Because our vocabulary's so poor...
They talk about '*jazz*' and '*musical*',
they say '*byebye*' and '*very well*'...
'*rock 'n' roll*' themselves hot and raw.

Wherever they are, they read
'*bestsellers*' from the '*USA*',
and forget they're German
at the end of the day.[55]

As the two poems above, published in a newsletter of the cadet corps old boys' association in 1974, can testify, the former cadets frequently felt completely alienated from post-war culture and society. How could everything have gone so terribly wrong for their beloved Germany that sermons could now be preached warning that 'being proud to be German' could lead to 'contempt for others'?[56] How could today's youth, or even fellow citizens, see ideas such as 'Fatherland, Nation, Duty, Obedience [and] Comradeship' as dirty words?[57]

The ex-cadets were desperate to be proud of their past, yet it seemed that both the press and the general public were far too prone to use the cadet corps as a scapegoat, conveniently culpable for the rise of militarism and right-wing nationalism which they saw as having ushered in Nazism and fuelled the Second World War. The former cadets thus felt themselves unfairly afflicted by others' attempts at 'mastering the past' (*Vergangenheitsbewältigung*). Some contemporary commentators publicly compared the cadet schools with concentration camps or even with hell,[58] while others (such as the author of an article published in *Der Spiegel* in the early 1970s) denounced former cadets as '*Militär-Roboter*' (military robots), blaming them explicitly for both World Wars and the Holocaust.[59] Other, more anonymous, outrages were perpetrated at dead of night, such as the defiling of cadet-corps memorials with faecal matter or neo-Nazi graffiti. The ex-cadets felt themselves embattled, but their will to prove their adversaries wrong and rebuff all hostile criticism was ineluctable. In this regard, one of the most frequently used weapons in their extensive rhetorical arsenal proved to be the continual proclamation of the 'Spartan' values inculcated by their cadet-school education.[60]

Thus, in response to an article in the *Frankfurter Allgemeine Zeitung* in May 1963 which depicted the cadet schools as anti-liberal 'convents of ancient Prussianism (*Altpreußentum*)',[61] one Dr. Detlev Rudelsdorff, a retired *Generalmajor*, defended the schools as follows:

> As well as the intellectual demands, one professed...a certain asceticism, which had as its basis an intensive physical training and structure with a conscious emphasis on soldierly requirements. As the standard for our thinking and behaviour, we – the so-called 'Spartan youths' – were taught to recognise duty as a categorical imperative... A sense of honour, obedience and hardship against ourselves were the principles for creating an enclosed...homogenous community...[62]

Some years later, Rudelsdorff gave a speech on the 250th anniversary of the founding of the Prussian Cadet Corps (5 May 1967), once again highlighting cadets' identification as '*Spartanerjünglinge*' and stating that the virtues of their education should still have a place in the modern *Bundeswehr* (the West-German army). He argued that, even though war had become so much more mechanised, officers in any day and age needed the timeless virtues of true soldierliness – courage, duty, and comradeship – with which the cadets had once been instilled.[63]

In a third speech, entitled '*Sinn und Wesen des Kadettentums*' (The meaning and character of cadet-hood), given at the 1975 *Bundeskadettentag* (cadets' annual reunion), Rudelsdorff explicitly traced the *mores* of the original cadets' education back to those 'principles of military discipline, convention and character traits...which the legendary Spartan lawgiver Lycurgus had already demanded.' This, he explains, can be seen with hindsight as the reason why the cadets were christened 'Spartan youths' (*Spartaner Jünglinge*).[64]

At the 1979 *Bundeskadettentag*, another former military man, Siegfried Fiedler, linked the current trend for *Vergangenheitsbewältigung* among the 'psychoanalytical posse', and the fact that cadet-school history was now a taboo subject, with the prevalent anti-elitism which decried any and all elite schools which forced their pupils to live in a Spartan fashion.[65] In a second speech, given in 1983 in response to the Defence Minister Hans Apel's prohibition against the *Bundeswehr* having a 'great tattoo' (*großer Zapfenstreich*) on their celebration day, because this constituted 'a relic of a pre-democratic age',[66] Fiedler argued that the destruction of tradition would leave the *Bundeswehr* with nothing, and the ex-cadets with worse than nothing. '*Kadettentum*' should be treated positively once more, as a vital link in the chain which connected Germany's living history with its distant past:

> After the catastrophe of 1945, the deep antagonism between historical views here in Germany could not have been expressed more crassly. The [younger] generations have never agreed on the continuity of historical comprehensibility. They feel such a consensus to be neither possible nor desirable... From the point of view of so-called pre-democratic traditions, i.e. those which are considered undemocratic, cadets are no longer an acceptable subject for another reason... [In the egalitarian society, elites become an embarrassment.] Consequently, all famous elite schools which constrain their pupils to live a Spartan life succumb to massive criticism, because they feel themselves bound to supra-individual values.[67]

Such ideas also came to the fore in the ex-cadets' constant struggle to avoid being tarred with the brush of 'militarism', as speeches at the Plön cadets' reunion in May 1968 show:

> Militarism and soldierliness are as little the same as nationalism and national consciousness... Therefore former cadets must not let anyone or anything rob them of their memories of their youthful experiences at Plön Castle! Their selfless love of the Fatherland must remain untouched by the tragic outcome of the last war... A former Plön cadet, General-Fieldmarshal von Manstein, said that in the time of the cadet corps the education had borne far more the traits of Sparta than those of Athens, viz. that development of military virtues stood more in the foreground than an all-round developed education. Yet there can be no doubt that in this place...virtues were cultivated, which redounded to any man's honour... [Any loss of this tradition] would be preposterous for soldiers, for tradition means the passing down of...moral and ethical values.[68]

Similar Spartan self-justification even found its way into eulogies at ex-cadets' funerals, as this extract from the service for Karl-Eberhard Struckmann, which was later published in the Hamburg old cadets' association newsletter in July 1977, reveals:

> Certainly, in the cadet corps we were brought up simply and strictly, and our education assuredly had more 'Spartan' than 'Athenian' traits. What the corps instilled us with, was a pronounced sense of honour, obedience – even when our duties might be disagreeable – strictness with ourselves, and a steadfast comradeship, which has lasted through all the highs and lows of our lifetime, right up to this day. – We were brought up to be '*Herren*' (masters) in the good sense of the word – and we learnt to keep a stiff upper lip.[69]

If the ex-cadets did admit that there had been any 'militaristic' elements in their education, they attempted to redefine the word so that it expressed only those aspects which they considered admirable – portraying the corps as providing a tough but wholly necessary education, which instilled them with love of their country and devotion to duty above all. Thus Werner Lübcke:

> For these former cadets, the goal of self-sacrifice meant more than mere empty words, but it only meant their identifying from childhood with the term *Vaterlandsliebe* (patriotism), and the necessary war readiness of men educated to lead their lives, and even their deaths, in exemplary fashion. If these ideas of loyalty, belief and pugnacity are included in the word 'militarism', then the former cadets were 'militarists' from their earliest youth, and they were rightly proud of this designation.[70]

In such a context, the spirit of Thermopylae could also be readily invoked, as is shown by a speech given by Senior Pastor Werner Hohenstein at the 1973 *Bundeskadettentag*:

> Our fallen comrades gave their lives in fulfilment of their duty, loyalty and obedience. But how often is it asked 'wasn't it all for nothing?' One can

> almost understand that in an age in which Christian belief is questioned, and in which *Volk*, Fatherland, Nation have become empty concepts... So we have kept the names of our comrades safely in a 'book of honour'. In an age which wishes to know nothing more of tradition, these names must proclaim the battles and sacrifices of past generations. The visitor to the treasure chamber of this castle must come to regard the cadet honour book...in the same sense as that memorial column which lists the 300 Spartiates who fell with King Leonidas at Thermopylae: '*Wanderer, kommst Du nach Sparta, verkündige dorten, du habest uns hier liegen gesehn, wie das Gesetz es befahl.*' ('Stranger, if you come to Sparta, declare to them that you have seen us lying here, as the law commanded.')[71]

The former cadets also saw their 'Spartan' education as one of the reasons why younger generations seemed incapable of understanding them, as a speech given by Walter Wenck at the 1969 *Bundeskadettentag* illustrates:

> When we old cadets find ourselves at a reunion like this, we think of our adolescence. Our youth was tough and Spartan. But I believe I can say that we look back on it happily. Perhaps more recent generations cannot understand us anymore; nevertheless, I want to emphasise that we – I believe – would not have survived the time after two lost wars, when we often had to choose a new career, if we had not been able to draw upon the education of our youth.[72]

It was precisely this Spartan school of hard knocks, Wenck implies, which made the cadets so resilient and capable of adjusting to the new challenges of the post-war era.

Such views were also shared by Hans Bruns in a speech given at an Oranienstein reunion ten years later:

> In loyalty and gratitude we avow ourselves now and always to our former place of education, where we were once trained Spartanly and simply! The education rested on the principles: love of the fatherland; fulfilment of duty; a sense of order; discipline; simplicity and humility! The principles were developed thus: to educate mind, body and character in the same fashion! They moulded us for our entire lives! To prove yourself a good comrade in all situations was our highest commandment! Today I should say, looking around, that we cadets, at our advanced age, trained in this way, have done our duty in our lives as useful men, whether in the military or in the civilian sector, in peace and in war![73]

Remembering the corps' *Spartanertum* could also simply be a form of fond nostalgia for times long past (a phenomenon also observable in some of the memoir literature discussed in Chapters 3 and 4). Seeing how one's old school had changed in the intervening years might awaken memories of the Spartan nature of the corps, as Werner Lübcke found at the Plön cadets' reunion in May 1978:

> The once Spartanly simple rooms with cupboards, the roughest tables and hard stools...had become snug living-rooms fitted out with all mod cons, in which the new generation is growing up. So it was only in our imagination and in our conversation that we saw the rooms once again as they had been when we left them...our little piece of home.[74]

Other former cadets from the Frankfurt old boys' association took more concrete steps to memorialise their former incarnation as *Spartanerjünglinge* – by painstakingly typing out Paul von Szczepański's novel and holding regular readings of it at their meetings, which they advertised proudly in the general *Mitteilungsblatt* (newsletter); the report of the first reading runs as follows:

> From the book provided by *Kamerad* (Comrade) Leder, *Spartanerjünglinge*, the first letter of *Kamerad* Gerhard von Gottwein to his "Mamming" from 20 August 1867 was read out. These readings will be continued.[75]

Particularly interesting to note is the way in which the hero of the novel is treated as being on a level with the other members of *Gruppe* Frankfurt (including *Kamerad* Leder, who presumably provided the typescript); he is simply '*Kamerad* Gerhard von Gottwein'. The phrasing of the report even seems to imply that the former cadets believed that the chapters of the work really were actual letters by a cadet who had lived during the 1860s.

During the later 1970s and the 1980s, as the average age of the surviving ex-cadets rose, their meetings and reunions were chronicled ever more regularly in local papers.[76] Very many of these reports describe the cadet-corps education as 'Spartan' (*vel sim.*), and it seems reasonable to assume that such descriptions were encouraged by the former cadets – even if they were not directly reported as making the connection themselves.[77] In other cases, the ex-cadets were captured on record referring to their own *Spartanertum*, as in the following excerpt from a Bensberg local paper: 'Dr Gerhard Saffran...added that, despite having lived at times as the Spartan youths did, [the cadets] had never experienced Draconian strictures.'[78]

Another instance of former cadets self-publicising their own 'Spartan' education can be found in many works by Dr. Albrecht Schott, including his guide to the 'cadet museum' (*Kadettenmuseum*), an exhibition which formed part of the *Militär-Museum*, *Schloss* Bartenstein.[79] Schott's identification of the cadet-corps education with that of Spartan youth was still evident even at the end of his life, when he left behind in his *Nachlass* a few pages of 'stream of consciousness'-type musings on his time at the cadet corps. One of the words which he identified in this document as conveying the very essence of cadet-school life was '*Spartanerjünglinge*'.[80]

Finally, in the former cadets' last ever official publication, the *Kadetten Abschluss-Chronik* (1991), a glossy A4 brochure put together by the last surviving members of the *Traditionsgemeinschaft*, which was proclaimed as their legacy to future generations, the following passage formed part of the section on the cadet-corps' 'education and training':

> Education and training in the cadet corps was arranged so that it trained courageous officers for the army, and responsible citizens for society. It was based on the principles which the two great kings of Prussia, Friedrich Wilhelm I and Frederick the Great, held as precepts for their behaviour: love of the fatherland, selfless service for people and state, fulfilment of duty, simplicity, self-discipline. It formed and moulded the young cadets for their entire lives. The education in the corps was tough, but certainly no harder than in the cadet schools of other countries. The title of '*Spartanerjünglinge*' applied to all the cadets.[81]

The former cadets' devotion to the 'Spartan' values with which the Prussian Cadet Corps had instilled them had evidently lasted until the end of their long and eventful lives. Whether it had been used to foil criticisms of the corps, to define what a 'good' type of militarism should entail, or even just to help revive and relive childhood memories, the Spartan *topos* had retained its power over the cadets' imaginations for more than seventy years after the cadet schools had ceased to exist.

Conclusions

Having considered the significant position of the Spartan *topos* within political debates and public perceptions regarding the cadet schools, it can be seen that the Spartan theme encapsulated a number of discourses, all dictated by contemporary concerns. From the point of view of the military Establishment, assertion of the schools' status as '*neu-Sparta*' could provide legitimisation and a form of safeguard for an institution which was increasingly seen as controversial by political reformers because of its highly reactionary, monarchist and anti-liberal ethos. However, in the hands of the cadet corps' liberal opponents, whose resistance became ever stronger until the schools were finally abolished, this discourse of Spartan 'legitimisation' became a target for mockery, vilification, and even curricular reform (if, following Nickol's account, we assume that debunking the Spartan paradigm was a high priority for the new Social Democratic authorities at the *Staatliche Bildungsanstalten* after 1920). Nevertheless, despite such criticisms, former cadets still clung to a Spartan identity (which they saw as embodying the true Prussian 'military spirit') as a highly politicised validation of their education in the corps. It is therefore impossible fully to comprehend the complexity of the political controversies surrounding the cadet corps if we ignore the role that this rhetoric of *Spartanertum* had to play, particularly during the twentieth century.[82] Meanwhile, on a personal level, identification with Spartan youths became a crucial aid in helping cadets to bear the hardships of military socialisation to which they were subjected, as well as reinforcing the idea of Sparta as an officially endorsed paradigm of undying military virtues, such as endurance and patriotic martyrdom.

While one might have expected a martial state cast in the Prussian mould to inculcate in her future officers certain inspiring episodes and anecdotes from Spartan history, such as the heroic self-sacrifice of Leonidas and the 300, or the 'with your shield or on it' apophthegms, the appropriation and idealisation of Spartan *mores* which we find in the cadet corps is of an altogether higher order. Contemporary ideas of Spartan education, and expectations of what one must do to 'become a young Spartan' – including normalisation of latterday brutalities which could almost mirror Plutarch's depictions of Spartan youths' sufferings at the temple of Artemis Orthia – actually formed a fundamental element of the cadet schools' comprehensive programme of socialisation and *Charaktererziehung* (character education), whether this was carried out by members of staff, or inflicted covertly by cadets themselves.

The Spartan paradigm therefore had a very significant influence on the educational formation of hundreds (if not thousands) of future Prussian officers, some of whom would in time become major players in world history – such as Paul von Hindenburg, Franz von Papen, Hermann Goering, and Erich Ludendorff. Whether or not German military history would have been appreciably different if many of her great commanders had not undergone such a 'Spartan' toughening can never be known. However, we can be certain that many of these men did indeed see their education as following a genuinely Spartan model, and that they identified themselves unreservedly as heirs of a latter-day Spartan ethos.

Notes

[1] Although this section discusses contemporary left-wing attitudes towards the cadet schools, and right-wing reactions to them, rather than dealing with specifically Communist ('Spartacist') attitudes, this title recalls a specific incident in Hanns Nickol's autobiographical novel *Der letzte Kadett* (1935), which is mentioned on p. 163 below. One of the protagonists, a former cadet called Krüger who has previously entertained pacifist sympathies, realises that, ultimately, he cannot escape the imperatives of his cadet-corps training, and runs away to join the Freikorps in a desperate battle against Spartacist troops.

[2] Clark 2006, 638–9.

[3] ibid., 638.

[4] cf. Schmitz 1997, 168, 172–4; Ulhorn 1919.

[5] Clark 2006, 623–4.

[6] ibid., 624–7.

[7] Schmitz 1997, 175ff.

[8] ibid., 180ff., 191–2.

[9] ibid., 185. For more on the political discussions which led to this step, see e.g. *Die Vorschläge über die Umwandlung der Kadettenanstalten in nichtmilitärische Staatsanstalten mit Internatscharakter* (July 1919) in GStAPK IV.HA Rep.13 Nr.84; *Preußische Landesversammlung*, 56. Sitzung (30/09/1919), 4452–3.

[10] Quoted in Schmitz 1997, 165.

[11] ibid., 199–201; cf. Clark 2006, 627.

[12] He is particularly notorious for his role in the assassination of Foreign Minister Walther Rathenau in 1922.

[13] Salomon 1930, 8–9.

[14] ibid., 11, 16. For another ex-cadet's similar feeling of hopelessness at this time, see Eckardt 1967, 39.

[15] At this time, the swastika was still a general symbol of German *völkisch* nationalism, not yet solely linked with the NSDAP, the Nazi party.

[16] Schmitz 1997, 197.

[17] ibid., 204–5.

[18] e.g. *Sitzungsberichte des preußischen Landtages* 1922, 126.-127. Sitzung (3-4/4/1922), 8961–9056.

[19] ibid., 9045.

[20] ibid., 8981.

[21] In this context, Oelze is probably referring to the idea of Sparta as a society made up of '*Männerbünde*'.

[22] ibid., 8985–8.

[23] Nickol 1935, 202.

[24] Although, as analysis by Schmitz has shown, the novel is certainly autobiographical, we should beware of any simplistic equation of Hartwig's character with that of the author himself, since Nickol also portrays very sympathetically other characters who are completely opposed to Hartwig's attitude.

[25] ibid., 8.

[26] ibid., 11.

[27] ibid., 12.

[28] ibid., 18.

[29] ibid., 19.

[30] ibid., 21.

[31] ibid., 19–20.

[32] ibid., 23–4.

[33] ibid., 30.

[34] ibid., 91.

[35] For more on this, and on the autobiographical nature of the work in general, see Schmitz 1997, 206–8.

[36] Nickol 1935, 95–8.

[37] ibid., 99–100.

[38] cf. Bux 1925; Pöhlmann 1925.

[39] Nickol 1935, 179ff.

[40] ibid., 187ff., 193.

[41] ibid., 193.

[42] ibid., 194–5.

[43] For a full list of references, see the Appendix below.

[44] *Deutsche Kadettenzeitung. Organ des Reichsbundes ehemaliger Kadetten.* Jg.1920, August-September, 1–2, 1. From Issue 3 onwards, the name was changed to *Reichskadettenblatt.*

[45] ibid., 2. It was also suggested that the former cadets should somehow try to inject their spirit back into the Stabilas (p. 6).

[46] ibid., 6.

[47] Boeckmann 1926, 99.

[48] Klingenburg 1928, 184.

[49] *Reichskadettenblatt* 13, April 1928, 176.

[50] Gruhl 1928, 1 (emphasis original).

[51] Henning 1928 [GStAPK IV.HA Rep.13 Nr.70, Bl.18]. It should be noted that the *Kreuzzeitung* was an extremely nationalist, right-wing newspaper – hence its open support of the cadet corps during this period.

[52] Kiock 1929, 1.

[53] Readers may wonder why very few sources from the Third Reich have been discussed here. During my research, I was able to find relatively few instances of the Spartan trope during this period, and the evidence for the *Reichsbund ehemaliger Kadetten* during the Third Reich in general is rather sparse. This may well be because large amounts of material were destroyed either by war damage or by post-war denazification processes. Additionally, former cadets may not have wished to have evidence of their pro-Nazi sympathies preserved in archival collections, and therefore may not have donated as many documents relating to their activities during this time to the *Bundesarchiv-Militärarchiv* and the *Geheimes Staatsarchiv*. For more on ex-cadets' attitudes towards the Nazi regime more generally, see Chapter 8 below.

[54] This new League of Former Cadets seems in reality to have been an umbrella organisation for many smaller overlapping groups or cells; some of these were based on where their members currently lived (e.g. *Gruppe* Frankfurt; *Gruppe* Hamburg), while others were formed of alumni from particular *Voranstalten*, such as Plön or Köslin.

[55] Two poems by 'E.L.', *Mitteilungsblatt* Nr.36, June 1974, 28 [GStAPK IV.HA Rep.13 Nr.21].

[56] GStAPK IV.HA Rep.13 Nr.135, Bl.15.

[57] GStAPK IV.HA Rep.13 Nr.121, Bl.38.

[58] cf. Hartmut von Hentig's introduction to a reprint of Leopold von Wiese's *Kindheit*, published in 1978; Werner Schreiber's afterword to Unruh 1983, 634, quoting an article from *Die Zeit* (5 April 1968).

[59] *Mitteilungsblatt* Nr.29, December 1972, 26–7.

[60] For a full list of Spartan references during this period, see the Appendix below.

[61] *FAZ* 14/05/1963, '*Eine Lanze für Kadetten-Anstalten*'.

[62] Rudelsdorff 1963, 4.

[63] Rudelsdorff 1967, 10–18.

[64] Rudelsdorff 1975.

[65] *Chronik des 11. Bundeskadettentages*, Nürtingen 1979, 20–34.

[66] *Die Welt*, 21/09/1982, '*Kein Zapfenstreich mehr beim feierlichen Gelöbnis*'.

[67] GStAPK IV.HA Rep.13 Nr.170, Bl.62–3.

[68] Plön *Kadetten-treffen* report, 10-12/05/1968 [GStAPK IV.HA Rep.13 Nr.121, Bl.17ff].

[69] *Hamburg Rundschreiben* 127, 18/07/1977, 2 [BA-MA MSG2/17021]. The speaker, Kurt-Christoph Voigt, was given a similar eulogy by Jobst Meyer-Schneidewind on 8 May 1988 at a reunion in Oranienstein. Meyer-Schneidewind praised the way of life at the corps, which all cadets had found 'very Spartan' (*die wohl von allen Kadetten...als sehr spartanisch empfundene Lebensweise*), as well as the way in which this life-style, and the high demands placed on the cadets, spurred comradeship. For more on cadets' self-defence against accusations of militarism, see Manteuffel 1958 and Schubert 1967.

[70] Lübcke n.d., 14. See further Müller 1946.

[71] *Chronik des Bundes-Kadettentages* 1973, Bornheim-Üdorf, 32–3. For a slightly different take on the Thermopylaean epigraph, see the following speech by Kamerad Wentscher, ibid., 38.

[72] Wagner 1969, 21.

[73] Bruns 1979 [GStAPK IV.HA Rep.13 Nr.35, Bl.63].

[74] Plön *Kadetten-treffen* report, 4-6/05/1978, 7 [GStAPK IV.HA Rep.13 Nr.121].

[75] The typescript itself can be found in BA-MA MSG2/17011. Report of the first reading: *Mitteilungsblatt* 24, August 1970, 16–17 [BA-MA MSG3/1186].

[76] This revival of interest may indicate a lessening of public hostility towards the former cadets, and the military caste which they were seen to represent. However, it also seems probable that this trend simply reflects the increased interest with which local journalists tend to regard the very elderly – the fewer and older the survivors at a reunion, the more noteworthy the occasion. This tendency can also be perceived in media coverage of surviving British war veterans.

[77] Some examples: *Lindauer Zeitung* 23/09/1978, '*Ein "Vorkorps-Appell" mit Herz und Gemüt*'; *Lahnzeitung* 16/11/1979, '*In Diez soll Erinnerung an Kadettenanstalt wach bleiben*'; *Lions Club Zeitung Diez* 02/1985, '*Königlich-Preußische Kadetten in Diez*'; *Rothenburg Stadt und Land*, ?1983, '*"Preußisch-deutsche Tradition". Königliche Hoheiten und hohe Offiziere beim Bundes-Kadettentreffen in der Reichsstadthalle. Der jüngste Teilnehmer am Treffen der 750 noch lebenden ehemaligen Kadetten ist 75 Jahre alt – Spartanisch erzogen*'.

[78] GStAPK IV.HA Rep.13 Nr.34, Bl.163 (20/02/1992). See also Noth 1978, as discussed in Chapter 2.

[79] Schott n.d., a; Schott n.d., b, Schott 1980, 7.

[80] Fritz D., private correspondence, 05/10/2010.

[81] *Kadetten Abschluss-Chronik*, December 1991, 10.

[82] For instance, how could a reader understand the full significance of Reitzenstein's entitling his longest and most harrowing cautionary tale 'Sparta' (when there is only one overt reference to *Spartanertum* in the whole story) without being aware of this all-encompassing socio-political context?

8

PERSONAL AND POLITICAL APPROPRIATIONS OF SPARTA AT THE *NATIONALPOLITISCHE ERZIEHUNGSANSTALTEN*: HISTORICAL CONTEXT

'Cadet Schools of the Third Reich'? The aims and ethos of the *Nationalpolitische Erziehungsanstalten* (1933–1945)

The Prussian Cadet Schools might have ceased to exist in 1920, but only 13 years later, the leaders of the 'new Germany' were to establish a new

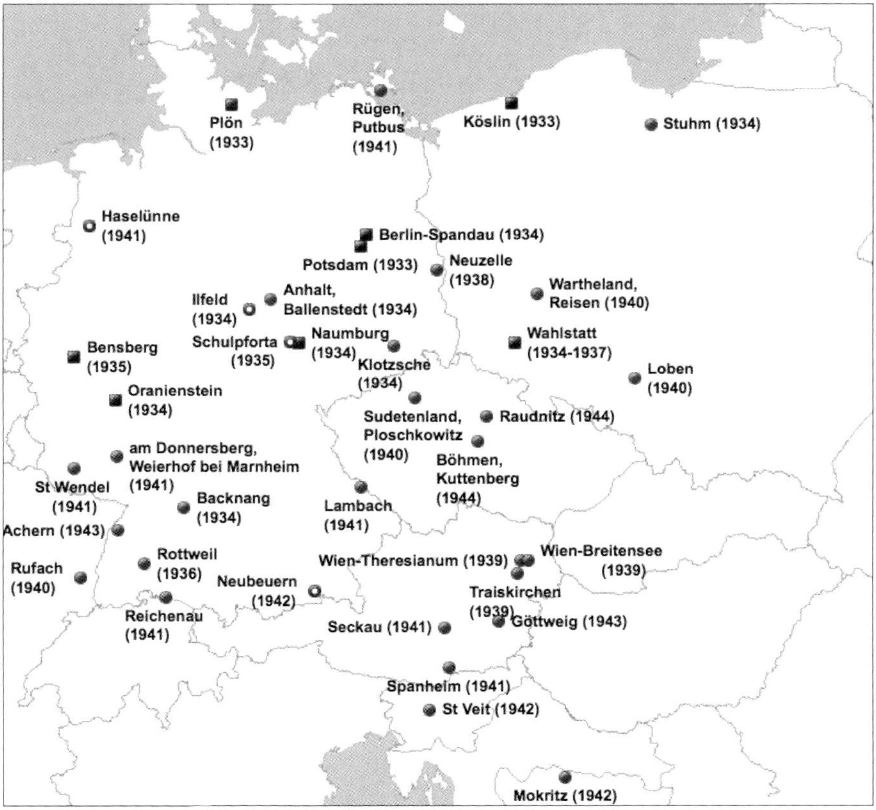

Fig. 20. Locations of the Napolas for boys and their dates of foundation (superimposed upon modern European state boundaries). N.B. Former cadet schools are marked with a square, and humanistic Napolas with a dotted circle.

type of elite educational institution: the *Nationalpolitische Erziehungsanstalten* or 'National Political Education Institutes', otherwise known as Napolas, or NPEA for short. Although the Napolas existed for only a handful of years compared with the cadet schools, they were widely considered to be of inestimable value in training the future leaders of the Third Reich during the twelve years of their existence.[1]

As Figure 20 shows, a number of these schools were founded on the premises of former cadet schools, and, albeit in a somewhat different fashion, they also appropriated the idea of Sparta as a model. These two chapters will therefore focus upon personal and political appropriations of Sparta at these institutions, including the ways in which the founders of the NPEA conceived of Sparta as a political paradigm for the schools, and the means whereby politicised portrayals of Sparta were used at the Napolas in order to foster the National Socialist worldview. Evidence from contemporary documentary material, memoirs, and eyewitness testimony will then be used to reconstruct a composite picture of the impact which such Spartan ideology had on Napola pupils on a personal level.

To begin with, this chapter will explore the continuities between the cadet schools and the NPEA, highlighting some of the ways in which both these institutions formed part of a shared tradition, despite their radically different political backgrounds. The general aims and ethos of the Napolas will also be summarised, including a brief account of everyday life at the schools. As discussed in the Introduction, some of the evidence which I have been able to collect during my research comes from correspondence and conversation with surviving ex-pupils of these schools, most of whom were in their mid-teens in 1945, and are in their eighties at the time of writing. This testimony has been used in particular when attempting to reconstruct the impact which the use of Sparta in National Socialist and Napola ideology had on pupils on a personal level, as well as to augment extant accounts of daily life at the schools, and illuminate contemporary teaching methods. It should, however, be stressed that individuals' experiences were not by any means uniform across all the schools – which could have widely differing traditions.[2] Even within one individual Napola, different classes or year-groups might experience their time at the school very differently, often due to the varied characters and attitudes of the teachers and *Erzieher* who were responsible for them.[3] Nevertheless, when using such testimony in conjunction with contemporary documentary evidence, we can gain a fairly clear picture of the schools' general atmosphere, and the life which pupils led there. The second half of the chapter will then examine the ways in which Spartan ideology was taken up by the founding fathers of the Napolas: namely, the Reich Education Minister Bernhard Rust; the first Inspector of the Napolas, Joachim Haupt; and the last, August Heißmeyer.

The *Nationalpolitische Erziehungsanstalten* were founded in 1933 by the then Prussian Culture Minister, Bernhard Rust, as a birthday present for the *Führer*. The first three Napolas to be established were founded on the sites of former cadet schools: Plön, Köslin and Potsdam. Pupils generally joined the schools at the age of 10, and were supposed to graduate at the age of 19. By 1945, the Napolas were educating a total of around 10,000 pupils (approximately 2% of the total number of school leavers); 46 schools had been founded, and it was intended that eventually there should be over 100.[4]

The Napolas were conceived as a special type of state boarding school which would educate the future elite of the Third Reich 'in the spirit of the National Revolution'.[5] Most followed the syllabus of a *Realgymnasium* (Latin was compulsory),[6] but their emphasis on physical and pre-military training was much more marked than at normal German secondary schools. The selection process was extremely rigorous; only those of 'Aryan descent, irreproachable character, pure racial health, full physical ability, and high intellectual prowess' were deemed eligible for the schools.[7] Boys with these credentials then underwent a week-long *Aufnahmeprüfung* (selection test), in which they had to prove not only their academic aptitude and physical fitness, but also sheer courage. One of my correspondents from Napola Rügen in Putbus, Hans P., writes:

> Non-swimmers had to jump from our diving platform (eighty metres out in the Baltic Sea, reached by a jetty) from a three-metre board into deep water. We older ones brought them out again. No one should hesitate! The swimmers had to jump out of a third-storey window into a blanket. Anyone who hesitated could go right home again.[8]

The schools were intended above all to create a new type of 'political soldier', dedicated to the National Socialist worldview, and ready to sacrifice all for *Volk* and *Führer*. This was to be achieved by moulding the pupils to a military-style way of life, based on subordination and control, toughness, and commitment to the community. *Kameradschaft* (comradeship) and *Gehorsam* (obedience) were considered crucial in order to create a strong, war-ready race of leaders; the individual had to be subordinated to the collective.[9] In order to emphasise the schools' military character, the nine classes were named '*Züge*' (platoons), organised into '*Hundertschaften*' (companies);[10] teachers were designated '*Zugführer*' (platoon commanders) or '*Hundertschaftsführer*' (company commanders), and the pupils themselves were called '*Jungmannen*'.[11]

The idea that these boys had been selected to form the future elite of the Third Reich in all walks of life was a given, and, even after the war, many former pupils went on to gain exalted positions in society and politics. However, it was emphasised that boys' social and financial background should play no role whatsoever in the selection process – the lowliest farmer's son was as welcome at an NPEA as the son of a Party bigwig, so long as he could demonstrate that he possessed the right character and physical attributes.[12]

Daily life at the schools followed a very strict timetable, which laid particular emphasis on physical training. However, during the last years of World War II, boys' education was often disrupted when they were sent as *Flakhelfer* to man anti-aircraft guns for months at a time, and all had to join the armed services at 16.

Clearly, the Napolas did exhibit certain continuities with the cadet schools.[13] The very first Napolas were all founded in cadet-school buildings, and others quickly followed – Naumburg, Wahlstatt, Oranienstein and Berlin-Spandau (the successor of the Lichterfelde HKA) in 1934, and Bensberg in 1935. These institutions' unhappy years as mere *Staatliche Bildungsanstalten* were quickly cast aside, as the new directors of the NPEA sought to remilitarise the schools, and to cement firm links with their previous glorious past as bastions of 'the greatness of the old Prussian spirit'.[14] As their founder, Bernhard Rust, put it:

> In these Prussian Cadet Schools, timeless German values were once nurtured...which must live once again; the soldierly spirit with its traits: courage, consciousness of duty, and frugality. For this reason, I have also effectively given all National Political Education Institutes the words of a great Prussian soldier [Moltke] for their legacy... '*Mehr sein als scheinen*' (be more than you seem).[15]

The only major difference between the two institutions, in Rust's view, was that the Napolas aimed to educate the future elite in all walks of life, not just the military. Although other members of the Inspectorate of the NPEA wished to emphasise discontinuities with the 'one-sided' education provided by the Prussian Cadet Corps,[16] and Himmler was later concerned at all costs to stop the *Wehrmacht* (the Third Reich's armed forces) from using the Napolas as 'a new type of cadet school' which would provide officers for the army in particular, since he wanted to bring the schools more and more under the SS's sphere of influence,[17] the 'positive values' of the 'cadet-school tradition' were generally seen as an important model by the schools' new directors.[18] Even the schools' new uniform was designed to incorporate the epaulettes of the cadet-corps uniform, with former cadet schools retaining their traditional colours.[19]

The former cadet-school Napolas also retained some continuity in personnel, and the first Inspector of the NPEA, Joachim Haupt, along with his adjutant Reinhard Sunkel, were both ex-cadets. Much of the Napolas' terminology also suggested connections with the cadet-school past, such as the titles of *Erzieher* and *Stubenältester*, as did the list of requisite 'Prussian' virtues which boys had to display. Even if these connections were felt more strongly by pupils of former cadet-school NPEA such as Spandau or Köslin than by those who attended Napolas in Southern Germany such as Backnang or Reichenau, the general public embraced the idea that the NPEA were simply '*Kadettenschulen*' in a new guise.[20] Families which had habitually sent their sons to the cadet schools in former times would often automatically enrol their children at a Napola, in the assurance that there they would receive a similar type of education.[21] Some boys were even inspired to join a Napola because they had previously been enthused by cadet literature, such as Ernst von Salomon's *Die Kadetten*.[22]

Many former cadets were overjoyed by the fact that their *almae matres* had been resurrected in recognisable form, and that current students even felt themselves to be 'old cadets' through and through, seeking to uphold cadet-corps traditions.[23] The *Reichskadettenblatt* urged ex-cadets to get in touch with their old schools once they had become Napolas,[24] and, in an article for *Das Jugend Regiment* in 1935, a contributor to the *Reichskadettenblatt* described the cadet schools as '*in der urwüchsigen Form nationalsozialistisch*' (National Socialist in their original form).[25]

On the Napolas' side, this forging of links was taken up no less eagerly. The NPEA old boys' networks explicitly encouraged ex-cadets to join them and attend their reunions, and former cadets were also invited to come and talk to Napola pupils, or to contribute to the schools' regular newsletters.[26] Some Napolas, such as Bensberg, even instituted a 'cadet tradition-room', where relics and documents from the cadet-school era could be studied and appreciated by boys and staff.[27] Therefore, for those pupils who attended former cadet-school Napolas, the cadets must have been, at least occasionally, a real presence – and perhaps also a model for emulation.

In some ways, daily life at the Napolas also followed a pattern not entirely dissimilar from that of the cadet schools. A wake-up call would precede half an hour or so of *Frühsport* (early morning sport – this often involved swimming lengths, or cross-country running), followed by breakfast and a morning of academic lessons, further physical activity and the private study

Fig. 21. Pupils at Napola Rügen attend a biology lesson (1941–2).

period took up the afternoon. The parade-ground drill demanded of the cadets also found its counterpart at the Napolas in the form of the frequent *Appelle* (military-style roll-calls), *Flaggenparaden* (ceremonies honouring the flag), and marching in formation.

Similarly, although some of the titles in the Napola hierarchy of command had changed, the structure remained almost identical. Alongside the unchanged office of the *Stubenältester*, who held absolute command over his '*Stubengemeinschaft*' of five to seven boys, we also find positions such as *Jungmann vom Dienst* (the equivalent of *Kadett vom Dienst*/duty cadet), *Jungmann-Gruppenführer* (equivalent to the rank of *Kadettengefreiter*/cadet NCO), *Jungmann-Zugführer* (equivalent to the position of *Klassenältester*/form captain) and *Jungmann-Hundertschaftsführer* (equivalent to the rank of *Kompagnieführer*/company commander).[28] As one of my correspondents from Napola Rügen, Dietrich Schulz, put it:

> Like the cadets, *Jungmannen* had to be brought up to be *Führer*-personalities, who were in a position to command and make independent decisions, and were meant to be 'an example worthy of imitation' to the troop or collective entrusted to them. Everyone in the *Zug* (class) would be *Jungmann vom Dienst* once, and had to prove his leadership abilities. He also had to decree punishments. The education to absolute obedience was all bound up with that. Special achievements in lessons, sport and institutional duties (*Anstaltsdienst*) were honoured with promotion to the rank of *Jungmann-Gruppen-/Zug-* and *Hundertschaftsführer*.[29]

Although this form of '*Selbsterziehung*' (self-education) fitted the Hitler Youth slogan 'youth must lead youth' admirably, the adult *Erzieher*,

Zugführer (class-commanders) and *Hundertschaftsführer* (company commanders) still possessed ultimate authority. Nevertheless, although the evidence suggests that the bullying found at the NPEA never attained quite the inventive and torturous heights which we saw employed by some cadets in Chapters 2–3, certain forms of hazing seem to have been resurrected at the Napolas in almost identical form, such as the *Kostümfest* (see p. 163 above), or being forced to do kneebends while balancing a heavy board piled with fragile items on one's outstretched arms.[30] Again, the 'constant supervision' exercised by the *Erzieher* did not necessarily extend to protecting the *Jungmannen* from each other – such toughening up was considered part and parcel of the training which would transform them all into '*ganze Kerle*' (real men), ready to serve the Reich, whatever hardships might befall.[31]

As at the cadet schools, *petzen* was considered the ultimate sin against the schools' cardinal virtue – comradeship.[32] Stealing from a comrade was taboo, but '*organisieren*' (appropriation) played a similar role to that which we have seen at the cadet schools – particularly during the final years of World War II, when provisions were becoming ever more scarce.[33] Karl L., formerly of Napola Naumburg, describes one such ploy:

> We were always hungry – particularly because the physical and sporting demands were high. Pre-military training played a big role in the final stages of the war. Only by honest sharing could we get by. We took care of additional nourishment through tricks. As a 'trumpeter', now and then in the evening I had to play the tattoo in front of the school. Finally, I had to check whether everywhere was well blacked-out (because of the air raids). Regularly, I 'discovered' cracks of light at the kitchen windows. In order for me not to have to report it, the dinner ladies gave me some leftovers (biscuits, peel with blancmange, bread), which I naturally shared with my friends afterwards. That these edibles were always lying there already [showed that] the women knew that the 'blackout problem' was only an alibi.[34]

However, it should not be supposed from this catalogue of similarities that the Napolas resembled the Prussian Cadet Corps in every regard. The cadet-school syllabuses had never contained designated slots for political teaching, such as the sessions on 'worldview' or 'national-political' education which formed a regular part of the routine at most NPEA. Furthermore, although the Napolas' entire curriculum was self-confessedly ideological, greater importance was placed on an all-round academic education at the Napolas than had ever been the case at the cadet schools.

Additionally, many of the Napolas placed a great emphasis on music or other extracurricular activities, such as amateur dramatics, or the cultivation

Fig. 22 and 23. Extracurricular activities during the early 1940s: orchestra practice at Napola Rügen, and camping – possibly during 'manoeuvres' (1944).

of hobbies.[35] Many of my correspondents recall everyone in their class being forced to take up a musical instrument and join an orchestra, wind band or choir, while others' photograph albums contain frequent snapshots of theatrical performances or model-building sessions, as well as programmes from professional theatrical or operatic performances which the *Jungmannen* were taken to see in nearby towns. Additionally, pupils were given the opportunity to go on numerous school trips to countries as far afield as Greece and Sweden, and – before the war – participated in regular exchanges with pupils from American academies or English public schools. Boys also took part in so-called '*Osteinsätze*' (Eastern Assignments) – part of the schools' 'Germanising' mission in newly-occupied Reich territories – during which they gained experience of helping *Volksdeutschen* (ethnic Germans) cope with farm work during the harvest. Older *Jungmannen* were even sent to work in mines and factories for a few weeks, in order that they should truly learn how 'the people', whom they would soon lead in peace or command in war, lived their humble existences.[36]

However, such hard graft was well made-up for by the number of exciting new sporting activities which were offered at the Napolas, and which formed one of their main attractions. Depending on the individual *Anstalt*, boys could learn to ride, drive, glide, fly light aircraft, row, sail, shoot or ski. The different schools competed against each other regularly at the Napola *Wettkämpfe* or 'manoeuvres', which were deliberately held in particularly beautiful parts of the Reich. Boys would live for a week or two in massive encampments, sleeping on pallets of straw, and eating meals prepared on primitive stoves known as *Gulaschkanonen*. *Jungmann* Ottho, writing in the tenth-anniversary edition of the Plön NPEA newsletter, describes the beginning of a typical day:

> At 6am sharp the Major's whistle shrilled through the sugar factory. Blearily, we crawled out of the straw. We ran immediately to the river and plunged into its cold currents.[37]

The highlight of the manoeuvres (which also formed an important part of individual schools' physical education programme throughout the year) were the '*Geländespiele*' (cross-country war games), in which boys were divided into different teams, each with a differently-coloured 'life-thread' tied round their wrists. One group would have to defend a tactical stronghold, while the other attempted to storm and gain control of it. The team with most surviving members (those who had not had their life-threads torn off by the enemy) were the winners. A report from the newsletter of Napola Köslin describes one such occasion in summer 1939:

> We had hardly come forward 100 metres, when suddenly the 'reds' appeared before us all over everywhere, and engaged us with a wild war cry. But the majority of our team was already there, and we rushed at the enemy all together. Everywhere one looked, tangles [of boys] were writhing on the ground... Here and there one saw bleeding noses and...shirts in tatters. Then the 'dead' were counted up. The totals gave us a resounding victory.[38]

Such fiercely-practised pre-military activities were deemed an excellent preparation for the boys' future military service for the fatherland – as were the gruelling cross-country running, athletics and assault course training which the *Jungmannen* often had to practise barefoot (even in snow) – which formed a regular part of the schools' physical education programme.

The atmosphere of the institutions in general, however, can perhaps best be summed up by this endorsement from one *Jungmann* Hägele of NPEA Backnang:

> Here, the community spirit (*Gemeinschaftsgeist*) works upon us directly. It demands that the individual give his all for victory, and conversely teaches him to relinquish his own glory and advantage for that of the team... Our way of life and our worldview demands that we endure many hardships and demonstrate iron-hard perseverance. These traits are systematically taught and nurtured in sport and *Geländesport.* As everywhere, here the best of the individual – his pride, his honour, and his healthy ambition – are invoked, on the assumption that he is sensitive and receptive to this. Then he gives of his very best... We will only truly be able to appreciate the full worth of this tough education when we have entered a new sphere of life... For our sojourn in this institution is really...a concentrated, systematic preparation and toughening up...for the essential coming battle for the great community of our people.[39]

Readers may have noticed in the preceding pages some features of Napola life which are somewhat reminiscent of depictions of Spartan education. The emphasis on bodily resilience, including barefoot exercise in skimpy clothing in all weathers, the 'tough hand-to-hand fighting',[40] and the declared aim of 'moulding self-sacrificing yet clear-eyed and iron-hard... warriors' with impeccable 'character', physical and mental toughness,[41] all have their echoes in the extant sources on Spartan education (as discussed in Chapter 4). This chapter will therefore conclude by examining the ways in which such an appreciation of the Spartan paradigm came to play an important role in the thought of the three founding fathers of the NPEA.

Sparta and the Creators of the NPEA

Three individuals in particular were to play a crucial role in the construction of the Napolas as an institution, and in the development of their specific ethos. As mentioned at the beginning of this chapter, Bernhard Rust, who had been appointed Prussian Culture Minister in 1933 and then Reich Education Minister in 1934, was the schools' original founder; in this regard, he was assisted by ex-cadet and staunch SA-man Joachim Haupt, whom he appointed the first 'Inspector of the NPEA'. However, following accusations of homoerotic attachments with Napola pupils, Haupt was dismissed and put on trial in 1936, whereupon August Heißmeyer, an SS official with a background in the pre-National Socialist *Jugendbund* youth movement, took over his position.

As we shall see, Rust, a Classicist by training and profession, seems to have had a particular penchant for Sparta as the ideal model to which a true National Socialist education should aspire. Haupt also held Sparta in high regard, due to his admiration for the Greek *Männerbund* as a pedagogical paradigm.[42] Though Heißmeyer, Haupt's successor, did not share his views on the beneficial educational effects of pederasty, he still almost always mentioned Sparta whenever he wrote programmatic memoranda and pamphlets on the schools. In these documents, Spartan education was frequently praised as one of the prime examples of the true *Gemeinschaftserziehung* (communal education) which Heißmeyer saw as the Napolas' aim.[43]

By exploring the various ways in which the Spartan paradigm was integrated into these men's conception of the NPEA, it is possible to demonstrate the extent to which Sparta may have played a part in their political programme. In some cases, Sparta could become a politicised tool, a pattern state which reflected those very virtues which the Napolas were intended to create in their young charges: anti-individualism; cooperation for the good of the community; physical prowess; readiness for war, and obedient self-sacrifice.

Born in 1883, Bernhard Rust gained his *Abitur* in 1904 from the Gymnasium Lyzeum II in Hanover, before pursuing further studies in Munich, Berlin, Göttingen and Halle an der Saale, where he concentrated on German Language and Literature and Classical Philology, including Greek history.[44] He was one of the few leading National Socialists to have higher education qualifications, and was even offered an extraordinary professorship at Halle University on the strength of his dissertation. Thereafter, he worked at various *Gymnasien* in Hanover, refusing many prestigious posts, including a position at Schulpforta, preferring to remain in his home town.[45] After the *Kampfzeit* (the period of the Nazi struggle for power during the late 1920s and early 1930s), he went on to become *Gauleiter* for Südhannover-Braunschweig, one of the most well organised and propagandistically effective *Gaue* (administrative sectors) of the

NSDAP in the period before the *Machtergreifung* (the Nazi seizure of power in 1933).[46] Rust is also said to have had phenomenal rhetorical abilities; even Goebbels himself conceded that their talents were comparable, whilst other observers claimed that Rust was actually a *better* speaker than the notorious Propaganda Minister.[47]

Fig. 24. Bernhard Rust (1934). Rust was appointed Prussian Minister for Culture in 1933, and Reich Education Minister in 1934.

When Rust founded the NPEA, he was determined that they should be directly under his jurisdiction as Education Minister, completely separate both from the general educational administration, and from the clutches of the NSDAP Party Organisation.[48] The 'Inspectorate of the NPEA', of which Rust was *Chef* (Chief), was therefore free to make its own decisions regarding the schools' management. As Heißmeyer put it in an article written for *Der Altherrenbund* in 1939, 'this personal and immediate subordination of the Inspectorate to the Minister guarantees a simplified command structure, and freedom of action...'[49] In general terms, Rust was seen as the schools' 'spiritual father', whose responsibility for and influence over the institutions was ultimately decisive.[50]

From this perspective, Rust's philhellenist sensibilities, and the knowledge of Greek and Spartan history with which his extensive Classical studies had provided him, could easily be brought to bear in terms of the formulation and imposition of school policy. Having been heavily influenced by Werner Jaeger's monumental work on Greek education, *Paideia* (1933), Rust saw communal education and physical training on a Greek model as all-important in attaining his National Socialist educational goals.[51]

Rust was also constantly concerned to convince his compatriots of Sparta's more general validity as the ultimate model for education in the new Germany. For instance, when opening a new teacher training college in Lauenburg, Pommern, in 1933, he declared:

> *I have no doubt but that we must rear a race of Spartans, and that any who are unwilling to espouse this Spartiate community* ***must relinquish forever their claim to be citizens of our state***.[52]

On another occasion, speaking at the 550th anniversary celebrations of the University of Heidelberg in June 1936, Rust asserted an absolute kinship of German youth with the heroic youth of Sparta.[53] He continued:

> The simple ways of life which form our youth today have not grown out of plagiarism of a previously intellectually-developed Greek example; on the contrary: the mystical tide of kindred blood, submerged for centuries, suddenly bursts forth once more... Suddenly, we sense a deep intimacy with the Greek people. The image of the Greek youth will be brought back to earth, without losing its sublimity. The core values of life, by which the German youth are beginning to shape their lives, appear to us here in a historical form.[54]

At another speech, given on 18 January 1941 at a *Gauleiter*'s handing-over ceremony, Rust drew a racial parallel between Sparta's mission and that of the Reich, even drawing an implicit comparison between Hitler and Lycurgus:

> Little Sparta was able to safeguard her power and individuality for nearly a thousand years; yet only her caste of leaders, the minority, were bound to this law. What future lies before the German people, then, now that they have found a great German lawgiver, if they safeguard these laws for the whole of their lives, inasmuch as one race can take over its knowledge and its will from another.[55]

As far as educational administration went, the syllabuses which Rust designed, both for use in secondary schools and at the Napolas, laid considerable emphasis on Spartan history, often at the expense of Athens. Tyrtaios gains a special mention in the sections on Classical literature, and the list of key themes in Greek history includes 'Sparta's *kosmos* (*Gesetzgebung*), and its racial, politico-social, military and socialist organisation'.[56]

Rust's appreciation of the Spartan model also came to the fore on some of his official visits to the NPEA. One ex-pupil from Napola Rügen recalls an instance from the early 1940s when Rust came to the school. He writes:

> I can still remember exactly an encounter with the then *Reichsminister* Rust at Putbus (I'd been allotted the task of doorman outside the biology classroom, and had to 'report' the class to him upon his visit), when he asked after my father. I replied to him that Father had died in 1940 as an SS Officer serving his Fatherland, in a reserve field hospital in Rostock, following a car accident. At which he said to me (practically word-for-word in my memory): 'Good, my boy! In ancient Sparta, too, sons had to take the place of their fathers...'[57]

In this case, the Spartan example seems to have been at the forefront of Rust's mind as a model for how 'his' pupils should conduct themselves (note the collocation of the recently bereaved Napola pupil with a theoretical Spartan boy). This laconophile aphorism was evidently intended to console, and spur its recipient on to match his father's valour.

Although it cannot be proved conclusively that the similarities between education at the Napolas and Spartan education were deliberately instituted at Rust's behest, it seems at least probable that Directors and teachers at the NPEA who knew of Rust's laconophile sympathies would have wished to stress or highlight the Spartan paradigm – a phenomenon which we shall see at work in the following chapter. In this way, *Erzieher* could have felt that they were not only following the implicit directions of their 'Chief', but also that they were 'working towards the *Führer*' – whose enthusiasm for Sparta has been mentioned briefly in the Introduction.[58]

However, Rust was by no means the only influential Napola official to have endorsed the Spartan example. We shall now turn to the laconophile sentiments attested in the work of the two Inspectors of the NPEA, beginning with Joachim Haupt.

Haupt was born in 1900; a member of the Prussian Cadet Corps until 1918, he then did a brief stint in the *Freikorps*.[59] Once it became clear that he would be unable to join the army, Haupt decided to go to university, studying at Frankfurt (where he first became involved with Nazi activism and pamphleteering), Greifswald, and Kiel, where he completed a doctorate in philosophy, graduating in 1926.[60] He then took up a teaching career, and in 1929 was nominated *Studienassessor* (junior teacher) and transferred to the *Schleswig-Holsteinische Bildungsanstalt* (the former cadet school) at Plön. During this period, Haupt had also begun to publish a series of National Socialist philosophico-pedagogical tracts (he had joined the NSDAP in 1922), and in 1931 he was disciplined and sent away from Plön because of his overt Nazi sympathies.[61] However, by 1934, he had gained a position as '*Ministerialdirektor*' (permanent secretary) in the Prussian Culture Ministry under Rust, turning his mind to more conceptual and programmatic educational problems.[62] Klaus Schmitz even suggests that the very first initiative for the foundation of the NPEA came from Haupt, before swiftly being taken up by Rust, who then gained all the credit.[63]

Haupt's educational ideals showed a strong inclination towards the model of the Greek *Männerbund*, and much of his work generally stresses the inseparability of *Griechentum* (Greekdom) and *Deutschtum* (Germandom). In a highly influential tract entitled *Sinnwandel der formalen Bildung*, published in 1935 under the pseudonym 'Winfrid', he declared that 'the task of German educational reform consists in the salvation and recreation of the Aryan Greeks' and Germans' cultural heritage'.[64] The Greeks had possessed the only true '*Knabenführung*' (leadership of boys),[65] since they took particular care over their blooming youth, and the future of the race – Greece should therefore function as a world-historical paradigm for all Nordic races:[66]

> Among the Greeks, every man was qualified and eager to take part in the education of the youths, and precisely the best and leading men among the Greeks competed formally for the love and fealty of worthy boys. This type of pedagogy, of leadership of boys by the leading men in the State, was underpinned by the correct idea that youth, with its core power and biological energy, is still unweakened by the injuries which the men's struggle for life and for the race have already inflicted upon them, nor is it encumbered with the failings and fatigues of their elders. Then, if ever, is the soul of the youth of the race given a possibility to gain the hard-won experience of manhood, not through ideas and books, but in realising the wisdom of the trainers and the higher embodiment of the coming generation of the people.[67]

The mistakes of the past two centuries, which had sacrificed such principles to the 'Jewish-Roman spirit', could only be remedied by a return to the common 'Aryan' origins of the German people. National Socialist education must therefore seek its true paradigm in the Greek warrior band (*Kampfbund*):[68] 'In Sparta and Athens the entire education of youth was a national-political education.'[69]

Although Haupt did not dwell so exclusively upon Sparta's paradigmatic importance as did Rust, she was certainly one of the Greek *poleis* which most aptly fitted his ideals – one can see clear links between, on the one hand, the ideas expressed in the quotation above and, on the other, those passages from Plutarch's *Lycurgus* or Xenophon's *Lakedaimoniōn Politeia* which stress the participation of all adult male citizens in the Spartan education process.[70] Similarly, Haupt's advocacy of officially endorsed pederastic educational relationships echo the Plutarchan and Xenophontic accounts of Sparta; no other ancient Greek educational practices, save perhaps those of Crete, seem to bear quite such a close resemblance to Haupt's professedly philhellenist ideals.[71] It may even be the case that Haupt had to some extent been influenced by the 'Spartan' culture of the cadet schools, though no evidence has yet been found to prove or disprove this suggestion.

However, the court which tried Haupt for his 'homoerotic relations' with pupils at NPEA Plön and Schulpforta was unimpressed by the positive gloss which it saw him as giving to Spartan pederasty:

> The court is too well acquainted with ancient Greek history, its authors and its truly sound ideals [to understand the evidence in this way]. The Greek ideal, i.e. the heroic spirit of the Spartans, also has nothing in common with the homoerotic dreamland of the accused, for his goings-on were reprehensible and immoral to the highest degree.[72]

Haupt's emphasis on the pederastic elements of Spartan educational methods had come into conflict with the homophobia inherent in mainstream Nazism, and been defeated by it. Haupt was dismissed from his post in 1935, and cast out of the Nazi party three years later. The *Spartabild* propagated by Haupt's successor would be of a rather different – and more virulent – mould.

August Heißmeyer was born in 1897, joining the NSDAP in 1925. He rose quickly in the ranks of the SA and then the SS, gaining promotion first to the position of 'Head of the SS Central Office' (*SS-Hauptamtstelle*) in 1935, and then to the rank of *SS-Obergruppenführer* in 1936, at the same time that he was appointed Inspector of the NPEA.[73] In many respects, Heißmeyer was the servant of two masters, for he was responsible not only to Rust (as far as the Napolas were concerned), but also, as an SS Officer and head of

Fig. 25. August Heißmeyer, Inspector of the Napolas from 1936–1945.

the *SS-Hauptamtstelle*, he was answerable ultimately to Himmler. As the war years progressed, this led to problems, as Rust (whose health was deteriorating due to a chronic condition of trigeminal neuralgia, exacerbated by excessive drinking) began to regard Heißmeyer with increasing distrust, suspecting him of playing a double game and concentrating influence over the Napolas into the hands of Himmler and the SS.[74] As Rust's health and political position grew more and more precarious, Heißmeyer's influence over the schools did indeed grow – however, his aim of turning all the Napolas into SS preparatory-schools was never realised.

One of Heißmeyer's most famous aphorisms neatly summarised his view of the Napolas' mission: 'Men make history – and we make the men!'[75] Less succinctly, in an internal party memo, he characterised some of the Napolas' educational aims as follows:

> *Erzieher* and *Jungmannen* form a firmly sworn comradeship, pervaded with discipline and order, which knows no arrogance; [they are] gladly willing to live under the law of authority and to master the tasks put before them. The *Jungmann* dedicates himself to his intellectual training and the improvement of his physical capabilities with identical enthusiasm... In boyish, though often tough battles, which are fought hand to hand; through cunning activity in the countryside; through conquering all hardships, whether in rain or sunshine, the *Jungmann* must prove himself to be a tough-minded person of sound character, with clear wits and an open heart...
>
> Through such a training, which includes many a tough trial of his nature and his ability, particularly in preparing him for the various functions of leadership, the *Jungmann* must be made capable and prepared for a combat-ready life of achievement in the service of the constitution of the entire people and its living space (*Lebensraum*). In his youth, [when he is] capable of development and receptive, he must steel his will, his courage, and his physical power in tough war games, in challenging cross-country field exercises, and in strenuous activity; he must strengthen his character, his courage and his attitude in the discipline of *Gemeinschaftsleben* and in his constant smaller life tasks; he must school his mind and his artistic abilities through the manifold tasks of learning and perception, and through the comradeship of our organisation of life and festivals...[76]

As we might suspect, given the rather Spartan nature of some of this description, one of the historical models to which Heißmeyer would return time and again in speeches, programmatic pamphlets, internal Party memos and radio broadcasts, was the educational system found in Sparta – often mentioned in conjunction with other, more recent, establishments – such as the Prussian Cadet Corps.[77]

In a tract on the Napolas' aims entitled '*Erziehung zur soldatischen Moral*' (1941), he writes:

> Peoples and races with the power of historical creativity, which were concerned to gain new blood for the caste which ruled the state, have always, through political instinct or political knowledge, focused upon a communal education (*Gemeinschaftserziehung*) for their youth – so for example Sparta and England, the Catholic Church and the Prussian Officer Corps...
>
> If we in Germany are going to get down to business in instilling those 'soldierly morals' which Nietzsche demanded, and of which the *Führer* provides the living example, then the training of our youth must be designed according to the view of life which Sparta..., Prussia-Germany, and the Reich of the *Führer* have brought to greatness. Therefore breeding, self-discipline, order, energy, a sense of community in personal matters, readiness to surrender oneself for *Volk* and Reich, pleasure in a dangerous and tough life and contempt for an easy life, must be our educational goals – which, through the manifold forms of training at the National Political Education Institutes, are striven for and made into reality.[78]

Similarly, in his programmatic pamphlet on the schools, *Die Nationalpolitische Erziehungsanstalten*, published in 1939, he wrote:

> The *Jungmann* must [through his education here] *become a man and a member of the troop*. But it is not the variety of the training and instruction which is important – this could also be an individualistic Renaissance ideal – but the character-moulding spirit of the training. Variety did not make the Spartan..., the Prussian, the National Socialist, but rather their *attitude*.

Heißmeyer is also on record as explicitly emphasising the Spartan example at speeches given when he visited the schools, and in unofficial conversations with Napola pupils.[79]

Many of the lesser members of the NPEA administrative hierarchy (such as Gustav Skroblin and Otto Calliebe) accepted these ideas, using them in their own speeches and articles on the schools.[80] Again, we might suggest that this embodied a form of 'working towards' Rust and Heißmeyer on the part of these subordinates, so that they were attempting to say what their superiors would have wanted to hear – not just about the goals of the Napolas in general, but also regarding the importance of Sparta as a political paradigm. Such admiration for Sparta as an ideal for the Napolas could then be put into practice in school life, both by pupils and teachers.

Notes

[1] e.g. BArch R43-II/956b, Bl.48-50 (see also R2/12711, R1501/624). N.B. The Napolas should not be confused with another type of Nazi elite school, the Adolf Hitler Schools, which were established in 1937 in order to train the future elite of the Nazi party. These schools were founded by Robert Ley, the Leader of the Party Organisation, and Baldur von Schirach, the Leader of the Hitler Youth, and were intended in part to compete with the Napolas. However, only around a dozen schools ever came into existence. For more on the Adolf Hitler Schools, and on their engagement with Sparta, see Roche 2012a; for a full account of their pedagogical practice, see Feller 2001.

[2] Dietrich Schulz notes that the *Kriegsanstalten* (Napolas founded during the Second World War) differed significantly from those founded earlier (private correspondence, 17/11/2009); Harald O. (private correspondence, 25/01/2010) stresses the overall importance of the '*genius loci*' – a school such as Schulpforta, with a humanistic, monastic tradition, would necessarily have had a very different ethos from that of a school such as his own, Traiskirchen, which had previously been an artillery cadet school of the Austro-Hungarian Empire.

[3] cf. Montanus 1998, 5; also private correspondence with Karl-Josef F. (30/07/2011). That there may have been more variation between individual Napolas than between individual cadet schools should not be considered particularly surprising, given that the cadet corps ultimately aimed to train all its pupils for exactly the same career, and that all the *Voranstalten* were founded and run by the military authorities with precisely this aim in mind. Meanwhile, the Napolas often took over schools with widely differing backgrounds (see n. 2 above), and also gave individual Directors great freedom to implement their own curricula and forge their own ethos – as long as this conformed ultimately to National Socialist principles. Thus, the intellectual atmosphere at NPEA Schulpforta would have been very different from that at NPEA Plön, where boys who did not bring home enough points from the Napola-wide sporting competitions (*Wettkämpfe*) would be summarily expelled (Paustian 1995, 28).

[4] Bouvier 2000, 59. Four *Mädchen*-Napolas were also established to educate girls, but since the ethos of these was rather different – they were largely intended to turn out 'intelligent mothers', rather than to train female leaders of the Third Reich – I have restricted my study to the boys' schools. For more on the *Mädchen*-Napolas, see Jodda-Flintropp 2010.

[5] Scholtz 1973, 29, quoting Rust's foundation speech.

[6] With the exception of Ilfeld, Schulpforta, Haselünne and Neubeuern, which all followed the curriculum of a humanistic *Gymnasium* (Greek was compulsory as well as Latin).

[7] *Aufnahmebedingungen der NPEA Naumburg*, 1935.

[8] Hans P., private correspondence, 04/12/2009.

[9] e.g. Heißmeyer n.d. For a programmatic pamphlet on the schools, see Kloppe 1934.

[10] *Hundertschaft* is an ancient Germanic term, used to denote a military unit of around a hundred men, loosely based on the Roman 'century'.

[11] This little-used term, the male form of '*Jungfrau*' (virgin/maiden), has strong connotations of the *Männerbund*.

[12] cf. Heißmeyer 1936.

[13] For a useful summary of the similarities and differences in organisation and focus of the two institutions, see Schmitz 1997, 282ff.

[14] *10 Jahre Nationalpolitische Erziehungsanstalt Köslin 1933 bis 1943*, 126; cf. Hobohm 1941, 224. Pupils who were suitable only for the namby-pamby '*Bildung*' (academic learning) which the Stabilas afforded, rather than the Napolas' true '*Erziehung zur Führerpersönlichkeit*' (training of *Führer*-personalities), were quickly excluded.

[15] Rust 1943b, 6.

[16] e.g. Helmut Trepte, quoted in Schmitz 1997, 245 n. 291; cf. Klare 1996, 6, 16; Förschler 2002, 64.

[17] See correspondence in spring 1940 between August Heißmeyer (the second Inspector of the NPEA) and Himmler, BArch NS19/1560.

[18] *Blätter der Nationalpolitischen Erziehungsanstalt Berlin-Spandau*, Jg.1934 (1), 18/12/1934, 3; BArch NS/5/VI 18842, Bl.21.

[19] Hans Günther Zempelin (2000, 51) recounts that, when Heißmeyer (cf. n. 17) suggested that individual schools' epaulettes should be replaced by a general design with the legend 'NPEA', there was an outcry – the cadet-school colours were seen as a paramount part of pupils' identity.

[20] Heinich 2007, 23.

[21] e.g. Leeb 2005, 25 (Rüdiger Freiherr von Wechmar), 202 (Mainhardt Graf Nayhauß-Cormons).

[22] Selke 1990, 5; cf. Bolte, n.d., 19.

[23] Selasinsky 1970, 242; cf. BA-MA MSG3/1295; MSG2/17012.

[24] *Reichskadettenblatt* 37, July 1936, 579.

[25] *Das Jugend Regiment* 22/12/1935 [GStAPK IV.HA Rep.13 Nr.152].

[26] *Naumburger Ring* Easter 1940, 2 [BA-MA MSG2/17024]; *Reichskadettenblatt* 38, October 1936, 599; *Mitteilungen der Nationalpolitischen Erziehungsanstalt Naumburg/Saale*, 22.Kriegsnummer, July 1944, 14–16. If the newsletter (*Rundbrief*) of the former Köslin cadets from December 1980 [GStAPK IV.HA Rep.13, Nr.109, Bl.233] is to be believed, the former Napolaner showed pride in being the cadets' successors even at post-war reunions.

[27] Former Bensberg cadets' newsletter, 01/01/1937 [BA-MA MSG3/1295].

[28] Zempelin 2000, 112; Vahl 2000, 3–4.

[29] Dietrich Schulz, private correspondence, 30/12/2009. It should be noted that the exact responsibilities inherent in these positions might vary between schools.

[30] e.g. Vahl 2000, 21; Kleinau 2000, 27.

[31] Vahl 2000, 22–3; on constant supervision, see Müncheberg 1991, 54.

[32] e.g. Montanus 1998, 144–9.

[33] Rüdiger Freiherr von Wechmar remarks that his thoughts of Spandau were always linked with hunger: 'Odd as it sounds, we *Jungmannen* were always hungry, even before the war!' (Leeb 2005, 32). See also a chant which Arne Heinich and other boys at NPEA Bensberg often used to sing: '*Wir haben Hunger, Hunger, Hunger, haben Durst; Wir wollen Käse, Käse, Käse, wollen Wurst*' – 'We're hungry, hungry, hungry, and we thirst; we want cheese, cheese, cheese, we want *Wurst* [sausage]' (Heinich 2007, 184).

[34] Karl L., private correspondence, 22/01/2010. For further thieving exploits, see correspondence with Günther P. (30/01/2010) and conversation with Ekkehard P. (03/01/2010).

[35] e.g. Morlang 2002, 46–51.

[36] For an example of this, see NPEA Plön 1942.

[37] *10 Jahre NPEA Plön*, 25.

[38] Quoted in Gélieu 1990, 86.

[39] Quoted in Förschler 2002, 120.

[40] Klare 1996, 50, quoting Vice-Inspector Otto Calliebe.

[41] *Die Brücke*, May 1944, 55.

[42] cf. Schmitz 1997, 287.

[43] e.g. R43-II/956b, Bl.52ff.

[44] Pedersen 1994, 22–3.

[45] ibid., 22.

[46] ibid., 87.

[47] ibid., 27.

[48] Scholtz 1973, 68.

[49] Heißmeyer 1939a, 203.

[50] e.g. *Chronik der Volksschule Diez* 1934, 246–7, quoted in Morlang 2002, 4.

[51] Scholtz 1973, 40.

[52] Rust 1935a, 45. All emphasis original.

[53] Frank 1936, 17.

[54] ibid., 17–18.

[55] Quoted in Pedersen 1994, 322.

[56] Rust 1938d, 232, 91.

[57] Klaus Schikore, private correspondence, 31/12/2009.

[58] For more on Hitler's laconophilia, see Roche 2012b, 104–6. 'Working towards the *Führer*' was a phrase first used by a Prussian civil servant in a speech given in 1934, and subsequently developed as a concept by Ian Kershaw in his biography, *Hitler 1889–1936: Hubris* (London 1998) 529–531, to express the idea that German state and party officials often took the initiative in devising policies to fulfil Hitler's supposed wishes, or attempted to turn his often loosely and indistinctly phrased views into actual policy.

[59] Heggen 1993, 25.

[60] Schmitz 1997, 254–6.

[61] ibid., 256–7; Heggen 1993, 25.

[62] Schmitz 1997, 258.

[63] ibid., 259.

[64] Winfrid 1935, 27.

[65] ibid., 54.

[66] ibid., 60.

[67] ibid., 60–1.

[68] ibid., 7; Schmitz 1997, 287.

[69] Haupt 1936, 19. It is intended that Haupt's particular relationship with philhellenism will be analysed more fully in future publications.

[70] e.g. *Lyc.* 16.5, 17.1; *L.P.* 2.10, 6.1.

[71] cf. *Lyc.* 17.1, 18.4; *L.P.* 2.12–14.

[72] BArch (ehem.BDC) SA Haupt Joachim, 7/4/1900, Bl.1728.

[73] Förschler 2002, 34–5.

[74] cf. BArch NS19/2498, secret memo to Himmler from the Chief of German Police, 21/08/1942.

[75] Quoted in Schäfer 1997, 29.

[76] Heißmeyer n.d., 7–9 [BArch R2/12710].

[77] Other examples can be found in *Der Altherrenbund* 1939, 1/8; an article in the *Frankfurter Zeitung*, 08/02/1939; Die *Innere Front N.S.K.* 19/04/1941; and Heißmeyer's speech at the foundation of NPEA Backnang, which was broadcast on all Reich radio stations and reported in the *Deutsche Allgemeine Zeitung* (22/04/1941).

[78] Heißmeyer 1942a, 52–3.

[79] Karl L., private correspondence, 22/01/10.

[80] e.g. Skroblin 1942.

9

'SPARTA'S SPIRIT LIVES!' SPARTA'S ROLE IN IDEOLOGY AND EVERYDAY LIFE AT THE NAPOLAS

'We demand firm, Spartan discipline!' Racial ideology, textbooks, and the Napolas' nazified view of Sparta

In April 1935, Schulpforta, the *alma mater* of Nietzsche, Fichte and Wilamowitz, and one of the oldest and most prestigious humanistic schools in Germany, was transformed into a Napola – the second to follow a Classical curriculum. At the school's annual celebration the following year, the Academic Director (*Unterrichtsleiter*), Dr. Kurt Person, made a programmatic speech which encapsulated the spirit of Schulpforta's new teaching, entitled 'What do the Greeks and Romans mean to us?' In this lengthy oration, subsequently published in the school newsletter, the *Pförtner Blätter*, Person outlined the ways in which he felt that the history and literature of Classical antiquity could usefully be analysed in terms of the National Socialist present. Ancient Greece and Rome had now become particularly relevant in historical terms, since their inhabitants were racially identical with the Nordic German people; they were 'brothers of our Germanic forefathers, recognisable in their appearance, origin, language, and psychological attitude'.[1]

During his speech, Person refers repeatedly to Sparta, the better to point up such pertinent parallels. Firstly, in order to emphasise the idea that the ancients' 'comportment in psychology and character' (*seelisch-charakterliche Haltung*) is supremely Aryan, he notes that the texts in question focus on deeds, rather than mere moralising:

> There, we see the Spartans at Thermopylae going to their certain death...in that terse, completely un-vainglorious, almost matter-of-fact way, which is well known to us from Germanic poetry.[2]

Later on, Person also praises the 'sense of duty towards the whole community of the people' which is to be found among the Spartans.[3] However, his peroration treats Sparta at still greater length, focusing upon the ways in which new National Socialist racial ideas can best be used to illuminate Spartan history:

> Who, in earlier times, would have seen so clearly that the Spartan character was so determined by biological heredity, and so consciously aimed at racial preservation, as we do today? How they must have skimmed over Thucydides' description of the battle for Sphacteria. In the sixth year of the war, the Athenians succeeded in laying siege to a Spartan detachment on the afore-mentioned island, an inconsequential battalion even by the standards of antiquity. And, immediately, the Spartans are ready to declare an armistice, make peace, and even beg the Athenians for an alliance. And all this, because – at first one thinks one must have read this wrongly – 181 Spartiates were among those under siege. 181, after six years of war, in which the losses on either side had reached high into the thousands. But *they* were Spartiates, members of that carefully-protected ancient Nordic warrior- and conqueror-caste, which only made up a very minimal fraction of the total population of Laconia, and which was so completely and carefully protected, because the State's destiny hung upon its racial preservation. When the 300 under Leonidas were picked out, those that were chosen for sacrificial death, contrary to the custom of other peoples and ages, were the fathers of families; the youths were sent back home! For the fathers had fulfilled their biological duty to the Fatherland for the preservation of the species![4]

In his enthusiasm to make Classical history – and particularly Spartan history – fit a National Socialist model, providing a useful paradigm for the present, Person was by no means alone, although his 'take' on Sparta was perhaps of a more scholarly mould than those of other Directors.[5] Another, less extended example can be found in the very first speech made by Dr. Adolf Schieffer, the new Director of Napola Köslin, upon the school's foundation on 1 August 1933. Here, he sets out his 'programme':

> Following on from the age-old tradition of the cadet schools, the outer framework of our institution will once again be a strictly military one. Here, comradeship, discipline and national sentiment will rule. Here the future leaders of the newer, better Germany must be brought up, not in terms of caste and class arrogance...but in terms of solidarity of the people. Whoever wishes some day to lead others must himself learn obedience and subordination first. For this reason I demand firm, Spartan discipline... I will place particular value on the pupils having a good military attitude...[6]

This passage is especially noteworthy because Schieffer's idea of 'Spartan discipline' appears to be linked with his conception of the cadet-school tradition, as well as with the very Spartan idea that one must learn to obey in order to command.[7] Interesting, too, is Schieffer's idea that the Napolas could improve upon this tradition by extending its benefits more widely; the 'Spartan' training provided by the NPEA was not to be the preserve of a solely aristocratic officer class, but was intended to embrace the whole potential caste of Nazi leaders, drawn from throughout the *Volk*.[8] When taken in conjunction with Person's speech, which was made on a similarly significant school occasion, these instances suggest that Sparta and *Spartanertum* were seen as being of considerable importance by some of those administrative officials who had most power to influence their respective schools' direction and future development.[9]

As the following pages will show, ideas about the significance of Sparta as a model for the Napolas appear to have been quickly taken up, both by external commentators, and at the schools themselves. Thus, in an article on the NPEA written for the periodical *Der Aufbau* in 1935, the anonymous author stressed the fact that 'history confirms that every heroic age needs a male educational order (*Männerordenserziehung*), just as in Spartan times.'[10] An article on NPEA Wahlstatt in the *Berliner Tageblatt* from 3 February 1934 also drew attention, in a sub-heading, to the 'Spartan education' which Wahlstatt had provided, which was founded, *mutatis mutandis*, upon 'the Spartan bases of the cadet-school education'. Meanwhile, distinguished professors might be invited to give edifying lectures on the Spartan constitution to the *Jungmannen*, as was the case at Schulpforta on 21 January 1939.[11] Two years later, in 1941, *Jungmann* Werner Querengässer even chose to do his final year dissertation – a piece of voluntary academic work which boys were encouraged to complete before they left Schulpforta, choosing a subject which particularly enthused them – on 'Spartan and Platonic Education'.[12]

However, the relevance of the Spartan nature of the Napolas was taken up yet more enthusiastically by one Dr. T. Goedewaagen, a Dutchman who, in an article written for the Dutch fascist periodical *Nieuw Nederland* in 1938, depicted his recent experiences at NPEA Bensberg in glowing terms. The article was intended to facilitate the spread of the Napolas to Holland, and Goedewaagen evidently conceived of the following endorsement as the best possible advertisement for the schools:

> These institutions aim to bring up loyal National Socialist Germans through an education in comradeship, in which body, soul and intellect are reared in organic unity through, and together with, a classy lifestyle. What in schools with a humanistic foundation is only a phrase (i.e. the nickname '*gymnasion*' for an institution in which nothing more is to be found of ancient *kalokagathia*, or the harmony of body and spirit, but in which youth is instead weighed down with trivial brain-ballast!) is at the NPEA a goal which is seriously striven for...
>
> It is as if the ancient Spartan spirit, the soldierly life-style, has been awakened to new life, but now with that typical nuance in which Germanic character reveals itself. In this organisation there lives a Germanic mysticism, a Germanic thought-world, a Germanic will to achieve. While

> Sparta had to abandon the refined culture of Athens, here refinement without decadence is coupled with power without brutality...[13]

In essence, Goedewaagen conceives of the NPEA as the only educational institution which can truly realise the promises of humanism – and, in so doing, reveals itself to be nothing other than a new, improved, and more Germanic Sparta.

In terms of teaching and the importance of Classics in general, Goedewaagen also had strong ideas:

> The choice of reading material from Greek and Roman authors will no longer be determined by classicising norms, but by the Nordic kinship of the Germanic and Classical cultural heritage. 'Greek teaching stands, as does all teaching, in the service of that task which has newly been given to us as Germans – self-education.' That men had a *völkisch* mindset in Greece and Rome is the cardinal theme of instruction. Anyone who sees that as restrictive should not forget that Classicism and Humanism have never done – or been able to do – anything other than bring to the fore an individual view of antiquity, in that they have also created their own version of antiquity.[14]

However, at the Napolas, it was undoubtedly a Nazified version of antiquity which held sway.

The rest of this section will focus upon the ways in which politicised versions of Spartan history were propagated at the NPEA, by examining portrayals of Sparta in a number of textbooks which we know to have been used at the Napolas – either because they were prescribed for all secondary schools by Bernhard Rust and the Education Ministry, or because eyewitnesses remember having used them. Particular attention will be given to the ways in which these textbooks' portrayals of Sparta were distorted to serve National Socialist ends or highlight resemblances between Sparta and the Third Reich.

As G. A. Rowan-Robinson, an Englishman who visited the Napolas for a period in the mid-1930s, put it, 'every single subject [at the NPEA] is taught with the sole idea of making the boys better Nazis... The children learned all the ordinary subjects, but they were no longer taught objectively. The whole teaching was coloured politically...'[15] Another English observer, J. W. Tate, also commented that:

> Even in those schools retaining the classical curriculum of the 'gymnasium', it is those qualities of the Greeks and Romans applicable to the new German citizen which are to be stressed. The relative value to National Socialism of different subjects is still *sub judice*, and is debated in the weekly masters' meetings.[16]

In this respect, the lessons followed the curricular framework provided by Rust in his pamphlets on 'Education and Teaching in German Secondary Schools'.[17] All the textbooks used at the schools had to follow these guidelines very closely, even possessing almost identical titles and topic headings. In one of these tracts, Rust also emphasises the importance of making history lessons as exciting as possible:

> History in its course must not seem like a chronicle to our youth, which places all occurrences in successive order, undifferentiated, but like a drama, in which only those events most significant and life-changing in their consequences should be presented...[18]

As far as teaching was concerned, boys would often have to prepare material in advance; teachers might retell it in an interesting way, or the pupils might have to answer questions upon it, but they should really have got to grips with all the material in the books, rather than merely parroting facts.[19] Karl-Josef F. describes the way in which lessons were often conducted: the *Jungmannen* would sit in pairs of desks set in parallel rows, while the teacher lectured from his rostrum at the front, sometimes writing things on the board or calling pupils up to answer questions, or pacing up and down among the rows of desks whilst making his points.[20]

The role of the textbook in all this can be elucidated admirably by Hans-Ulrich Horn, in an article entitled '*Die Neuordnung des Schulbuchwesens und Schulbuchfragen im Kriege*', published in the periodical *Deutsche Schulerziehung* in 1941–2:

> [The history textbook] is the most political school book which we possess; free from any problematisation..., it must reveal the historical genesis of the German people in its great lines of development, its vivid highs and lows, in terms of National Socialist views and values, free from any falsification, and make every young German person become conscious of the mission of our Reich for Europe under Adolf Hitler.[21]

With this programme – or warning – in mind, then, we shall turn to the ways in which these 'most political of school books' were used to portray the history and *mores* of the ancient Spartans, linking these wherever possible with the tasks and worldview of their contemporary National Socialist 'descendants', with whom they were supposedly linked in undying 'racial brotherhood'.

The textbooks which will be discussed here are Walther Gehl's *Geschichte für höhere Schulen. Mittelstufe: Ein Hilfsbuch zu geschichtlicher Anschauung. 1. Heft: Altertum* (1933); Bernhard Kumsteller's *Geschichtsbuch für die deutsche Jugend. Für die Jüngeren* (1936); Walther Hohmann's and Wilhelm Schiefer's *Volk und Reich der deutschen. Klasse 6. Von der Vorgeschichte bis zum Ende der Stauferzeit* (1940); Johannes Silomon's and Walther Franke's *Volk und Führer. Deutsche Geschichte für Schulen. Ausgabe für Oberschulen und Gymnasien. Klasse 6. Von der Vorgeschichte bis zum Ende der Staufenzeit* (1940 and 1943), Hans Bartels', Karl Klotzsch's and Hans Lüdemann's *Volkwerden der Deutschen. Von der Vorgeschichte bis zum Ende der Stauferzeit* (1941) and Paul Schmidthenner's and Friedrich Fliedner's *Führer und Völker. Geschichtsbuch für Höhere Schulen, sechste Klasse. Von der Vorgeschichte bis zum Ende der Stauferzeit* (1943).[22] As noted above, all textbooks had to be approved by the Education Ministry before distribution, and also had to follow government guidelines concerning their overall span and content – hence the obvious duplication in the titles of works written by different authors, as well as the designation of the class which should use them (in this instance, primarily the Sexta).

In almost all these works, the introduction to Spartan history portrays the 'Dorian Migration' (*dorische Wanderung*) as a legitimate conquest of the weaker Mycenaean races by an Aryan caste of Germanic farmer-warriors.[23] Thus Bartels, Klotzsch and Lüdemann in their *Volkwerden der Deutschen. Von der Vorgeschichte bis zum Ende der Stauferzeit*:

> Only in *one* place in Greece did the Dorian migration lead to the formation of a great power. In Laconia, in the south-east of the Peloponnese, parts of the tribe, in which Nordic warriorhood and the Nordic species were preserved at their purest, seized the fertile Eurotas plain, with *Sparta* at its midpoint, and from here conquered the entire countryside with healthy ambition for power, and a born understanding for the importance of this as the existential basis of the people. The earlier, Achaean inhabitants, [who had become] strongly mixed with Near Eastern elements, became thralls, slaves of the state, 'helots', and were divided up amongst their new masters, the 'Spartiates'... They were warrior farmers, tied to the land...[24]

Bernhard Kumsteller, in his *Geschichtsbuch für die deutsche Jugend*, treats the same material with an even more palpable sense of (over-)excitement:

> What beacons burn over the towers of the ancient Greek royal castles; how the farmers flee for protection within the thick castle walls! Hostile hordes are there, from the rugged northern Balkan peninsula, with wife and child, with dogs, horses, goats and carts... The oaken club is their weapon. They call themselves *Dorians*, and they honour *Heracles* as their patron.
>
> War all over Greece! See, already these wild bands are hurling their battle-chariots against the Mycenaean knights and destroying them in their impetuosity... The men whom they leave alive must serve them as 'helots' (slaves); they set themselves up as lords of the Peloponnese. Many inhabitants of the countryside flee before them, in order to seek a new homeland in another Greek valley... That was the Dorian migration.[25]

While Silomon and Franke, the authors of the relevant volume of *Volk und Führer*, also highlight the fact that the Spartans preserved the purity of the Aryan invaders' blood most effectively,[26] this link with the ancient Germanic peoples is then brought repeatedly to the fore throughout their treatment of Spartan history. Thus, they remark that 'the Spartan *assembly* of all Spartiates over 30 still corresponded exactly to the ancient Germanic council of war (*Heeresgemeinde*).'[27]

Similarly, in their conclusion to the section entitled 'The Nordic Character', Silomon and Franke state categorically that:

> The Spartan polity is a conscious creation of the Nordic spirit [which] wanted, through state socialism...to guarantee for the minority of the racially pure conquering people an enduring supremacy over a great majority of subjects, and the preservation of the purity of their blood.[28]

Sparta's decision to enslave Messenia is simply portrayed as the absolute right of such a powerful community of rulers, and, later on, the Platonic or Aristotelian criticism that Sparta might have subordinated cultural values in pursuit of excellence in war is brushed aside with the assertion that Sparta was '*the birthplace of the heroic idea of the State*' in terms of 'iron consistency' and the 'fanatical will to form a political community'.[29] The implication seems to be that Sparta was in fact the original birthplace of an *Ur*-form of National Socialism, in stark contrast to the 'Ionian states in the capitalist mould.'[30] These are then compared with Sparta – very unfavourably:

> In the verses of Tyrtaios lives the idea of the Spartan warrior state, the ideal of the Nordic man, who fulfils himself in his action and death for his state, and who knows only one glory: the continuation of his memory within the community for which he lived and died.
>
> How very different a picture is presented by the *Ionic cities of Asia Minor* and their citizens!...[31]

Silomon and Franke go on to complain that, for the Ionians, wealth was seen as the only measure of men's worth; the decadence of the Ionians' warrior instinct can be proved merely by contrasting the content of Tyrtaios' poetry with that of Archilochus.[32] The crisis of the farming class before the advent of Solon is seen as being due to 'the development of capitalism' at Athens; Solon's reforms could never have been successful in the long term, due to the capitalist underpinning of Athens' economy.[33] The dangerous growth of the slave and metic proportion of the Athenian population engendered by Solon's reforms is placed in stark contrast with Sparta's continued maintenance of racial purity and financial integrity:

> Despite all his good intentions, Solon had dug the grave of Athens' Nordic conception of the state, inasmuch as he introduced the penetration of capitalism into the state's power. Lasting peace could not be achieved in this fashion...[34]

Sparta's destruction only came about when she attempted to engage with the grasping Athenians on their own terms, crucially reducing her citizen numbers so that she was reduced to breeding with helots, and was soon overtaken by mercenary capitalist sentiments.[35]

In general terms, the textbooks also portray the Spartans as obeying National Socialist racial tenets to the letter, as exemplified by the account in Schmidthenner's and Fliedner's *Führer und Völker (6. Klasse)*:

> The Spartiates were far outnumbered by the subject population. The consciousness of superiority (*Herrenbewusstsein*) which lived within them, and the inner necessity of guaranteeing their ruling position, held them far from mixing blood with their subjects. Their position led them to give themselves a constitution which brought their warrior spirit to the highest fulfilment...
>
> The Spartans consciously set out to preserve a powerful race. On the principle that a person who did not possess a healthy, strong body was of just as little value to himself as he was to the state, the racial elders dictated whether a newborn child should live or not. Only physically flawless, healthy children were brought up; those of no racial value (*minderwertige*) were exposed on Mount Taygetos. Childless marriages could be dissolved; celibacy was forbidden. Relationships of Spartiates with women who were not their racial equals were threatened with punishment.[36]

Here, the language used by the authors resonates throughout with the language and technical terminology of Nazi propaganda and racial laws. Just as the Germans in the greater Reich were far outnumbered by the 'racially inferior' Slavic peoples whom they had conquered and forced to do their bidding, but were nevertheless able to rule them due to their supposed innate racial superiority and *Herrenbewusstsein*, so too were the Spartans able to ensure their supremacy over fellow Greeks. The Spartans are portrayed as being equally concerned to avoid 'blood mixing' (*Blutmischung*) through sexual contact with inferior elements, and any infants who are physically imperfect are left to die because they are *minderwertig* (racially inferior) – a key term in National Socialist racial vocabulary, which was also used to describe all the handicapped or mentally ill persons who were put to death under the Nazis' '*Aktion* T4' euthanasia programme (1939–1941).[37] Spartan marriage customs are also recast to fit a racial model; Germans could also be subject to punishment if they defiled the race through sexual relations with Slavs, Jews, or other supposedly racially inferior categories of humanity.

The Spartan way of life, and in particular the educational system, were also treated in depth; these, too, were often linked with Sparta's exalted status as an 'Aryan' warrior state. The textbooks in question often seem deliberately to emphasise (or even make up) traits of the *agōgē* which cause it more closely to resemble the ideal National Socialist education. Thus Bernhard Kumsteller:

> The greatest among the Greek states was Dorian *Sparta*. – It is about 600 BC. The sun has just risen over the snow-covered mountains. There, troops of fifteen to twenty youths march out of Sparta singing, to bathe in the nearby River Eurotas. An older comrade whom they have chosen is their leader. After their bath, they exercise heartily and do gymnastics on the meadow. Woe to the clumsy and the disobedient; they are ruthlessly punished by their leader with whippings. Once again, the *Jungmannschaft* return to the town, singing, and arrange their common meal; each one must bring something along to it. Lots of talking is forbidden whilst eating. Talk must be militarily short and succinct. At sundown the youths fetch reeds from the river, in order to make their common pallet-beds anew. Thus they live until their twentieth year, when the hotly desired day draws near, on which they will be accepted into the army.[38]

Here, in accordance with the best Hitler Youth principles, youth are being led by youth, singing as they go. Unlike Spartan boys in the ancient accounts on which the passage is evidently partly based, they go for cold baths in the Eurotas, and the exercises which they then pursue take the form of drills and gymnastics – those activities most akin to those of a National Socialist youth troop. Similarly, not only are all religious connotations of the 'whippings' removed, but it is now the leading boy himself, rather than the adult *paidonomos* or his aides, who administers the punishment. What is more, the group of Spartan boys is explicitly termed a '*Jungmannschaft*' – a term which the Napolaner would probably have seen as implying some sort of identity with themselves, as *Jungmannen*.

A similarly modernised portrayal can be found in *Führer und Völker*:

> *The* Erzieher *was the State*. Until the beginning of their seventh year, the children of the Spartiates stayed with their mothers, but then the boys entered the 'herds', which, divided according to age-grades, were under the command of an older youth. Gymnastic exercises and contests of all kinds, a modest life, for example sleeping on reeds and simple, rough food, the 'black soup', annual whippings at the altar of Artemis, and other means, had to serve the purpose of toughening, physical strength and agility, practice in the use of weapons, courageous and warriorly sentiment. Obedience and reverence for elders were held to be valuable virtues. In his twentieth year, the young Spartiate joined the army... Physical exercises to preserve war-capability were also assiduously cultivated among the men... *Subordination to the State, obedience*

> *to the laws, courage before the enemy, were the virtues of these tough men, for whom it was the highest commandment, either to return from the battle with their shield or on their shield, and for whom there could be no greater shame than flight in the face of the enemy.*[39]

Here also, we can see a similar focus upon those elements of Spartan education and Spartan life which match National Socialist virtues, such as 'toughness, physical power', 'subordination to the State' and total obedience. However, Silomon's and Franke's account of Spartan education even goes so far as to discard almost any relation to the ancient peculiarities of the *agōgē*. Instead, they replace these with a catalogue of activities which would almost all have seemed very familiar to the *Jungmannen* – so much so, in fact, that the passage could almost have been lifted from one of Heißmeyer's programmatic tracts on the Napolas:

> From their 7th year onwards, the *boys* were no longer brought up by their families, but as a collective, in the strictest military discipline, which was designed above all to awaken their sense of honour.[40] In a way of life which was completely dedicated to gymnastics, exercises, sport, hunting and all types of war games, which already, before they were put to the test in earnest, had as its great high point regular *Wettkämpfe*, *soldierly virtues* were developed in them: courage, endurance, obedience, alert quick-wittedness and unconditional comradeship.[41]

Such soldierly virtues were also brought to the fore in textbooks' accounts of Thermopylae and the heroic deaths of Leonidas and the 300 [*sic*], as exemplified by Silomon and Franke:

> In Spring 480, the Persians advanced once again with a land army and a fleet. Since the northern Greek tribes had collapsed, the Persians succeeded in marching unhindered through Thessaly to the Thermopylae pass. All the Persians' frontal attacks came to grief through the heroic bravery of the Greeks, but a traitor led the Persian troops to their rear. The Greek army saw that they were surrounded and had to marshal for the retreat. The withdrawal of the main army was covered by *Leonidas* with 300 Spartiates and 700 Thespians, right to their last breath. They all found death, but they won undying glory. On the spot where they fought their heroic battle, the Spartans erected a monument to them, and as long as men live, the saying that stands engraved there as their last greeting to their homeland will never be forgotten: '*Wanderer, kommst Du nach Sparta, verkündige dorten, du habest / Uns hier liegen gesehn, wie das Gesetz es befahl!*' ('Stranger, if you come to Sparta, declare to them that you have seen us lying here, as the law commanded!')[42]

*

In this brief examination, it has only been possible to consider a few of the most common ways in which Sparta was treated in an ideological fashion in some of the textbooks used at the Napolas.[43] Nevertheless, it becomes clear that a particular, Nazified version of Sparta does emerge from all of these works – as we might expect, perhaps, given that all textbooks published during this period had to be approved by the Reich Education Minister before permission was given for their distribution.

To sum up, then: wherever possible, Spartan history was forced to fit National Socialist views of race, and the Spartans themselves were interpreted as following a Third Reich-style programme of eugenic policies, as well as cultivating all those warrior virtues which were most prized both by the ancient Germans, and by their twentieth-century National Socialist counterparts. Spartan education and *mores*, including the heroism of Leonidas and the 300, were also presented in such a way as to emphasise the similarities between the Lacedaemonian polity and the Third Reich's '*neu Sparta*'.[44]

Role-models of heroism and self-sacrificial death: Memories of Spartan teaching at the Napolas

It will now be demonstrated that such ideas about the validity of the Spartan example for the Third Reich were also brought to life by individual teachers during lessons at the Napolas, using evidence both from published memoirs, and from my correspondents' recollections. By exploring this aspect of Spartan influence at the Napolas, it is possible to appreciate the variety of ways in which politicised views of Sparta became common currency at some of the NPEA.

The true extent of this politicised use of Sparta is impossible to ascertain, due to the paucity of available evidence. It should be noted that a small number of the eyewitnesses wished to emphasise strongly the fact that they remembered nothing about any Spartan influence at their schools, or that they did not remember the adjective 'Spartan' as having had any particular relationship with ancient Sparta.[45] It seems at least possible that pupils at some schools, such as Oranienstein, may simply have been less exposed to such ideas, and that at other schools, exposure may have depended more upon the attitudes of individual teachers. It is notable, however, that some of those correspondents who took this approach still gave (sometimes quite detailed) examples of Leonidas and the 300 Spartans at Thermopylae being held up as an example.[46]

However, even though Sparta was not held up as a paradigm at all of the Napolas all of the time, it seems that admiration of Sparta *was* sufficiently widespread for us to categorise this tendency as a distinct phenomenon, which has thus far been completely neglected in modern scholarship.

In general, teachers' attitudes were to play a very significant role in the Napolas' dissemination and reception both of Nazified versions of Spartan history, and of laconophile ideology. As at the cadet schools, the *Erzieher* lived alongside their charges, and were generally young (in their early twenties) – although older replacements commonly had to be found during the war years, as more and more able-bodied *Erzieher* were called up, despite Rust's attempts to gain them exemption from military service because of the 'militarily decisive significance' (*kriegsentscheidende Bedeutung*) of their educational work.[47]

NPEA teaching staff were all supposed to be convinced National Socialists and members of the SA or SS – at schools such as Plön which underwent a transformation from Stabila to Napola, any staff who were insufficiently committed to the aims and ideals of National Socialist elite education were asked to leave.[48] Once appointed, all *Erzieher* were supposed to attend further politically-oriented subject training and schooling in the correct worldview (*weltanschaulichpolitische Schulung*), or even to perform functions in other party and government organisations and departments.[49] As well as living together with the *Jungmannen*, the *Erzieher* had to take part in *Geländespiele* and other school activities alongside them, in order to build up an unbreakable bond of comradeship. Hans Günther Zempelin notes that there were three main types of *Erzieher*: some were more '*bürgerlich*'; others were strong, sport-oriented idealists, while yet

Fig. 26. '*Zugführer* Knapp and his lads' training on the coast of Rügen (c.1944).

others were deeply convinced National Socialists whose forte was training boys in the correct 'worldview' (*weltanschauliche Bildung*).[50]

Since the Napolas had no common, unified timetable or curriculum, there was a good deal of freedom for Directors and *Erzieher* to teach what they wanted, focusing upon those aspects of their subject which most interested them.[51] In this way, both the content and form of academic lessons could be very much determined by individual teachers, and there were manifold possibilities for them to play not only to their strengths – but also to their hobby-horses. Ernst G. of Napola Spandau recalled that 'One Gerhard Stock (Olympic victor 1936) managed, unchallenged, to occupy himself and us for a whole school half-year with the geography of Sweden!'[52] However, other teachers preferred to focus on Sparta as their 'special subject' – even if that meant using Latin lessons in order to teach material from Greek history.[53]

At Napola Naumburg, indeed, it appears that a great many of the teachers were concerned to instil their charges with the Spartan example; one history teacher in particular made a great impression. Karl L., who entered the school in 1943, gives an account of Sparta's role in the history teaching there:

> In history in the first year at the Napola (10–11) we were taught: Greek history; Roman history; German history, Part 1. In lessons, Greek history was covered particularly extensively, and here Sparta and *Spartanertum* were *particularly* emphasised. Boys of this age-group are especially susceptible and receptive to this type of subject matter. Although the academic and artistic achievements of the Athenians were acknowledged, at the same time their tendency towards weakness, deterioration of war readiness and supposed decadence was made clear. *Spartanertum*, on the other hand, was held up as a glowing example for the development of a healthy, powerful ethnic character (*Volkstum*); their war-ready way of life etc. was emphasised, a paradigm for our 'National Socialist *Volkstum*'.
>
> Thus the Spartan education of youth was on the agenda. For examples and evidence [one can take, for example,] the selection test, the trials of courage, the early morning sport, physical toughening, cross-country exercises, manoeuvres, war games etc. Sparta was constantly and explicitly emphasised as an example by the teachers and *Erzieher*. One example should prove the high value of this '*Vorbildwirkung*' (role model):
>
> We had to learn a text *by heart*, even though it didn't rhyme. We mastered it so thoroughly, that I can repeat it word for word, even now, after well over 60 years. I can't say what literary source it comes from:
>
> 'What did the troop of sunburned boys sing, who marched in lock-step into the Eurotas valley, in Laconia, to the sound of flute-music?
>
> "*Auf in den Kampf, ihr Enkel des unbezwungenen Herakles, streitet getrost! Noch nie wand euch den Rücken der Gott. Nimmer erschreck' euch die Menge des Feindes, noch*

fass' euch ein Zagen, nein, geradeaus mit dem Schild stürmt auf den Vordersten an! Denn schön ist's für den Tapfern, im vordersten Glied zu fallen, wenn er, den Seinen ein Hort, kämpft für den heimischen Herd. Aber unendliche Schmach, wenn den Fliehenden, der das Getümmel meidet, des Feindes Geschoss hinten im Rücken ereilt. Schreite denn jeder beherzt vorwärts, in den Boden die Füße fest eindrückend, die Zähne über die Lippen geklemmt, Brust und Schulter und zumal hinabwärts Hüften und Schenkel hinter des mächtigen Schildes eherner Wölbung gedeckt. Hoch her schwing' er zum Wurf in der Rechten die wuchtige Lanze, und Furcht weckend vom Haupt flattre der Busch ihm herab! Fuß an Fuß mit dem Gegner und Schild andringend dem Schilde, dass sich der Helm streift und der Busch mit dem Busch, Brust an Brust dann such' er im Kampf ihn niederzustrecken, sei's mit des Schwerthiebs Kraft oder dem ragenden Speer."

"Into battle, you descendants of unconquered Heracles, fight with confidence! The god has never turned his back upon you. Never let the mass of the enemy terrify you, nor consider hesitating; no, onwards with your shields, attack the foremost! For it is a beautiful thing for the brave man to fall in the frontmost ranks, when, a shelter to his own, he fights for his home and hearth. But unending shame, if the man who flees, who shuns the mêlée, is overtaken by an enemy shot in the back. So let every man stride forwards valiantly, feet firmly crushing the ground, teeth bared, breast and shoulder and especially below, hips and thighs sheltered behind the brazen curve of the mighty shield. High in his right hand he shall swing the weighty spear to throw it, and the plume shall awaken fear, quivering down from his head. Foot to foot with the enemy and shield pressing upon shield, so that helmet brushes against helmet and plume against plume, breast to breast then shall he seek to fell him in battle, whether with the power of the sword-stroke or the lofty spear."

Sparta's youth trekked out into the countryside, barefoot and clad only in flimsy tunics. With a crisp step, they passed through the fields. These were divided into equally fertile plots and allotted to the citizens of Sparta by the State... In the countryside they would then train rigorously for hours on end, and also fought each other one-on-one. Wearily, the young troop returned at midday. They were put hard at work out in the fields. They had to prove not only their strength and agility, but also their resilience and toughness, particularly as far as pain was concerned. Even at dinner-time they stayed together, just as at the communal dining places of the men. Straight after dinner the ringleader (*Rottenführer*) put his boys back to work. First they sang songs about the great deeds of their forebears, then they had to answer questions laconically (i.e. concisely).

"Why does our city-state have no walls?"

"Our bodies are its walls!"

At night the boys and youths made their makeshift beds out of hay, which they had to break without a knife from the reeds on the bank of the Eurotas. Sometimes they were sent out in the night-time, to steal vegetables or hunting-kill, to prove how wily they were. Anyone who was so clumsy as to let himself get caught was severely beaten.

> A steel-hard race of proud warriors grew up in Sparta. They lived under harsh discipline, as if the whole city were a barracks. They retained their spirit of comradeship through thick and thin. The arts and sciences found no place in Sparta, but in times of need, she was the saviour of all Greece!'[54]

The fifteen lines of the text which follow the initial rhetorical question about what the youths are singing are, in fact, nothing less than an abridged Hölderlin-style translation of Tyrtaios' poem, Fragment 11 West.[55] When I asked Dr. L. about this, he replied:

> The whole class had to learn the text about the Spartan youths over the Christmas holiday period 1943/44. Unfortunately I can't remember the name Tyrtaios.
>
> It was our *Hauptzugführer*, Wilhelm Riefenstahl, who gave us the 'Sparta-text' to learn by heart – not as a punishment, mind you! [He] sometimes called us, as encouragement, 'my brave little Spartans'. I should mention at this point that history was my favourite subject at that time; I really imbibed the material which was presented to me.
>
> We boys just had the textbook. The teacher had literature, pictorial material, maps etc. at his disposal. The lessons were formulated in a very emotionally-arousing manner; we cooperated intensively and enthusiastically.
>
> The Sparta-text probably came from a book, perhaps even the textbook. Herr Riefenstahl himself couldn't have written it, in my opinion. Further I can't say.[56]

Dr. L. also remembers that, even outside Herr Riefenstahl's lessons, many of the other teachers treated emulating the Spartans and living up to their educational standards as a favourite theme. He writes:

> Our Director Alfred Männich, one of the few teachers who was disliked, whom we called the '*Goldfasan*' (golden pheasant), because he always wore all the party medals, decorations and braiding, and emphasised his National Socialist attitude, explicitly emphasised the 'Spartan education' of the Napola *Jungmannen* in his official speech at the tenth anniversary celebrations of the founding of the *Nationalpolitische Erziehungsanstalt* Naumburg. I remember that absolutely clearly. He had certainly consciously 'planned' the 'Spartan education'.
>
> Our beloved *Hundertschaftsführer*, Dr. Friedrich Dubslaff, blond, small but very nimble and sporty, with bushy eyebrows and often with a little pipe, taught us Sport and German. He constantly emphasised that as war-ready brave German boys, it was our duty to live a Spartan way of life. Perhaps he also wanted to 'comfort' us with this [sentiment], and help us to bear more easily the fact that in the last two years of the war, food, heating, broken nights due to air raid warnings, power cuts etc., everything became scarce and circumscribed. [Therefore...] the emphasis on '*Spartanertum*' probably also served to make our lives, which were made so hard by the exigencies of the final stages of the war, more bearable... The Spartans, our role-models, had also lived such a frugal existence.[57]

> In certain situations, it was usual for him to make comments which made it clear that as far as his subject, Sport, was concerned, Spartan education stood in high regard. Firstly, when he wanted to spur us on to the highest possible achievements, or praise us; secondly, when he wanted to console us or cheer us up...if we were complaining about...physical exhaustion. Some examples [of the first type]: 'Pull yourselves together, give it your last effort, like the little Spartans...'; 'You've proved that you're true warriors, brave Hitler Youths, courageous Spartans!' (we were really proud when he praised us so!). When we were...completely worn out, at the end of our tether [...he might say]: 'The Spartans had to go hungry now and then; they didn't have regular mealtimes like you do! They had to go barefoot through the wilderness!' [or] 'Would a Spartan have moaned about a couple of bleeding blisters on his feet?'[58]
>
> We had history for a short time with Heinz Eckardt, a sportingly elegant teacher, who was also the *Ortsgruppenleiter* (regional group leader) of the NSDAP for Naumburg at the same time. He was a strict National Socialist. He too spoke of the 'Spartan education'. I should mention here that one of our teachers, I believe it was H. Eckhardt, told us (as we understood it as 11–12-year-olds), that the Spartans were racially related to us. They were supposedly descended from the Dorians, who had come from the North. I only present it as we understood it at the time.[59]

From this, and from further testimony given by another pupil from Napola Naumburg, Günther P., it appears that emphasis on the relevance of the Spartan example became more and more marked as World War II progressed. As Dr. L. has suggested, this could partly have been an attempt on the part of the *Erzieher* in question to palliate the hardships and shortages which the war made inevitable. However, we could also posit a link with Goering's and Goebbels' collocation of Stalingrad with Thermopylae, and the ensuing propaganda campaign, as discussed in the Introduction ('*Kommst du nach Deutschland, so berichte, du habest uns in Stalingrad kämpfen gesehen, wie das Gesetz, das Gesetz für die Sicherheit unseres Volkes, es befohlen hat.*' 'When you reach Germany, tell them that you have seen us fighting at Stalingrad, as the law, the law of the safety of our people, commanded us.'). Günther P., who was a couple of years older than Karl L., remembers that Leonidas' last stand at Thermopylae was an important part of what made Sparta an attractive example:

> At a relatively late point in time, when Germany's fortunes in the war had already changed a lot, one or other of the *Erzieher* would frequently name the Spartans as 'the paradigm' of a particularly warlike, 'disciplined' race of the Greeks who – particularly in the example of the defence of the Thermopylae pass – had saved the remaining Greeks from conquest by the Persians under Xerxes. In memory of their 'heroic and sacrificial bravery', over 2,000 years later, there now stood there a memorial with the

> (obviously Greek) inscription: '*Wanderer, wenn du kommst nach Sparta, sage: Du habest uns hier liegen gesehen, wie das Gesetz es befahl.*' ('Stranger, if you come to Sparta, say: you have seen us lying here, as the law commanded.') Following on from this, there very seldom failed to be a piece of advice along the lines of: 'A nation, a people, that provides such special benefits, chances, and training for a group of its members, can also demand from them the readiness to undertake more in the way of duties and achievements!'[60]

In similar fashion, Günter O., a pupil who attended two of the humanistic Napolas, Schulpforta and Neubeuern, between 1938 and 1945, remembers the way in which Spartan history was ideologically presented in Greek lessons, explicitly stating that '...I had the impression that, the longer the war went on, the more often the Battle of Thermopylae was presented as an act of heroic self-sacrifice':[61]

> The Battle of Thermopylae in 480 BC was duly treated as an outstanding incident, and sacrificial death for the community was emphasised. In my memory the famous verse has continued to stick – in Greek as well – '*Wanderer kommst Du nach Sparta verkünde den Lakedämoniern, Du habest uns hier liegen gesehen, wie das Gesetz es befahl.*' ('Stranger, if you come to Sparta, tell the Lacedaemonians that you have seen us lying here, as the law commanded.') The Second World War had also demanded many sacrifices from among the teachers and *Jungmannen*. We often heard this verse at commemoration ceremonies for the war dead. More haunting for us were the accounts about the sacrificial death of young German volunteers in the First World War at Langemarck/Ypres/West Flanders...
>
> Greek History wasn't taught at Schulpforta. Of course, incidents that were charged with history were extensively discussed in language lessons, such as the Battle of Thermopylae. In connection with this, the position of the two kings, the importance of the Spartiates and the social position of the helots were gone into. The official duty of those who belonged to the different classes of the population to serve in the army also found a mention. The education of the boys and the rights and opportunities of the women were handled inasmuch as this was necessary in order to understand the Greek texts... At the time that the Greek teaching was carried out intensively, we pupils were 13–15 years old.

Hans W., an ex-pupil of Napola Loben/Annaberg, describes another such instance:

> At our NPEA...Sparta was always a theme. The Spartan way of life, soldierly life, warriorly courage and readiness for self-sacrifice, toughness and robustness, sense of responsibility and self-discipline were demanded ever more. The Spartans served as a role model... [As far as languages were concerned] we only had English and Latin. And in these Latin lessons, which were given by our Director (sadly, I have never again experienced such wonderful teaching) we mostly learned about Greco-Roman history.

> Leonidas and his battle at Thermopylae took centre stage. We knew the inscription: '*Erzähle, Wanderer, wenn Du nach Sparta kommst, dass wir, seinem Gesetz gehorsam, hier gefallen sind.*' ('Tell them, stranger, when you come to Sparta, that we fell here, obedient to their laws.') At our weapon presentation ceremony on 6 June 1944, our readiness to sacrifice ourselves for the Fatherland was ceremonially appealed to in terms of the Spartans. On 15 April 1945 we went straight from the school bench to the Front. I returned [to Germany] from being a Russian prisoner of war for the first time in 1950, as a twenty-one-year-old. We had fought until 12 May 1945.[62]

In general, a considerable number of my correspondents recalled Thermopylae and the heroic self-sacrifice of Leonidas and the 300 as one of the most memorable aspects of Spartan history, often recalling the Schiller-Simonides epigram (or variants thereof) verbatim.[63] This was still the case even when the correspondents in question wished to suggest that Sparta had not played a particularly large role in history teaching at their respective schools.[64]

Other aspects of Spartan history (as presented by teachers at the NPEA) which had been retained in my correspondents' memories included the murder of disabled children by exposure or throwing them off city walls [*sic*] or down ravines, presented in terms of 'destruction of unworthy life';[65] the Spartans' 'black soup' as a praiseworthy example of a frugal lifestyle;[66] the idea that the Spartans needed no walls to defend their city;[67] the contrast between Sparta and Athens, often presented in terms of Spartan warrior virtue and Athenian weakness and decadence,[68] and the whole gamut of 'Spartan' qualities which fitted in with the Napola ethos. Erwin K. and Rüdiger B. of Napola Spandau give some examples of these:

> In my memory, according to what I heard, the Spartans were a very sporty, if not to say pugnacious people, who laid a great value on health and a healthy life-style, physical toughening – how else should I put it – Spartan/ascetic life in the most simple form, and along with it, endurance of whatever hardships and sufferings might ensue.[69]

> At that time the Spartans were regarded as courageous, tough, frugal, persevering, unfailing and loyal role-models and idols to be emulated.[70]

Helmuth Z. of Napola Rügen concurs with this view:

> Even general history teaching in the Third Reich emphasised the exemplary role-model of Sparta. Events in Sparta were generally presented as a paradigm for a soldierly way of life, which should be imitated.[71]

Karl-Josef F., an ex-pupil of Napola Wartheland, suggests some reasons why Sparta might have held such a privileged position in terms of teaching:

> My own ideas of Sparta at that time (1941–45) could have been these: After a defeat (Versailles) it behoves all parts of the conquered people to strengthen their efficiency and power in war, in order to become free from interference and suppression. There existed an unspoken agreement that our military power had to be strengthened... In this regard it was not the privileged social position which was meant, but the much emphasised 'duty to the people'... Sparta was...a means to the end of cultivating and underpinning the '*Volkstum*'. This is my estimation of the attitudes of Rust, Heißmeyer, and also of Otto Calliebe... Not a search for Spartan education as an 'aim', but as a 'means' of attempting to attain some 'clout' for our people which could also contend with the outside world. In fact, this 'Spartan education' not only formed part of the so-called 'elite schools', but also the most varied organisations of the entire '*Volk*'. Just think of the '*Winterhilfswerk*' (Winter Relief Fund), 'One-pot Sunday', and the countless treatments on the radio, in the press, and on film.[72]

Meanwhile, Reinhard Wagner, who wrote a memoir of his time at NPEA Rottweil in the late 1990s, highlighted the racial elements of Spartan history which had been presented to his class, both in History and in Biology lessons:

> That the Nordic man was predominant was shown by history everywhere. Thus the Indogermanic Dorians and Achaeans who migrated from the North to Greece were clearly superior to the races already resident there... But the real role-model in ancient Greece, everyone knew that, that was the state of the Spartans. It was founded 'on fulfilment of duty in service to the community', and it was strong, so long as a warrior elite created through selective breeding ruled over the mass of shiftless helots. Struggle was the father of all things! The *Jungmannen* knew that. Adolf Hitler was cited: 'Whoever wants to live, will fight, and anyone who does not wish to fight in this world of eternal struggle, has not earned the right to live'. That meant struggle against enemies, against the rigours of nature, and also against...one's weaker self. The old boys at the Front had proved that they were ready and capable of fighting.[73]

In general, we can see that those National Socialist themes which were highlighted in depictions of Spartan history in the textbooks discussed in the previous section – race, toughness, war readiness, and self-sacrifice (as exemplified by Leonidas and the 300) – were also pointed out by the *Erzieher* and used to spur the *Jungmannen* on, whether in lessons which explicitly had some connection with antiquity, such as History, Greek, or Latin, or in other, non-academic, contexts such as sports lessons, or ceremonies honouring the war dead. Ex-pupils often remembered that certain *Erzieher* would focus particularly on Sparta as a paradigm, whilst others preferred to focus on other aspects of history or the Classics.[74]

The rest of this chapter will therefore consider the ways in which boys at the Napolas themselves engaged with the Spartan example on a personal level, and the extent to which they saw the NPEA as recreating an ancient Spartan ethos, whether deliberately or otherwise.

'*Spartas Geist lebt!*': Napola pupils' personal identifications with Sparta

In 1936 and 1938, two groups of *Jungmannen* from NPEA Schulpforta and Ilfeld embarked upon pilgrimages to Greece, in order to 'experience the land of the Hellenes' for themselves.[75] As *Zugführer* Büssow of Schulpforta explained, revealing the rationale behind the expeditions, it was necessary that the *Jungmannen* should learn to know modern Greece, in order to recognise the eternal face of Hellas, 'which has now come closer to us than ever, for we are more clearly conscious of the communality of our blood heritage and destiny than ever before... The trip does not serve the purpose of aesthetic enjoyment, but of national-political, that is to say *völkisch*, education.'[76]

That the expeditions made a great impression on the pupils involved, particularly as far as their respective visits to Sparta were concerned, can be illustrated both by contemporary reports and by later memoirs written by some of the participants. Hugo Selke, then a *Jungmann* at Schulpforta, describes a promising visit which his class had made to see the work of German archaeologists at Athens during their two-week stay in Attica, where an alumnus, Dieter Ohly (assistant to Professor Wilhelm Dörpfeld) showed them the fruits of their labours:

> The famous graves of the Spartans confirmed for us what imposing figures (*Recken*) the ancient Spartans must have been; some of them were two metres long – the optimum height![77]

However, when the boys finally made the pilgrimage to the Peloponnese, they were terribly disappointed to find 'hardly a trace of the heroic ancient inhabitants. They had left behind nothing except their epic glory, of which they had proudly said that their bodies were a better protection for their city than walls.'[78] In a report on the trip, Selke wrote:

> [Sparta] today is a small town with angular streets of bleak, square houses, anticlimactically boring. In vain we sought the remains of the ancient Spartan settlement, but nothing has remained except a few stones. We were disappointed...[79]

Selke's extreme disappointment, expressed both at the time of the visit and many years later, is telling, in that it shows how very much the boys cared about finding relics of the ancient Spartans.

Jungmann Gauß, who was in the Obersekunda at NPEA Ilfeld at the time of his visit in 1936, wrote an even more impassioned description of the boys' visit to Sparta, which was then selected for publication in the school newsletter, the *Ilfelder Blätter*:

> Mighty, snow-covered rocks ring the plain, looking silently and majestically down upon it. Their gloomy walls stab upwards towards the glowing peaks. They throw long shadows over the land, through which the broad river-bed threads. The earth is fertile. The small-leaved trees stand close together. In the middle of the valley lies the city of Sparta! Short and brief it is, this word. It sounds like a word of command, like an imperious order, like steel and iron. Sparta!... Yes, hard and imperious were they, the men from the cold Northland, with eyes like the grey sea, with hair like glimmering gold. Strong races were reared. Their breeding remained pure, pure and undefiled. Then the small, dark ones were oppressed, who groaned under the yoke...
>
> But the years, decades, centuries passed over the land. Still the mountains stand forever; still the river snakes forever through the plain. But where does the ancient city remain, tough and frugal? No more, annihilated, destroyed, a few old lumps of stone, pillars... And the men? Seek them on land and sea, in the whole of the Peloponnese, in Attica, in Macedonia, in Sicily, in Asia Minor, you will find nothing, nothing... gone with the wind... Only the river rushes as before, spreading fruitfulness; softly the wind blows through the olive-trees' crowns, from afar off the rocks appear grim and defiant, as even the sun goes down behind them.
>
> Sunk in this sight, we stand, and stand right long; only here and there is a word spoken. Our spirits become completely still before the greatness and holiness of this place. Pride fills us: they were truly men of our blood, who fought and died here. Fought... tough and determined for their race... until they flagged for ever, and did not draw boundaries so clearly and unambiguously between themselves, the masters, and the others, and also until they bled to death on the battlefields of Hellas. We grasp the entire, mighty tragedy of this death. – Slowly we descend the hill, while the night casts its shadows over rocks and river, over trees and houses. High above in the starry sky, the stars shine in southern glory... They appear to us as a symbol of Sparta's glory, alone, enthroned high above all else, understood only by a few – until their fate was fulfilled, and it became dark. But the belief is within us despite all darkness, the belief that
>
> Sparta's spirit lives![80]

Here we can see an almost religious veneration of Lacedaemon's erstwhile inhabitants, as implied by the language of belief (*Glaube*) and holiness (*Heiligkeit*) which Gauß employs. He seems to have been completely convinced of – and humbled by – the idea that Spartan blood (as well as the all-important Spartan spirit) was flowing once again in German veins.

However, such adulation of the ancient Spartans and their values was not only stirred in the hearts of pupils at Ilfeld when they trod the hallowed earth of Lacedaemon. One *Jungmann* Komoß (in the Unterprima in 1936) was moved to praise Spartan simplicity in the context of an exchange visit with Kingswood School in Bath, analysing the differences between English and German boys' attitudes to education in another article for the *Ilfelder Blätter*:

> The child, the young man, who has learnt to subordinate himself, is also capable of leading, and of setting the tone himself. The German attempts, in this connection, to set the individual on his own two feet as early as possible, in order to train him to be independent. The Englishman has a fundamentally different opinion on this matter. The young men are led and guided for as long as possible; the way is smoothed for them. They must not have it hard; everything is done for them as much as possible. Just as the youth of a people grows, so does the future of that people grow, and our people will remain great, as long as its youth is hard on itself, lives Spartanly, and always tries to 'be more than it seems'... [An English boy here joked, shockingly, that the Officer Training Corps is 'the greatest arbiter of peace ever', since it makes you never want to fight again. And yet they are permitted to use weapons!] We all long to become weapon bearers for our nation, and cannot wait at all for the moment in which, for the first time, we can lay our hands on weaponry.[81]

Additionally, some former *Jungmannen* who had already set off to fight also seemed to have internalised the Spartan paradigm.[82] At Napola Naumburg, quotations from old boys' writings which praised *Spartanertum* were published as epigraphs to various wartime editions of the school newsletter, the *Mitteilungen der Nationalpolitischen Erziehungsanstalt Naumburg/Saale* – testimony not only to the fact that the Napolaner considered the collocation important, but also that the school authorities wished to draw still further attention to the parallel, placing the quotations so prominently that all present and past Naumburger who received the newsletter would see them.

The first instance, an extract from an old boy's letter, was published in autumn 1943 on the front page of the 16th/17th *Kriegsnummer* (war-time edition) of the *Mitteilungen*:

> We are far too soft and spoiled. We Germans must be tougher and more ruthless against ourselves. – Train up the lads for us with a self-abnegatory, Spartan hardness! Only those who will be the toughest, both now and in coming years, will win this bitter fight! Stalingrad and Tunis must be burnt into the heart of every German to such an extent that at last he completely gives up his creature comforts, softnesses and half-measures.[83]

The second, in similar vein, was apparently taken originally from an entry in the old boys' visitors' book (*Buch der Altkameradschaft*):

> Soldierly thinking proclaims: to treat things harshly is to treat them well – yourself above all! To live as a Spartan for a couple of years gives you guts

> your whole life long, and even if your bones get broken for the Fatherland, it's no shame; they'll be all the healthier for it.[84]

Here, the toughness of the Spartans is brought to the fore, as might be expected at an NPEA which had gained the nickname '*Napola Zackig*' (Napola 'Snap-to-it!') because of its particularly harsh and militaristic way of life.

However, some similar reflections can be found in memoirs written by pupils at other Napolas, such as Dietrich Steinkopf of Schulpforta, who commented that 'during the ten-year Napola interregnum, Sparta ruled instead of Athens',[85] or Günther Lamprecht of Napola Wartheland, who stated, in the conclusion to a historical compendium of memories about the school, that 'the methods of education at the Napola were *Spartan*, and weaklings fell by the wayside.'[86] Herbert Bessel, an alumnus of Napola Ilfeld (1935–1941), when considering which individual images had stayed with him from his time there, even ended up with a partly Spartan-influenced stream of consciousness: 'Mucius Scaevola! Thermopylae! Marathon! "...with the shield or on the shield..." Pathos – heroism – kitsch: what was real!'[87] One *Jungmann* from Napola Köslin, Martin Köhler, describing the school's evacuation to Napola Rügen at the end of January 1945, also related the very particular way in which he and his room-mates decided to shock the Russian invaders who would soon take over the building – namely, by decorating the insides of their cupboards with National Socialist emblems and indictments of the Russians and their 'helot character' (*Helotenwesen*).[88]

Meanwhile, Manfred Peter Hein, in an autobiographical novel about his time at Napola Stuhm, described the *Spartanertum* of the Napolaner both as a positive way in which they could be distinguished from the ordinary Hitler Youth, and as a reason for the hazing which the boys were so often forced to undergo:

> But at least we weren't *Jungvolk*. Wearing an open collar in summer as in winter... The real Spartans...who ran barefoot over knife-sharp karst, through moon-craters. For that reason we were hazed. And for cleanliness, for order to the centimetre in the cupboards, on tables, benches, chairs and stools, in marching- and attack-baggage.[89]

Here we find some similarities with the personal appropriations of Sparta found at the cadet schools, in a not entirely dissimilar autobiographical context. The Napolaner in Hein's depiction are the '*echten Spartiaten*' (real Spartiates) because they can bear the '*spartanern*'-type hardships of cold and discipline, unlike the measly *Jungvolk* (the 10–14-year-old members of the regular Hitler Youth).

In similar vein, several autobiographies and reminiscences draw attention to the 'Spartan toughness' and 'Spartan' nature of life and living arrangements at various Napolas, in a way that seems somewhat akin to the 'rationalisation' of hardship found in the cadet-school literature.[90] Thus, in his autobiography, Kurt Schwechheimer of Napola Wartheland frequently referred to the Napolaners' accommodation and bedding (including sea-grass mattresses) as 'Spartan'; Harry Bolte, who attended Napola Ilfeld between 1936 and 1943, expressed similar sentiments. Schwechheimer also characterised certain punishments which he and his comrades were forced to undergo during one Pentecost-holiday as instilling '*spartanische Härte*' (Spartan toughness).[91] Klaus Montanus of Napola Rügen also conceived of the 'Spartan principles' of schooling at the NPEA as glorifying 'merciless harshness', regarding the Spartan and Prussian traditions as well-nigh interchangeable.[92]

The composer Gottfried von Einem even recalled an unpleasant incident at Plön, just after it had become a National Socialist foundation, in which an older student told him in a hate-filled tone that, had he lived in Sparta, he would have been exposed and killed.[93] Einem believes this to have been because, as a foreigner, he had attracted opprobrium by remaining the only non-uniformed pupil in the whole school. In this instance, his tormentor appears to be using a Spartan example for his own (nefarious) ends – as at the cadet schools – rather than the Spartan paradigm having been simply imposed from above by enthusiastic Nazi teachers and *Erzieher*.

Moving on from memoirs to the eyewitness evidence given by my correspondents, however, an even wider variety of Spartan identification can be found – ranging from the idea of Sparta as a useful parable, acknowledged as important, yet not crucial to the functioning of the system, to an extreme self-identification with 'the Spartan people, who were victorious in the end'.[94] Even former pupils who had not actually been taught about Sparta in lessons would often state that they had experienced their education at the Napolas as 'Spartan'. Thus Dietrich Schulz of Napola Rügen:

> I always experienced our life in Putbus as absolutely Spartan...
>
> We slept in unheated dormitories, so that – especially in the Siberianly-cold winter of 1941–42, during which the soldiers on the Eastern Front gained their popular nickname 'the *Gefrierfleisch-Orden*' (the Order of the Frozen Meat) – we used every trick in the book to smuggle our spare tracksuits into the dormitories, mostly without success!
>
> – On waking, a morning run around the Circus (450m). Washing and brushing of teeth in cold water only. Although after sports lessons we normally had warm showers.

> Tests of courage; e.g. diving from a diving platform for non-swimmers, or jumping from a height of 5m into a blanket. Boxing naturally also belonged in this category (but with boxing gloves).
>
> Endurance-training in the form of forest runs and marches with baggage, with one and two bricks in the rucksacks, each according to his age.
>
> Field exercises, where rivers had to be traversed in full uniform...
>
> The entire day ran to timetable, military-style!
>
> Because I became a cadet of the new age of my own free will, and with enthusiasm, I felt that this Spartan discipline was essential and athletic, even if one often had to grit one's teeth...
>
> At that time I had no background knowledge about Sparta and her society, as the history of Classical Antiquity was first designated for the *Abitur* classes. None of us reached this class, because we were called up already at 16 to the *Heimatflak* (anti-aircraft defence) and then at 17 to the *Reichsarbeitsdienst* (Reich Labour Service) and the *Wehrmacht* – war conditions. The Spartans performed the function of role-models, although no reference to their society and their way of life remained for us.[95]

This could suggest that even those boys who had not yet had the opportunity to learn about Sparta absorbed ideas of *Spartanertum* which did, to some extent, match ideas of an ancient Spartan ethos based on textbooks or the Classical texts.

Meanwhile, Klaus Schikore, also a *Jungmann* at Napola Rügen from 1942–1945, but who had already gained some knowledge of Spartan history in lessons, writes in similar vein:

> I too experienced the institutional life in Putbus as 'Spartan', not just as a mere cliché, but as a feeling that the daily duties at the school were *in no way* that of a civilian life; early rising, military regimentation; punctuality; self-discipline. Besides, it became ever clearer to me as I went up the school that our life unfolded similarly to that in ancient Sparta, which we knew all about from our history lessons. This became even more clear to me, since in history lessons at today's German *Gymnasien* it's almost exclusively 'democratic Athens' (in opposition to Sparta) which gets prime treatment – as the precursor and paradigm of our present-day democracy.[96]

Karl L. of Napola Naumburg also gave (unprompted) a complete catalogue of characteristics of Napola life which, in his view, were consciously constructed as Spartan by the authorities:

> The Spartan way of life and Spartan conduct were ever more explicitly emphasised by the teachers and *Erzieher*. We also lived 'spartanly' in a certain sense.
>
> – We slept in our plain beds with...only a couple of woollen blankets in winter; there were no eiderdowns.
>
> – Immediately after the wake-up call, early morning sport was on the agenda, in plain sportswear.

> – In new-fallen snow we had to go cross-country running *barefoot.*
> – The meals were (particularly towards the end of the war), though just about sufficient, utterly meagre...
> – Strict subordination, iron discipline, and the hierarchy of command corresponded to the Spartan example.
> – the 'spirit of community' was emphasised and instilled to an extreme degree.
> We were to be trained as 'political soldiers'; the Spartan way of life and the National Socialist worldview were to meld together to form political warriors.
> As teaching materials there were history books, maps, pictures and plentiful literature provided in the reading room. I remember a picture, in which (in Sparta) naked youths were fighting naked maidens, which naturally made a particular impression on us, as eleven-year-olds.
> It also counted as Spartan often to drink cold water, to fight on after minor injuries, to bear pain, to mobilise one's last efforts etc. Tests of courage played an ever greater role...[97]

Theodor K., an ex-pupil of Napola Rottweil, also believed that the authorities there had deliberately devised the Napolas according to a 'Spartan' model:

> Without any doubt at all, the life in our boarding school was designed with a Spartan impetus, and that the Spartan part was consciously willed – and that it was also called by the name 'Spartan' – was known to us all. And was accepted by all of us also. Without acceptance by the pupils, a school of this type would have been unable to function at all. Training and subordination aren't successful in the long run, if effected through imposed violence and

Fig. 27. Pupils at Napola Rügen preparing to run barefoot (1943).

Fig. 28. The reading room at Napola Rügen (1943). Many Napolas possessed similar recreation rooms.

> whipping. And, seen in this way, Sparta surely had a greater significance for us all than we were conscious of at the time.[98]

In a letter ruminating on my research to another correspondent, Herr K. wrote:

> It's true that, on occasion, we Napolaner felt spiritual similarities and sympathies with the courageous people of Sparta, though we never had the feeling that the character of our school would have been a jot different if the Spartan people had not existed 2,500 years before... The deeper I get into this topic, the more I see that the influence continues to work upon us much more strongly than I suspected at first... We former pupils can, however, only present the facts about how our time at boarding school played itself out; Miss Roche may then draw conclusions regarding the parallels.[99]

Another element of my correspondents' personal memories of Sparta involved the invocation of Spartan soldierly and self-sacrificial duty to try to alleviate their anxiety about the possible outcome of the Second World War in its closing stages. Thus Helmuth Z. of Napola Rügen:

> We ourselves held fast to the idea that the present looked a bit different from what we'd been led to believe. When I was called up to the *Flakhelferdienst* (anti-aircraft defence duties) in January 1944, and to the *Reichsarbeitsdienst* (Reich Labour Service) in 1945, people jeered...at our claims to re-embody the Spartan people, who were victorious in the end.[100]

Klaus E. of Napola Rottweil was even more vehement in his affirmation of the importance of the Spartan and Thermopylaean example:

> Certainly we also had 'Sparta' before our eyes: '*Wanderer, kommst Du zurück in die Heimat, so verkündige dorten, du habest uns liegen gesehen – wie die Pflicht es befahl*' ('Stranger, if you return to the homeland, then declare to them that you have seen us lying dead – as duty commanded.'). Duty, obedience and discipline were generally very high values – everything else would have been real squandering of powers and resources, and gone in the face of our goal – the goal being to achieve the best possible contribution to effect the victory, the defence of our homeland and the preservation of the threatened existence of our people.
>
> The school comrades of the older year-groups were soldiers with the army, air force and navy; we read their letters and mourned for them when they fell; we were proud of their deeds and their courage in surviving against a world of powerful enemies. Our fathers before us had been soldiers in the Great War, and not a few of them were now once again wearing military uniform.
>
> We read books which told of the bloody battles and the cruel hardships of the First War – Ettighoffer, Beumelburg, Zöberlein, Jünger, Wittek, Flex, Dwinger, and sought to develop a manner which corresponded to the spiritual models of our people, Frederick the Great, Arndt, Fichte, Kant, Scharnhorst and Bismarck. We were born in a time of deep necessity and then experienced years of political and economic renewal, taking part in which was already in my childhood a deep experience.
>
> I wanted to learn to bear my own physical and intellectual weaknesses, to overcome them and to come out of it strengthened, as a thankful member of a community of equals, upstanding and courageous men. We were still children, as our homeland went up in flames around us, as our cities fell into soot and ashes, and fanatical enemies thought up ever-more original ways of tormenting our people and physically annihilating them. The image of Thermopylae was already very soon no saga of the past, but daily bitter reality; in order to learn harshness against ourselves, we had our reality, which demanded so much of everyone.
>
> Sparta was only a parable for us, a slogan – but there we stood...with the task of commanding ourselves, in order to vanquish inertia, cowardice and self-interest, and to serve, sacrifice and bleed. Even during the time of victories this was not easy – but how hard it was, when the laurels withered and fell in a blaze of phosphorus! When all was lost and it was our lot to endure years of disenfranchisement after the war, hungering behind barbed-wire and undergoing drudgery, the time of extreme testing for the '*Spartanerjünglinge*' seemed to have utterly come to pass.[101]

In this passage, we can see what high emotions were linked with this invocation of the Spartan paradigm, and the way in which Herr E. (and, to a lesser extent, Herr Z.) had utterly internalised the Nazified teaching about the necessity of Spartan self-sacrifice in the service of the Third Reich, particularly as the war drew to a close. However, in a sense, we have also come full circle – back to the idea of the *Spartanerjünglinge*, and their position in the continuing tradition of German military education.

Conclusions

It may have been the case that a great many Napolaner did indeed conceive of themselves as *Spartanerjünglinge* in similar fashion to – or even in emulation of – the cadets, on whom their lives were partly modelled.[102] The vagaries of *Vergangenheitsbewältigung* (attempts to 'master' the Nazi past), and the short duration of the Napolas' existence compared to that of the cadet schools (only twelve years, as opposed to over two centuries) mean that we will never possess a comparable corpus of Napola memoirs and Nazi elite-school stories, whilst the newsletters and documentary material of the Napola old boys' associations have yet to be discovered and archived, if indeed they ever will be. However (even leaving the evidence of the eyewitnesses aside), given the number of references to the Spartans and the importance of *Spartanertum* in the relatively few Napola memoirs which I have had the opportunity to consult (whether in publicly- or privately-published form), it seems that a number of correlations can be perceived between the appropriations of Sparta found at the Napolas and those of the Prussian Cadet Corps.

Those traits of Spartan life and the Spartan educational system which were emphasised above all were, firstly, those which enabled boys better to bear the hardships of the present, whether in terms of hazing, insufficient food, or gruelling programmes of physical training. Although the Napola evidence does not allow us to construct such a complete pattern as the cadet-school evidence, it nevertheless seems reasonable to suggest that ideas of Sparta were used, both by *Erzieher* and *Jungmannen*, to assist in the 'rationalisation' process which was involved in adapting to life at a total – and, in this case, totalitarian – institution.

However, in terms of the Napolas, certain elements of *Spartanertum* came rather more to the fore than they had at the cadet schools. Thus, the racial relationship between the 'Aryan' Spartans and their 'Germanic brother-race', which had not been posited in any (official or unofficial) cadet-school sources, was emphasised at the Napolas, in order both to present the Spartans as a paradigm for the new Reich, and to portray them as a warning of the dangers of racial degradation which had brought about Sparta's eventual downfall.

The heroic self-sacrifice of Leonidas and the 300 was also a crucial part of Sparta's characterisation in National Socialist and Napola ideology, and was explicitly presented to the *Jungmannen* as an ideal model for self-identification, in order to spur them on to fight and die for *Führer* and Fatherland in the Second World War. Although we find elements of such idealisation of the Thermopylae fighters in the cadet-school literature, it does not seem to have played quite such a crucial role in cadets' later depictions of the Spartan elements of their education system, or in their self-identification with young Spartans. In this regard, we may also note the quantity and variety of translations of the Thermopylaean epigram which my ex-Napola informants were still able to remember, many decades after the war's end. This degree of internalisation suggests a widespread, personalised acceptance of the formula, rather than its having been construed as a mere meaningless propaganda slogan.[103]

Nevertheless, as with the ex-cadets' clinging to their pride in being *Spartanerjünglinge* even in extreme old age, the effectiveness of the use of the Spartan paradigm to instil National Socialist values in the Napola *Jungmannen* is attested by the large number of ex-Napola eyewitnesses who still remember what they were taught about Sparta very vividly, well over 60 years after they had left the schools. During the Third Reich, Sparta had become an exemplar of physical and ethical excellence to which these boys were often encouraged to aspire – one which has, ultimately, remained with many of them for the rest of their lives.

Notes

[1] Person 1936, 15.

[2] ibid., 16.

[3] ibid., 18.

[4] ibid., 21.

[5] For a detailed case-study of the ideological use of Sparta in another type of Nazi elite school, the Adolf Hitler Schools, see Roche 2012a.

[6] Quoted in Gélieu 1990, 47, 50.

[7] cf. *Lyc.* 16.5–6.

[8] This is a theme which also recurs to some extent in some of the eyewitness testimonies quoted in the rest of this chapter. Compare Franz Baron von Weyssenhoff's comment in the foreword to Kurt von Borcke's *Das sind wir*, where he explicitly acknowledges the '*Spartanertum*' of the cadet-school tradition, whilst applying its principles to the new National Socialist foundation of the NPEA: 'The Spartan education to frugality, the early instruction of the boys in unquestioning dutifulness, in truthfulness and in voluntary dedication to the Fatherland form the basis of the attitude of the pre-war German Officer Corps. A great number of important army commanders and leaders of the old army and the new German *Wehrmacht* are from the [Prussian] cadet corps. One can say without hyperbole that the cadet corps has...made up a crucial part of the army's constitution, and hence of the Reich... We National Socialists took over many good educational methods from former times in our

National Political Education Institutes, but we eradicated class-prejudice and caste-arrogance, placing in their stead the concept of a true and absolute national community (*Volksgemeinschaft*)...' (Borcke 1940, 7–8).

[9] See further examples below. This is not to say that all Napola Directors leaned so strongly towards Sparta as a model; however, given the tiny proportion of such speeches which have survived, it is impossible to say whether Directors such as Schieffer, Person and Männich (Naumburg) were in a minority. This caveat holds true of many of the other types of contemporary evidence adduced in these pages.

[10] *Der Aufbau* 20/21, 01/08/1935, *NPEA Nationalpolitische Erziehungsanstalten* [BArch NS/5/VI 18840, Bl.21]; see also BArch NS/5/VI 18841, Bl.71.

[11] *Pförtner Blätter*, 4.Jg. Heft 1, July 1939, 9. The speaker was Professor Erich Burck of Kiel University.

[12] *Pförtner Blätter*, 5.Jg. Heft 3, April 1941, 87. For further examples from Schulpforta, see *Pförtner Blätter* 6.Jg. Heft 3, August 1942 (8. Kriegsnummer), 69; *Die Pforte*, 17.Jg, Heft 2, 74.

[13] BArch NS15/205, Bl.73, 82–3.

[14] ibid., Bl.84

[15] Rowan-Robinson 1938, 241, 250.

[16] Tate 1937, 169.

[17] e.g. Rust 1938d.

[18] ibid., 70.

[19] ibid., 72.

[20] Karl-Josef F., private correspondence, 07/08/2011. Although many of my correspondents experienced interruptions to their education, when they were drafted at 16 (or even younger) to man anti-aircraft guns, or dig trenches, bunkers and tank traps in the East as a last line of defence against the advancing Russians, the authorities attempted (with varying degrees of success) to ensure that their academic education was kept up, even if this meant that the Flak batteries were used as classrooms by day and engine-rooms of destruction by night.

[21] Horn 1943, 82.

[22] N.B. All emphases in quotations from these works are original. It is perhaps worth noting here that the textbook specifically on Sparta commissioned by the Adolf Hitler Schools, entitled *Sparta: Der Lebenskampf einer nordischen Herrenschicht* (Vacano 1942), was almost certainly never made available to the general public, despite requests to the Inspector of the schools, Kurt Petter, for its wider distribution (Roche 2012a, 335). It is therefore unsurprising that there is no evidence for this particular textbook having been used at the Napolas.

[23] It should be noted that the terms 'Nordic' and 'Aryan' were used interchangeably in Nazi rhetoric.

[24] Bartels 1941, 55.

[25] Kumsteller 1936, 9. In his general descriptions of the rise of the Greek *poleis*, Sparta is the only *polis* which Kumsteller describes in such a flamboyant style, couching the whole of his depiction of Spartan life in the vivid present. The parallel passage on Athens is written much more soberly, and, we might conjecture, would therefore have seemed less exciting to Kumsteller's young readership.

[26] Silomon 1940, 64.

[27] ibid.

[28] ibid., 66.

[29] ibid., 67.

[30] ibid. In the National Socialist lexicon, 'capitalism' was an extremely dirty word, inextricably linked with notions of 'Judaeo-Bolshevik' global financial conspiracies and cultural degradation. In a sense, then, whilst Sparta is playing the role of Germany, Athens is forced to fit the mould of her capitalist opponents – perhaps in particular the USA.

[31] ibid.

[32] ibid., 68–70.

[33] ibid., 71.

[34] ibid., 72–3.

[35] ibid., 66.

[36] Schmidthenner 1943, 50–1.

[37] For discussion of a parallel in Hitler's own thought about Sparta, in which he praises her destruction of infants who are *minderwertig*, seeing this as programmatic for his own vision of Germany's future, see Roche 2012b, 105.

[38] Kumsteller 1936, 10–11.

[39] Schmidthenner 1943, 50–1.

[40] The importance of 'honour' as a guiding principle at the Napolas has been noted by very many of my correspondents, and, in interviews, the idea that the Napolas' education was aimed at instilling a fundamental sense of honour and comradeship was repeatedly stressed.

[41] Silomon 1940, 65. Even the extract from Plutarch's *Lycurgus* which is printed above this passage feels almost as if it could have been lifted from a National Socialist tract, such as Hitler's famous speech, given on 2 December 1938, on the all-embracing nature of National Socialist education, '*Und sie werden nicht mehr frei ihr ganzes Leben*' ('And they will no longer be free for their whole lives'): 'These Spartiates felt themselves to be a master-caste; they brought up their children in this way, and thus did they live themselves: "None was free, nor could he live as he wished, but, as in an army camp, each man in the *polis* had his strictly-regimented way of life and occupation with the State's tasks, and one was ever conscious that one *did not belong to oneself, but to the Fatherland*." (Plutarch, *Lycurgus* [24.1])'

[42] Silomon 1943, 71–2. Interestingly, the last three sentences of this passage, including the Simonides-Schiller epigraph, were absent from the 1940 edition – which implies that they may well have been added for propaganda purposes after the collapse of Stalingrad and Goering's speech to the Third Army on 31 January 1943, which drew an explicit parallel between the two battles (cf. p. 23 above). For more on this, see Roche 2012b, Watt 1985; for a similar treatment in the context of an Adolf Hitler School textbook, see Roche 2012a. Most of the other textbooks (listed on pp. 207–8 above) cite the epigraph in some form, most often in Schiller's translation.

[43] During my research, I have also explored the use of Sparta in a number of Nazi educational periodicals (which might well have been read by Napola *Erzieher*), in which I found many similarities to the tropes which have been examined here. In general, Spartan history seems to have been considered an important subject in these articles; I hope to have the opportunity to analyse this corpus of material more thoroughly in the future.

[44] Bogner 1935, 13. See further Roche 2012b.

[45] Thus Kurt L., private correspondence, 17/09/2010; Lothar J., private correspondence, 13/09/2011; Karl L., private correspondence, 05/08/2010 (all from Oranienstein); Wolfgang V., private correspondence, 01/07/2010 (Plön); Günther P., private correspondence, 10/09/2010 (Naumburg), and, to a lesser extent: Harald O., private correspondence, 25/01/2010 (Traiskirchen); Paul F., private correspondence, 09/04/2010 (Rottweil); Peter B., private correspondence, 06/05/2010 (Plön); Gerhard F., private correspondence, 06/06/2010 (Backnang).

[46] See further p. 220 and n. 64 below. This reaction could possibly also stem from a desire on some of the correspondents' part to distance themselves from the way in which Sparta was manipulated during the Third Reich in general (or at some of the Napolas in particular). See also pp. 11–12 above.

[47] See further correspondence between Rust and Wilhelm Stuckart (State Secretary in the German Interior Ministry) during the year 1943 (BArch R1501/624).

[48] Kasdorff 1968, 118.

[49] Heißmeyer 1939a, 202–3.

[50] Zempelin 2000, 57.

[51] Klare 1996, 14.

[52] Ernst G., private correspondence, 20/12/2009.

[53] e.g. Hans W., private correspondence, 02/04/2010 (see pp. 219–220); Bernhard G., private correspondence, 17/12/2009. In another letter (10/01/2010), Herr G. (an ex-pupil of Napola Köslin) notes that Sparta was also treated in the discussion of '*weltanschauliche Fragen*' (questions of worldview) in German lessons. Rüdiger B. of Napola Spandau also remembers hearing about 'Leonidas and the Battle of Thermopylae etc.' not only in history lessons, but also in '*Heimabenden*' (social evenings) which had a similar function (private correspondence, 11/06/2010). For more on the reception of Thermopylae at the NPEA, see pp. 218–20.

[54] Karl L., private correspondence, 13/01/2010.

[55] An almost identical, unabridged translation of this fragment can in fact be found in Hans Philipp's *Vor- und Frühgeschichte des Nordens und des Mittelmeerraumes* (Berlin, 1936), a history of antiquity heavily influenced by Nazi racial typology, which may well have been the source on which Herr Riefenstahl had drawn. However, the original source of the translation seems to be Emanuel Geibel's *Klassisches Liederbuch. Griechen und Römer in deutscher Nachbildung* (Leipzig, 1875). Here, Geibel combined Fragment 11 West and part of Fragment 12 West to form a single '*Schlachtgesang*' (battle ode). In general, the lines from Fragment 11 West which do not appear in Karl L.'s version are those which place most emphasis upon death (ll. 5–10 and 19–20). Though it is impossible to know, we might conjecture that, rather than merely reflecting a lapse in Karl L.'s memory, these lines were deliberately excised from the text which the boys had to learn because they could be seen as highlighting the more negative aspects of battle.

[56] Karl L., private correspondence, 22/01/2010 and 01/02/2010.

[57] Karl L., private correspondence, 01/02/2010.

[58] Karl L., private correspondence, 30/08/2010. Interestingly, Dietrich Schulz, who was a pupil at Napola Rügen during the early 1940s, describes a similar admonition from his own sports teacher. The *Erzieher* in question forced the class to swim in the ice-cold Baltic Sea, and when they emerged with chattering teeth and blue lips, he would shout: 'Stop looking like that! What do you think the ancient Spartans would have to say about that?!' (private correspondence, 30/12/2009).

[59] Karl L., private correspondence, 01/02/2010.

[60] Günther P., private correspondence, 22/01/2010.

[61] Günter O., private correspondence, 08/09/2010. During an interview conducted in 2001 by a then student, Hans Rettkowski, another Schulpforta alumnus, recollected similar emphases during his time at the school: '...in a Greek lesson, the Battle of Thermopylae was portrayed as a glowing example. Just as the Spartans had had to fight there, so now would we, too, although death was certain.

[Interviewer]: *The formulation was that explicit?*

H.R.: Yes, the belligerent, heroic side of the Romans and Greeks was always proclaimed more and more as exemplary...' (*Die Pforte* 2001, 32).

[62] Hans W., private correspondence, 02/04/2010. The unconditional surrender to the Allies took place on 7 May 1945.

[63] e.g. Joachim D., private correspondence, 30/12/2009 (Neubeuern); Hans F., private correspondence, 22/01/2010; Klaus Schikore, private correspondence, 31/12/2009 (both Rügen); Rudolf B., private correspondence, 26/06/2010 (Spandau).

[64] e.g. Klaus-Jürgen B., private correspondence, 07/10/2010 (Oranienstein); Peter B., private correspondence, 06/05/2010 (Plön); Arnulf P., private correspondence, 02/02/2011 (Spandau).

[65] e.g. Wilfried K., private correspondence, 20/06/2010 (Spandau); Karl-Josef F., private correspondence, 30/07/2011 (Wartheland).

[66] e.g. Joachim D., private correspondence, 30/12/2009 (Neubeuern).

[67] e.g. Erwin K., private correspondence, 24/06/2010 (Spandau).

[68] e.g. Ernst G., private correspondence, 20/10/2009; Rudolf Arendt, private correspondence, 23/06/2010 (both Spandau).

[69] Rüdiger B., private correspondence, 11/06/2010.

[70] Erwin K., private correspondence, 24/06/2010.

[71] Helmuth Z., private correspondence, 25/12/2009.

[72] Karl-Josef F., private correspondence, 07/08/2011.

[73] Wagner 1998, 109–110.

[74] For a description of an *Erzieher* who was obsessed with the ancient Romans, see Wagner 1998, 94.

[75] cf. Selke 1938.

[76] *Pförtner Blätter*, 3.Jg. Heft 2, November 1938, 36.

[77] Selke 1990, 41.

[78] ibid., 45.

[79] Selke 1938, 9.

[80] Gauß 1936. All ellipses are original.

[81] *Ilfelder Blätter*, Heft 3, Easter 1938, 65–6.

[82] e.g. *Pförtner Blätter* 6.Jg. Heft 3, August 1942, 69.

[83] Note once again the reference to Stalingrad.

[84] *Mitteilungen der Nationalpolitischen Erziehungsanstalt Naumburg/Saale*, 22. Kriegsnummer, July 1944, 1.

[85] Leeb 2005, 78.

[86] Lamprecht 2007, 201.

[87] Bessel 1999, 529. Interestingly, in his autobiography *Mehr sein als scheinen* (1998), Reinhard Wagner of NPEA Rottweil remembered a war memorial in Welun (now Wieluń, Poland), where his class were helping with the harvest, which always reminded

him of the monument to the Spartans at Thermopylae because of its inscription '*Wanderer verweile in Andacht und gedenke der Toten*' (Stranger, bide awhile in prayer and remember the dead). The *Jungmannen* were marched there every Sunday for a '*Gedenkappell*' (p. 89).

[88] Köhler n.d., 10.

[89] Hein 1999, 67–8.

[90] See also Lamprecht 2007, 49.

[91] Schwechheimer n.d., 22, 24, 71, 89; Bolte n.d., 3. Similar characterisations of Napola life and accoutrements as 'Spartan' can be found in Müncheberg 1991, 44, 118 (although here the adjective is used by the author's aunt and mother respectively, rather than by the narrator himself).

[92] Montanus 1998, 6–7, 163; private correspondence, 21/02/2010.

[93] Eickhoff 1998, 22.

[94] See p. 229 below.

[95] Dietrich Schulz, private correspondence, 17/11/2009 and 30/12/2009.

[96] Klaus Schikore, private correspondence, 31/12/2009.

[97] Karl L., private correspondence, 13/01/2010.

[98] Theodor K., private correspondence, 04/03/2010.

[99] Theodor K., private correspondence with Paul F., 18/02/2010.

[100] Helmuth Z., private correspondence, 25/12/2009.

[101] Klaus E., private correspondence, ?/02/2010.

[102] In this regard, it is noteworthy that an ex-pupil of Napola Plön, Klaus-Christoph Marloh, actually published a new edition of *Spartanerjünglinge* in 1994, praising the Prussian spirit of loyalty, community and self-sacrifice which lay at the heart of the work, and expressing the hope that this code of honour might some day become a German hallmark once again (Marloh 1994, 5). In correspondence with a fellow Plöner, Marloh wrote: 'The "Spartanerjünglinge" accompanied me my whole life long (I was born in 1923); they escaped the pillaging of my home and my kitbag on [U-boat] U-2506.' (Klaus-Christoph Marloh, private correspondence with Uwe Lamprecht, 25/08/1994).'

[103] Interestingly, one might argue that, at the Napolas, the idea of Sparta-as-paradigm was more broadly staff-sponsored – particularly by convinced and fanatical National Socialist teachers – than had been the case at the cadet corps. It would appear that, very often, a Nazified vision of Sparta, replete with the ideology of racial struggle, was imposed upon the *Jungmannen* from above, and only then accepted and internalised. At the cadet schools, on the other hand, it seems that cadets devised their own forms of '*spartanern*', playing more of an active role in developing their self-identification as *Spartanerjünglinge*. However, this does not rule out the possibility that further evidence could come to light in the future which might show either that staff at the cadet schools had played as great a role in facilitating such identification and appropriation, or that some Napolaner might have had more control over their personal appropriations of a Nazified *Spartabild*. This difficulty is compounded by the fact that Napola eyewitnesses might be more likely to portray absorption of a National Socialist view of Sparta as beyond their control, rather than as something which they eagerly espoused. In any case, the general paucity of extant evidence relating to the administration of the cadet corps, in relation to the evidence for Nazi official policies, means that these ideas will probably always remain mere conjecture.

10

CONCLUSION

It is now a commonplace of Spartan reception to observe, as Ernst Kirsten did in 1936, that 'Sparta has detached herself from reality, and become an idea. *Spartiatentum* (Spartiate-hood) has become a concept, a judgment, a paradigm.'[1] One of the fundamental aims of this monograph has been to illuminate one particular aspect of this phenomenon, commonly known as the *mirage spartiate*,[2] and to analyse it in detail.

For this purpose, I have taken one of the more generally observable trends in the Prusso-German Spartan tradition – that of Spartan idealisation within the military Establishment, and thence in the sphere of militaristic elite education – and provided a pair of detailed case-studies which show that ideas of ancient Sparta did indeed have an influence upon generations of Prusso-German military commanders, as well as providing an ideological underpinning for the training of the future leaders of the Third Reich. Whilst these tendencies have been treated briefly in recently published work both by Volker Losemann and myself,[3] this strand of identification with Sparta finds no mention whatsoever in Elizabeth Rawson's magisterial overview of the Spartan tradition in European thought (1969) – as Stephen Hodkinson and Ian Macgregor Morris have rightly noted.[4] In these case-studies, however, we have a substantial volume of rich and varied evidence which shows that the Spartan paradigm, even in recent history, has had untold power to mobilise German martial and ideological forces – even if the portrayals of Sparta in the relevant traditions have departed radically from what we can recover of ancient realities.[5] In the following section, the contributions which this work can make to a number of academic fields will be suggested, beginning with the study of the 'Spartan tradition'.

Firstly, this analysis demonstrates the malleability and multifaceted nature of the Spartan paradigm, in that Sparta was appropriated in very different ways by the two regimes in question, though for somewhat similar ends. The Spartan self-identifications found in the Prussian Cadet Corps can be strikingly contrasted with the ideas of racial kinship and self-sacrifice which featured at the Napolas. Through these two case-studies, we can therefore gain insight into the rich palette and ever shifting spectrum of

Spartan exemplarity, in which different aspects of the Spartan *topos* are brought to the fore as varying social and political exigencies allow – or dictate.[6]

However, this is by no means a recent phenomenon originating in nineteenth-century Germany, but rather a particular manifestation of what we might call a deeply rooted *mythos* of Spartan education, which lent itself to such idealisations even in the ancient world.[7] A manifestation of this *mythos* in antiquity might be the 're-creation' of allegedly Classical Spartan educational practices during the Roman Imperial period, partly in order to provide a sort of 'theme park' for Roman 'sado-tourists'.[8] Yet these re-creations of 'ancient Spartan' educational ideals can be seen to be bound up with the re-creation of a Spartan identity *per se*, with legitimisation and the bolstering of self-worth – motivations which can also be found in the later German appropriations of supposedly Spartan educational ideals, as discussed above.

In a sense, then, this idea (or ideal) of Spartan pedagogy and *mores* as providing a paradigm of military training and socialisation, both as presented in the ancient sources, and as adopted by later educational systems, runs deeper than any of its individual manifestations. It can be used for praise or blame, by widely differing regimes, in succession or concurrently, without losing any of its power. This tendency may also be noted in recent American attitudes to Sparta; during the Cold War, the Americans styled the Russians as Spartans who were opposing, with atomic tyranny, their Athenian freedom.[9] In recent years, however (at least according to Adam Sherwin, writing in *The Times* on 27 August 2008), copies of Paul Cartledge's *The Spartans* have been compulsory kit for all U.S. Marines doing basic training. From being seen as an avatar of the 'red peril', the Spartans have, within the span of a few decades, become the Americans' allies beyond the grave in the 'War on Terror'.

But can our understanding of Sparta's more modern appropriations actually bring us any closer to understanding the history of ancient Sparta herself? Can this research on German elite education, and its conclusions, serve the study of Classics, as well as Classical Reception?

Firstly, it seems that the sociological model of the 'total institution' (as discussed in Chapter 5) could usefully be applied to an analysis of Spartan education – this is not a concept that has been mentioned much (if at all) in previous scholarship on Sparta. Although some aspects of Goffman's theory would certainly be inapplicable to the social institutions of an ancient society, there could still be some fruitful parallels to be drawn. Such analysis could also be applied to the extant scholarship and textbooks on Sparta, in order to determine the extent to which authors from differing periods and nations tended to portray Spartan education as following most closely the patterns followed by the 'total institutions' of their own day.[10] T. Rutherford-Harley's 'The Public School of Sparta' (1934), which explicitly compares Spartan pedagogy with that of the English public school, provides a classic example of this tendency.[11]

Secondly, we can – up to a point – use social practices at the two modern institutions under discussion to make informed inferences and build useful hypotheses about pedagogical experiences in ancient Sparta herself, based on an appreciation of the universals of human psychology.[12] For instance, Anton Powell has suggested, regarding the themes of pederasty as comfort amid emotional deprivation, and of cruelty suffered becoming cruelty later inflicted by the former sufferer, that these German cases can usefully disprove a negative generalisation: that ancient accounts of Spartan endurance must be largely exaggerated, because such hardships would not be tolerable in human society. The sources discussed here show, however, that such hardships can indeed be tolerated, and we might then suggest that responses to such cruel and emotionally isolating circumstances could have cross-cultural resonance. Thus, 'the pederastic couples [described in Chapter 4 above] should make us look again at what was happening in emotionally deprived Sparta.'[13] This is not to say that the German cases can ever prove anything precise about Sparta, but only that the cross-cultural nature of the work can possibly provide some psychological insights into an ancient system of education which shares some very general attributes with these more modern educational institutions, such as the prioritisation of hardship and physical toughness.

However, this work can also make a contribution to modern historical scholarship – both in terms of general nineteenth- and twentieth-century Prusso-German history, and in the spheres of educational, military, and cultural history.

Firstly, as mentioned in the Introduction, during this research, a corpus of documentary, literary and eyewitness evidence regarding these institutions has been amassed and investigated, the analysis of which can make an original contribution to the sparse scholarly literature on both the Prussian Cadet Corps and the Napolas.

Additionally, due to the vagaries of postwar *Vergangenheitsbewältigung* in Germany, such engagement with the Spartan values prevalent in elite education during the Third Reich has often been 'passed over in silence in pedagogical scholarship'.[14] I have therefore been able to touch upon aspects of German educational experience which have previously been left undiscussed in the scholarly literature, not least because, as the authors of

Das Erbe der Napola have noted, it is often difficult for German researchers to maintain objectivity when dealing with this period: '*Every* piece of research on Nazism [in Germany] releases massive anxieties in the researchers – particularly if those in question are Germans whose parents were adults during this period.'[15] In fact, a key element in the willingness of many of the former Napolaner to give me evidence on this subject, whether in written or oral form, was their belief that, as a non-German, I could consider the case of the Napolas more objectively, without a reaction of detestation and disgust (which could indeed be observed when I discussed the topic with some of my German contemporaries).

Moreover, this new evidence can also advance our knowledge of educational history during the Third Reich. As Saul Robinsohn has remarked, 'studies on history syllabuses and textbooks...have shown that it is from such information on the reality of the school and its institutions that we gain some of the most valuable insights into the intentions of National Socialist "education".'[16] In this case, such analysis of documentary pedagogical material has been enhanced and illuminated by ex-pupils' testimony regarding the ways in which such material was presented in the classroom – or even on the assault course. In more general terms, this work also enables us the better to consider the continuities and discontinuities between the cadet schools and the Napolas, and the degree to which the creation of a new type of school necessarily culminated in a reinvention of the old.[17] Meanwhile, it is hoped that the more general elucidations of personal life and political controversies at and about both these institutions will provide useful material and insights for all those with an interest in elite or military education, as well as those studying youth and culture in Prussia and the Third Reich – even if the material is often presented from a Spartologist's perspective.[18]

Similarly, it could be argued that existing discussions of the relationship between politics and Prussian militarism, especially regarding political debates in parliament over the role of the military (both before and after the *Verfassungskonflikt*) can benefit from taking the debates and controversies surrounding the role of the Prussian Cadet Corps (as mentioned above) into account.

As far as military scholarship is concerned, although the ways in which Western societies have prepared the leaders of their armed forces to deal with war is both a major topic in history and a pressing current issue, it is also a startlingly neglected one.[19] Yet, as authors spanning a wide chronological range have noted, the relationship between an army and its educational establishments is supremely close; understanding one institution is therefore key to understanding the other.[20] Thus, since the

Prussian Cadet Corps is barely mentioned in German military histories or in the biographies of famous commanders, the fact that this work draws attention back towards the corps as a real historical institution with an important political and cultural impact should be of some value. One might even suggest that contemporary problem-solvers and strategists of the *Bundeswehr*, such as Elmar Wiesendahl, the author of a recently-published thinktank pamphlet entitled *Athen oder Sparta – Bundeswehr quo vadis?* (2010), might find it useful to know how Spartan and Athenian values were once construed in Prusso-German military circles.[21]

In any case, in order to gain a fuller understanding of the cadet schools and the mindset of the commanders which they produced (who, as we have seen, were predominantly successful in their military careers), we have to take into account their pervasive identification with *Spartanerjünglinge*, and the way that this accords with the Prussian military adulation of Sparta which was more broadly prevalent at the time.[22] In particular, the socialisatory effect of this Spartan identification, and the inurement to brutality which it seems successfully to have facilitated, seem to go beyond any analogous instances to be found at, for instance, British public schools.[23]

At the Napolas, this tradition was transmuted. Although less pervasive, it nevertheless demonstrated above all the educational domination of the Nazi regime, which constantly used racialised ideologies in order to acquire historical legitimacy for its own ends.[24] The Spartan model here can thus be understood as underpinning the schools ideologically – alongside other models such as the cadet schools themselves, the English public schools, and the Jesuit Academies.[25] We might perhaps see in these two manifestations of the Spartan paradigm a gradual transition from the use of Sparta as an immediately practical model to her use as an ideological trope which could be placed without contradiction alongside other tropes, all of which were intended to legitimise the strength and superiority of the German race in 'biological' terms. Or perhaps we might surmise that the original Prussian vision of Sparta had been partially subsumed into the National Socialist worldview (as were other elements of 'Prussianism'), where it was reconstituted in a fittingly ideologised and racialised fashion.[26]

However, we can also consider these two refractions of the Spartan mirage as granting insight into the essential nature of the regimes in question. Although it might be suggested that the exceptionalism implicit in Spartan culture resonated well with the exceptionalism of both Prussia and the NSDAP,[27] we can also perceive the ways in which these regimes' respective appropriations corresponded to their underlying characteristics. Under the strong, military-oriented Prussian government, the pedagogical appropriation of Sparta by the military Establishment was pervasive and coherent (though still subject to liberal criticism). In Nazi Germany, however, these pedagogical appropriations were far more fragmented, differing widely between various schools and teachers, and dependent upon their respective attitudes to Sparta and their perception of her position in the ongoing power-struggle over education. They thus mirrored the fundamental disorganisation at the heart of the Nazi regime, in which political and administrative procedure constantly centred on personal struggles for power at the expense of other individuals and governmental organisations.

There remains one fundamental question which lies at the heart of this book – why Sparta, and why to such a degree? I have attempted to answer this question in various ways throughout the work, but here I wish to put forward two more comprehensive – though perhaps less substantiable – suggestions.

It has been noted by Anton Powell – and, I believe, rightly – that one of the greatest advantages of ancient Sparta was that she 'offered to children the image of a child as a model, indeed as hero. The ideal usually offered to children, of the adult they *may* become if they keep straight for 15 or so more years, is weakened by its remoteness: there's much unreality for a child about the prospect of themself as adult. But you can be a good little Spartan already!'[28] This idea could be key to explaining the supremely tenacious quality of Spartan ideology in German elite pedagogy during this period; certainly, it sheds light on the (perhaps initially surprising) alacrity with which cadets embraced an identification as *Spartanerjünglinge*, despite the painful trials which this might involve, and also on the pride experienced by many of the Napolaner when they were designated as 'brave young Spartans' (*vel sim.*) by members of staff.[29]

The second possible explanation has more far-flung roots in the Prusso-German historical context. In this model, which can be linked to the broader currents of philhellenism which were prevalent from the later eighteenth century onwards,[30] we can see the appropriation of Sparta as a response to the humiliations of the Napoleonic Wars, and an attempt to construct a new, secure identity which could legitimise the authority of this '*jugendliche Heerwesen*' (youthful military system).[31] In what had already become, thanks to the Great Elector and Frederick the Great, a strong military power, yet one which was desperately trying to rebuild her military prowess and self-confidence after the humiliations and shame of the Napoleonic invasion,[32] where better to seek out an ancient model for the training of young officers and the spirit with which to imbue the army, than the greatest ancient Greek military state – for the model of the Roman Empire was too tainted by its association with France.[33] Recasting the Prussian Officer Corps – including the cadet corps – as a form of *neu-Sparta* could thus be seen as one of the most practical applications of German philhellenism, and one with an enduring impact on those senior Officers who commanded in the Austro-Prussian, Franco-Prussian, and colonial wars, as well as the two World Wars.

Nowadays, we have fallen out of love with Sparta, convinced, perhaps, that Spartanness can mean nothing other than physical discomfort and dangerous militarism – our cultural memory, and our scholarship, cannot quite forgive Sparta for her appropriation by Nazi Germany. Besides, now that liberal democracy is the perennial rallying-cry of the West, Athens holds sway over what few Hellenic yearnings we still possess. In a way, this loss of affection for the Spartan ideal makes the tale which this work has to tell both more striking and more significant. At a time when the idea of Sparta as a state worthy of admiration, adulation, and imitation can seem at best bizarre, at worst misguided and masochistic, to explore the reasons why the inhabitants of one of Europe's greatest states deemed Sparta worthy of such whole-hearted identification can surely give us further insight into the nature of that state's history.

Such explorations also encourage us to pass beyond our own twenty-first century perspective, limited by cultural freedoms which do more than we might suppose to prevent a full understanding of the 'cruel', 'restrictive' past. Militaristic discipline may be anathema now to most Western Europeans, but in both nineteenth-century Prussia and Nazi Germany attitudes were very different, and if one way to turn young boys into loyal servants of their Fatherland was to inure them to bearing the most extreme hardships, invoking the Spartan youths of old as they did so, this phenomenon demands serious investigation, not ridicule.

In essence, that is what this monograph has aimed to achieve – to provide an answer to the question of how such mythologisation, such self-identification with ancient Spartan counterparts, functioned in Prusso-German pedagogical practice at these two elite educational institutions, over a period of nearly two centuries.

Notes

[1] Kirsten 1936, 385–6.

[2] After François Ollier's eponymous (and seminal) two-volume monograph (Paris 1933).

[3] Namely, in our respective contributions to *Sparta in Modern Thought*, ed. Stephen Hodkinson, Ian Macgregor Morris (Losemann 2012, Roche 2012a). However, I do disagree strongly with Losemann's (completely unsubstantiated) conclusion that 'in the National Socialist elite education [Sparta] was far more deeply rooted than in the education of the Prussian *Spartanerjünglinge*' (Losemann 2012, 281). The evidence clearly shows that Spartan influence was all-pervasive at the cadet schools, and that Spartan self-identification was consistently embraced by the cadets over a wide geographical and chronological span. Meanwhile, at the Napolas, diffusion of Spartan ideology seems to have relied far more upon the attitudes and predilections of individual politicians, Directors and members of staff – based on the available evidence, it would be erroneous to claim that a Spartan influence was prevalent at all of the Napolas all of the time (see further pp. 180 and 213 above). Moreover, even if further evidence were discovered which could prove that Sparta was appropriated at the Napolas in a more wholesale fashion, Losemann's conclusion would still be untenable on chronological grounds; since the Napolas were active for only twelve years, their influence could only ever have worked upon around 20 year-groups, and in any case, many of the schools actually existed for a far shorter duration than this (see Fig. 20 above).

[4] Hodkinson and Macgregor Morris 2012, xxiii, n. 31.

[5] For the most comprehensive attempt in modern scholarship to recover the ancient realities of Spartan education, see Ducat 2006.

[6] It should be noted that the Spartan influence discovered at the Napolas might have existed (to a lesser extent, perhaps) at other, non-elite, schools throughout the Third Reich. However, to prove this empirically would require a vast amount of further research. In this instance, then, the Napola eyewitnesses have provided an easily identifiable, specific subsection of individuals who were of school age during the National Socialist era.

[7] cf. Rawson 1969, Ollier 1973, Tigerstedt 1974. Birgalias (1999) provides the most comprehensive study of the idealisation of Spartan education *per se*.

[8] Cartledge 2002, 21.

[9] cf. Hodkinson 2012.

[10] cf. also p. 122 n. 1 above.

[11] cf. Powell 1989, 174.

[12] On this point, I share the view of psychological universals put forward by Steven Pinker (1997, 2002).

[13] Anton Powell, private correspondence, 14/01/2012.

[14] Rudolf Lennert, *Neue Sammlung* 1961, 433.

[15] Schneider 1996, 23. Emphasis original.

[16] Robinsohn 1966, 229.

[17] This, too, is a topic which I hope soon to consider in more detail.

[18] One subject which I would have liked to touch upon, had space and time permitted, was the role which these pedagogical ideas of *Spartanertum* may have had to play in more general Prusso-German discourses of *Männlichkeit* (masculinity) and

Körperkultur (culture of the body) during the period in question. This, I believe, would be a fruitful area for further scholarly exploration. For discussion of such discourses in general, see Hagemann 2002, Schilling 2002, Dahlke 2006.

[19] Kennedy 2002, 1.

[20] e.g. Crousaz 1876, 40; Ostertag 1990, 5–6. Ostertag also suggests that institutionalised military education is crucial to forming the fundamental phenomena of a national '*ousia*', and that the selection and training of future commanders therefore has a great significance for the whole society – in that the basic selection criteria form social barriers and determine the values which are considered most important by that society: 'An age and its society is mirrored in its elite.'

[21] It is obvious that Wiesendahl has no idea of the historical tradition into which his composition pleasingly – if somewhat ironically – falls.

[22] See pp. 16–22 above; also Roche 2012d.

[23] Again, I would ideally have liked to pursue a more 'transnational' approach, comparing the incidence and extent of Spartan identification to be found at English public schools or at military schools in other states, such as Austria, Bavaria and Switzerland; however, the scope of the project precluded this. Anton Powell hopes to treat Spartan influences in the English public schools in a future publication, however.

[24] cf. Roche 2012a.

[25] cf. Heißmeyer 1939a, 1942.

[26] On general appropriations of 'Prussianism' by the Nazi regime, see Simms 2001. For a particular instance of the Nazis appropriating an incident from the history of the Prussian Cadet Corps for the purposes of an anti-Bolshevik propaganda film, see Abels 2002.

[27] Anton Powell, private correspondence, 14/01/2012.

[28] ibid.

[29] See Chapter 9 above.

[30] As mentioned in the Introduction.

[31] Crousaz 1876, 10.

[32] On these humiliations, and in particular the catastrophic Prussian defeat at the Battle of Jena (1806), see Garnier 1998, John 1998; also Simms 1998, 75–9.

[33] cf. O'Boyle 1968.

APPENDIX:

INSTANCES OF THE SPARTAN *TOPOS* RELATING TO THE PRUSSIAN CADET SCHOOLS, ARRANGED CHRONOLOGICALLY

In order to contextualise the considerable number of references to the Spartan *topos* relating to the Prussian Cadet Corps, and to situate them clearly within the time-span of over 200 years to which they refer, this appendix presents a list of the references arranged chronologically, followed by further graphic representations and discussion of the various patterns (chronological, typological and geographical) which can be deduced from the data.

It should be noted that these are only the instances of the *topos* which I have uncovered during my doctoral research; more could potentially come to light at any time. To try to exhaust every avenue of enquiry which might lead to the discovery of further Spartan references regarding the Prussian Cadet Corps could be a lifetime's work; the fruits of the past four years' research must therefore suffice, as far as this monograph is concerned. If readers know of other instances of the *topos* which are not listed here, I would be delighted to hear of them.

*** denotes information concerning attendance at a *Voranstalt* (if known) by an author who uses the Spartan *topos* to describe the cadet corps in later writing.

Foundation dates of *Voranstalten*:
Culm – 1776 (1818); Potsdam – 1822; Wahlstatt – 1838; Bensberg – 1840; Oranienstein – 1867; Plön – 1868; Köslin (from Culm) – 1890; Karlsruhe – 1892; Naumburg – 1900

1770
– Frederick the Great writes the *Dialogue de Morale à l'Usage de la jeune Noblesse*

1818 – REORGANISATION OF THE CADET CORPS

1820s
***Otto von Corvin attends *Voranstalt* Potsdam (early 1820s)

1840s
***August Kühne (ps. Johannes van Dewall) attends *Voranstalt* Bensberg (early 1840s)

1850s

***Graf von Holleben attends *Voranstalt* Potsdam (early 1850s); he was later appointed as Commander of the Cadet Corps during the 1860s, and then as Commander of *Voranstalt* Potsdam (1879–1884)

***Eugen Jany-Hamburg attends *Voranstalt* Culm (1854–1857)

– 1857: Adolf von Crousaz publishes *Geschichte des Königlich Preußischen Kadetten-Corps*

1860s

***Paul von Hindenburg attends *Voranstalt* Wahlstatt (1859–1863)

***Graf von Haslingen probably attends *Voranstalt* Potsdam (early 1860s); he was later appointed as Commander of *Voranstalt* Wahlstatt (1900–1903) and *Voranstalt* Potsdam (1903–1910); as well as being appointed Commander of the Cadet Corps (1905–1908).

***Paul von Szczepański probably attends *Voranstalt* Culm (late 1860s)

***Alfred von Boeckmann attends *Voranstalt* Potsdam (c.1869–1870)

– 1861: Otto von Corvin publishes *Aus dem Leben eines Volkskämpfers*

– 1862: August Gertner publishes *Bensberg und sein Kadettenhaus*

1871 – GERMAN UNIFICATION

1870s

***Viktor von Arent attends *Voranstalt* Bensberg (1871–1876)

***Emil von Ilgner attends *Voranstalt* Culm and *Voranstalt* Bensberg (1872–1877)

***von Altrock attends *Voranstalt* Potsdam and *Voranstalt* Oranienstein (mid-1870s)

***Paul von Schoenaich attends *Voranstalt* Culm (late 1870s)

– 1871: Otto von Corvin publishes *A Life of Adventure. An Autobiography*

– 1873: Dünheim's article '*Die Central-Kadettenanstalt zu Lichterfelde*' published in *Daheim*

– 1877: Johannes van Dewall publishes *Aus meinen Kadettenjahren*

– 1878: Pelet-Narbonne publishes *Die Haupt-Kadetten-Anstalt zu Lichterfelde*

1880s

[1880: Otto von Corvin publishes *Illustrirte Geschichte des Alterthums* (Vol.1), which describes the education of young Spartans in a way that is somewhat reminiscent of cadet-school life.]

***Leopold von Wiese attends *Voranstalt* Wahlstatt (late 1880s)

– 1889: Louis von Scharfenort publishes *Bilder aus der Geschichte des Kadetten-Korps für Alt und Jung*

1890s

***Franz von Papen attends *Voranstalt* Bensberg (1891–1895)

***Friedrich-Wilhelm von Isenburg attends *Voranstalt* Plön and the *Prinzenschule* (1894–1900)

***Kurt von Borcke attends *Voranstalt* Karlsruhe (c.1893–1898)

***Balthasar von Aulock-Radau attends *Voranstalt* Wahlstatt (1896–1900)

***Magnus von Eberhardt attends *Voranstalt* Potsdam (1896–c.1900)

***Erich Werner attends *Voranstalt* Potsdam (1897–1901)

– 1890: School reform conference

1900s

***Fritz von Unruh attends *Voranstalt* Plön and the *Prinzenschule* (1894–1905)
***Erich von Manstein attends *Voranstalt* Plön (1900–1902)
***Peter von Heydebreck attends *Voranstalt* Köslin (c.1900–1905)
***Horst von der Goltz attends the HKA (c.1900)
***Herbert Maisch attends *Voranstalt* Oranienstein and *Voranstalt* Karlsruhe (1901–1906)
***Henning von Koss attends *Voranstalt* Köslin (1901–1904)
***Hans-Joachim von Reitzenstein probably attended the cadet corps around this point.
– 1901: Paul von Szczepański publishes *Spartanerjünglinge*
– 1901: Ernst von Faller publishes *Der Offizier*
– 1906: Graf von Haslingen publishes *Geschichte des Kadettenhauses in Potsdam*
– 1907: Ludwig Thoma publishes *Tante Frieda*

1910s

***Hans-Ulrich Neumann attends *Voranstalt* Köslin (1910–1914)
***Ernst von Salomon attends *Voranstalt* Karlsruhe (1913–1917)
***Walther Wenck attends *Voranstalt* Naumburg (1911–c.1917)
***Kurt-Christoph Voigt attends *Voranstalt* Plön (1913–1918)
***Hans Bruns (Oranienstein), Ernst Kiock (Wahlstatt), Werner Lübcke (Plön), Herbert Nimz (Köslin), Albrecht Schott (Wahlstatt) and Siegfried Fiedler, Hans Friedrich Heuser, Werner Hohenstein, Friedrich Carl Lengerke, Karl Lorentz, Detlev Rudelsdorff, and Jobst Meyer-Schneidewind probably attended their respective *Voranstalten* during this period
– 1917: Horst von der Goltz publishes *My Adventures as a German Secret Agent*
– 5 May 1917: Reichstag debate
– August 1917: The *Tägliche Rundschau* publishes '*Die Spartaner von Lichterfelde*'
– 1919: Hindenburg's recollections (quoted in Brand 1981, 265–7)

1920 – THE PRUSSIAN CADET CORPS IS DISBANDED

1920s

***Hanns Nickol attends the Stabila (former HKA) Berlin-Lichterfelde (c.1920)
– 1920: Hans-Joachim von Reitzenstein publishes *Vergitterte Jugend*
– March 1920: The *Deutsches Offizier-blatt* publishes an 'obituary' of the cadet corps
– August 1920: Kurt Tucholsky publishes '*Kadettenliteratur*' in *Die Weltbühne*
– August-September 1920: *Deutsche Kadettenzeitung* Nr.1 editorial; reprinting of cadet-corps 'obituary' from the *Deutsches Offizier-blatt*
– 1922: M. Masberg publishes *Entstehen und Werden des Potsdamer Kadettenhauses*
– 3 April 1922: *Landtag* Debate
– 1924: Leopold von Wiese publishes *Kindheit. Erinnerungen aus meinen Kadettenjahren*
– 1924: Otto von Corvin's *Ein Leben voller Abenteuer* is published
– March 1925: von Altrock publishes '*Aus dem Kadettenleben*' in the *Reichskadettenblatt* (= RKB)
– May 1925: Alfred von Boeckmann publishes '*Erinnerungen eines alten Potsdamer Kadetten*' in the *Deutsches Adelsblatt*
– September 1925: H.F.H. [probably Hans Friedrich Heuser] publishes '*Vogel Wiedehopf*' in the RKB

– 1926: Paul von Schoenaich publishes *Mein Damaskus. Erlebnisse und Bekenntnisse*
– March 1926: Eugen Jany-Hamburg publishes '*Erinnerungen eines Uralten*' in the RKB
– October 1926: The RKB reprints Boeckmann's '*Erinnerungen*'
– 1 October 1927: *Die Woche* publishes '*Der Kadett Hindenburg*'
– 4 March 1928: Sermon by Chaplain Kostorz at the former cadets' ceremony honouring the war-dead, published in the RKB in April 1928
– April 1928: Pastor Klingenburg publishes '*Neues Leben im Bensberger Schloss*' in the RKB
– 17 September 1928: 50th anniversary of the HKA: Cadet Pastor Gruhl's speech, reported in the *Neue Preußische [Kreuz-] Zeitung* by Klaus-Ulrich Henning
– October 1928: Gruhl's speech is published in the RKB
– September 1929: Magnus von Eberhardt publishes '*Aus der Kadettenzeit*' in the RKB
– September 1929: *Gaugruppe* Pommern report in the RKB
– December 1929: Ernst Kiock publishes '*Der Kadett in Zivil*' in the RKB

1930s
– October 1930: G. von Unruh publishes his version of '*Die Spartaner von Lichterfelde*' in the RKB
– 1931: Peter von Heydebreck publishes *Wir Wehrwölfe*
– 1932: Emil Ilgner publishes *Kadettenerinnerungen*

1933 – THE NATIONAL SOCIALISTS COME TO POWER

– 1933: Ernst von Salomon publishes *Die Kadetten*
– 1935: Hanns von Nickol publishes *Der letzte Kadett*
– 3 February 1937: Article entitled '*Wahlstatts "Yorckscher Geist"*' is published in the *Berliner Tageblatt*
– 1939: Publication of *Festschrift, herausgegeben aus Veranlassung der ersten großen Zusammenkunft ehemaliger Kadetten in Stuttgart am 4. März 1939*

1940s
– 1940: Kurt von Borcke publishes *Das sind wir*
– endorsement by Franz von Weyssenhoff in the preface to *Das sind wir*
– December 1940: comment by Viktor von Arent in the RKB (*Ortsgruppe* Görlitz report)
– 6 December 1940: *Wahlstätter Ring* report in *Nachrichten für alte Kadetten* Nr.1
– 1941: Ernst Zander publishes *Bensberg als militärischer Standort*

1945 – *STUNDE NULL*

– 1947: Richard Feiber writes *Leben und Treiben im Königlich Preußisch Kadettenhaus Bensberg*
– including a contribution by a former Bensberg cadet under the pseudonym 'v. Chr.'

1950s
– 1952: Franz von Papen publishes *Der Wahrheit eine Gasse* (*Memoirs*)
– 30 August 1953: Article on the HKA in the *Tagesspiegel*: '*Casanova wollte nicht Kadettenlehrer werden*'
– 1955: Erich von Manstein publishes *Verlorene Siege*
– 1955: Balthasar von Aulock-Radau writes '*4 Jahre Kadett in Wahlstatt (1896–1900)*'

– 1957: Fritz von Unruh publishes *Der Sohn des Generals*
– 1958: Erich von Manstein publishes *Aus einem Soldatenleben 1887–1939*
– 1958: Friedrich-Wilhelm von Isenburg publishes *Kadettenleben*
– endorsement by Erich von Manstein in the foreword to *Kadettenleben*

1960s

– December 1963: Detlev Rudelsdorff publishes '*Gedanken über die Erziehungsgrundsätze des ehem. Kadettenkorps in Hinblick auf die Frage des Offiziernachwuchs unserer Zeit*' in the *Mitteilungsblatt*
– 1967: Fritz von Unruh publishes *Im Haus der Prinzen*
– 5 May 1967: Rudelsdorff gives a speech commemorating the 250th anniversary of the Prussian Cadet Corps
– 1968: Herbert Maisch publishes *Helm ab – Vorhang auf*
– 10–12 May 1968: Speech at Plön cadets' reunion
– 1969: Speech at dedication of cadets' memorial by Walther Wenck – later published in *Das Ehrenmal der Kadetten auf der Burg Hohenzollern*, ed. Horst Wagner

1970s

– 1970: Heuser writes a modernised version of Crousaz's history
– May 1970: *Gruppe* Frankfurt make a typed version of Szczepański's *Spartanerjünglinge*
– 6 June 1970: *Gruppe* Frankfurt start holding readings of *Spartanerjünglinge* at their regular meetings (reported in the August *Mitteilungsblatt*)
– 8 February 1971: correspondence between Friedrich Carl Lengerke and Werner Hosse
– 1973: Werner Hohenstein gives a memorial speech at the *Bundeskadettentag*, reprinted in *Chronik des Bundes-Kadettentages* 1973, ed. Albrecht Schott
– December 1973: Henning von Koss publishes his reminiscences in the Köslin cadets' *Rundbrief* (newsletter)
– 29–31 August 1975: Rudelsdorff gives a speech at the *Bundeskadettentag*, reprinted in the *Chronik des Bundeskadettentages* 1975, and in a military newspaper in December 1975.
– 21 November 1975: Speech given at the ceremony inaugurating an exhibition on the cadet corps in the Plön *Heimatmuseum* (local history museum), reported both in the Hamburg *Rundschreiben* (newsletter) on 27 November 1975 and in *Der Plöner* in December 1975.
– c.1975: Erich Werner writes *Lebenserinnerungen aus meiner Kadettenzeit in Potsdam und Berlin-Lichterfelde 97/01, 01/03*
– 1976: Henning von Koss publishes further reminiscences in Nimz's *Das Kadettenhaus Culm-Köslin 1776–1920*
– 1976: Hans-Ulrich Neumann's *Erinnerungen an das Kgl. Pr. Kadettenkorps* are made available after his death
– July 1977: eulogy by Kurt-Christoph Voigt, celebrating the life of Karl-Eberhard Struckmann at his funeral, reprinted in the Hamburg *Rundschreiben*
– May 1978: Werner Lübcke reports on a Plön reunion
– 23 September 1978: The *Lindauer Zeitung* reports on a Naumburg reunion
– 8 October 1978: Rudolf Noth of the *Berliner Morgenpost* reports on the *Bundeskadettentag*
– 1979: Herbert Nimz publishes '*Das Kadettenhaus Köslin*' in the journal *Pommern*

– 17 June 1979: Hans Bruns speaks at an Oranienstein reunion
– 28–30 August 1979: Siegfried Fiedler speaks at the *Bundeskadettentag*, reprinted in the *Chronik des 11. Bundeskadettentages*, ed. Albrecht Schott
– 16 November 1979: The *Lahnzeitung* reports on an Oranienstein reunion

1980s
– 1980: Albrecht Schott publishes '*Erziehungsgrundsätze im Kadettenkorps*' in *Steglitzer Heimat*; an article by Schott in the *Deutsches Adelsblatt* was probably also published around this time
– 1 June 1980: Friedrich-Wilhelm Gloatz speaks at an Oranienstein commemoration ceremony
– July 1980: Karl Lorentz publishes '*Der Pamsch – und wie er enden musste*' in the *Mitteilungsblatt*
– 1981: Karl-Hermann Brand publishes *Kadetten. Aus 300 Jahren deutscher Kadettenkorps. Band I.*
– 1982: Köslin cadets reprint the first page of the *Deutsche Kadettenzeitung* 1920 in their *Rundbrief*
– November 1982: '*Der Kadett Hindenburg*' (from *Die Woche* 1927) is reprinted in *Der Plöner*
– 8 May 1983: report on an exhibition about the cadet school in Karlsruhe published in the Köslin cadets' *Rundbrief*
– 7 September 1983: Siegfried Fiedler speaks at the *Bundeskadettentag*
– 1983: *Rothenburg Stadt und Land* reports on the *Bundeskadettentag* 1983*;* see also *Soldaten schreiben für Soldaten* (n.d.)
– c.1985: Albrecht Schott writes a museum guide entitled '*Kadetten ihrer Könige*', which is cited in the Diez *Lions Club Zeitung* in February 1985
– 1988: Klaus-Rainer Woche publishes an article entitled '*Von Kadetten, Kanonieren und Kasernen*' in *Steglitzer Heimat*
– 8 May 1988: Kurt-Christoph Voigt's life is remembered by Jobst Meyer Schneidewind at a reunion at Oranienstein; Schneidewind's speech is reprinted in *Kadettentage in Oranienstein* (ed. Albrecht Schott)

1990s
– 1991: The life of Frank Weller (1901–1991, who attended Oranienstein) is remembered in the *Nachrichtenblatt des Traditionsverbandes Jaeger-Regiment*
– 1991: publication of the *Kadetten Abschluss-Chronik*, part of which is reprinted in *Preußische Mitteilungen*
– 20 February 1992: Bensberg reunion reported in local paper: '*Kuchendieb auf der Geistertreppe*'
– Albrecht Schott's *Nachlass*

N.B. It should be understood that all the data and graphs below refer only to this list of references, and are therefore entirely provisional, given that (as mentioned above) new references to the *topos* could potentially come to light at any time.

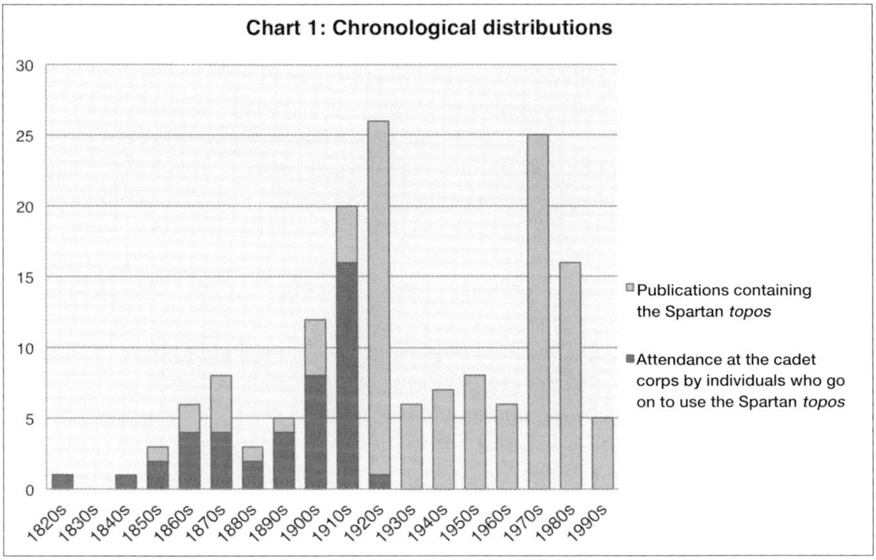

Commentary

It is impossible to make any definitive comments based on the patterns revealed by the data above, since there is simply less evidence available generally from some periods and from some *Voranstalten* than from others. For instance, much depends on how many alumni each *Voranstalt* produced in each generation who were famous enough – or simply interested and talented enough – to publish reminiscences or autobiographies describing their time at the corps. However, it is clear that pupils at Potsdam, Bensberg and Karlsruhe (Corvin, Dewall [Kühne], and Borcke respectively) remember engaging with cadet-school *Spartanertum* almost immediately after their respective *Voranstalten* had been opened. Very often, the first works of literature to come to light regarding other *Voranstalten* (Culm, Köslin, Wahlstatt and Plön) also mention the *topos*, even if the works in question were produced by pupils who only attended the schools some years after they opened.

The fact that a steady stream of Spartan references can be found in the 1920s which did not exist to the same extent beforehand can in part be explained by the fact that, for the first time, former cadets who were not blessed with particular literary or military talent now possessed both a forum and a sympathetic audience for their reminiscences and their opinions. One suspects that far more Spartan references would survive from before 1920 if there had then existed an organ such as the *Reichskadettenblatt*, in which similar autobiographical anecdotes could have been published. However, from 1920 onwards, as never before, former cadets were uniformly encouraged to dilate upon their time in the corps in nostalgic fashion, since disseminating *Erinnerungsschriften* (remembrance literature) as widely as possible was one of the expressed aims of the *Reichsbund ehemaliger Kadetten*, as set out in the first issue of the *Deutsche Kadettenzeitung*, later renamed the *Reichskadettenblatt* (see pp. 164 and

176 n. 44 above). This tendency also appears to have been exacerbated by the political tensions surrounding the dissolution of the cadet corps in particular, and the rise of the Weimar Republic in general. As well as forming an element of former cadets' reminiscences similar to that found in cadet-school literature published before the First World War, the Spartan *topos* could now be used even more as a means of self-definition by the former cadet community, part of their reaction in righteous anger to the destruction of the cadet corps by its hated left-wing detractors.[1] The white columns referring to the 1920s–1940s in Chart 2 below show roughly the proportion of material published by the *Traditionsgemeinschaft* during this period which had a more political – as opposed to nostalgic – bent (although sometimes the two elements are hard to disentangle).

Following a relative dearth of evidence from the Third Reich (see p. 176 n. 53 above), more Spartan references begin to come to light in the 1950s, with a number of autobiographical works by the generation of cadets who were educated at the turn of the century (Franz von Papen, Erich von Manstein, Fritz von Unruh *et al.*), and then with the foundation of the new League of Former Royal Prussian and Royal Saxon Cadets, whose newsletter (the *Mitteilungsblatt*) was first published in 1963. The first reference to the Spartan *topos* in the publications of the League appeared in December of that year, in the form of an article by Detlev Rudelsdorff (referred to in Chapter 7 above). References then peak once more in the 1970s – again, at a time when the former cadets perceived themselves to be enduring hostility from politicians, and even the general public, but also when many were beginning to enter that stage of their lives which heralds the 'reminiscence bump' (see p. 11 above), when memories from one's youth are more easily and readily recalled. Not all of the Spartan references from this period have been discussed in Chapter 7, since some are fairly fleeting, while others merely involve the reprinting of articles from earlier periods which happened

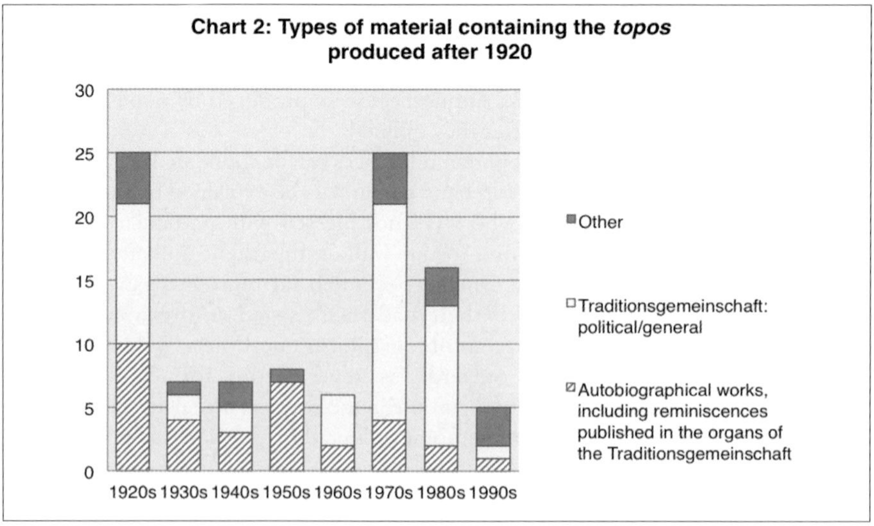

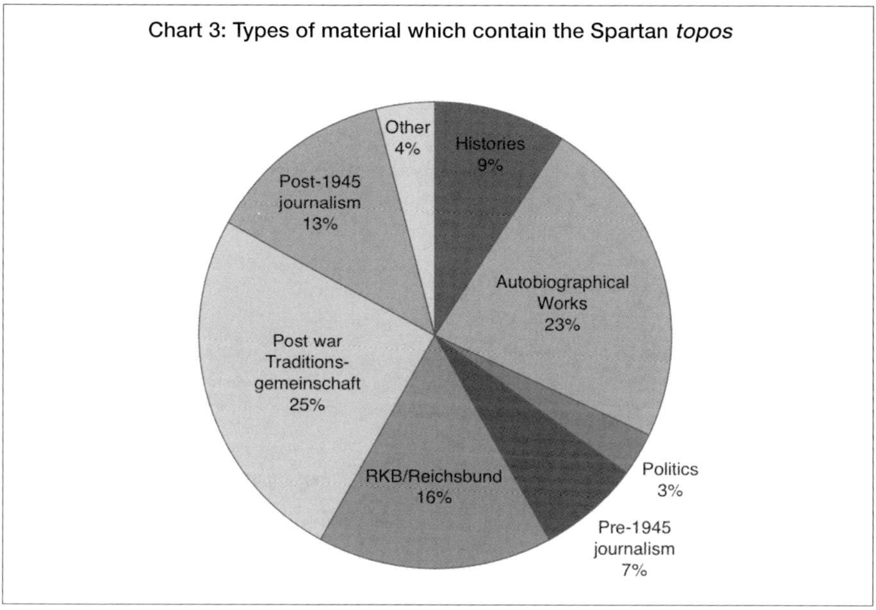

to contain the *topos* (such as the first article printed in the *Deutsche Kadettenzeitung*), or the publication of a contemporary speech or piece of writing containing the *topos* in another context or periodical (see the list of references above). Gradually, during the later 1970s and 1980s, the political elements with which the discussion had been infused slowly grew less pressing, and the *topos* was more likely to be mentioned in nostalgic fashion, or taken up by reporters for local newspapers enthusing over the average age of those attending the cadet-corps reunions. Finally, in 1991, the League was formally disbanded, as the last of the former cadets – even those who had still been at the *Voranstalten* in 1918 – succumbed to old age and death.

As discussed above, any attempt to conduct a statistical analysis regarding how large a proportion of the evidence on the cadet corps in general contains the *topos* is deeply problematic, given the vast amounts of material which have been lost, or those which are currently inaccessible.[2] The only areas where a statistical analysis can realistically be attempted are those of autobiographical literature and history. Out of 47 autobiographical works consulted, 26 referred to the *topos* (55%) – however, it should be borne in mind that there might have been certain reasons why, after the Second World War, some authors might have felt it politic not to mention cadet-school Spartanism in any form, given the way in which ideas of Sparta were used during the Third Reich. One might even suggest that this potential problematisation makes the prevalence of the *topos* in cadet-school memoirs and newsletters during the postwar period even more remarkable. Meanwhile, out of 16 histories – dealing with the cadet corps as a whole or with individual schools – 10 referred to the *topos* (63%). During the years for which we possess a complete run of issues of the *Reichskadettenblatt* (up to 1930), 10 out of 21 issues refer to the *topos* (48%), though it should be noted that some issues included more than one article which contained a Spartan reference.

As mentioned above, the distribution of references is somewhat arbitrary, since some schools seem to have produced more alumni who became famous, or who later wished to immortalise their cadet-school experiences in literature – such as Karlsruhe, which inspired both Ernst von Salomon and Kurt von Borcke, or Plön, whose alumni included Fritz von Unruh and Erich von Manstein. However, if the amount of time during which each *Voranstalt* existed is taken into account, the statistics seem to suggest a degree of comparability (if the figures for Culm and Köslin are added together – these were, in effect, one school which simply relocated – the total is 12%, an identical figure to that of the HKA, which had also been serving the new dispensation since 1818). The relative predominance of references from Plön relative to the length of time that the school existed can partially be explained by the fact that newsletters from the Plön old boys' network were more readily available in the archives. The very small number of references from Naumburg can also be explained by the fact that only about half a dozen complete year groups who had attended the school would have graduated from the HKA before the First World War.

Chart 4: Topographical distribution of the Spartan *topos* (approximate)

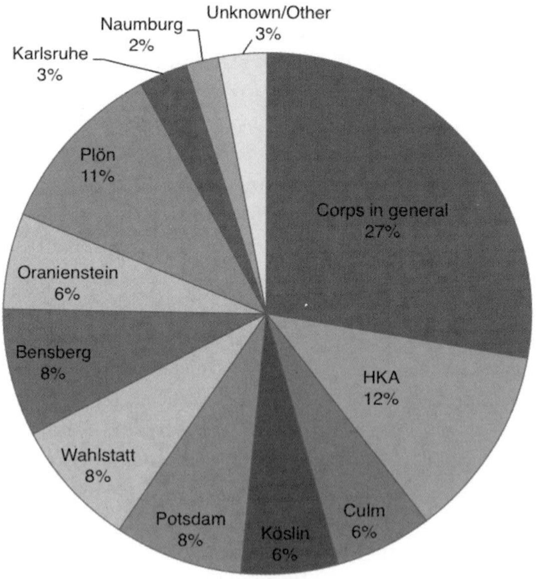

A note on the Napolas

All references to the Spartan *topos* at the Napolas which are contained in sources other than eyewitness correspondence or interviews have already been mentioned in the text or notes. The chronological and topographical distribution of these references has generally been dictated by the sources which were available (for instance, more material can be discussed from Schulpforta because many sources concerning the school's time as a Napola have been preserved in the archives of the current *Landesschule zur Pforta*). Further instances of the *topos* might well come to light in sources from various German regional archives, or in memoirs which have not yet been published or brought to the author's attention. It would in any case be premature to attempt to catalogue this type of material in any comprehensive fashion, since much documentation is still in the hands of former pupils and has not yet been archived. It is envisaged that any further such references will be incorporated into a second, paperback edition of this volume, if appropriate.

Notes

[1] N.B. It could be argued that this type of self-definition was prevalent to some extent anyway, but that the sources which could have attested to this before the creation of the *Reichskadettenblatt* do not exist in sufficient number.

[2] For instance, it is highly probable that further references to the *topos* could be found in other local newspapers, both before and after the cadet schools were abolished. However, the amount of research involved in tracing references to the cadet corps in all of these would have been impractical for this project.

GLOSSARY

agela – the name used by several authors of Classical texts on Sparta (including Plutarch) to denote a group of Spartan boys.[1]

bōmolochia – a ritual conducted in Sparta at the altar of the goddess Artemis Orthia, involving the flagellation of Spartan youths (either by their peers, who attempted to prevent them from stealing cheeses which were laid upon the altar, or as a test of endurance).[2]

eirēn – a Spartan youth over the age of twenty, entrusted with authority over his juniors.

Erzieher – trainer/educator. At the Prussian Cadet Schools, *Erzieher* were young regular army officers (usually in their mid-twenties) whose task was to supervise and train the cadets. At the Napolas, *Erzieher* were usually men of a similar age and with a similar function, though they took more part in teaching, and were supposed to be loyal National Socialists.

Gymnasium – a type of German secondary school which followed a humanistic curriculum (focusing upon Latin and ancient Greek).

Hauptkadettenanstalt (HKA) – the central cadet school in Berlin, which educated cadets between around the ages of 15 and 19, covering the classes Untersekunda, Obersekunda, Unterprima, and Oberprima, and also including the Selekta – a special fast-track class for the most gifted cadets, which allowed them to gain their commission without attending the *Kriegsschule*, the war academy.

Hundertschaftsführer – (company commander) a Napola teacher with responsibility for one of the units of around a hundred boys into which each school was generally divided.

Jungmann – the official designation for a boy attending a Napola.

paidonomos – the Spartan magistrate responsible for boys' education.

Realschule – a type of German secondary school which focused upon modern languages and science subjects (Latin was usually taught, but not Greek).

Reichswehr – the German armed forces between 1921–1935. From 1935–1945 these were called the *Wehrmacht*; in the post-war Federal Republic of Germany, they then became the *Bundeswehr*.

Schnappsack (sometimes shortened to *Sack*) – derogatory term for a new pupil in the cadet corps.

Stube – room: the smallest division in the cadet schools, usually containing ten cadets, who would work and relax in the room allocated to them. This form of organisation was then taken over by the Napolas.

Stubenältester – room captain: an older cadet or *Jungmann*, who was in charge of the boys in his *Stube*.

Volk – people / race / nation.

völkisch – racial / ethnic / national.

Voranstalt – preparatory cadet school which fed into the *Hauptkadettenanstalt*, educating boys from the age of ten to fifteen (covering the year-groups Sexta, Quinta, Quarta, Untertertia and Obertertia). Year-groups in German secondary schools usually ran from the Sexta (age 10–11) to the Oberprima (age 18–19).

Zug – (platoon) the name for a year-group at the Napolas, replacing the civilian term *Klasse* (class).

Zugführer – (platoon commander) a Napola teacher responsible for a particular class or year-group.

Notes

[1] See further Ducat 2006, 77–81.

[2] See further Ducat 2006, 249–60.

ARCHIVAL SOURCES

Bundesarchiv Lichterfelde (BArch)

Collections:

NS6	Parteikanzlei der NSDAP
NS/5/VI	Deutsche Arbeitsfront; Bildungs- und Schulwesen
NS12	Hauptamt für Erzieher/Reichsverwaltung des NS-Lehrerbundes
NS15	Der Beauftragte des Führers für die Überwachung der gesamten geistigen und weltanschaulichen Schulung und Erziehung der NSDAP
NS19	Persönlicher Stab Reichsführer SS
NS26	Hauptarchiv der NSDAP
R2	Reichsfinanzministerium
R43-II	Neue Reichskanzlei, Serie Schulwesen
R1501	Reichsministerium des Innern
R4901	Reichsministerium für Wissenschaft, Erziehung und Volksbildung

Personnel files (formerly held at the Berlin Document Center):

Personalakten Otto Calliebe
BArch (ehem. BDC) SSO 125, Calliebe Otto, 15/5/1893

Personalakten Joachim Haupt
BArch (ehem. BDC) SA Haupt Joachim, 7/4/1900
BArch (ehem. BDC) SA (7-A) Haupt Joachim, 7/4/1900
BArch (ehem. BDC) OPG Haupt Joachim, 7/4/1900 (D0119)

Personalakten August Heißmeyer
BArch (ehem. BDC) SSO 80-A, Heißmeyer August, 11/1/1897

Personalakten Kurt Person
BArch (ehem. BDC) SSO[369A] Person, Kurt, 24/4/1898

Personalakten Bernhard Rust
BArch (ehem. BDC) DS A0059, Rust Bernhard, 30/9/1883
BArch (ehem. BDC), PK K0121, Rust Bernhard, 30/9/1883

Personalakten Reinhard Sunkel
BArch (ehem. BDC) DS Sunkel, Reinhard 9/2/1900
BArch (ehem. BDC) SA Sunkel Reinhard 9/2/1900

Geheimes Staatsarchiv Preußischer Kulturbesitz (GStAPK)

Collections:

GStAPK IV.HA Preußische Armee, Rep.13 Militär-Erziehungs- und Bildungswesen, Kadettenkorps (referred to in notes as GStAPK IV.HA Rep.13)

Archival sources

GStAPK I.HA. Rep.76, Kultusministerium
GStAPK I.HA Rep.84a, Justizministerium
GStAPK I.HA Rep.89, Geh. Zivilkabinett, jüngere Periode

Bundesarchiv-Militärarchiv Freiburg (BA-MA)
Collections:

MSG2	Militärgeschichtlicher Sammlungsbestand
MSG3	Sammlung von Verbandsdruckgut
PH21	Akademien, Schulen, Kadettenanstalten

Archiv der Landesschule Pforta
Material relating to the school's incarnation as a *Nationalpolitische Erziehungsanstalt* (1935–1945)

SELECT BIBLIOGRAPHY

Primary sources

Anon.

1798 'Wäre es möglich den patriotischen Heldengeist der preußischen Nation noch mehr zu erheben?', *Jahrbücher der preußischen Monarchie* 1798 (3), 245–56.

1848 *Das Kadettenkorps sonst und jetzt. Zur richtigen Beurtheilung dieser Anstalt*, Berlin.

1889 'Drei Jahre im Kadettencorps (1758–1760)', *Jahrbuch für die Deutsche Armee und Marine* (April), 87–92.

1898 'Das Berliner Kadettenhaus in den Märztagen 1848', *Der Bär* 24 (3), 34–5.

1914 *The German Army from Within. By a British Officer who has served in it*, London.

1972 *Also sprach der Kadett...*, Bornheim.

n.d. 'Das Preußische Kadettenkorps, seine Wirkung im 200 jährigem Bestehen und sein Ende. Sind seine Erziehungsformen auch heute noch Zukunftsweisend?' [BA-MA MSG 2/17007].

∴ [The author's pseudonym]

1894 *Unsere Kadettenkorps* (2nd edn.), Leipzig.

Abbt, T.

1765a 'Drey hundert und ein und zwanzigster Brief', *Briefe, die neueste Litteratur betreffend*, 113–36.

1765b 'Drey hundert und zwei und zwanzigster Brief', *Briefe, die neueste Litteratur betreffend*, 137–46.

Abercron, H. von

1938 *Offizier und Luftpionier. Tatberichte und Erinnerungen 1869–1938*, Stuttgart.

Altrock, Generalleutnant von

1925a 'Aus dem Kadettenleben (Teil 1)', *Reichskadettenblatt* 4 (March), 38–41.

1925b 'Aus dem Kadettenleben (Teil 2)', *Reichskadettenblatt* 5 (September), 51–3.

1931 'Peter Murr über das preußische Kadettenkorps', *Reichskadettenblatt* 21 (March), 314–15.

Aulock-Radau, B. von

1955 '4 Jahre Kadett in Wahlstatt (1896–1900)' [BA-MA PH21/20].

Barnard, H.

1871 *National Education. Systems, Institutions and Statistics of Public Instruction in different countries. Part I – Europe – German States*, New York.

1872 *Military Schools and Courses of Instruction in the Science and Art of War in France, Prussia, Austria, Russia, Sweden, Switzerland, Sardinia, England, and the United States. Drawn from recent official reports and documents*, New York.

Bartels, H., Klotzsch, K., and Lüdemann, H.

1941 *Volkwerden der Deutschen. Von der Vorgeschichte bis zum Ende der Stauferzeit* (2nd edn.), Leipzig.

Basdorf, H.
1953 'Casanova wollte nicht Kadettenlehrer werden. Vor 80 Jahren Grundsteinlegung zur HKA in Lichterfelde – Kassette macht Geschichte lebendig', *Tagesspiegel*, 30 August 1953.

Beard, C. A.
1936 'Education under the Nazis', *Foreign Affairs. An American Quarterly Review* 14 (3), 437–52.

Becker, W.
2000 *Erinnerungen an die Napola Naumburg: ein über die "Kadette Naumburg" hinausgehender Beitrag zur Geschichte der NPEA*, Neustrelitz.

Bensberg, Kadettenhaus
n.d. (c.1906?) *Vorschriften für die Erzieher des Kadettenhauses in Bensberg*, Bergisch-Gladbach.

Benstatt-Wahlberg, M.
1882 *Aus den Voranstalten des Kadetten-Corps und der Hauptkadettenanstalt zu Lichterfelde*, Hanover.

Berkun, A.
c.1930 *Also sprach der Kadett... 500 Worte Kadettensprache*, Berlin.

Berve, H.
1934 'Antike und nationalsozialistischer Staat', *Vergangenheit und Gegenwart* 24, 257–72.
1937 *Sparta*, Leipzig.
1941 'Vier Sparta-Bücher', *Gnomon* 17, 1–11.

Bessel, H.
1999 'Hat Ilfeld mich geprägt?', in *Die Nationalpolitische Erziehungsanstalt Ilfeld. Sammlung der von 1934 bis 1944 herausgegebenen Ilfeld-Blätter – Ein Beitrag zur Zeitgeschichte*, Vol. 2, n.p., 529–32.

Besser, H.-E. von
1934 *Wahlstätter. Kadettengeschichten*, Gütersloh.
1942 *Zum Soldat geboren. Die Geschichte eines Wahlstätter Kadetten*, Leipzig.

Billib, H.
1978 'Das letzte Kadettenjahr in Wahlstatt. Erinnerungen', in E. Kiock (ed.) *Wahlstatt und seine Kadetten*, Dortmund, 41–60.

Boeckmann, A. von
1926 'Erinnerungen eines alten Potsdamer Kadetten', *Reichskadettenblatt* 8 (October), 99–101.

Bogner, H.
1935 'Die Behandlung der Antike im nationalsozialistischen Geschichtsunterricht', *Vergangenheit und Gegenwart*, 9. Ergänzungsheft, 13–25.

Bolte, H.
n.d. *Ilfelder Erinnerungen 1936–1943*, n.p.

Borcke, K. H. von
1940 *Das sind wir. Biographie einer Jugend*, Leipzig.

Bormann, M.
1981 *Hitlers politisches Testament*, Hamburg.

Bösser
1897 *Erziehung und Unterricht im Königlich preußischen Kadettenkorps*, Berlin.

Brandis, C. von
1966 *Vor uns der Douamont. Aus dem Leben eines alten Soldaten*, Leoni am Starnberger See.
Braunburg, R.
1989 *Hinter Mauern. Eine Jugend in Deutschland*, Reinbek bei Hamburg.
Breysig, T.
1876 *Das Königliche Kadettenhaus zu Culm 1776–1876. Nach urkundlichen Quellen bearbeitet*, Culm.
Bruck, M. van den
1916 *Der Preußische Stil*, Breslau.
Bruns, H.
1979 'Grusswort des Betreuers der ehem. Oraniensteiner Kadetten an die Bürger der Stadt Diez/Lahn aus Anlass der 650 Jahrfeier im Rahmen des Empfangs für geladene Gäste im Hotel "Hof von Holland" am 17. Juni 1979' [GStAPK IV.HA Rep.13 Nr.35, Bl.63–4].
Bürgener, M.
1934 'Spartanische Jugend', *Wille und Macht* 2 (4), 2–5.
Bux, E.
1925 'Zwei sozialistische Novellen bei Plutarch', *Klio* 19, 413–31.
Calliebe, O.
1940 'Die nationalpolitischen Erziehungsanstalten', *Deutsche Schulerziehung* 1940, 248–57.
Corvin, O. von
1861 *Aus dem Leben eines Volkskämpfers*, Vol.1, Amsterdam.
1871 *A Life of Adventure. An Autobiography*, Vol.1, London.
1880 *Illustrirte Geschichte des Alterthums* (Illustrirte Weltgeschichte, Vol. 1), Leipzig.
1924 *Ein Leben voller Abenteuer*, Frankfurt am Main.
Crousaz, A. von
1857 *Geschichte des Königlich Preußischen Kadetten-Corps, nach seiner Entstehung, seinem Entwicklungsgange und seinen Resultaten*, Berlin.
1876 *Das Offizier-Corps der Preußischen Armee nach seiner historischen Entwickelung, seiner Eigenthümlichkeit und seinen Leistungen*, Halle an der Saale.
Darré, R. W.
1929 *Das Bauerntum als Lebensquell der nordischen Rasse*, Munich.
1933 'Sparta. Ein Staatsgedanke aus Blut und Boden (Grundlagen, Aufstieg, Niedergang)', in Losemann 2005.
Degen, A. von
1890 *Aus der Kadettenzeit*, Leipzig.
Deichmann, P.
1979 *Der Chef im Hintergrund. Ein Leben als Soldat von der preußischen Armee bis zur Bundeswehr*, Hamburg.
Deussen, W.
n.d. (c.1922) *Ernstes und Heiteres aus dem Kadettenleben zu Großlichterfelde. Ein Buch der Erinnerung*, Berlin.
Dewall, J. van
1878 *Kadettengeschichten. Erinnerungen aus meinen Kadettenjahren*, Stuttgart and Leipzig.
1884 *Aus meinen Kadettenjahren. Lose Blätter* (2nd edn.), Stuttgart and Leipzig.

Dünheim, W. von
1873 'Die Central-Kadettenanstalt zu Lichterfelde', *Daheim* [GStAPK IV.HA Rep.13 Nr.72, Bl.11].
Eberhardt, W. M. von
1929 'Aus der Kadettenzeit', *Reichskadettenblatt* 16 (September), 236–40.
Eckardt, F. von
1967 *Ein unordentliches Leben. Lebenserinnerungen*, Düsseldorf.
Eisenhofer, H.
1932 *Einst gab's Kadetten!*, Munich.
Faller, E.
1901 *Der Offizier. Das Buch der Berufe. Ein Führer und Berater bei der Berufswahl*, Hanover.
Feiber, R.
1939 *Auszug aus der Chronik des Kadettenhauses Bensberg* [BA-MA MSG2/16992].
1947 *Leben und Treiben im Königlich Preußisch Kadettenhaus Bensberg* (unpublished manuscript), Bergisch Gladbach [BA-MA MSG2/16995].
Foth, W.
1935 'Im alten Kadettenhaus Karlsruhe', *Reichskadettenblatt* 33 (May), 522–3.
Frank, W. (ed.)
1936 *Das nationalsozialistische Deutschland und die Wissenschaft. Heidelberger Reden von Reichsminister Rust und Prof. Ernst Krieck* (Schriften des Reichsinstituts für Geschichte des neuen Deutschlands), Hamburg.
Franke, K.-J.
n.d., a *Erinnerungen aus den Jahren 1941–1945*, n.p.
n.d., b *Einzelkind kein Musterknabe*, n.p.
Frederick the Great
1770 *Dialogue de Morale à l'Usage de la Jeune Noblesse*, Berlin.
Freundeskreis ehemaliger Ilfelder Lehrer und Schüler
1999 *Die Nationalpolitische Erziehungsanstalt Ilfeld. Sammlung der von 1934 bis 1944 herausgegebenen Ilfeld-Blätter – Ein Beitrag zur Zeitgeschichte*, 2 vols, n.p.
Frick, W
1933 'Richtlinien für die Geschichtslehrbücher, 29/07/33' [BArch NS12/810, Teil 2].
Gauß, H.
1936 'Sparta. Aus der Griechenlandbericht unserer Jungmannen', *Ilfelder Blätter* 1936 (4), 104–5.
Gehl, W.
1933 *Geschichte für höhere Schulen. Mittelstufe: Ein Hilfsbuch zu geschichtlicher Anschauung. 1. Heft: Altertum* (6th edn.), Breslau.
Gertner, A.
1862 *Bensberg und sein Kadettenhaus*, Siegen.
Glinicke, K. A. Prusz von
n.d. *Aus den Memoiren eines Leibpagen*, Hamelin.
Goedewaagen, T.
1938 'Die Nationalpolitische Erziehungsanstalten in Deutschland', *Nieuw Nederland* [BArch NS15/205, Bl.75–84].

Goltz, C. von der
1932 *Denkwürdigkeiten* (2nd edn.), Berlin.
Goltz, H. von der
1917 *My Adventures as a German Secret Agent*, New York.
Görnandt, R.
1966 *Rabenschloß und Rote Mauern. Geschichte und Geschichten um Kadetten*, Düsseldorf.
Gruhl
1928 'Fünfzigjähriger Gedenktag an das Bestehen der Hauptkadettenanstalt Lichterfelde', *Reichskadettenblatt* 14 (October), 1–3.
Günther, J.
1980 'Untertanen, keine Ritter. Leopold von Wiese: "Kadettenjahre"', *Die Zeit,* 24 October 1980.
H. F. H.
1925 '"Vogel Wiedehopf"', *Reichskadettenblatt* 5 (September), 54–5.
Halkett, G. R.
1939 *The Dear Monster*, London.
Haslingen, von
1906 *Geschichte des Kadettenhauses in Potsdam*, Berlin.
Haupt, J.
n.d. *Völkisch oder national? Eine grundlegende Auseinandersetzung mit der deutsch-"nationalen" Oberschicht* (Völkisches Rustzeug, Flugschriftenreihe), Munich.
1921 *Vom deutschen Nationalsozialismus*, Frankfurt am Main.
1933 'Das Bildungsziel im nationalsozialistischen Staat', *Nachrichtenblatt des N.S.L.B., Gau Südhannover-Braunschweig* 1 (1), 3–6.
1935 'The educational ideals of the German National Socialist movement', *The Yearbook of Education*, 923–30.
1936 *Nationalerziehung*, Langensalza.
Hazen, W. B.
1872 *The School and the Army in Germany and France*, New York.
Hein, M. P.
1999 *Fluchtfährte. Erzählung*, Zürich.
Heinich, A.
2007 *"Niemand entgeht seiner Zeit". Erziehung, Lernen und Leben in der Nationalpolitischen Erziehungsanstalt (Napola) Bensberg bei Köln. September 1942 bis April 1945*, Norderstedt.
Heinz, G. von
1908 *Kadettenliebe. Erzählung*, Dresden and Leipzig.
Heißmeyer, A.
n.d. 'Die national-politischen Erziehungsanstalten' [BArch R2/12710].
1936 'Auslese an den Nationalpolitischen Erziehungsanstalten', *Internationale Zeitschrift für Erziehung* 5, 222.
1939a 'Über die Nationalpolitischen Erziehungsanstalten', *Der Altherrenbund* 1 (8), 201–3.
1939b *Die Nationalpolitischen Erziehungsanstalten*, Berlin.
1939c 'Wieviele Nationalpolitische Erziehungsanstalten gibt es?', *Weltanschauung und Schule* 3, 334–6.

1940 'Bericht über die Nationalpolitischen Erziehungsanstalten' [BArch R43-II/956b].
1942a 'Erziehung zur soldatischen Moral. Das Ziel der Nationalpolitischen Erziehungsanstalten. Sonderdruck aus "*Die Innere Front*", Pressedienst der NSDAP', *Die Pforte. Neue Folge des "Alten Pförtners"; Zeitschrift des Pförtner-Bundes* 18 (2), 51–4.
1942b 'Denkschrift an Reichsführer-SS – Erziehernachwuchs' [BArch NS19/1531].
Henning, K.-U.
1928 'Die alten Kadetten in Lichterfelde. Die 50-Jahrfeier der Übersiedlung der Hauptkadettenanstalt', *Neue Preußische [Kreuz-] Zeitung*, 17 September 1928.
Herrig, L.
1878 *Die Haupt-Cadetten-Anstalt zu Lichterfelde. Skizzen*, Berlin.
Heydebreck, P. von
1931 *Wir Wehr-Wölfe. Erinnerungen eines Freikorps-führers*, Leipzig.
Hillard, G.
1954 *Herren und Narren der Welt*, Munich.
Hiller, F. (ed.)
1935 *Deutsche Erziehung im neuen Staat*, Langensalza.
Hindenburg, P. von
1920 *Out of my Life*, trans. F.A. Holt, London.
Hinzpeter, G.
1888 *Kaiser Wilhelm II. Eine Skizze nach der Natur gezeichnet*, Bielefeld.
Hitler, A.
1943 *Mein Kampf* (855th edn.), Munich.
1961 *Hitlers Zweites Buch*, ed. G.L. Weinberg, Stuttgart.
Hobohm, K.
1941 'Über Geist und Arbeit der Nationalpolitischen Erziehungsanstalt. Bericht von einer Besichtigung der Nationalpolitischen Erziehungsanstalt Potsdam', *Die Erziehung* 16, 223–5.
Hohenlohe-Ingelfingen, Prinz K. zu
1897 *Aus meinem Leben*, Berlin.
Hohmann, W. and Schiefer, W.
1940 *Volk und Reich der deutschen Klasse 6. Von der Vorgeschichte bis zum Ende der Stauferzeit*, Berlin.
Holleben, von
1902 'Die wissenschaftliche Grundlagen für den Offizier und die Reorganisation des Kadetten-Korps', *Militärische Zeitfragen* 11 (5), 25–40.
Holtze, F. and Berduschek, H.
1899 *Übersicht der Weltgeschichte* (14th edn.), Berlin.
Horn, H.
1943 'Die Neuordnung des Schulbuchwesens und Schulbuchfragen im Kriege', *Deutsche Schulerziehung* 1941/42, 77–88.
Howard, E.
1915 *Potsdam Princes*, London.
Humboldt, W. von
1809 'Über Kadettenhäuser', in A. Flitner and K. Giel (eds) *Wilhelm von Humboldt. Schriften zur Politik und zum Bildungswesen*, Darmstadt (1964), 90–3.

Ilgner, E.
1932 *Kadetten-Erinnerungen*, Berlin.
Im Auftrage des Ministers der geistlichen, Unterrichts- und Medizinal-Angelegenheiten
1891 *Verhandlungen über Fragen des höheren Unterrichts. Berlin, 4. bis 17. Dezember 1890*, Berlin.
1972 *Verhandlungen über Fragen des höheren Unterrichts. Berlin, 6. bis 8. Juni 1900*, Glashütten im Taunus.
Isenburg, F.-W.
1958 *Kadettenleben. Erinnerungen an meine Jugendjahre am großen Plöner See*, Hamburg.
Jany-Hamburg, E.
1926 'Erinnerungen eines Uralten', *Reichskadettenblatt* 6 (March), 67–8.
Jochmann, W. (ed.)
1980 *Adolf Hitler. Monologe im Führerhauptquartier 1941–1944*, Hamburg.
Justizministerium
1848 'Bericht der Fachkommission für Heereswesen und Militair-Reform über die Kadetten-Institute (30 September 1848)' [GStAPK I.HA Rep.84a, Justizministerium, Nr.11552].
Kadetten, ehemalige
1939 *Festschrift. Herausgegeben aus Veranlassung der ersten großen Zusammenkunft ehemaliger Kadetten in Stuttgart am 4. März 1939*, Stuttgart.
1967 *250 Jahre Königlich-Preußisches Kadettenkorps 1717–1967. Dokumente zur Geschichte des Königlich-Preußischen Kadettenkorps*, Düsseldorf.
Karlsruhe, Kadettenhaus
n.d. *Hausordnung des Kadettenhauses Karlsruhe*, Karlsruhe.
Keller, J.
n.d. (c.1899?) *Wünsche zur bevorstehenden Reform der Gymnasien*, Wittenberg.
Kinsky, F.
1891 'Des Grafen Franz Kinsky Ansichten über die Anordnung des Unterrichts in Geschichte und Erdbeschreibung', *Militair-Wochenblatt,* Issue 82, 2111–2.
Kiock, E.
1929 'Der Kadett in Zivil', *Reichskadettenblatt* 17 (December), 1–4.
Kiock, E. (ed.)
1978 *Wahlstatt und seine Kadetten*, Dortmund.
Kirsten, E.
1936 'Die Entstehung des Spartanischen Staates', *Neue Jahrbücher für Wissenschaft und Jugendbildung*, 385–400.
Klein, L. E.
1985 'Königlich-Preußische Kadetten in Diez', *Lions Club Zeitung*, February 1985.
Kleinau, K.
2000 *Im Gleichschritt, marsch! Der Versuch einer Antwort, warum ich von Auschwitz nichts wusste. Lebenserinnerungen eines NS-Eliteschülers der Napola Ballenstedt*, Hamburg.
Klingenburg
1928 'Neues Leben im Bensberger Schloss', *Reichskadettenblatt* 13 (April), 184–5.
Klinz, A.
1935 'Nationalsozialistisches Gedankengut im Lektüreplan des griechischen Unterrichts', *Die deutsche höhere Schule* 2, 332–8.

Kloppe, F.
1934 *Nationalpolitische Erziehungsanstalten*, Leipzig.
Klüver, W.
1954 *Plön. Grundzüge und Hauptdaten seiner Geschichte*, Eutin.
Köhler, M.
n.d. *Als Jungmann in der Napola Köslin 1942 bis zum bitteren Ende 1945*, n.p.
Kohlrausch, F.
1841 *Chronologischer Abriss der Weltgeschichte, zunächst für den Jugend-Unterricht* (12th edn.), Leipzig.
Köslin, NPEA
1939–1944 *Die Brücke. Nachrichten von der Nationalpolitischen Erziehungsanstalt Köslin.*
Koss, H. von
1973 ['Erinnerungen'], *Ehemalige kgl. preußische Kösliner Kadetten, Rundbrief* 3, 2–3 [GStAPK IV.HA Rep.13 Nr.109].
Kostorz
1928 'Die Heldengedenkfeier am 4. März 1928', *Reichskadettenblatt* 13 (April), 174–8.
Krieck, E.
1933 *Nationalpolitische Erziehung* (4th edn.), Leipzig.
Kumsteller, B.
1936 *Geschichtsbuch für die deutsche Jugend. Für die Jüngeren* (39th edn.), Leipzig.
Lamprecht, Günther (ed.)
2007 *Wie es damals war. Napola Schloss Reisen, Wartheland. Erinnerungen und Berichte*, Hamburg.
Lankheit, K. (ed.)
1994 *Hitler: Reden, Schriften, Anordnungen, Band III Teil 2*, Munich.
Leeb, J.
2005 *"Wir waren Hitlers Eliteschüler": ehemalige Zöglinge der NS-Ausleseschulen brechen ihr Schweigen* (7th edn.), Munich.
Lenski, F. von
1922 *Aus den Leutnantsjahren eines alten Generalstabsoffiziers. Erinnerungen an den Rhein und die Reichshauptstadt aus den 80er und 90er Jahren des 19. Jahrhunderts*, Berlin.
Lettow-Vorbeck, P. von
1957 *Mein Leben*, Biberach am Riß.
Lichtenstein, P.
1890 *Die Central-Cadetten-Anstalt und die Entstehungs-Geschichte des Vorortes Groß-Lichterfelde*, Berlin.
Lindner, F.
1900 *Zur Jahrhundertwende. Festrede, gehalten am 21.Dez.1899 im Feldmarschallsaale der Königlichen Hauptkadettenanstalt zu Großlichterfelde*, Berlin.
Lorentz, K.
1980 'Der Pamsch – und wie er enden musste', *Mitteilungsblatt* 46, 23 [GStAPK IV.HA Rep.13 Nr.71, Bl.48].
Lorentzen, V.
1977 *Naumburg. Kadettenheimat an der Saale*, n.p.

Lübcke, W.
c.1980 *Kadetten in Deutschland* (unpublished typescript) [GStAPK IV.HA Rep.13 Nr.55].
Ludendorff, E.
1933 *Mein militärischer Werdegang. Blätter der Erinnerung an unser stolzes Heer*, Munich.
Ludendorff, M.
1929 *My Married Life with Ludendorff*, trans. R. Somerset, London.
Maisch, H.
1968 *Helm ab – Vorhang auf. Siebzig Jahre eines ungewöhnlichen Lebens*, Emsdetten.
Männig, H.-J.
1998 'Schulpforta: NPEA im Krieg', *Die Pforte. Schulpforta-Nachrichten. Zeitschrift des Pförtner Bundes e.V.* 51, 15–19.
Manstein, E. von
1955 *Verlorene Siege*, Bonn.
1958 *Aus einem Soldatenleben 1887–1939*, Bonn.
Manteuffel, H. von
1958 *Zur Erinnerung an die Einweihungsfeier einer Kadettengedenktafel an der ehemaligen Hauptkadettenanstalt am 10. September 1958* [BA-MA MSG3/3038].
Marloh, K.-C. (ed.)
1994 *Spartanerjünglinge. Eine Kadettengeschichte in Briefen, von Paul von Szczepański; Der jüngste Leutnant, von Detlev von Liliencron*, Seevetal.
Masberg, M.
n.d. *Entstehen und Werden des Potsdamer Kadettenhauses*, n.p.
n.d. (c.1970) *Bildband. 200 Jahre Potsdamer Kadetten. Potsdam und seine Kadetten. Eine Bildfolge*, n.p.
Menge, H.
1999 *Chronik der ehemaligen Nationalpolitischen Erziehungsanstalt Rügen in Putbus für die Zeit von Oktober 1944 bis Mai 1945. Zusammengestellt nach den Erinnerungen ehemaliger Schüler*, Schwanewede.
2008 'Die Nationalpolitische Erziehungsanstalt Rügen 1941 bis 1945', in Förderverein Fürstliches Pädagogium zu Putbus (ed.) *Über 170 Jahre Bildungstradition am Putbusser Circus. Die Geschichte des Königlichen Pädagogiums zu Putbus und seiner nachfolgenden Einrichtungen*, Putbus, 50–61.
Menne, A.
1939 *Preußische Jugend. Erzählung*, Leipzig.
Meuer, P,
1991 *Linien des Lebens. Eine Kindheit und Jugend im Schwäbischen und anderswo*, Stuttgart.
Meyer, K. (ed.)
1944 *NPEA Ilfeld. Blätter der Ilfelder Kameradschaft. Sonderheft zum 10jährigen Bestehen der Anstalt*, Nordhausen.
Militair-Wochenblatt
1821 'Alt-Griechische Tapferkeit, oder die denkwürdigen Tage von Marathon, Thermopylä, Salamis und Platäa, hinsichtlich der Kriegeszucht und Stellordnung der alten Griechen', *Militair-Wochenblatt*, 1994–8, 2004–6, 2009–14, 2020–2, 2026–30, 2035–8, 2043–6, 2050–4.

1873a 'Wissenschaft und Militair-Bildung (Eine Entgegnung)', *Militair-Wochenblatt,* Issue 21, 194–8.
1873b 'Die Mittel zum Neubau der Central-Kadetten-Anstalt bei Lichterfelde', *Militair-Wochenblatt*, Issue 36, 320–5.
1890 'Organisation des Kadettenkorps etc. gemäß der Allerhöchsten Kabinetts-Ordre vom 13. Februar 1890', *Militair-Wochenblatt,* Issue 20, 581–8.
1891a 'Vaterländischer Geschichtsunterricht', *Militair-Wochenblatt,* Issue 91, 2347–50.
1891b 'Über die Auswahl der Offiziere als Erzieher am Kadettenkorps', *Militair-Wochenblatt*, Issue 112, 2915–18.
1896 'Geschichte des Militär-Erziehungs- und Bildungswesens in Preußen (Schluß)', *Militair-Wochenblatt*, Issue 60, 1622–8.
1899 'Kadettenerzieher', *Militair-Wochenblatt*, Issue 89, 2273–5.

Militärische Gesellschaft zu Berlin
1860 *Ueber den Militairischen Geist, mit besonderer Rücksicht auf die Preußische Armee. Ein Vortrag, gehalten in einem Kreise von Offizieren*, Berlin.
1899 'Das Offizierkorps und die Geselligkeit', *Militair-Wochenblatt,* Issue 100, 2525–9; Issue 101, 2545–8.

Military Education Commission
1870 *Accounts of the Systems of Military Education in France, Prussia, Austria, Bavaria and the United States*, London.

Mönch, O.
1913 'Einiges über Berlin-Lichterfelde und die Kadettenanstalt', *Mitteilungen des Vereins für die Geschichte Berlins* 30 (6), 85–89.

Montanus, K.
1998 *Die Putbusser – Kadetten unter dem Hakenkreuz. Ein Napola-Schüler erzählt*, Frankfurt am Main.

Müffling, K.
1853 *Passages from my Life, together with Memoirs of the Campaign of 1813 and 1814*, London.

Müller, W.
1946 'Wie sah ich kurz nach dem 2. Weltkrieg – 1946 – vor 29 Jahren meine Erziehung im Kadettenkorps (1912–1919). Auszug aus meinem Tagebuch des Jahres 1946 (Bitte bei Wertung beachten!)' [BA-MA MSG2/15327].

Müncheberg, H.
1991 *Gelobt sei, was hart macht. Aus dem Leben eines Zöglings der Nationalpolitischen Erziehungsanstalt Potsdam*, Berlin.

Murr, P.
1931 *Hinter den roten Mauern von Lichterfelde. Erlebnisse in der Kadettenanstalt*, Leipzig.

Musil, R.
1955 *Young Törless*, trans. E. Kaiser, E. Wilkins, London.

Naumburg, NPEA
1944 *10 Jahre Nationalpolitische Erziehungsanstalt Naumburg a. d. Saale*, Naumburg.

Neuber, F.
1903 *Zum fünfundzwanzigsten Jahrestage der Übersiedelung der Hauptkadettenanstalt von Berlin nach Groß-Lichterfelde*, Berlin.

Neubourg, E.
1890 *Bensberg und sein Cadettenhaus. Zum fünfzigjährigen Stiftungsfeste des Cadettenhauses*, Berlin.
Neumann, H.-U.
n.d. *Erinnerungen an das Kgl. Pr. Kadettenkorps* [GStAPK IV.HA Rep.13 Nr.57].
Nickol, H.
1935 *Der letzte Kadett*, Stuttgart.
Nimz, H.
1976 *Das Kadettenhaus Culm-Köslin 1776–1920. Eine Gründung Friedrichs des Großen*, n.p.
1979 'Das Kadettenhaus Köslin', *Pommern* (4), 5–10.
Noth, R.
1978 'Noch heute treffen sich 50 ehemalige Kadetten', *Berliner Morgenpost,* 8 October 1978 [GStAPK IV.HA Rep.13 Nr.71, Bl.150].
Ollech, K. R. von
1862 *Friedrich der Große und die Kadetten-Anstalten. Ein Vortrag gehalten in der Militairischen Gesellschaft zu Berlin am 24. Januar 1862* (Militair-Wochenblatt Beiheft 6), Berlin.
Oranienstein, Kadettenhaus
1908 *Hausordnung für das Kadettenhaus in Oranienstein*, Cassel.
1910 *Dienstanweisung für die Erzieher des Kadettenhauses in Oranienstein* [incomplete], Cassel.
Overweg, R.
n.d. *Brüderchen. Ein Kadettendrama in drei Akten*, Leipzig.
Papen, F. von
1952 *Memoirs*, trans. B. Connell, London.
Pelet-Narbonne, G. von
1878 *Die Haupt-Kadetten-Anstalt zu Lichterfelde bei Berlin nebst einem Rückblick auf die Entwicklung des Königlich Preußischen Kadettenkorps* (Militair-Wochenblatt Beiheft 7), Berlin.
Person, K.
1936 'Was bedeuten uns die Griechen und Römer? Rede des Unterrichtsleiters Dr. Person zum Schulfest am 21. Mai 1936', *Pförtner Blätter* 1 (1/2), 12–24.
1943 '400 Jahresfeier in Schulpforta. Rede des Anstaltsleiters Dr. Kurt Person am 21. Mai 1943', *Pförtner Blätter* 7 (3), 69–79.
Picker, H.
1976 *Hitlers Tischgespräche im Führerhauptquartier*, Stuttgart.
Plön, Kadettenhaus
1911 *Hausordnung des Königlichen Kadetten-Hauses in Plön mit Anhang (Allgemeine Bestimmungen zur Beachtung für die Kadetten und deren Angehörige)*, Plön.
Plön, NPEA
1942 'Bergwerkseinsatz des Zuges "Walter Clausen" der Nationalpolitischen Erziehungsanstalt Plön' [BArch NS26/349].
Pöhlmann, R.
1925 *Geschichte der sozialen Frage und des Sozialismus in der antiken Welt. 1. Band* (3rd edn.), Munich.

Poten, B.

1896 *Geschichte des Militär-Erziehungs- und Bildungswesens in den Landen deutscher Zunge; Band 4: Preußen*, Berlin.

Potsdam, Kadettenhaus

1914 *Hausordnung des Königlichen Kadettenhauses Potsdam*, Potsdam.

Priebatsch, F.

1919 *Geschichte des preußischen Offizierkorps*, Breslau.

Prussia

1844 *Grundzüge der Organisation der Königl. Cadetten-Corps*, Berlin.

1849 *Bestimmungen über die Umgestaltung des Kadetten-Corps*, Berlin.

1877 *Aufnahme-Bestimmungen und Lehrplan des Königlichen Cadettencorps*, Berlin.

1880/81 *Wissenschaftliche Anforderungen für die Aufnahme in das Kadettenkorps*, Berlin.

1883/84 *Wissenschaftliche Anforderungen für die Aufnahme in das Kadettenkorps*, Berlin.

1887 *Aufnahme-Bestimmungen und Lehrplan des Königlichen Cadettencorps*, Berlin.

1893 *Aufnahme-Bestimmungen und Lehrplan des Königlichen Cadettencorps*, Berlin.

1899 *Aufnahme-Bestimmungen und Lehrplan des Königlichen Kadettenkorps*, Berlin.

1902a *Bestimmungen über die Versetzung der Zöglinge des Kadettenkorps*, Berlin.

1902b *Ordnung der Reifeprüfung*, Berlin.

Prussia, H.R.H. Princess Friedrich Leopold of

1939 *Behind the Scenes at the Prussian Court*, London.

Putzar, A. H. K.

1998 *Im Schatten einer Zeit*, Schwerin.

Rahden, W. von

1846 *Wanderungen eines alten Soldaten*, Berlin.

Rauschning, H.

1939 *Hitler Speaks: A series of political conversations with Adolf Hitler on his real aims*, London.

Redwitz, O. von

1928 'Beim Münchner Kadettenkorps, Erinnerungen eines alten Generals', *Reichskadettenblatt* 12 (January), 157–62.

Reichskadettenblatt

1936 '"Eine harte, aber gute Schule". Ministerpräsident Göring über das ehemalige Kadettenkorps', *Reichskadettenblatt* 36, 569–70.

Rein, W.

1897a 'Militär-Erziehungs- und Bildungswesen', in W. Rein (ed.) *Encyklopädisches Handbuch der Pädagogik* (Band 4), Berlin.

1897b 'Militarismus und Schulerziehung', in W. Rein (ed.) *Encyklopädisches Handbuch der Pädagogik* (Band 4), Berlin.

Reitzenstein, H.-J. von

1920 *Vergitterte Jugend. Geschichten aus dem Kadettenkorps*, Berlin.

Rhyn, A. von

1920 'Zum Geleit', *Deutsche Kadettenzeitung. Organ des Reichsbundes ehemaliger Kadetten* 1 (1/2), 1.

Rothenburg Stadt und Land

1983 '"Preußisch-deutsche Tradition": Königliche Hoheiten und hohe Offiziere beim Bundes-Kadettentreffen in der Reichsstadthalle. Der jüngste

Teilnehmer am Treffen der 750 noch lebenden ehemaligen Kadetten ist 75 Jahre alt – Spartanisch erzogen' [GStAPK IV.HA Rep.13 Nr.99, Bl.150].

Rott

1902 'Das Kadettenkorps und seine Ziele', *Militair-Wochenblatt*, Issue 4, 89–92.

Röttger

1941 'Warum Latein auch an Nationalpolitische Erziehungsanstalten?', *Der Deutsche Erzieher* (11), 326–7.

Rowan-Robinson, G. A.

1937 'The German Nationalpolitische Erziehungsanstalt and the English Public School: I. Comparison', *Internationale Zeitschrift für Erziehung* 6, 162–5.

1938 'The training of the Nazi leaders of the future', *International Affairs* 17, 233–50.

Rudelsdorff, D.

1963 'Gedanken über die Erziehungsgrundsätze des ehem. Kadettenkorps in Hinblick auf die Frage des Offiziernachwuchs unserer Zeit', *Mitteilungsblatt* 1 (4), 3–7 [BA-MA MSG3/1186].

1967 'Das Königlich-Preußische Kadettenkorps. Festansprache von Generalmajor a.D. Bürgermeister i.R. Dr. jur. Detlev Rudelsdorff zum 250. Jahrestag (1717) der Gründung des preußischen Kadettenkorps, Freitag 5/5/1967 in Berlin' [GStAPK IV.HA Rep.13 Nr.170].

1975 'Sinn und Wesen des Kadettentums [speech given at the *Bundeskadettentag*, Goslar, August 1975]', December 1975 [GStAPK IV.HA Rep.13 Nr.170].

Russell, J. E.

1899 *German Higher Schools. The History, Organisation and Methods of Secondary Education in Germany*, New York.

Rust, Bernhard

1934 'Rust-Rede, gehalten am 15. November 1934 beim Diplomaten-Empfang des Außenpolitischen Amtes' [BArch R4901/11913].

1935a 'Rede des Preuß. Kultusministers Rust bei der Einweihung der landgebundenen Hochschule für Lehrerbildung in Lauenburg (Pommern) am 24. Juni 1933', in F. Hiller (ed.) *Deutsche Erziehung im neuen Staat*, Langensalza, 41–5.

1935b 'Die Grundlagen der nationalsozialistischen Erziehung', *Hochschule und Ausland* 13 (1), 1–18.

1937 'Hellas und das neue Deutschland', *Weltanschauung und Schule* 1, 401–6.

1938a 'Betrifft: Zusammenarbeit zwischen Hochschulen für Lehrerbildung und Nationalpolitische Erziehungsanstalten (08/03/1938)' [BArch R4901/11913].

1938b 'Erziehung und Unterricht in der höheren Schule', *Weltanschauung und Schule* 2, 97–104.

1938c 'Das Manifest von Lauenburg. Aus der Rede zur Einweihung des Neubaues der Hochschule für Lehrerbildung am 29.5.1938', *Weltanschauung und Schule* 2, 241–2.

1938d *Erziehung und Unterricht in der höheren Schule*, Berlin.

1938e 'Education in the Third Reich', in J. von Ribbentrop (ed.) *Germany Speaks. By 21 Leading Members of Party and State*, London, 97–117.

1938f 'Wissenschaft und Glaube. Rede in der Feierstunde der Universität am 26. Juni 1937', in Georg-August-Universität Göttingen (ed.) *Wissenschaft und Glaube. Reden und Ansprachen zur 200-Jahrfeier der Georg-August-Universität zu Göttingen im Juni 1937*, Oldenburg, 11–19.

1938g 'Freiheit und Ordnung. Rede bei der Kundgebung der Studenten auf dem Ehrenhof der Universität am 28. Juni 1937', in Georg-August-Universität Göttingen (ed.) *Wissenschaft und Glaube. Reden und Ansprachen zur 200-Jahrfeier der Georg-August-Universität zu Göttingen im Juni 1937*, Oldenburg, 20–27.

1940a *Reichsuniversität und Wissenschaft. Zwei Reden, gehalten in Wien am 6. November 1940*, Berlin.

1940b *Erziehung und Unterricht in der Volksschule*, Berlin.

1943a 'Musische Erziehung', *Völkische Musikerziehung* 9, 1–6.

1943b 'Erziehung zur Tat', *Deutsche Schulerziehung* 1941/42, 3–12.

Rutherford Harley, T.

1934 'The Public School of Sparta', *Greece and Rome* 3 (9), 129–39.

Salomon, E. von

1930 *Die Geächteten*, Berlin.

1933 *Die Kadetten*, Berlin.

1954 *The Answers of Ernst von Salomon to the 131 questions in the Allied Military Government 'Fragebogen'*, trans. C. Fitzgibbon, London.

Sander, M.

1915 *25 Jahre in Köslin 1890–1915. Erinnerungsblätter*, Köslin.

Sch., Dr.

1917 'Die Spartaner von Lichterfelde', *Tägliche Rundschau,* August 1917, 5 [GStAPK IV.HA Rep.13 Nr.70, Bl.16].

Schaarschmidt, von (ed.)

1911/12 *Jahrbuch für Kadetten*, Oldenburg.

Schäfer, H.

1997 *NAPOLA. Die letzten vier Jahre der Nationalpolitischen Erziehungsanstalt Oranienstein bei Diez an der Lahn 1941–1945. Eine Erlebnis-Dokumentation*, Frankfurt am Main.

Schäfer, Otto

1942 'Ziel und Gestalt der Nationalpolitischen Erziehungsanstalten', *Nationalsozialistisches Bildungswesen* 7 (1), 19–31.

Scharenberg, E. (ed.)

1979 *Kadetten-generale von 1717–1919. Teil I*, Döhle.

Scharfenort, L. von

1889 *Bilder aus der Geschichte des Kadetten-Korps für Alt und Jung*, Berlin.

1891 'Friedrich der Große über die Erziehung der militärischen Jugend (Vortrag, gehalten am 26.Nov.1890 in der Militärischen Gesellschaft zu Berlin von v. Scharfenort, Hauptmann a.D., Bibliothekar an der Haupt-Kadettenanstalt zu Groß-Lichterfelde und Lehrer an der Kriegsakademie)', *Militair-Wochenblatt,* Issue 7, 203–23.

1892 *Das Königlich Preußische Kadettenkorps 1859–1892 unter den Kaisern und Königen Wilhelm I., Friedrich III., Wilhelm II.*, Berlin.

Schieffer, A.

1935 'Die Pforte als nationalpolitische Erziehungsanstalt. Bericht des Leiters

der Nationalpolitischen Erziehungsanstalt Schulpforta, Oberregierungsrat Dr. Schieffer, vom 5. September 1935', *Die Pforte. Neue Folge des "Alten Pförtners"; Zeitschrift des Pförtner-Bundes* (4), 223.
1936 'Erziehungsziele der Nationalpolitischen Erziehungsanstalt Schulpforta. Rede des Anstaltsleiters, SS.-Standartenführers Dr. Schieffer, zum Schulfest am 21. Mai 1936', *Pförtner Blätter* 1 (1/2), 3–12.

Schikore, K.
1994 *Kennungen. Landmarken einer Wandlung* (2nd edn.), Aachen.

Schillmann, R.
1881 *Vorschule der Geschichte. Sagen und Geschichten zum Schulgebrauch bearbeitet*, Berlin.

Schmidt, C. and Floß, A.
1894 *Griechische Sagen*, Berlin.

Schmidthammer, K.
1809 'Vergleichung der Lycurgischen und Solonischen Verfassung', *Minerva* 2, 274–90.

Schmidthenner, P. and Fliedner, F.
1943 *Führer und Völker. Geschichtsbuch für Höhere Schulen, sechste Klasse. Von der Vorgeschichte bis zum Ende der Stauferzeit* (2nd edn.), Leipzig.

Schoenaich, P.
1926 *Mein Damaskus. Erlebnisse und Bekenntnisse*, Berlin-Hessenwinkel.

Schott, A. (ed.)
1973 *Chronik des Bundes-Kadettentages 1973*, Bornheim-Üdorf.
1979 *Chronik des 11. Bundeskadettentages der ehem.kgl.preuß.u.sächs.Kadetten vom 28. bis 30. August 1979 in Goslar*, Nürtingen.
1991 *Kadetten Abschluss-Chronik* [GStAPK: Bibliothek]

Schott, A.
n.d., a 'Kadetten ihre Könige', from the *Begleitheft "Führung durch das Kadetten-Museum"* [GStAPK: Bibliothek].
n.d., b 'Abschrift aus dem Adelsblatt. Erziehungsgrundsätze im Kadettenkorps' [GStAPK IV.HA Rep.13 Nr.101, Bl.227–8].
1980 'Erziehungsgrundsätze im Kadettenkorps', *Steglitzer Heimat*, 6–10.

Schrökh, J. M.
1788 *Algemeine Weltgeschichte für Kinder. Erste Theil. Alte Geschichte*, Brünn.

Schubert, T.
1967 *Die deutschen Kadettenkorps*, Hanover.

Schulenburg, W. von der
1919 *Meine Kadettenerinnerungen (1892–1899). Ein Beitrag zur Lösung einer Zeitfrage [1901]*, Munich.

Schulze, W.
1922 *Damals, als ich Kadett war*, Leipzig.

Schwechheimer, K.
n.d. *Mein Leben*, n.p.

Selasinsky, von
1970 'Aus meiner Kadettenzeit (I – Vorkorps Oranienstein)', *Deutsches Soldatenjahrbuch* 18, 241–54.
1971 'Aus meiner Kadettenzeit (II – H.K.A. Berlin-Lichterfelde), Persönliche Erinnerungen', *Deutsches Soldatenjahrbuch* 19, 81–9.

Selke, H.

1938 *Frühlingsfahrt durch Griechenland. Deutsche Jungen erleben das Land der Hellenen*, n.p.

1990 *Auch eine Jugend in Deutschland. Meine Schulzeit in Ilfeld und Schulpforte 1935–1939*, n.p.

Sidgwick, C.

1937 'The German Nationalpolitische Erziehungsanstalt and the English Public School: III. German Journey: To Backnang!', *Internationale Zeitschrift für Erziehung* 6, 170–3.

Silomon, J. and Franke, W.

1940 *Volk und Führer. Deutsche Geschichte für Schulen. Ausgabe für Oberschulen und Gymnasien. Klasse 6. Von der Vorgeschichte bis zum Ende der Staufenzeit* (1st edn.), Frankfurt am Main.

1943 *Volk und Führer. Deutsche Geschichte für Schulen. Ausgabe für Oberschulen und Gymnasien. Klasse 6. Von der Vorgeschichte bis zum Ende der Staufenzeit* (4th edn.), Frankfurt am Main.

Skroblin, G.

1942 'Tradition und Zukunft. Aufgabe der Nationalpolitischen Erziehungsanstalten. Sonderdruck aus "*Westermanns Monatsheften*" Dezember 1941', *Die Pforte. Neue Folge des "Alten Pförtners"; Zeitschrift des Pförtner-Bundes* 19 (1), 3–6.

1943 'Die Nationalpolitischen Erziehungsanstalten', *Deutsche Schulerziehung* 1941/42, 211–18.

Sohr

1897 *Zur Hundertjahrfeier 1897. Festrede gehalten im Feldmarschallsaale der Königlichen Hauptkadettenanstalt*, Berlin.

Spandau, NPEA

1944 *Blätter der Nationalpolitischen Erziehungsanstalt Berlin-Spandau. 1934–1944*, [including] *10 Jahre N.P.E.A. Berlin-Spandau, Jg. 1944, Heft 1, 30. Januar 1944. Verstärkte Ausgabe anläßlich des zehnjährigen Bestehens der Anstalt, enthaltend die Kriegsausgabe 23*, Spandau.

Spranger, E.

1932 *Volk. Staat. Erziehung. Gesammelte Reden und Aufsätze*, Leipzig.

Stacke, L.

1894 *Griechische Geschichten. Erzählungen aus der alten Geschichte in biographischer Form* (27th edn.), Oldenburg.

Staf. [Brunk, H.]

1943 *10 Jahre NPEA Plön. Sonderheft der Kameradschaft*, Kiel.

Stuhm, Nationalpolitische Erziehungsanstalt

1938 *Nationalpolitische Erziehungsanstalt Stuhm im Aufbau*, Königsberg.

Sudetenland, NPEA

1940 *Festschrift zur feierlichen Eröffnung der Nationalpolitischen Erziehungsanstalt Sudetenland am 10. Oktober 1940*, Ploschkowitz.

Szczepański, P. von

n.d., a *Spartanerjünglinge*, Leipzig.

n.d., b *Spartanerjungen*, Leipzig.

1904 *Neu-Berlin. Erzählungen*, Leipzig.

1910 'Letters from a Cadet to his Mother', in W. D. Lowe (ed. and trans.) *Inner Life of the Prussian Cadet*, London.

Tanera, C.

1895 *Hans von Dornen, des Kronprinzen Kadett. Eine Erzählung aus d. Deutsch-Französisch. Kriege 1870/71* (2nd edn.), Bielefeld and Leipzig.

Tate, J. W.

1937 'The German Nationalpolitische Erziehungsanstalt and the English Public School: II. The Public Schools of Germany', *Internationale Zeitschrift für Erziehung* 6, 165–70.

Teuchert, K. (ed.)

1930–1933 *Blätter der Hans-Richert-Schule. Staatliche Bildungsanstalt Berlin-Lichterfelde*, Berlin.

Thoma, L.

1907 *Tante Frieda. Neue Lausbubengeschichten*, Munich.

Trotha, T. von

1912 'Offizierberuf und Offizierlaufbahn', *Militärische Zeit- und Streitfragen* 21, 1–35.

Tucholsky, K.

1920 'Kadettenliteratur', *Die Weltbühne* 35, 26/08/1920, 236.

1924 'Eine deutsche Kindheit', *Die Weltbühne* 46, 11/11/1924, 734.

Ulhorn, O.

1919 *Das Kadettenhaus Plön und die Revolution*, Rostock.

Ulrich, H. H.

1909 *Blutsbrüder. Kadettengeschichten*, Dresden.

United States War Department

1896 *The Military Schools of Europe, and other papers selected for publication*, Washington.

Unruh, Friedrich Franz von

1967 *Ehe die Stunde schlug: Eine Jugend im Kaiserreich*, Bodensee.

Unruh, Fritz von

1957 *Mächtig seid ihr nicht in Waffen*, Nuremberg.

1961 *Wir wollen Frieden. Die Reden und Aufrufe 1960/61*, Düsseldorf.

1967 *Im Haus der Prinzen*, Frankfurt am Main.

1979 *Opfergang, Politeia, Biographien. Erinnerungen, Aufsätze, Vorträge*, Berlin.

1983 *Der Sohn des Generals* (2nd edn.), Berlin.

Unruh, G. von

1930 'Die Spartaner von Lichterfelde', *Reichskadettenblatt* 20 (October), 297–99.

Upton, E.

1878 *Armies of Asia and Europe*, New York.

Vacano, O.-W. von

1943 *Sparta: Der Lebenskampf einer nordischen Herrenschicht* (2nd edn.), Kempten.

Vahl, H.

2000 *Napola Schulpforta 1933–1945. Erinnerungen eines Schülers*, Hamburg.

Vereinigung ehemaliger Kadetten von Groß-Berlin

1920 *Ein Erinnerungsblatt an die Auflösung der H.K.A.*, Berlin.

Vizetelly, H.

1879 *Berlin Under the New Empire*, 2 vols., London.

Vogel, E.

2007 *Wanderungen in Deutschland. Lebensstationen 1935–1948*, Berlin.

Wagner, H.

1969 *Das Ehrenmal der Kadetten auf der Burg Hohenzollern*, Bonn.

Wagner, R.

1998 *Mehr sein als scheinen. Vier Jahre Jungmann in der NPEA Rottweil*, Ditzingen.

Wassermann, E.

1998 'Schulpforta 1935–1945: Nationalsozialistische Erziehung unter humanistischem Deckmäntelchen oder Kontinuität humanistischer Bildungstradition hinter NS-Fassade?', *Die Pforte. Schulpforta-Nachrichten. Zeitschrift des Pförtner Bundes e.V.* 51, 12–15.

Weber, G.

1847 *Lehrbuch der Weltgeschichte, mit Rücksicht auf Cultur, Literatur und Religionswesen, und einem Abriß der deutschen Literaturgeschichte als Anhang, für höhere Schulanstalten und zur Selbstbelehrung*, Leipzig.

Wegelin, J.

1763 *Politische und moralische Betrachtungen über die Spartanische Gesetzgebung des Lycurgus*, Lindau.

Wehrhan, K.

1935 'Nationalpolitische Erziehung, insbesondere die nationalpolitischen Erziehungsanstalten', *Die neue Deutsche Schule* 9, 99–105.

Weihe, J.

1990 'Die Erziehung in der Nationalpolitischen Erziehungsanstalt Schulpforte', *Die Pforte. Schulpforta-Nachrichten. Zeitschrift des Pförtner Bundes e.V.* 43, 24–8.

1994 'Die Nationalpolitische Erziehungsanstalt Schulpforta 1935 bis 1945', in H. Heumann (ed.) *Schulpforta. Tradition und Wandel einer Eliteschule*, Erfurt, 231–58.

Weitershausen, von

1919 'Die Erziehung des Offiziers im neuen Volksstaat', *Militair-Wochenblatt*, Issue 100, 1787–90.

Werner, E.

n.d. *Lebenserinnerungen aus meiner Kadettenzeit in Potsdam und Berlin-Lichterfelde 97/01, 01/03* [GStAPK IV.HA Rep.13 Nr.158].

Wiese, L.

1886 *Lebenserinnerungen und Amtserfahrungen*, 2 vols. (2nd edn.), Berlin.

Wiese, L. von

1924 *Kindheit. Erinnerungen aus meinen Kadettenjahren*, Hanover.

1954 'Über militärische Erziehung', in *Spätlese*, Opladen, 39–50.

Wildenbruch, E. von

1909 *Vice-Mama*, Berlin.

1910 'A Story of Cadet Life' (translation of *Das Edle Blut*), in W. D. Lowe (ed. and trans.) *Inner Life of the Prussian Cadet*, London.

William II

1926 *My Early Life*, London.

Winfrid [Haupt, J.]

1935 *Sinnwandel der formalen Bildung*, Leipzig.

Winterfeld, A. von

1865 *Cadetten-geschichten*, Berlin.

Wolffradt, M. H. von
1913 'Aus dem Berliner Kadettenkorps zur Zeit Friedrichs des Großen', *Mitteilungen des Vereins für die Geschichte Berlins* 30 (6), 89–91.
Wülfingen, A. B. von
1894 *Die geschmähten Kadettenkorps. Ein Wort der Entgegnung zu der Schrift "Unsere Kadettenkorps" von* ∴, Dresden.
Zander, E.
1941 *Bensberg als militärischer Standort. Sonderdruck aus "Köln als befestigte Stadt und militärischer Standort"*, Cologne.
Zapp, A.
1887 *Im modernen Sparta. Erbauliche Zeitbilder*, Berlin.
1888 *Im neuen Sparta*, Berlin.
Zempelin, H. G.
2000 *Des Teufels Kadett. Napola-Schüler von 1936 bis 1943. Gespräch mit einem Freund*, Frankfurt am Main.
Zobeltitz, F. von
1900 *Besser Herr als Knecht*, Berlin.
c.1913? *Aus dem alten Berliner Kadettenkorps. Kleine Erinnerungen*, n.p.
1934 *Ich hab so gern gelebt. Lebenserinnerungen*, Berlin.
Zobeltitz, H. von
1896 *The King's Recruits*, trans. S. M. S. Clarke, London.

Secondary sources

Abels, K.
2002 *Kadetten: Preußenfilm, Jugendbuch und Kriegslied im "Dritten Reich"*, Bielefeld.
Albertz, A.
2006 *Exemplarisches Heldentum. Die Rezeptionsgeschichte der Schlacht an den Thermopylen von der Antike bis zur Gegenwart*, Munich.
Albisetti, J. C.
1983 *Secondary School Reform in Imperial Germany*, Princeton.
Alkemeyer, T.
1996 *Körper, Kult und Politik. Von der "Muskelreligion" Pierre de Coubertins zur Inszenierung von Macht in den Olympischen Spielen von 1936*, Frankfurt am Main.
Apel, H. J. and Bittner, S.
1994 *Humanistische Schulbildung 1890–1945. Anspruch und Wirklichkeit der altertumskundlichen Unterrichtsfächer*, Cologne.
Assmann, J.
1995 'Collective memory and cultural identity', *New German Critique* 65, 125–33.
Barnett, C.
1967 'The education of military elites', *Journal of Contemporary History* 2, 15–35.
Baumeister, S.
1997 *NS-Führungskader. Rekrutierung und Ausbildung bis zum Beginn des Zweiten Weltkriegs 1933–1939* (Konstanzer Schriften zur Schoáh und Judaica 4), Konstanz.
Bayer, P. R.
1996 'Die ehemalige Andrews-Kaserne zu Berlin-Lichterfelde: Ein Blick zurück –

Eine Arbeit zur Erlangung des Diploms an der Fachhochschule Potsdam, Fachbereich Archiv-, Bibliotheks-, und Dokumentationswesen' [GStAPK IV.HA Rep.13 Nr.166].

Bedford, S.
1954 *A Legacy*, London.

Bendele, U.
1984 *Krieg, Kopf und Körper: Lernen für das Leben – Erziehung zum Tod*, Frankfurt am Main.

Berger, S.
2000 'Prussia in history and historiography from the eighteenth to the nineteenth century', in P. G. Dwyer (ed.) *The Rise of Prussia 1700–1830*, Harlow, 27–47.
2001 'Prussia in history and historiography from the nineteenth to the twentieth centuries', in P. G. Dwyer (ed.) *Modern Prussian History 1830–1947*, Harlow, 21–40.

Bergerson, A. S.
2004 *Ordinary Germans in Extraordinary Times. The Nazi Revolution in Hildesheim*, Bloomington and Indianapolis.

Bernett, H.
1966 *Nationalsozialistische Leibeserziehung. Eine Dokumentation ihrer Theorie und Organisation* (Theorie der Leibeserziehung 1), Schorndorf.

Bertram, J. (ed.)
1969 *Die Bildung des Offiziers. Dokumente aus vier Jahrhunderten* (Schriftenreihe Innere Führung 5), n.p.

Bialas, W. and Rabinbach, A. (eds)
2007 *Nazi Germany and the Humanities*, Oxford.

Birgalias, N.
1999 *L'odyssée de l'éducation spartiate*, Athens.

Blatz, C. W. and Ross, M.
2009 'Historical memories', in P. Boyer and J. V. Wertsch (eds) *Memory in Mind and Culture*, Cambridge, 223–37.

Blee, K.
1998 'Evidence, empathy and ethics. Lessons from oral histories of the Klan', in R. Perks and A. Thomson (eds) *The Oral History Reader*, London, 333–43.

Blesse, H.
2009 'Die Anfänge der Rudolf-Schröter-Schule, Staatliche Nationalpolitische Erziehungsanstalt Klotzsche', in Dresdner Geschichtsverein (ed.) *Zwischen Reform und Restriktion. Sächsische Schulgeschichte im 20. Jahrhundert*, Dresden, 54–63.

Boberach, H.
1984 *Meldungen aus dem Reich. Die geheimen Lageberichte des Sicherheitsdienstes der SS 1938–1945*, Vol. 12, Herrsching.

Boog, H.
1998 'Civil education, social origins, and the German Officer Corps in the nineteenth and twentieth centuries', in E. V. Converse (ed.) *Forging the Sword. Selecting, Educating, and Training Cadets and Junior Officers in the Modern World*, Chicago, 119–34.

Bouvier, H. and Géraud, C.
2000 *NAPOLA. Les écoles d'élites du troisième Reich*, Paris.
Boyer, P. and Wertsch, J. V. (eds)
2009 *Memory in Mind and Culture*, Cambridge.
Bradley, D.
1982 *Walther Wenck. General der Panzertruppe*, Osnabrück.
Brand, K.-H. von
1981 *Kadetten. Aus 300 Jahren deutscher Kadettenkorps. Band I. Geschichte des Königlich Preußischen Kadettenkorps*, Munich.
Briesen, D. and Gans, R.
1993 'Über den Wert von Zeitzeugen in der deutschen Historik. Zur Geschichte einer Ausgrenzung', *BIOS* 6 (1), 1–32.
Buruma, I.
1994 *The Wages of Guilt. Memories of War in Germany and Japan*, London.
Butler, E. M.
1935 *The Tyranny of Greece over Germany*, Cambridge.
Carsten, F. L.
1957 'Germany: from Scharnhorst to Schleicher: The Prussian officer corps in politics, 1806–1933', in M. E. Howard (ed.) *Soldiers and Governments: Nine studies in civil-military relations*, Westport, 73–98.
Cartledge, P. A.
2001 *Spartan Reflections*, London.
2001a 'The politics of Spartan pederasty', in Cartledge 2001, 91–105.
2002 *The Spartans: An Epic History*, London.
Charlton, T. L., Myers, L. E., and Sharpless, R. (eds)
2006 *Handbook of Oral History*, Oxford.
Christ, K.
1996 'Spartaforschung und Spartabild', in *Griechische Geschichte und Wissenschaftsgeschichte* (*Historia* Einzelschriften 106), Stuttgart, 9–58.
Clark, C.
1996 'The wars of liberation in Prussian memory: Reflections on the memorialisation of war in early nineteenth-century Germany', *Journal of Modern History* 68, 550–76.
2006 *Iron Kingdom. The Rise and Downfall of Prussia, 1600–1947*, London.
Clemente, S. E.
1992 *For King and Kaiser! The Making of the Prussian Army Officer, 1860–1914*, Westport.
Confino, A.
1997 'Collective memory and cultural history: Problems of method', *American Historical Review* 102, 1386–403.
Confino, A. and Fritzsche, P. (eds)
2002 *The Work of Memory. New Directions in the Study of German Society and Culture*, Urbana and Chicago.
Conradt, M.
1994 *Vom Königlichen Württembergischen Lehrerseminar zum Staatlichen Aufbaugymnasium des Landes Baden-Württemberg. 1912 bis 1994 in Rottweil: eine Schulchronik*, Rottweil.

Converse, E. V. (ed.)
1998 *Forging the Sword. Selecting, Educating, and Training Cadets and Junior Officers in the Modern World*, Chicago.

Craig, G. A.
1955 *The Politics of the Prussian Army 1640–1945*, Oxford.

Dahlke, B.
2006 *Jünglinge der Moderne. Jugendkult und Männlichkeit in der Literatur um 1900*, Cologne.

Degner, U.
2012 'Spartanic verses: Hölderlin and the role of Sparta in German literary hellenism, c. 1800', in S. Hodkinson and I. Macgregor Morris (eds) *Sparta in Modern Thought. Politics, History and Culture*, Swansea, 231–51.

Demandt, A.
2002 'Klassik als Klischee: Hitler und die Antike', *Historische Zeitschrift* 274, 281–313.

Demeter, K.
1965 *The German Officer-Corps in Society and State 1650–1945*, trans. A. Malcolm, London.

Devantier, S.
2008 'Das Heeresarchiv Potsdam. Die Bestandsaufnahme in der Abteilung Militärarchiv des Bundesarchivs', *Archivar. Zeitschrift für Archivwesen* 61 (4), 361–9.
2010 '"Was hat der Mensch dem Menschen Größeres zu geben als Wahrheit?" Zur Gründung des Reichsarchivs vor 90 Jahren in Potsdam', *Archivar. Zeitschrift für Archivwesen* 63 (1), 54–6.

Dithmar, R.
2003 *Schule und Unterricht im Dritten Reich*, Ludwigsfelde.

Doerfel, M.
1989 'Der Griff des NS-Regimes nach Elite-Schulen. Stätten klassischer Bildungstradition zwischen Anpassung und Widerstand', *Vierteljahrshefte für Zeitgeschichte* 37 (3), 401–55.

Dorfmüller, P. and Konetzny, R.
1993 *"Damit es an gelahrten Leuten in unsern Landen nicht Mangel gewinne." Schulpforta 1543–1993: Ein Lesebuch*, Leipzig.

Driftmann, H. H.
1980 *Grundzüge des militärischen Erziehungs- und Bildungswesens in der Zeit 1871–1939*, Regensburg.

Ducat, J.
1999 'Perspectives on Spartan education in the Classical period', in S. Hodkinson and A. Powell (eds) *Sparta: New Perspectives*, London, 43–66.
2006 *Spartan Education. Youth and Society in the Classical Period*, trans. E. Stafford, P.-J. Shaw and A. Powell, Swansea.

Dwyer, P. G.
2000 *The Rise of Prussia 1700–1830*, Harlow.
2001 *Modern Prussian History 1830–1947*, Harlow.
2001a 'Modern Prussia – continuity and change', in Dwyer 2001, 1–20.

Eickhoff, T.
1998 *Politische Dimensionen einer Komponisten-Biographie im 20. Jahrhundert – Gottfried von Einem* (Beihefte zum Archiv für Musikwissenschaft 43), Stuttgart.

Eike, S. J.
n.d. *Die Jungmannen-Kadetten – Eliten im Vergleich*, Hamburg.

Evans, R. J.
2000 *In Defence of History* (2nd edn.), London.
2002 *Telling Lies About Hitler. The Holocaust, History and the David Irving Trial*, London.
2003 *The Coming of the Third Reich*, London.
2006 *The Third Reich in Power*, London.
2009 *The Third Reich At War*, London.

Fairburn, M.
1999 *Social History. Problems, Strategies and Methods*, London.

Feller, B. and Feller, W.
2001 *Die Adolf-Hitler-Schulen. Pädagogische Provinz versus Ideologische Zuchtanstalt*, Vienna.

Fentress, J. and Wickham, C.
1992 *Social Memory. New Perspectives on the Past*, Oxford.

Fesser, G. and Jonscher, R. (eds)
1998 *Umbruch im Schatten Napoleons. Die Schlachten von Jena und Auerstedt und ihre Folgen* (Jenaer Studien 3), Jena.

Fetscher, I.
1998 *"Wollt ihr den totalen Krieg?" Joseph Goebbels im Berliner Sportpalast 1943*, Hamburg.

Fleischer, H.
1988 'Siegfried in Hellas. Das nationalsozialistische Griechenlandbild und die Behandlung der griechischen Zivilbevölkerung seitens der deutschen Besatzungsbehörden, 1941–1944', in A. Kerker (ed.) *Griechenland – Entfernung in die Wirklichkeit*, Hamburg, 26–48.

Flessau, K.-I.
1977 *Schule der Diktatur. Lehrpläne und Schulbücher des Nationalsozialismus*, Munich.
1987 'Schulen der Partei(lichkeit)? Notizen zum allgemeinbildenden Schulwesen des Dritten Reichs', in K.-I. Flessau, E. Nyssen, and G. Patzold (eds) *Erziehung im Nationalsozialismus. "...und sie werden nicht mehr frei ihr ganzes Leben!"*, Cologne, 65–82.

Förschler, A.
2002 *Die Nationalpolitische Erziehungsanstalt Backnang. Eine Eliteschule im Dritten Reich* (MA thesis), Stuttgart.

Frevert, U.
2004 *A Nation in Barracks. Modern Germany, Military Conscription and Civil Society*, trans. D. Brückenhaus, A. Boreham, Oxford.

Fröhlich, E.
2005 'Die drei Typen der nationalsozialistischen Ausleseschulen', in J. Leeb (ed.) *"Wir waren Hitlers Eliteschüler": ehemalige Zöglinge der NS-Ausleseschulen brechen ihr Schweigen* (7th edn.), Munich, 241–63.

Führ, C.
1980 'Die preußischen Schulkonferenzen von 1890 und 1900. Ihre bildungspolitische Rolle und bildungsgeschichtliche Bewertung', in P. Baumgart (ed.) *Bildungspolitik in Preußen zur Zeit des Kaiserreichs*, Stuttgart, 189–223.

Fulbrook, M.
1999 *German National Identity after the Holocaust*, Cambridge.
2011 *Dissonant Lives. Generations and Violence through the German Dictatorships*, Oxford.

Gamm, H.-J.
1964 *Führung und Verführung. Pädagogik des Nationalsozialismus*, Munich.

Garnier, J.
1998 'Jena und die Erneuerung Preußens', in G. Fesser and R. Jonscher (eds) *Umbruch im Schatten Napoleons. Die Schlachten von Jena und Auerstedt und ihre Folgen* (Jenaer Studien 3) Jena, 15–24.

Gelhaus, D. and Hülter, J.-P
2003 *Die Ausleseschulen als Grundpfeiler des NS-Regimes*, Würzburg.

Gélieu, B. von
1990 *1890 – 1990. Culm – Köslin. Kadettenhaus/Stabila/NPEA*, Butzbach-Maibach.

Gersdorff, U. von
1965 'Zum Bild des Kadettenhauses in der deutschen Literatur', *Wehrwissenschaftliche Rundschau* (September), 524–8.

Gies, H.
1992 *Geschichtsunterricht unter der Diktatur Hitlers*, Cologne.

Gilbert, M.
1994 *First World War*, London.

Glassberg, D.
1996 'Public history and the study of memory', *Public Historian* 18, 7–23.

Goeldel, P.
1936 'Die Charaktererziehung im preußischen Kadettenkorps', *Archiv für Körpererziehung*, Beiheft 1, 73–96.

Goffman, E.
1961 *Asylums. Essays on the Social Situation of Mental Patients and Other Inmates*, London. (2nd edition, London, 2007).

Grele, R. J.
1998 'Movement without aim. Methodological and theoretical problems in oral history', in R. Perks and A. Thomson (eds) *The Oral History Reader*, London, 38–52.
2006 'Oral history as evidence', in T. L. Charlton, L. E. Myers, and R. Sharpless (eds) *Handbook of Oral History*, Oxford, 43–101.

Hagemann, K.
2002 *"Mannlicher Muth und Teutsche Ehre". Nation, Militär und Geschlecht zur Zeit der Antinapoleonischen Kriege Preußens*, Paderborn.

Hausmann, F.-R.
2007 *"Deutsche Geisteswissenschaft" im Zweiten Weltkrieg. Die "Aktion Ritterbusch" (1940–1945). Dritte, erweiterte Ausgabe*, Heidelberg.

Heggen, A. (ed.)
2004 *300 Jahre Gymnasium in Plön 1704–2004. Festschrift*, Neumünster.

Heggen, A. and Kloos, V. (eds)
1993 *125 Jahre Erziehung auf Schloss Plön (1868–1993)*, Plön.
Herwig, H. H.
1998 '"You are here to learn how to die": German subaltern officer education on the eve of the Great War', in E. V. Converse (ed.) *Forging the Sword. Selecting, Educating, and Training Cadets and Junior Officers in the Modern World*, Chicago, 32–46.
Heumann, H. (ed.)
1994 *Schulpforta. Tradition und Wandel einer Eliteschule*, Erfurt.
Heydorn, H.-J. and Koneffke, G.
1973 *Zur Bildungsgeschichte des deutschen Imperialismus. Einleitungen zur Neuherausgabe der Preußischen Schulkonferenzen 1890/1900 und der Reichsschulkonferenz von 1920*, Glashütten im Taunus.
Hinchliffe, P.
1999 *Schnaufer: Ace of diamonds. The Biography of Heinz Wolfgang Schnaufer: Germany's top-scoring night fighter of World War II*, Stroud.
Hodkinson, S.
1999 'An agonistic culture? Athletic competition in archaic and classical Spartan society', in S. Hodkinson and A. Powell (eds) *Sparta: New Perspectives*, London, 147–87.
2006 'Was classical Sparta a military society?', in S. Hodkinson and A. Powell (eds) *Sparta and War*, Swansea, 111–62.
2010 'Sparta and Nazi Germany in mid-20th-century British liberal and left-wing thought', in A. Powell and S. Hodkinson (eds) *Sparta: The Body Politic*, Swansea, 297–342.
2012 'Sparta and the Soviet Union in U.S. Cold War foreign policy and intelligence analysis', in S. Hodkinson and I. Macgregor Morris (eds) *Sparta in Modern Thought*, Swansea, 343–92.
Hodkinson, S. and Macgregor Morris, I. (eds)
2012 *Sparta in Modern Thought. Politics, History and Culture*, Swansea.
Hoffmann, A. M. and Hoffmann, H. S.
2006 'Memory theory: Personal and social', in T. L. Charlton, L. E. Myers, and R. Sharpless (eds) *Handbook of Oral History*, Oxford, 275–96.
Hofmann, H. H. (ed.)
1977 *Das Deutsche Offizierkorps 1860–1960*, Boppard.
Höhn, R.
1963 *Die Armee als Erziehungsschule der Nation. Das Ende einer Idee*, Bad Harzburg.
Jodda-Flintropp, S.
2010 *"Wir sollten intelligente Mütter werden". Nationalpolitische Erziehungsanstalten für Mädchen*, Norderstedt.
Johann, K.
2003 *Grenze und Halt: Der Einzelne im "Haus der Regeln". Zur deutschsprachigen Internatsliteratur*, Heidelberg.
John, J.
1998 '"Jena 1806" – Symboldatum der Geschichte des 19. und 20. Jahrhunderts', in G. Fesser and R. Jonscher (eds) *Umbruch im Schatten*

Napoleons. Die Schlachten von Jena und Auerstedt und ihre Folgen (Jenaer Studien 3), Jena, 177–95.

Jureit, U.

1999 *Erinnerungsmuster. Zur Methodik lebensgeschichtlicher Interviews mit Überlebenden der Konzentrations- und Vernichtungslager* (Forum Zeitgeschichte 8), Hamburg.

Kansteiner, W.

2002 'Finding meaning in memory: A methodological critique of collective memory studies', *History and Theory* 41, 179–97.

Kasdorff, H. and Schmidt, E. (eds)

1968 *100 Jahre Erziehung der Jugend auf Schloss Plön. 1868–1968*, Plön.

Kattago, S.

2001 *Ambiguous Memory. The Nazi Past and German National Identity*, Westport.

Kaufhold, K. H. and Sösemann, B. (eds)

1998 *Wirtschaft, Wissenschaft und Bildung in Preußen. Zur Wirtschafts- und Sozialgeschichte Preußens vom 18. bis zum 20. Jahrhundert.* (*Vierteljahrsschrift für Sozial- und Wirtschaftsgeschichte* Beiheft 148), Stuttgart.

Keim, W.

1995 *Erziehung unter der Nazi-Diktatur Band I: Antidemokratische Potentiale, Machtantritt und Machtdurchsetzung*, Darmstadt.

1997 *Erziehung unter der Nazi-Diktatur Band II: Kriegsvorbereitung, Krieg und Holocaust*, Darmstadt.

Kennedy, G. C. and Neilson, K. (eds)

2002 *Military Education: Past, present, and future*, Westport.

Kennell, N. M.

1995 *The Gymnasium of Virtue. Education and Culture in Ancient Sparta*, Chapel Hill.

Kershaw, I.

2011 *The End: Hitler's Germany 1944–45*, London.

Kiernan, B.

2009 'Hitler, Pol Pot, and Hutu power: Distinguishing themes in genocidal ideology', *The Holocaust and the United Nations Outreach Programme Discussion Papers Journal*, 19–31.

Klare, A.

1996 'Die Nationalpolitische Erziehungsanstalt Potsdam 1933–1945', Diplomarbeit der Fachhochschule Potsdam.

Kneller, G. F.

1941 *The Educational Philosophy of National Socialism*, New Haven.

Lambert, A. J., *et al.*

2009 'How does collective memory create a sense of the collective?', in P. Boyer and J. V. Wertsch (eds) *Memory in Mind and Culture*, Cambridge, 194–217.

Lieven, D.

2009 *Russia against Napoleon. The Battle for Europe, 1807 to 1814*, London.

Losemann, V.

1977 *Nationalsozialismus und Antike. Studien zur Entwicklung des Faches Alte Geschichte 1933–1945*, Hamburg.

2005 '"Ein Staatsgedanke aus Blut und Boden": R. W. Darré und die Agrargeschichte Spartas', *Laverna* 16, 67–120.

2007 'Sparta in the Third Reich', in N. Birgalias, K. Buraselis, and P. Cartledge (eds) *The Contribution of Ancient Sparta to Political Thought and Practice*, Athens, 449–63.

2012 'The Spartan tradition in Germany, 1870–1945', in S. Hodkinson and I. Macgregor Morris (eds) *Sparta in Modern Thought*, Swansea, 253–314.

Lumnis, T.

1998 'Structure and validity in oral evidence', in R. Perks and A. Thomson (eds) *The Oral History Reader*, London, 273–83.

Luserke, M.

1999 *Schule erzählt. Literarische Spiegelbilder im 19. und 20. Jahrhundert*, Göttingen.

Maier, C. S.

1993 'A surfeit of memory? Reflections on history, melancholy and denial', *History and Memory* 5, 136–52.

Marchand, S. L.

1996 *Down from Olympus. Archaeology and Philhellenism in Germany, 1750–1970*, Princeton.

Markmann, H.-J.

1984 *Kadetten – Militärische Jugenderziehung in Preußen*, Berlin.

Marrou, H.-I.

1956 *A History of Education in Antiquity*, trans. G. Lamb, London.

Matthes, A. (ed.)

1976 *"Schwarzseher dulde ich nicht, und wer sich zur Arbeit nicht eignet, der scheide aus, und wenn er will, suche er sich ein besseres Land." Reden Kaiser Wilhelms II*, Munich.

McCann, P. (ed.)

1977 *Popular Education and Socialisation in the Nineteenth Century*, London.

Meier-Welcker, H.

1964 *Offiziere im Bild von Dokumenten aus drei Jahrhunderten*, Stuttgart.

Messerschmidt, M.

1976 *Die Preußische Armee. Handbuch zur deutschen Militärgeschichte 1648–1939, IV.2. Militärgeschichte im 19. Jahrhundert 1814–1890: Strukturen und Organisation*, Munich.

1978 'Militär und Schule in der wilhelminischen Zeit', *Militärgeschichtliche Mitteilungen* 1/23, 51–76.

1995 '"Zur Aufrechterhaltung der Manneszucht". Historische und ideologische Grundlagen militärischer Disziplin im NS-Staat', in N. Haase and G. Paul (eds) *Die anderen Soldaten. Wehrkraftszersetzung, Gehorsamsverweigerung und Fahnenflucht im Zweiten Weltkrieg*, 19–36.

Minder, R.

1962 'Kadettenhaus, Gruppendynamik und Stilwandel von Wildenbruch bis Rilke und Musil', *Kultur und Literatur in Deutschland und Frankreich. Fünf Essays*, Frankfurt am Main, 73–93.

Moeller, R. G.

1996 'War stories: The search for a usable past in the Federal Republic of Germany', *American Historical Review* 101, 1008–48.

Moncure, J.

1993 *Forging the King's Sword. Military Education between Tradition and Modernisation – The Case of the Royal Prussian Cadet Corps, 1871–1918*, New York.

Morina, C.
2011 *Legacies of Stalingrad. Remembering the Eastern Front in Germany since 1945*, Cambridge.
Morlang, A.
2002 *"Neuer Stil im alten Schloss". Die Napola/NPEA Oranienstein 1934–1945*, Diez.
Moser, A.
1997 *Die Napola Reichenau. Von der Heil- und Pflegeanstalt zur nationalsozialistischen Eliteerziehung (1941–1945)*, Konstanz.
Mosse, G.
1964 *The Crisis of German Ideology: Intellectual origins of the Third Reich*, London.
Müller, J.-W. (ed.)
2002 *Memory and Power in Post-War Europe. Studies in the Presence of the Past*, Cambridge.
Muth, J.
2011 *Command Culture: Officer education in the U.S. Army and the German armed forces, 1901–1940, and the consequences for World War II*, Denton.
Naake, E.
1971 'Zur Theorie und Praxis der Erziehung in den Nationalpolitischen Erziehungsanstalten und ähnlichen faschistischen "Eliteschulen"' (unpublished dissertation), Jena.
Näf, B.
1986 *Von Perikles zu Hitler? Die athenische Demokratie und die deutsche Althistorie bis 1945*, Bern.
Näf, B. (ed.)
2001 *Antike und Altertumswissenschaft in der Zeit von Faschismus und Nationalsozialismus*, Mandelbachtal and Cambridge.
O'Boyle, L.
1968 'Klassische Bildung und soziale Struktur in Deutschland zwischen 1800 und 1848', *Historische Zeitschrift* 207, 584–608.
Ollier, F.
1973 *Le mirage spartiate: étude sur l'idéalisation de Sparte dans l'antiquité grecque de l'origine jusqu'aux cyniques; et étude sur l'idéalisation de Sparte dans l'antiquité grecque du début de l'école cynique jusqu'à la fin de la cité* (combined edition), New York.
Ostertag, H.
1990 *Bildung, Ausbildung und Erziehung des Offizierkorps im deutschen Kaiserreich 1871 bis 1918. Eliteideal, Anspruch und Wirklichkeit*, Frankfurt am Main.
Overesch, M., *et al.* (eds)
1991 *Das Dritte Reich im Gespräch*, Hildesheim.
Parker, P.
2007 *The Old Lie. The Great War and the Public-School Ethos*, London.
Passerini, L. (ed.)
1992 *Memory and Totalitarianism* (*International Yearbook of Oral History and Life Stories* 1), Oxford.
Paustian, M.
1995 *Die Nationalpolitische Erziehungsanstalt Plön 1933–1945*, Rostock.

Pedersen, U.
1994 *Bernhard Rust: Ein nationalsozialistischer Bildungspolitiker vor dem Hintergrund seiner Zeit* (Steinhorster Schriften und Materialen zur regionalen Schulgeschichte und Schulentwicklung 6), Braunschweig.

Perks, R. and Thomson, A. (eds)
1998 *The Oral History Reader*, London.

Pinker, S.
1997 *How the Mind Works*, London.
2002 *The Blank Slate. The Modern Denial of Human Nature*, London.

Powell, A. (ed.)
1989 *Classical Sparta: Techniques behind her success*, London.

Rawson, E.
1969 *The Spartan Tradition in European Thought*, Oxford.

Rebenich, S.
2001 'Alte Geschichte zwischen Demokratie und Diktatur. Der Fall Helmut Berve', *Chiron* 31, 457–96.
2002 'From Thermopylae to Stalingrad: The myth of Leonidas in German historiography', in S. Hodkinson and A. Powell (eds) *Sparta: Beyond the mirage*, Swansea, 323–49.

Rehm, W.
1936 *Griechentum und Goethezeit. Geschichte eines Glaubens*, Leipzig.

Ritchie, D.
2003 *Doing Oral History. A Practical Guide* (2nd edn.), Oxford.

Ritter, G.
1969 *The Sword and the Scepter. The Problem of Militarism in Germany. Vol.I: The Prussian tradition 1740–1890*, trans. H. Norden, Miami, Florida.

Robinsohn, S. B.
1966 'On National-Socialist education', *Comparative Education* 2 (3), 225–32.

Roche, H. B. E.
2012a '*Spartanische Pimpfe:* The importance of Sparta in the educational ideology of the Adolf Hitler Schools', in S. Hodkinson and I. Macgregor Morris (eds) *Sparta in Modern Thought. Politics, History and Culture*, Swansea, 315–42.
2012b '"*In Sparta fühlte ich mich wie in einer deutschen Stadt*" (Goebbels): The leaders of the Third Reich and the Spartan nationalist paradigm', forthcoming in F. Rash, G. Horan, and D. Wildmann (eds) *English and German Nationalist and Anti-Semitic Discourse (1871–1945)*, Oxford, 99–115.
2012c 'Spartan supremacy: A "*ktêma es aei*"? Reconstructing Lakedaimonian expectations of Sparta's enduring ascendancy', forthcoming in A. Powell (ed.) *Hindsight, or Unfulfilled Expectations in Antiquity*, Swansea.
2012d '"Go, tell the Prussians...": The Spartan paradigm in Prussian military thought during the long nineteenth century', *New Voices in Classical Reception Studies* 7, 25–39.
2012e 'Youth of Sparta and Youth of Mars: Uses and abuses of Classics at the Prussian Cadet Schools (1818–1920)', unpublished paper, presented at the Classical Association Annual Conference, University of Exeter, 12/04/2012.
2012f 'Critique of the portrayal of the Prussian Cadet Corps in Jörg Muth's

Command Culture (2011)', blog post dated 17/08/2012, accessible at http://helenroche.com/news/joerg-muth-command-culture-review.

Röhl, J. C. G.

1998 *Young Wilhelm. The Kaiser's Early Life, 1859–1888*, Cambridge.

Rosenthal, G.

1986 *Die Hitlerjugend-Generation. Biographische Thematisierung als Vergangenheitsbewältigung* (Gesellschaftstheorie und Soziale Praxis 1), Essen.

1990 *"Als der Krieg kam, hatte ich mit Hitler nichts mehr zu tun": Zur Gegenwärtigkeit des "Dritten Reiches" in Biographien*, Opladen.

1991 'German war memories: Narrability and the biographical and social functions of remembering', *Oral History* 19 (2), 34–41.

Rubin, H. J. and Rubin, I. S.

1995 *Qualitative Interviewing. The Art of Hearing Data*, London.

Samuel, R. and Thompson, P. (eds)

1990 *The Myths We Live By*, London.

Sardina, A.-M.

2010 *Die Nationalpolitischen Erziehungsanstalten (NAPOLAs) als Beleg für widersprüchliche NS-Erziehungskonzeptionen im Dritten Reich*, Norderstedt.

Schilling, R.

2002 *"Kriegshelden". Deutungsmuster heroischer Männlichkeit in Deutschland 1813–1945*, Paderborn.

Schleunes, K. A.

1989 *Schooling and Society. The Politics of Education in Prussia and Bavaria 1750–1900*, Oxford.

Schlink, B.

2010 *Guilt About the Past*, London.

Schmitz, K.

1997 *Militärische Jugenderziehung. Preußische Kadettenhäuser und Nationalpolitische Erziehungsanstalten zwischen 1807 und 1936* (Deutsches Institut für Internationale Pädagogische Forschung. Studien und Dokumentationen zur deutschen Bildungsgeschichte 67), Frankfurt am Main.

Schneider, C., Stillke, C., and Leineweber, B.

1996 *Das Erbe der Napola: Versuch einer Generationengeschichte des Nationalsozialismus*, Hamburg.

Scholtz, H.

1973 *Nationalsozialistische Ausleseschulen. Internatsschulen als Herrschaftsmittel des Führerstaates*, Göttingen.

Schreckenberg, H.

2001 *Erziehung, Lebenswelt und Kriegseinsatz der deutschen Jugend unter Hitler. Anmerkungen zur Literatur*, Münster.

Schubert-Weller, C.

1988 'Vormilitärische Jugenderziehung', in C. Berg (ed.) *Handbuch der deutschen Bildungsgeschichte – Band IV: 1870–1918. Von der Reichsgründung bis zum Ende des Ersten Weltkriegs*, Munich, 503–15.

Schulz, K.

1995 *Fast ein Revolutionär. Fritz von Unruh zwischen Exil und Remigration (1932–1962)* (*Cursus* Band 11. Texte und Studien zur deutschen Literatur), Munich.

Schulze, H.
2000 'The Prussian military state, 1763–1806', in P. G. Dwyer (ed.) *The Rise of Prussia 1700–1830*, Harlow, 201–19.

Schwirkmann, K.
1992 *Königlich-Preußisches Kadettenhaus Karlsruhe. Aus der Vergangenheit der heutigen Dienstgebäude der Oberfinanzdirektion Karlsruhe an der Moltkestrasse* (2nd edn.), Karlsruhe.

Shanahan, W. O.
1945 *Prussian Military Reforms 1786–1813*, New York.

Showalter, D.
2000 'Prussia's army: continuity and change, 1713–1830', in P. G. Dwyer (ed.) *The Rise of Prussia 1700–1830*, Harlow, 220–36.
2001 'Prussia's military legacy in Empire, Republic and Reich, 1871–1945', in P. G. Dwyer (ed.) *Modern Prussian History 1830–1947*, Harlow, 230–52.
2002 '"No officer rather than a bad officer": Officer selection and education in the Prussian/German Army, 1715–1945', in G. C. Kennedy and K. Neilson (eds) *Military Education: Past, present, and future*, Westport, 36–61.

Simms, B.
1998 *The Struggle for Mastery in Germany, 1779–1850*, London.
2001 'Prussia, Prussianism and National Socialism, 1933–1947', in P. G. Dwyer (ed.) *Modern Prussian History 1830–1947*, Harlow, 253–73.

Simpson, K.
1985 *History of the German Army*, London.

Sperber, J. (ed.)
2004 *Germany 1800–1870*, Oxford.

Stargardt, N.
1994 *The German Idea of Militarism. Radical and Socialist Critics, 1866–1914*, Cambridge.

Steinbach, L.
1995 *Ein Volk, ein Reich, ein Glaube? Ehemalige Nationalsozialisten und Zeitzeugen berichten über ihr Leben im Dritten Reich*, Bonn.

Stone, D.
2006 *Fighting for the Fatherland. The Story of the German Soldier from 1648 to the Present Day*, London.

Street, D., Vinter, R. D., and Perrow, C.
1966 *Organization for Treatment*, Glencoe, Ill.

Strohmeyer, A.
2006 *Dichter im Waffenrock. Erhart Kästner in Griechenland und auf Kreta 1941 bis 1945*, Mähringen.

Stübig, H.
1983 'Leopold von Wieses *Kadettenjahre*. Zum System der kasernierten Anstaltserziehung im 19. Jahrhundert', *Vierteljahrsschrift für wissenschaftliche Pädagogik* 59, 493–510.
1987 'Das Militär als Bildungsfaktor', in C. Berg (ed.) *Handbuch der deutschen Bildungsgeschichte – Band III: 1800–1870*, Munich, 362–77.
1988 'Der Einfluss des Militärs auf Schule und Lehrerschaft', in C. Berg (ed.), *Handbuch der deutschen Bildungsgeschichte – Band IV: 1870–1918. Von der Reichsgründung bis zum Ende des Ersten Weltkriegs*, Munich, 515–23.

1993 'Kadettenanstalt und Kriegsschule Potsdam. Bildung und Erziehung in den Streitkräften des Kaiserreichs', in B. R. Kroener (ed.) *Potsdam. Staat, Armee, Residenz in der preußisch-deutschen Militärgeschichte*, Berlin, 393–407.

1998 'Das höhere militärische Bildungswesen zwischen Professionalisierung und sozialer Abgrenzung. Zur Entwicklung der Kriegsschulen und der Kriegsakademie in Preußen während des 19. Jahrhunderts', in K. H. Kaufhold and B. Sösemann (eds) *Wirtschaft, Wissenschaft und Bildung in Preußen. Zur Wirtschafts- und Sozialgeschichte Preußens vom 18. bis zum 20. Jahrhundert*, Stuttgart, 191–212.

Sünderhauf, E. S.

2004 *Griechensehnsucht und Kulturkritik. Die deutsche Rezeption von Winckelmanns Antikenideal 1840–1945*, Berlin.

Thompson, P.

2000 *The Voice of the Past. Oral History* (3rd edn.), Oxford.

Tigerstedt, E. N.

1974 *The Legend of Sparta in Classical Antiquity*, 2 vols., Uppsala.

Tonkin, E.

1992 *Narrating our pasts. The social construction of oral history*, Cambridge.

Tournier, M.

1972 *The Erl-King*, trans. B. Bray, London.

Trox, E.

1990 *Militärischer Konservativismus. Kriegervereine und "Militärpartei" in Preußen zwischen 1815 und 1848/49* (Studien zur modernen Geschichte 42), Stuttgart.

Ueberhorst, H.

1969 *Elite für die Diktatur. Die Nationalpolitischen Erziehungsanstalten 1933–1945. Ein Dokumentarbericht*, Düsseldorf.

Ullrich, H.-J.

1954 'Zur Geschichte des alten Berliner Kadettenhauses', *Zeitschrift für Heeres- und Uniformkunde* 136 (3), 38–41.

Villard, P.

1972 'Antiquité et Weltanschauung Hitlérienne', *Revue d'histoire de la deuxième guerre mondiale* 88, 1–18.

Wakeford, J.

1969 *The Cloistered Élite. A Sociological Analysis of the English Public Boarding School*, London.

Watt, R.

1985 '"Wanderer, kommst du nach Sparta": History through propaganda into literary commonplace', *The Modern Language Review* 80 (4), 871–83.

Weiler, I.

2001 'Zur Rezeption des griechischen Sports im Nationalsozialismus: Kontinuität oder Diskontinuität in der deutschen Ideengeschichte?', in B. Näf (ed.) *Antike und Altertumswissenschaft in der Zeit von Faschismus und Nationalsozialismus*, Mandelbachtal and Cambridge, 267–84.

Weinberg, I.

1967 *The English Public Schools. The Sociology of Elite Education*, New York.

Weiß, H. (ed.)

1998 *Biographisches Lexikon zum Dritten Reich*, Frankfurt am Main.

Wertsch, J. V.
2002 *Voices of Collective Remembering*, Cambridge.

Wiesendahl, E.
2010 *Athen oder Sparta – Bundeswehr quo vadis?* (WIFIS [Wissenschaftliches Forum für Internationale Sicherheit] Aktuell 44), Bremen.

Willems, E.
1986 *A Way of Life and Death. Three Centuries of Prussian-German Militarism – An Anthropological Approach*, Nashville.

Williams, H. L. and Conway, M. A.
2009 'Networks of autobiographical memories', in P. Boyer and J. V. Wertsch (eds) *Memory in Mind and Culture*, Cambridge, 29–61.

Wistrich, R. S.
1995 *Who's Who in Nazi Germany*, London.

Yow, V. R.
2005 *Recording Oral History. A Guide for the Humanities and Social Sciences* (2nd edn.), Lanham and Oxford.

Zabel, J.-K.
1978 *Das preußische Kadettenkorps. Militärische Jugenderziehung als Herrschaftsmittel im preußischen Militärsystem* (Studien zur Politikdidaktik 5), Frankfurt am Main.

LIST OF FORMER NAPOLA PUPILS WHO HAVE PROVIDED EYEWITNESS TESTIMONY

Most of the eyewitnesses preferred to be named by their forename and initial. Names listed in square brackets are aliases provided by those who did not wish any part of their real name to be disclosed. Some eyewitnesses particularly requested that their full names should be used; these are also listed below.

NPEA Backnang
Gerhard F.
Kurt S.

NPEA Bensberg
Eike G.
Arne Heinich

NPEA Köslin
Joachim D.
Bernhard G.
Kurt K.

NPEA Klotzsche
Roman R.

NPEA Loben/Annaberg
Hans W.

NPEA Naumburg
Karl L.
Ekkehard P.
Günther P.
Heiner S.

NPEA Neubeuern
Joachim D.
Günter O.

NPEA Oranienstein
Klaus-Jürgen B.
Lothar J.
Kurt L.
Karl L.

NPEA Plön
Peter B.
Uwe L.
Harald R.
Wolfgang V.

NPEA Rügen/Putbus
Hans F.
Günther M.
Klaus Montanus
Hans P.
Dietrich Schulz
Jürgen S.
Klaus Schikore
Helmuth Z.

NPEA Reichenau and Rottweil
Gerhard B.
Fritz D.
Günter E.
Klaus E.
Paul F.
Klaus H.
Theodor K.
Paul S.
Wolfgang T.

NPEA Berlin-Spandau
Rudolf Arendt
Rüdiger B.
Manfred F.
Ernst-Christian G.
Heinrich H.

List of former Napola pupils who have provided eyewitness testimony

Erwin K.
[Hermann K.]
Wilfried K.
Gerhard L.
Hans M.
Arnulf P.
[Otto R.]
Gerhard R.
Anon.

NPEA Stuhm
Eckhard R.

NPEA Schulpforta
Günter O.
Hans R.
Hartmut V.

NPEA Traiskirchen
Harald O.

NPEA Wartheland
Wolfgang E.
Karl-Josef F.

INDEX